OBJECTIVE	CHAPTER

Section 4: Concurrency

Write code to define, instantiate, and start new threads using both java.lang .Thread and java.lang.Runnable.	5
Recognize the states in which a thread can exist, and identify ways in which a thread can transition from one state to another.	5
Given a scenario, write code that makes appropriate use of object locking to protect static or instance variables from concurrent access problems.	5
Given a scenario, write code that makes appropriate use of wait, notify, or notifyAll.	5

Section 5: OO Concepts

Develop code that implements tight encapsulation, loose coupling, and high cohesion in classes, and describe the benefits.	6
Given a scenario, develop code that demonstrates the use of polymorphism. Further, determine when casting will be necessary and recognize compiler vs. runtime errors related to object reference casting.	6
Explain the effect of modifiers on inheritance with respect to constructors, instance or static variables, and instance or static methods.	6
Given a scenario, develop code that declares and/or invokes overridden or overloaded methods and code that declares and/or invokes superclass, or overloaded constructors.	6
Develop code that implements "is-a" and/or "has-a" relationships.	6

Section 6: Collections/Generics

Given a design scenario, determine which collection classes and/or interfaces should be used to properly implement that design, including the use of the Comparable interface.	7
Distinguish between correct and incorrect overrides of corresponding hashCode and equals methods, and explain the difference between == and the equals method.	7
Write code that uses the generic versions of the Collections API, in particular, the Set, List, and Map interfaces and implementation classes. Recognize the limitations of the non-generic Collections API and how to refactor code to use the generic versions. Write code that uses the NavigableSet and NavigableMap interfaces.	7

Develop code that makes proper use of type parameters in clas̄
declarations, instance variables, method arguments, and returi
write generic methods or methods that make use of wildcard t̥
understand the similarities and differences between these two

x®
.... ımprint of
⊕WILEY

OBJECTIVE	CHAPTER
Use capabilities in the java.util package to write code to manipulate a list by sorting, performing a binary search, or converting the list to an array. Use capabilities in the java.util package to write code to manipulate an array by sorting, performing a binary search, or converting the array to a list. Use the java.util.Comparator and java.lang.Comparable interfaces to affect the sorting of lists and arrays. Furthermore, recognize the effect of the "natural ordering" of primitive wrapper classes and java.lang.String on sorting.	7

Section 7: Fundamentals

Given a code example and a scenario, write code that uses the appropriate access modifiers, package declarations, and import statements to interact with (through access or inheritance) the code in the example.	1
Given an example of a class and a command line, determine the expected runtime behavior.	1
Determine the effect upon object references and primitive values when they are passed into methods that perform assignments or other modifying operations on the parameters.	1
Given a code example, recognize the point at which an object becomes eligible for garbage collection, determine what is and is not guaranteed by the garbage collection system, and recognize the behaviors of the Object.finalize() method.	1
Given the fully-qualified name of a class that is deployed inside and/or outside a JAR file, construct the appropriate directory structure for that class. Given a code example and a classpath, determine whether the classpath will allow the code to compile successfully.	1
Write code that correctly applies the appropriate operators including assignment operators (limited to: =, +=, -=), arithmetic operators (limited to: +, -, *, /, %, ++, --), relational operators (limited to: <, <=, >, >=, ==, !=), the instanceof operator, logical operators (limited to: &, |, ^, !, &&, ||), and the conditional operator (? :), to produce a desired result. Write code that determines the equality of two objects or two primitives.	1

Exam specifications and content are subject to change at any time without prior notice and at Sun Microsystems' sole discretion. Please visit Sun's website (www.sun.com/training) for the most current information on their exam content.

Sybex®
An Imprint of
WILEY

OBJECTIVE	CHAPTER

Use capabilities in the java.util package to write code to manipulate a list by sorting, performing a binary search, or converting the list to an array. Use capabilities in the java.util package to write code to manipulate an array by sorting, performing a binary search, or converting the array to a list. Use the java.util.Comparator and java.lang.Comparable interfaces to affect the sorting of lists and arrays. Furthermore, recognize the effect of the "natural ordering" of primitive wrapper classes and java.lang.String on sorting.

7

Section 7: Fundamentals

Given a code example and a scenario, write code that uses the appropriate access modifiers, package declarations, and import statements to interact with (through access or inheritance) the code in the example.

1

Given an example of a class and a command line, determine the expected runtime behavior.

1

Determine the effect upon object references and primitive values when they are passed into methods that perform assignments or other modifying operations on the parameters.

1

Given a code example, recognize the point at which an object becomes eligible for garbage collection, determine what is and is not guaranteed by the garbage collection system, and recognize the behaviors of the Object.finalize() method.

1

Given the fully-qualified name of a class that is deployed inside and/or outside a JAR file, construct the appropriate directory structure for that class. Given a code example and a classpath, determine whether the classpath will allow the code to compile successfully.

1

Write code that correctly applies the appropriate operators including assignment operators (limited to: =, +=, -=), arithmetic operators (limited to: +, -, *, /, %, ++, --), relational operators (limited to: <, <=, >, >=, ==, !=), the instanceof operator, logical operators (limited to: &, |, ^, !, &&, ||), and the conditional operator (? :), to produce a desired result. Write code that determines the equality of two objects or two primitives.

1

Exam specifications and content are subject to change at any time without prior notice and at Sun Microsystems' sole discretion. Please visit Sun's website (www.sun.com/training) for the most current information on their exam content.

Sybex®
An Imprint of
WILEY

SCJP: Sun Certified Programmer for Java Platform, SE6 Study Guide

CX-301-065 Exam Objectives

OBJECTIVE	CHAPTER
Section 1: Declarations, Initialization and Scoping	
Develop code that declares classes (including abstract and all forms of nested classes), interfaces, and enums, and includes the appropriate use of package and import statements (including static imports).	2
Develop code that declares an interface. Develop code that implements or extends one or more interfaces. Develop code that declares an abstract class. Develop code that extends an abstract class.	2
Develop code that declares, initializes, and uses primitives, arrays, enums, and objects as static, instance, and local variables. Also, use legal identifiers for variable names.	2
Develop code that declares both static and non-static methods, and—if appropriate—use method names that adhere to the JavaBeans naming standards. Also develop code that declares and uses a variable-length argument list.	2
Given a code example, determine if a method is correctly overriding or overloading another method, and identify legal return values (including covariant returns), for the method.	2
Given a set of classes and superclasses, develop constructors for one or more of the classes. Given a class declaration, determine if a default constructor will be created, and if so, determine the behavior of that constructor. Given a nested or non-nested class listing, write code to instantiate the class.	2
Section 2: Flow Control	
Develop code that implements an if or switch statement; and identify legal argument types for these statements.	3
Develop code that implements all forms of loops and iterators, including the use of for, the enhanced for loop (for-each), do, while, labels, break, and continue; and explain the values taken by loop counter variables during and after loop execution.	3
Develop code that makes use of assertions, and distinguish appropriate from inappropriate uses of assertions.	3

Sybex®
An Imprint of
WILEY

OBJECTIVE	CHAPTER
Develop code that makes use of exceptions and exception handling clauses (try, catch, finally), and declares methods and overriding methods that throw exceptions.	3
Recognize the effect of an exception arising at a specified point in a code fragment. Note that the exception may be a runtime exception, a checked exception, or an error.	3
Recognize situations that will result in any of the following being thrown: ArrayIndexOutOfBoundsException,ClassCastException, IllegalArgumentException, IllegalStateException, NullPointerException, NumberFormatException, AssertionError, ExceptionInInitializerError, StackOverflowError or NoClassDefFoundError. Understand which of these are thrown by the virtual machine and recognize situations in which others should be thrown programmatically.	3

Section 3: API Contents

Develop code that uses the primitive wrapper classes (such as Boolean, Character, Double, Integer, etc.), and/or autoboxing and unboxing. Discuss the differences between the String, StringBuilder, and StringBuffer classes.	4
Given a scenario involving navigating file systems, reading from files, writing to files, or interacting with the user, develop the correct solution using the following classes (sometimes in combination), from java.io: BufferedReader, BufferedWriter, File, FileReader, FileWriter, PrintWriter, and Console.	4
Develop code that serializes and/or de-serializes objects using the following APIs from java.io: DataInputStream, DataOutputStream, FileInputStream, FileOutputStream, ObjectInputStream, ObjectOutputStream and Serializable.	4
Use standard J2SE APIs in the java.text package to correctly format or parse dates, numbers, and currency values for a specific locale; and, given a scenario, determine the appropriate methods to use if you want to use the default locale or a specific locale. Describe the purpose and use of the java.util.Locale class.	4
Write code that uses standard J2SE APIs in the java.util and java.util.regex packages to format or parse strings or streams. For strings, write code that uses the Pattern and Matcher classes and the String.split method. Recognize and use regular expression patterns for matching (limited to: . (dot), * (star), + (plus), ?, \d, \s, \w, [], ()). The use of *, +, and ? will be limited to greedy quantifiers, and the parenthesis operator will only be used as a grouping mechanism, not for capturing content during matching. For streams, write code using the Formatter and Scanner classes and the PrintWriter.format/printf methods. Recognize and use formatting parameters (limited to: %b, %c, %d, %f, %s) in format strings.	4

Sybex®
An Imprint of
WILEY

OBJECTIVE	CHAPTER

Section 4: Concurrency

Write code to define, instantiate, and start new threads using both java.lang.Thread and java.lang.Runnable.	5
Recognize the states in which a thread can exist, and identify ways in which a thread can transition from one state to another.	5
Given a scenario, write code that makes appropriate use of object locking to protect static or instance variables from concurrent access problems.	5
Given a scenario, write code that makes appropriate use of wait, notify, or notifyAll.	5

Section 5: OO Concepts

Develop code that implements tight encapsulation, loose coupling, and high cohesion in classes, and describe the benefits.	6
Given a scenario, develop code that demonstrates the use of polymorphism. Further, determine when casting will be necessary and recognize compiler vs. runtime errors related to object reference casting.	6
Explain the effect of modifiers on inheritance with respect to constructors, instance or static variables, and instance or static methods.	6
Given a scenario, develop code that declares and/or invokes overridden or overloaded methods and code that declares and/or invokes superclass, or overloaded constructors.	6
Develop code that implements "is-a" and/or "has-a" relationships.	6

Section 6: Collections/Generics

Given a design scenario, determine which collection classes and/or interfaces should be used to properly implement that design, including the use of the Comparable interface.	7
Distinguish between correct and incorrect overrides of corresponding hashCode and equals methods, and explain the difference between == and the equals method.	7
Write code that uses the generic versions of the Collections API, in particular, the Set, List, and Map interfaces and implementation classes. Recognize the limitations of the non-generic Collections API and how to refactor code to use the generic versions. Write code that uses the NavigableSet and NavigableMap interfaces.	7

Develop code that makes proper use of type parameters in clas
declarations, instance variables, method arguments, and retur
write generic methods or methods that make use of wildcard t
understand the similarities and differences between these two

SCJP
Sun Certified Programmer for Java® Platform, SE6
Study Guide

SCJP
Sun Certified Programmer
for Java® Platform, SE6
Study Guide

Richard F. Raposa

Wiley Publishing, Inc.

Acquisitions Editor: Jeff Kellum
Development Editor: Jennifer Leland
Technical Editor: James Nuzzi
Production Editor: Christine O'Connor
Copy Editor: Elizabeth Welch
Production Manager: Tim Tate
Vice President and Executive Group Publisher: Richard Swadley
Vice President and Publisher: Neil Edde
Media Project Manager 1: Laura Moss-Hollister
Media Associate Producer: Shawn Patrick
Media Quality Assurance: Angie Denny
Book Designer: Judy Fung, Bill Gibson
Proofreader: Nancy Bell
Indexer: Robert Swanson
Project Coordinator, Cover: Lynsey Stanford
Cover Designer: Ryan Sneed

For general information on our other products and services or to obtain technical support, please contact our Customer Care Department within the U.S. at (877) 762-2974, outside the U.S. at (317) 572-3993 or fax (317) 572-4002.

Wiley also publishes its books in a variety of electronic formats. Some content that appears in print may not be available in electronic books.

Library of Congress Cataloging-in-Publication Data

Raposa, Richard F.
  SCJP Sun certified programmer for Java platform, SE6, study guide / Richard F. Raposa. — 1st ed.
      p.   cm.
    ISBN 978-0-470-41797-3 (paper/cd-rom)
      1. Electronic data processing personnel — Certification.   2. Operating systems (Computers) — Examinations — Study guides.   3. Java (Computer program language) — Examinations — Study guides.
  I. Title.
  QA76.3.R357 2009
  005.13'3—dc22
                                                                              2008054906

10 9 8 7 6 5 4 3 2 1

Dear Reader,

Thank you for choosing *SCJP: Sun Certified Programmer for Java Platform, SE6 Study Guide*. This book is part of a family of premium-quality Sybex books, all of which are written by outstanding authors who combine practical experience with a gift for teaching.

Sybex was founded in 1976. More than thirty years later, we're still committed to producing consistently exceptional books. With each of our titles we're working hard to set a new standard for the industry. From the paper we print on, to the authors we work with, our goal is to bring you the best books available.

I hope you see all that reflected in these pages. I'd be very interested to hear your comments and get your feedback on how we're doing. Feel free to let me know what you think about this or any other Sybex book by sending me an email at nedde@wiley.com, or if you think you've found a technical error in this book, please visit http://sybex.custhelp.com. Customer feedback is critical to our efforts at Sybex.

Best regards,

Neil Edde
Vice President and Publisher
Sybex, an Imprint of Wiley

To Susan, Megan, Ryan, Katelyn, Emma and Sara.

Acknowledgments

A lot of time and energy goes into a book like this, and my wife and kids will be the first ones to attest to that fact! I owe them many thanks for their patience and understanding during the months that went into this project.

I also want to thank Jennifer Leland, the Developmental Editor, for putting up with my complete inability to learn when to use the appropriate styles. Everyone who reads this book owes James Nuzzi a big thank you for his meticulous job as Technical Editor. The text and sample questions involve a lot of code, and James did an amazing job finding errors and typos. Thanks also to Jeff Kellum, Pete Gaughan, Christine O'Connor, and everyone at John Wiley & Sons, Inc., who helped make this book a reality.

And last but not least, I want to thank all of you who are reading this book in hopes of learning Java and passing the SCJP Exam. I hope all of you find this book informative and indispensable wherever your Java adventures take you. Good luck!

About the Author

Rich Raposa runs a Java training firm, JLicense, Inc., based out of Rapid City, SD. He is a Sun Certified Java Programmer as well as a Sun Certified Java Instructor, and has spent the past 11 years delivering Java training courses to businesses across the United States. He has written dozens of Java courses ranging from introductory Java to advanced topics like Enterprise JavaBeans, Java Web development, and Java Web Services. He enjoys playing poker and playing the guitar (though he does not claim to be good at either).

Contents at a Glance

Contents

Introduction

The Sun Certified Programmer for Java Platform, Standard Edition 6 (Java SE 6) certification exam is for programmers experienced using the Java programming language. Achieving this certification provides clear evidence that a programmer understands the basic syntax and structure of the Java programming language and can create Java technology applications that run on server and desktop systems using Java SE 6.

How Do You Become SCJP Certified?

Pass the exam! You need to achieve a 65% (47 of 72 questions) or higher to pass the SCJP exam, and once you pass it, then you are a Sun Certified Java Programmer for the particular version of the exam that you passed. The latest SCJP exam is for JavaSE 6.0, which is the exam this book covers.

The SCJP Exam

The SCJP exam consists of 72 questions and you are given three and one-half hours to complete it. You take the exam at an Authorized Worldwide Prometric Testing Center. You take the SCJP exam on a computer using the mouse to display questions and answers. The questions appear on the screen one at a time, and you can navigate forward and backward at any time to view any question or modify your answer. Longer questions do not fit on the screen and require you to click on the scroll bar. You answer a question by clicking the appropriate answer.

You are not allowed to bring anything into the exam room, including a pen and paper. Most testing centers do not allow scratch paper and instead provide a small white board and a dry-erase marker. Most testing centers have security cameras as well, and it is likely that other people will be in the exam room taking different exams.

Types of Exam Questions

The SCJP exam consists of the following types of questions:

Multiple choice A majority of the questions are multiple choice. The number of answers given varies for each question, but typically you are given five to six answers. If a question has more than one answer, the question specifically states exactly how many correct answers there are for the question. For example, a question might have five answers and state that two of them are correct. The exam software only allows you to select two answers for that particular question.

Drag and drop About 10 to 15 of the exam questions involve filling in the blanks of a question. The answers are given in a list or box on the screen, and you drag and drop an answer into the blank. Some of the drag-and-drop questions have the exact same number of blanks as answers, and some of them have more answers than blanks.

When you navigate from one question to the next during the exam, the multiple choice questions simply appear on the screen. If the question is drag and drop, you do not see the actual question initially when you navigate to the question. Instead, you click a button that displays the question and answers, and when you have finished answering the question, you close the display and return to the navigation screen, where you can continue to the next question.

Tips for Taking the SCJP Exam

The most important tip I can give you for passing the exam is to practice answering questions. Study all of the sample questions that appear at the end of each chapter, as well as the bonus exam questions and the Assessment Test later in this Introduction. I tried to write questions that were indicative of the questions on the exam as far as knowledge and difficulty level. Between this book and its accompanying CD, you have over 400 questions to prepare you for the exam. Try to answer the questions to the best of your ability without "cheating" and looking back through the chapters, and practice a group of questions at a time without checking the answers right away. This will help simulate the taking of the actual exam.

Some questions on the SCJP exam are easier than others and require less time, while other questions might take several minutes to answer. You should average about 30 questions an hour. This pace will leave you with an hour or so at the end to go back and review your answers. If you start running out of time, make sure you at least answer every question on the exam, even if you have to guess. There is no penalty for a wrong answer, so do not leave a question blank.

Do not underestimate the exam objectives or try to guess what will or won't be on the exam. Because the number of objectives outnumbers the exam questions, not every exam objective has a corresponding exam question. Therefore, your best plan of action is to understand every exam objective. If you find yourself struggling with a particular topic, then write some code! Writing code and making mistakes along the way are the best way to understand any programming topic.

Also, expect the newer concepts of the Java language to appear on the exam. For example, I can guarantee that you will see a question on generics and enumerations. These are newer concepts in the language and they separate the new SCJP exam from the previous versions.

One unpleasant issue that I ran into with the drag-and-drop questions is that you cannot review the answer after you move on to the next question. If you go back to a drag-and-drop question and click the button to display the question and answers, your answer is lost and you have to re-answer the question in its entirety. Some of these drag-and-drop questions took some time to determine the answer, and I found that I did not always remember what my initial answer was, so I had to rethink the question all over again! If you are getting close to the end of your allotted time and you are trying to review all your answers, you might want to be judicious about whether to rework through a drag-and-drop question.

If you have to retake the exam, keep in mind that there are several versions of the exam and the questions will be different each time you take the exam.

Exam Registration

The price of the exam in the United State is $300 and you can purchase a voucher online at http://www.sun.com/training/catalog/courses/CX-310-065.xml. This URL is for the Java SE 6.0 exam. If you are taking a different version of the exam, you can find the corresponding registration page at http://www.sun.com/training/catalog/courses/. If you reside outside of the United States, visit http://www.sun.com/training/world_training.html to purchase a voucher for the exam.

After you purchase your exam voucher, you have up to one year from the date of purchase to use it. Each voucher is valid for one exam and can only be used at an Authorized Prometric Testing Center in the country for which it was purchased. Please be aware that exam vouchers are nonrefundable for any reason.

An exam voucher contains a unique number that you provide to Prometric when scheduling the exam. To schedule the exam, contact Prometric at (800) 795-3926 (United States and Canada). You can also visit the Prometric Web site at http://www.2test.com.

When you arrive at the testing facility to take the exam, you need to bring two forms of identification. One must be a current, government-issued photo ID, such as a valid passport or driver's license, with a photo that looks like you. Be sure the names on your ID are displayed the same way it is displayed on your exam record, and that both IDs have a current signature that looks like yours. Examples of other pieces of ID are credit cards and check cashing cards. The test will not be delivered without the appropriate form of identification. Prometric Test Center Administrators have the right to refuse seating you for the exam if they are unable to properly identify you.

Do not bring notes, pens, pencils, paper, large purses, or backpacks to the test center. Supplies needed for taking the exam are provided by the testing center. Prometric recommends that you arrive at the testing center at least 30 minutes before the test is scheduled to begin to allow time to complete the sign-in process.

Is This Book for You?

If you want to become certified as a Java programmer, this book is definitely for you. If you want to acquire a solid foundation in Java and your goal is to prepare for the exam by learning how to program and develop in Java, this book is for you. You'll find clear explanations of the concepts you need to grasp and plenty of help to achieve the high level of professional competency you need in order to succeed in your chosen field.

However, if you just want to attempt to pass the exam without really understanding Java, this study guide is not for you. It is written for people who want to acquire hands-on skills and in-depth knowledge of programming Java.

What's in the Book?

What makes a Sybex Study Guide the book of choice for hundreds of thousands of SCJPs? We took into account not only what you need to know to pass the exam, but also what you need to know to take what you've learned and apply it in the real world. Each book contains the following:

Objective-by-objective coverage of the topics you need to know   Each chapter lists the objectives covered in that chapter.

 The topics covered in this Study Guide map directly to Sun's official exam objectives. Each exam objective is covered completely.

Assessment Test   Directly following this Introduction is an Assessment Test that you should take. It is designed to help you determine how much you already know about the Java Platform, Standard Edition 6. Each question is tied to a topic discussed in the book. Using the results of the Assessment Test, you can figure out the areas where you need to focus your study. Of course, we do recommend you read the entire book.

Exam Essentials   To highlight what you learn, you'll find a list of Exam Essentials at the end of each chapter. The Exam Essentials section briefly highlights the topics that need your particular attention as you prepare for the exam.

Glossary   Throughout each chapter, you will be introduced to important terms and concepts that you will need to know for the exam. These terms appear in italic within the chapters, and at the end of the book, a detailed Glossary gives definitions for these terms, as well as other general terms you should know.

Review questions, complete with detailed explanations   Each chapter is followed by a set of Review Questions that test what you learned in the chapter. The questions are written with the exam in mind, meaning that they are designed to have the same look and feel as what you'll see on the exam.

Real World Scenarios   Because reading a book isn't enough for you to learn how to apply these topics in your everyday duties, we have provided Real World Scenarios in special sidebars. These explain when and why a particular solution would make sense, in a working environment you'd actually encounter.

Interactive CD   Every Sybex Study Guide comes with a CD complete with additional questions, flashcards for use with an interactive device, and the book in electronic format. Details are in the following section.

What's on the CD?

With this new member of our best-selling Study Guide series, we are including quite an array of training resources. The CD offers bonus exams and flashcards to help you study for the exam. We have also included the complete contents of the Study Guide in electronic form. The CD's resources are described here:

The Sybex E-book for *SCJP: Sun Certified Programmer for Java Platform, SE6 Study Guide*   Many people like the convenience of being able to carry their whole Study Guide on a CD. They also like being able to search the text via computer to find specific information quickly and easily. For these reasons, the entire contents of this Study Guide are supplied on the CD, in PDF. We've also included Adobe Acrobat Reader, which provides the interface for the PDF contents as well as the search capabilities.

The Sybex Test Engine   This is a collection of multiple-choice questions that will help you prepare for your exam. There are three sets of questions:

- Two bonus exams designed to simulate the actual live exam.

- All the questions from the Study Guide, presented in a test engine for your review. You can review questions by chapter, or you can take a random test.

- The Assessment Test.

    Here is a sample screen from the Sybex Test Engine:

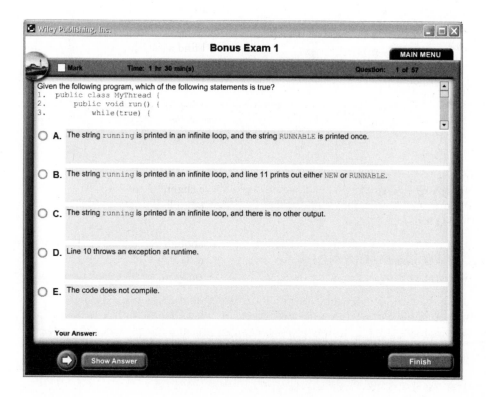

Sybex Flashcards for PCs and Handheld Devices The "flashcard" style of question offers an effective way to quickly and efficiently test your understanding of the fundamental concepts covered in the exam. The Sybex Flashcards set consists of 100 questions presented in a special engine developed specifically for this Study Guide series. Here's what the Sybex Flashcards interface looks like:

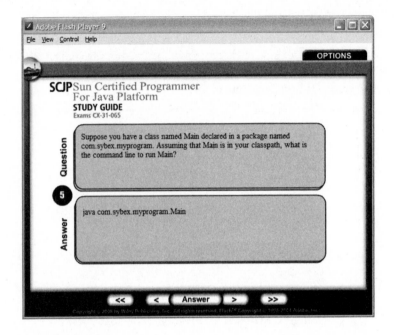

Because of the high demand for a product that will run on handheld devices, we have also developed, in conjunction with Land-J Technologies, a version of the flashcard questions that you can take with you on your Palm OS PDA (including the PalmPilot and Hand-spring's Visor).

How to Use This Book

This book is loaded with valuable information, and you will get the most out of your studying time if you understand how I put the book together. Here's a list on how to approach studying it so you get the most out of it:

1. Take the Assessment Test immediately following this introduction. It's okay if you don't know any of the answers—that's what this book is for! Carefully read over the explanations for any question you get wrong and make note of the chapters where that material is covered.

2. Study each chapter carefully, making sure that you fully understand the information and the test objectives listed at the beginning of each one. Again, pay extra-close attention to any chapter that includes material covered in questions you missed on the Assessment Test.

3. Answer all of the Review Questions related to each chapter. Specifically note any questions that confuse you and study those sections of the book again. And don't just skim these questions—make sure you understand each answer completely!

4. Try your hand at the bonus exams included on the companion CD. The questions in these exams appear only on the CD.

5. Test yourself using all the flashcards on the CD.

If you follow the steps listed here and study and practice the Review Questions, bonus exams, and the electronic flashcards, you should do fine.

Assessment Test

1. The following code appears in a file named `Book.java`. What is the result of compiling this source file? (Select one answer.)

```
1.  public class Book {
2.      private int pageNumber;
3.
4.      private class BookReader {
5.          public int getPage() {
6.              return pageNumber;
7.          }
8.      }
9.  }
```

A. The code compiles successfully and one bytecode file is generated: `Book.class`.

B. The code compiles successfully and two bytecode files are generated: `Book.class` and `BookReader.class`.

C. The code compiles successfully and two bytecode files are generated: `Book.class` and `Book$BookReader.class`.

D. A compiler error occurs on line 4.

E. A compiler error occurs on line 6.

2. Given the following TV class:

```
1.  public class TV {
2.      private String make;
3.      private String model;
4.
5.      public TV(String make, String model) {
6.          this.make = make;
7.          this.model = model;
8.      }
9.
10.     public boolean equals(TV other) {
11.         return make.equals(other.make) &&
12.                 model.equals(other.model);
13.     }
14.
15.     public int hashCode() {
16.         return make.length() * 10 + model.length();
17.     }
18. }
```

what is the result of the following statements?

```
TV a = new TV("Philips", "42PFL5603D");
TV b = new TV("Philips", "42PFL5603D");
if(a.equals(b)) {
    System.out.println("equal");
} else {
    System.out.println("not equal");
}
```

A. equal

B. not equal

C. Line 10 causes a compiler error.

D. Line 11 causes a compiler error.

E. Line 15 causes a runtime exception to occur.

3. When does the String object "hi" instantiated on line 2 become eligible for garbage collection?

```
1.  public class Hello {
2.      String greeting = "hi";
3.
4.      public static void main(String [] args) {
5.          Hello h = new Hello();
6.          h.greeting = null;
7.          System.gc();
8.          return;
9.      }
10. }
```

A. Immediately after line 5

B. Immediately after line 6

C. Immediately after line 7

D. Immediately after line 8

E. Immediately after line 9

4. What is the result of the following code?

```
6.  byte x = 23, y = 4;
7.  int z = 23 % 4;
8.  System.out.println(z);
```

A. 3

B. 4

C. 4.75

> **D.** Compiler error on line 6
>
> **E.** Compiler error on line 7

5. What is the result of the following program?

```
1.  public class Vehicle {
2.       public boolean used;
3.       public String make;
4.
5.       public static void main(String [] args) {
6.            Vehicle v = new Vehicle();
7.            if(v.used) {
8.                System.out.println(v.make);
9.            } else {
10.               System.out.println(v.make.length());
11.           }
12.      }
13. }
```

> **A.** null
>
> **B.** 0
>
> **C.** Line 7 generates a compiler error.
>
> **D.** Line 8 generates an exception at runtime.
>
> **E.** Line 10 generates an exception at runtime.

6. Given the following class definition:

```
1.  public class PrintStrings {
2.       public static void print(String... values) {
3.            for(String value : values) {
4.                System.out.print(value);
5.            }
6.       }
7.  }
```

which of the following statements are valid method calls to print?

> **A.** PrintStrings.print();
>
> **B.** PrintStrings.print("abc");
>
> **C.** PrintStrings.print('a', 'b', 'c');
>
> **D.** PrintStrings.print("a", "b", "c");
>
> **E.** PrintStrings.print(new java.util.Date());

7. Given the following `Football` class definition:

```
1.  package my.sports;
2.
3.  public class Football {
4.      public static final int teamSize = 11;
5.  }
```

and also the following `FootballGame` class:

```
1.  package my.apps;
2.
3.
4.
5.  public class FootballGame {
6.      public int getTeamSize() {
7.          return teamSize;
8.      }
9.  }
```

which of the following statements can appear on line 3 so that the `FootballGame` class compiles successfully?

A. `import static my.sports.Football;`

B. `import my.sports.Football;`

C. `import static my.sports.Football.*;`

D. `import static my.sports.*;`

E. No import statement is necessary.

8. What is the result of the following statements?

```
28. Integer i = 5;
29. switch(i) {
30.     case 1: System.out.print(1); break;
31.     case 3: System.out.print(3);
32.     case 5: System.out.print(5);
33.     case 7: System.out.print(7); break;
34.     default: System.out.print("default");
35. }
```

A. 5

B. 57

C. 57default

D. Compiler error on line 28

E. Compiler error on line 29

9. What is the result of the following code?

```
3.  Boolean m = true;
4.  int n = 14;
5.  do {
6.      n = n >> 1;
7.      if(n < 4) {
8.          m = new Boolean(false);
9.      }
10. }while(m);
11. System.out.println(n);
```

A. 0

B. 2

C. 3

D. An infinite loop

E. Line 10 generates a compiler error.

10. Given the following class definition:

```
1.  public class AssertDemo {
2.      public static void main(String [] args) {
3.          Integer x = 10;
4.          assert x == null && x >= 0;
5.          System.out.println(x);
6.      }
7.  }
```

and given the following command line, which one of the following statements is true?

`java AssertDemo`

A. Line 3 generates a compiler error.

B. Line 4 generates a compiler error.

C. Line 4 throws an `AssertionError` at runtime.

D. The output is 10.

11. Which of the following statements are true? (Select two.)

A. All string literals are automatically instantiated into a `String` object.

B. The `StringBuilder` and `StringBuffer` classes define the exact same public methods.

C. In a multithreaded environment, use `StringBuilder` instead of `StringBuffer`.

D. A `StringBuilder` object is immutable.

E. A `StringBuffer` object cannot change its length once it is instantiated.

12. Suppose you need to write data that consists of char values and String objects to a file that maintains the format of the original data. The data needs to be buffered to improve performance. Which two java.io classes can be chained together to best achieve this result?

A. FileWriter

B. FileOutputStream

C. BufferedOutputStream

D. BufferedWriter

E. PrintWriter

F. PipedOutputStream

13. What is the result of the following code?

```
14. DecimalFormat df = new DecimalFormat("#,000.0#");
15. double pi = 3.141592653;
16. System.out.println(df.format(pi));
```

A. 3.141592653

B. 0,003.14

C. ,003.1

D. 003.14

E. 00.04

14. What is the result of the following program?

```
1.    public class PrintX implements Runnable {
2.        private int count;
3.
4.        public PrintX(int count) {
5.            this.count = count;
6.        }
7.
8.        public void run() {
9.            for(int i = 1; i <= count; i++) {
10.               System.out.print("x");
11.           }
12.       }
13.
14.       public static void main(String [] args) {
15.           Thread t = new Thread(new PrintX(3));
16.           t.start();
17.           System.out.print("y");
```

```
18.            t.start();
19.        }
20. }
```

A. xxxyxxx

B. yxxxxxx

C. Six xs and one y printed in an indeterminate order

D. The code throws an exception at runtime.

E. The code does not compile.

15. What is the result of the following statements?

```
4.  Thread t = new Thread() {
5.      public void run() {
6.          System.out.println(
7.              Thread.currentThread().getState());
8.      }
9.  };
10. t.start();
```

A. NEW

B. RUNNABLE

C. BLOCKED

D. TERMINATED

E. The state of the thread is indeterminate.

16. Given the following class definitions:

```
1.  public class Student implements java.io.Serializable {
2.      private String name;
3.
4.      public static void main(String [] args) {
5.          _____ s = new Senior();
6.      }
7.  }
8.
9.  class Senior extends Student {}
10.
11. class Junior extends Student {}
```

which of the following answers can fill in the blank on line 5 and have the code compile successfully? (Select three.)

A. Object

B. Junior

C. Student

D. String

E. java.io.Serializable

17. What is the result of the following program?

```
1.  public abstract class Message {
2.      public String recipient;
3.
4.      public abstract final void sendMessage();
5.
6.      public static void main(String [] args) {
7.          Message m = new TextMessage();
8.          m.recipient = "6055551212";
9.          m.sendMessage();
10.     }
11. }
12.
13. class TextMessage extends Message {
14.     public final void sendMessage() {
15.         System.out.println("TextMessage to "
16.                             + recipient);
17.     }
18. }
```

A. TextMessage to 6055551212

B. TextMessage to null

C. Compiler error on line 1

D. Compiler error on line 4

E. Compiler error on line 9

18. Given the following Parent class definition:

```
1.  public class Parent {
2.      Object doSomething(int x) {
3.          return null;
4.      }
5.  }
```

which of the following methods could appear in a child class of Parent? (Select three answers.)

A. `public void doSomething(int x)`

B. `protected String doSomething(int x)`

C. `private Thread doSomething(int x)`

D. `private Thread doSomething(short x)`

E. `public double doSomething(int y)`

19. What is the result of the following statements?

```
23. List<Number> data = new Vector<Number>();
24. data.add(10);
25. data.add("4.5F");
26. data.add(new Double(56.7));
27. for(Number number : data) {
28.     System.out.print(number);
29. }
```

A. `104.556.7`

B. `104.5F56.7`

C. `10` followed by a `ClassCastException`

D. Compiler error on line 25

E. Compiler error on line 27

20. Given the following Box class definition:

```
1.  public class Box<T> {
2.      T value;
3.
4.      public Box(T value) {
5.          this.value = value;
6.      }
7.
8.      public T getValue() {
9.          return value;
10.     }
11. }
```

what is the result of the following statements?

```
15. Box<String> one = new Box<String>("a string");
16. Box<Integer> two = new Box<Integer>(123);
17. System.out.print(one.getValue());
18. System.out.print(two.getValue());
```

A. Compiler error on line 1

B. Compiler error on line 2

C. Compiler error on line 16

D. a `string123`

E. The code compiles but throws an exception at runtime.

21. Given the following statements:

```
30. Set<Object> objects = new HashSet<Object>();
31. String one = "hello";
32. int two = 2;
33. Boolean three = new Boolean(true);
34. objects.add(one);
35. objects.add(two);
36. objects.add(three);
37. objects.add(three);
38. for(Object object : objects) {
39.     System.out.print(object);
40. }
```

which of the following statements are true? (Select two.)

A. The code compiles successfully.

B. The output is `hello`, 2 and `true` in an indeterminate order.

C. The output is `hello`, 2, `true` and `true` in an indeterminate order.

D. Line 35 generates a compiler error.

E. Line 37 throws an exception at runtime.

22. Suppose a class named `com.mypackage.MyProgram` contains the `main` method of a stand-alone Java application, and `MyProgram.class` is in the following directory:

`\my\classes\com\mypackage`

Which of the following commands successfully executes `MyProgram`? (Select two answers.)

A. `java -classpath \my\classes com.mypackage.MyProgram`

B. `java -classpath \my\classes\com\mypackage MyProgram`

C. `java -classpath=\my\classes com.mypackage.MyProgram`

D. `java -classpath \my\classes\com mypackage.MyProgram`

E. `java -cp \my\classes com.mypackage.MyProgram`

23. What is the result of the following program?

```
1.  public class MathFunctions {
2.       public static void addToInt(int x, int amountToAdd)
3.       {
4.            x = x + amountToAdd;
5.       }
6.
7.       public static void main(String [] args) {
8.            int a = 15;
9.            int b = 10;
10.           MathFunctions.addToInt(a, b);
11.           System.out.println(a);
12.       }
13. }
```

A. 25

B. 15

C. 10

D. A compiler error occurs on line 4.

E. A compiler error occurs on line 10.

24. Given the following interface and class definitions:

```
1.  //Readable.java
2.  public interface Readable {
3.       public void read();
4.       public int MAX_LENGTH = 10;
5.  }
```

```
1.  //MyReader.java
2.  public class MyReader implements Readable {
3.       public void read() {
4.            Readable.MAX_LENGTH = 25;
5.            System.out.println(Readable.MAX_LENGTH);
6.       }
7.  }
```

what is the result of the following statement?

```
new MyReader().read();
```

A. 25

B. 10

C. Compiler error on line 3 of Readable.java

D. Compiler error on line 4 of `Readable.java`

E. Compiler error on line 4 of `MyReader.java`

25. Given the following enum declaration:

```
1.  public enum Toppings {
2.      PEPPERONI, SAUSAGE, ONION, OLIVES, CHEESE;
3.  }
```

what is the result of the following statements?

```
8.  Toppings [] choices = Toppings.values();
9.  System.out.println(choices[1]);
```

A. PEPPERONI

B. SAUSAGE

C. The code compiles but the output is indeterminate.

D. Line 8 generates a compiler error.

E. Line 9 generates a compiler error.

26. What is the result of the following code?

```
21. final byte b = 1;
22. int value = 2;
23. switch(value) {
24.     case b : System.out.print("A");
25.             break;
26.     case 2 : System.out.print("B");
27.     case 3 : System.out.print("C");
28.     default : System.out.print("D");
29.             break;
30. }
```

A. Compiler error on line 24

B. B

C. BC

D. BCD

E. Compiler error on line 29

27. Given the following class definition:

```
1.  public class EchoInput {
2.      public static void main(String [] args) {
3.          if(args.length <= 3) {
4.              assert false;
5.          }
```

```
6.              System.out.println(args[0] + args[1]
7.                              + args[2]);
8.      }
9.  }
```

what is the result of the following command line?

```
java EchoInput hi there
```

A. hithere

B. The assert statement on line 4 throws an AssertionError.

C. Line 7 throws an ArrayIndexOutOfBoundsException.

D. The code compiles and runs successfully, but there is no output.

E. The code does not compile.

28. What is the result of the following code?

```
46. NumberFormat nf =
47.         NumberFormat.getCurrencyInstance(Locale.US);
48. double value = 123.456;
49. System.out.println(nf.format(value));
```

A. $123.456

B. $123.45

C. $123.46

D. 123.45

E. 123.46

29. Given the following code:

```
3.  Pattern p = Pattern.compile(".+es");
4.  String [] words = {"unless", "guesses",
5.                      "boxes", "guest"};
6.  for(String word : words) {
7.      if(p.matcher(word).matches()) {
8.          System.out.println(word);
9.      }
10. }
```

which of the following strings is output? (Select all that apply.)

A. unless

B. guesses

C. boxes

D. guest

E. None of the above

30. What state can a NEW thread transition into? (Select all that apply.)

   A. WAITING

   B. RUNNABLE

   C. BLOCKED

   D. TIMED_WAITING

   E. TERMINATED

31. What is the output of the following program?

```
1.  public class Worker extends Thread {
2.      public void run() {
3.          System.out.print("N");
4.      }
5.
6.      public static void main(String [] args) {
7.          Thread worker = new Worker();
8.          worker.run();
9.          System.out.print("O");
10.     }
11. }
```

   A. The output is always NO.

   B. The output is always ON.

   C. The output varies and is either NO or ON.

   D. The code does not compile.

32. Fill in the blank: When an object performs a collection of closely related tasks, this is referred to as _____.

   A. The is-a relationship

   B. The has-a relationship

   C. Tight encapsulation

   D. Loose coupling

   E. High cohesion

33. What is the result of the following code?

```
1.  public class Beverage {
2.      private void drink() {
3.          System.out.println("Beverage");
4.      }
5.
6.      public static void main(String [] args) {
7.          Beverage b = new Coffee();
```

```
8.              b.drink();
9.       }
10. }
11.
12. class Coffee extends Beverage {
13.      public void drink() {
14.          System.out.println("Coffee");
15.      }
16. }
```

    A. Beverage

    B. Coffee

    C. Compiler error on line 2

    D. Compiler error on line 8

    E. Compiler error on line 13

34. Given the following variable declaration:

```
Set<? extends RuntimeException> set = _____;
```

which of the following statements can appear in the blank line so that the statement compiles successfully? (Select all that apply.)

    A. new HashSet<? extends RuntimeException()

    B. new TreeSet<RuntimeException>()

    C. new TreeSet<NullPointerException>()

    D. new LinkedHashSet<Exception>()

    E. None of the above

Answers to Assessment Test

1. **C.** The code compiles fine, so D and E are incorrect. The bytecode file for the outer class Book is Book.class, and the bytecode file for the inner class BookReader is Book$BookReader.class, so the answer is C. For more information, see Chapter 2.

2. **A.** The code compiles fine, so C, D, and E are incorrect. Based on the definition of the equals method, two TV objects are equal if they have the same make and model fields, so the line a.equals(b) evaluates to true and equal is output, so the answer is A. For more information, see Chapter 1.

3. **B.** The String on line 2 is created in memory after line 5 executes, and the greeting reference points to it. After line 6, no references point to "hi" anymore and it immediately becomes eligible for garbage collection then, so the answer is B. For more information, see Chapter 1.

4. **A.** The code compiles fine, so D and E are incorrect. The value of z is the remainder of 23 divided by 4, which is 3. Therefore, the answer is A. For more information, see Chapter 1.

5. **E.** The code compiles fine, so C is incorrect. The used field initializes to false and the make field initializes to null for the new Vehicle v. Therefore, line 7 is false and line 10 executes. Because v.make is a null reference, attempting to invoke its length method results in a NullPointerException at runtime. Therefore, the answer is E. For more information, see Chapter 2.

6. **A, B, and D.** The print method can take in any number of String objects, including zero, so A, B, and D are valid statements. C attempts to pass in chars, which is not valid and generates a compiler error. D also generates a compiler error attempting to pass in a Date object. For more information, see Chapter 2.

7. **C.** The code does not compile without a proper import for the teamSize variable on line 7, so E is incorrect. A is not a valid statement. B is a valid statement but does not import teamSize, so B is incorrect. D causes a compiler error because sports is not a class or interface name. C is valid and imports all static members of the Football class, so C is the correct answer. For more information, see Chapter 2.

8. **B.** You cannot switch on an Integer, but because of Java's autoboxing, i is converted to an int, so lines 28 and 29 are valid, which means D and E are incorrect. The value of i is 5, so the case on line 32 executes and prints 5. Because there is no break, 7 is printed. The break on line 33 causes control to break out of the switch, so the output is 57 and the answer is B. For more information, see Chapter 3.

9. **C.** Line 10 compiles fine, so E is incorrect. Line 6 right shifts n by 1, which is equivalent to integer division by 2. The first time through the loop, n becomes 14/2 = 7; the second time through n becomes 7/2 = 3. Because 3 < 4 is true, m is set to false and the loop terminates. The value of n is 3, which is printed on line 11, so the answer is C. For more information, see Chapter 3.

10. D. The code compiles, so A and B are incorrect. The command line does not enable assertions, so C cannot happen. Line 5 executes and prints out 10, so the answer is D. For more information, see Chapter 3.

11. A and B. String literals are automatically instantiated into String objects, so A is true. B is also true; the two classes contain the same methods. The only difference between StringBuilder and StringBuffer is that StringBuffer is thread-safe, which is why C is false. You should use StringBuffer if using mutable strings in a multithreaded application. D is false; the StringBuilder and StringBuffer classes represent mutable character sequences. E is false; a StringBuffer and StringBuilder can grow and shrink to match the number of characters in the sequence. For more information, see Chapter 4.

12. A and D. The data to be output consists of strings and characters, so writer classes are the best choice. FileWriter is needed to write to the file, and BufferedWriter is needed to buffer the data, so the best choices are A and D. For more information, see Chapter 4.

13. D. The DecimalFormat object calls for at least three digits before the decimal point, so two leading 0s appears before the 3. The format also calls for at least one digit past the decimal but no more than two. Therefore, the output is 003.14 and the answer is D. For more information, see Chapter 4.

14. D. The code compiles fine, so E is incorrect. However, a Thread object cannot be started twice, so line 18 throws an IllegalThreadStateException and D is the correct answer. For more information, see Chapter 5.

15. B. The state of the currently running thread must be RUNNABLE, so the answer is B. For more information, see Chapter 5.

16. A, C, and E. A and C are valid because Object and Student are both parent classes of Senior. B and D are not valid because Junior and String are not compatible with Senior. E is valid because Senior is of type Serializable—a type inherited from Student. For more information, see Chapter 6.

17. D. The code does not compile, so A and B are incorrect. The problem with this code is the Message declares the sendMessage method as both abstract and final, which does not make sense. An abstract method must be overridden, and a final method cannot be overridden. Using abstract and final on the same method results in a compiler error, so the answer is D. For more information, see Chapter 6.

18. B and D. A is incorrect because void is an incompatible return type with Object. (If the return type is changed, it must be a subclass of the return type in the parent class.) B is a valid overriding of doSomething in Parent because it is more accessible and String is a subclass of Object. C is incorrect because it assigns a weaker access, which is not allowed. D is valid because it is not overriding doSomething in Parent—it is overloading the method instead. E is not valid because double is not a subclass of Object. Therefore, the answers are B and D. For more information, see Chapter 6.

19. D. The code does not compile, so A, B, and C are incorrect. E is also incorrect; line 27 compiles fine because data contains Number objects. Line 25 does not compile because data is instantiated using generics; only Number objects can be added to data and "4.5F" is a String. Therefore, the answer is D. For more information, see Chapter 7.

20. D. The compiles and runs fine, so A, B, C, and E are incorrect. The Box class uses a generic type named T. For one, the generic type is a String. For two, the generic type is an Integer. The two value fields are printed out on lines 17 and 18, which print a string123, so the answer is D. For more information, see Chapter 7.

21. A and B. The code compiles and runs fine, so D and E are incorrect and A is true. Line 37 attempts to add the same object to the set, which does not alter the set. Therefore, C is incorrect. The for loop on line 38 outputs the objects in an indeterminate order, so the other correct answer is B. For more information, see Chapter 7.

22. A and E. A assigns the -classpath flag to the appropriate directory. E also sets the class path correctly except -cp is used. C uses an equals sign, =, with the -classpath flag, which is not the correct syntax. B and D set the class path to the wrong directory and also incorrectly refer to the MyProgram class without its fully qualified name. Therefore, the answers are A and E. For more information, see Chapter 1.

23. B. The code compiles successfully, so D and E are incorrect. The value of a cannot be changed by the addToInt method, no matter what the method does, because only a copy of a is passed into the parameter x. Therefore, a does not change and the output on line 11 is 15, so the answer is B. For more information, see Chapter 1.

24. E. The Readable interface compiles fine, so C and D are incorrect. However, the MyReader class does not compile, so A and B are incorrect. Fields in an interface are implicitly final, so attempting to set MAX_LENGTH to 25 on line 4 of MyReader is not allowed and generates a compiler error. Therefore, the answer is E. For more information, see Chapter 2.

25. B. The code compiles fine, so D and E are incorrect. The values method of an enum returns an array containing the elements in the enum, in the order they are declared in the enum. The element at index 1 is SAUSAGE, which is printed at line 9. Therefore, the answer is B. For more information, see Chapter 2.

26. D. The code compiles fine, so A and E are incorrect. The case on line 26 is satisfied, so B is printed. There is no break, so line 27 executes and C is printed. Because there is no break, the default block executes and D is printed on line 28. Therefore, the output is BCD and the answer is D. For more information, see Chapter 3.

27. C. The code compiles fine, so E is incorrect. The command line has only two arguments, so args.length is 2 and line 3 is true. However, because assertions are not enabled, line 4 does not throw an AssertionError, so B is incorrect. Line 7 attempts to print args[2], which generates an ArrayIndexOutOfBoundsException, so the answer is C. For more information, see Chapter 3.

28. C. The currency format rounds decimals up to two decimal places, so 123.456 is rounded up to 123.46 and printed in the U.S. locale. The output is $123.46, and therefore the answer is C. For more information, see Chapter 4.

29. B and C. The regular expression .+es matches character streams that start with any number of characters and end in es. Two of the strings in the array match this pattern: guesses and boxes. Therefore, the answers are B and C. For more information, see Chapter 4.

30. B. A NEW thread can only transition into the RUNNABLE state, so the answer is B. For more information, see Chapter 5.

31. A. The code compiles fine and runs fine, so D is incorrect. On line 8, the run method of the new Worker thread is invoked. However, the run method does not start a new thread in the process. (Only a call to start starts a new thread.) In other words, this program is not multithreaded and the call to run occurs within the main thread. The output of this program is always NO and therefore the answer is A. For more information, see Chapter 5.

32. E. The definition of high cohesion is when an object performs a collection of closely related tasks, so the answer is E. For more information, see Chapter 6.

33. A. The code compiles fine, so C, D and E are incorrect. A private method cannot be overridden, so drink in Coffee is not overriding drink in Beverage. The method call to drink on line 8 is referring to the private method on line 2, and that is also the method that gets invoked at runtime because it is not overridden. Therefore, the output is Beverage and the correct answer is A. For more information, see Chapter 6.

34. B and C. The reference set declares an upper bound of RuntimeException on the generic, so D is not valid because Exception is a parent class of RuntimeException. A is not valid because a new statement cannot declare a wildcard in the generic type. B is valid because TreeSet implements Set. C is valid because TreeSet implements Set and NullPointerException is a subclass of RuntimeException. Therefore, the answers are B and C. For more information, see Chapter 7.

Chapter
1

Fundamentals

✓ Given a code example and a scenario, write code that uses the appropriate access modifiers, package declarations, and import statements to interact with (through access or inheritance) the code in the example.

✓ Given an example of a class and a command line, determine the expected runtime behavior.

✓ Determine the effect upon object references and primitive values when they are passed into methods that perform assignments or other modifying operations on the parameters.

✓ Given a code example, recognize the point at which an object becomes eligible for garbage collection, determine what is and is not guaranteed by the garbage collection system, and recognize the behaviors of the Object .finalize() method.

✓ Given the fully-qualified name of a class that is deployed inside and/or outside a JAR file, construct the appropriate directory structure for that class. Given a code example and a classpath, determine whether the classpath will allow the code to compile successfully.

✓ Write code that correctly applies the appropriate operators including assignment operators (limited to: =, +=, -=), arithmetic operators (limited to: +, -, *, /, %, ++, --), relational operators (limited to: <, <=, >, >=, ==, !=), the instanceof operator, logical operators (limited to: &, |, ^, !, &&, ||), and the conditional operator (? :), to produce a desired result. Write code that determines the equality of two objects or two primitives.

Java is an interpretive, object-oriented programming language that Sun Microsystems developed. A considerable benefit of writing Java applications is that they run in a Java Runtime Environment (JRE) that is well defined. As a Java programmer, you know your Java program is going to run on a Java Virtual Machine (JVM), regardless of the device or operating system. Consequently, you know an `int` is 32 bits and signed, a `boolean` is `true` or `false`, method arguments are passed by value, and the garbage collector cleans up your unreachable objects whenever it feels like it. (Okay, not every aspect of Java is an exact science!) The point is that Java runs in a precise environment, and passing the SCJP exam requires a strong knowledge of these well-defined Java fundamentals.

This chapter covers the fundamentals of Java programming, including writing Java classes, running Java applications, creating packages, defining classpath, and using the Java operators. We will also discuss the details of garbage collection and call by value.

Writing Java Classes

The exam objectives state that you need to be able to "write code that uses the appropriate access modifiers, package declarations, and imports statements." In other words, you need to be able to write Java classes, which makes sense because Java is an object-oriented programming (OOP) language and writing classes is an essential aspect of OOP. Your executable Java code will appear within the definition of a class. A *class* describes an object, which is a noun in your program. The object can either represent something tangible, like a television or an employee, or it can represent something less obvious but just as useful in your program, like an event handler or a stream of data being read from a file.

An *object* is an instance of a class. Think of a class as a blueprint for a house, and the object as the house. Another common analogy is to think of a class as a recipe for cookies, and the objects are the cookies. (We will discuss the details of instantiating objects in Chapter 2, "Declarations, Initialization, and Scoping.") Because classes are a fundamental aspect of Java programming, the certification exam assumes you are familiar with the rules for writing them, and in this section we cover these details.

For starters, a Java class must be defined in a text file with a `.java` extension. In addition, if the class is declared `public`, then the name of the file must match the name of the class. Consequently, a `.java` file can only contain at most one top-level `public` class. For example, the following class definition must appear in a file named `Cat.java`:

```
public class Cat {
  public String name;
  public int weight;
}
```

Compiled Java code is referred to as *bytecode*, and the name of the bytecode file matches the name of the class. Compiling the Cat.java source file creates a bytecode file named Cat.class.

Line Numbers

Java source files do not contain line numbers. However, the classes on the exam display line numbers. If the numbering starts with a 1, then the entire definition of a source file is being displayed. If the numbering starts with some other value, then only a portion of a source file is being displayed. You will see this explanation in the instructions at the beginning of the SCJP exam.

Java allows multiple classes in a single .java file as long as no more than one of the top-level classes is declared public. The compiler still generates a separate .class file for each class defined in the .java file. For example, suppose a file named Customer.java contains the following two class definitions:

```
1.   public class Customer {
2.      public String name;
3.      public String address;
4.   }
5.
6.   class Order {
7.      public int partNumber;
8.      public int quantity;
9.      public boolean shipped;
10.  }
```

Compiling Customer.java generates two files: Customer.class and Order.class. Note that the Order class cannot be public because Customer is already public, nor can Order be protected or private because Java does not allow top-level classes to be protected or private. Therefore, Order must have the default access, often referred to as friendly or package-level access, meaning only classes within the same package can use the Order class. (We discuss packages in the next section.)

Access Specifiers for Top-Level Classes

A top-level class has two options for an access modifier: public or package-level access (often called the default access). Keep an eye out for exam questions that declare a top-level class as private or protected. For example, the following code will not compile:

```
//Generates a compiler error: "modifier private not allowed here"
private class HelloWorld {
    public static void main(String [] args) {
        System.out.println(args[1] + args[2]);
    }
}
```

Multiple Classes in a Single File

Java allows multiple top-level classes to be defined in a single file, but in the real world this is rarely done. We typically want our classes to be public, and only top-level classes can be public. That being said, the exam might contain questions that define multiple classes in a single source file because it is convenient and many questions on the exam involve more than one class.

Packages

The exam objectives state that you need to be able to "write code that uses the appropriate package declarations and import statements," and I can assure you there will be more than one question on the exam testing your knowledge of the package keyword and its effect on a Java class. This section discusses the details you need to know about Java packages. A *package* is a grouping of classes and interfaces. It can also contain enumerations and annotated types, but because these are special types of classes and interfaces, I will refer to items in a package as simply classes and interfaces for brevity. This grouping of classes and interfaces is typically based on their relationship and usage. For example, the java.io package contains classes and interfaces related to input and output. The java.net package contains the classes and interfaces related to networking. There are two key benefits of using packages in Java:

- Packages organize Java programs by grouping together related classes and interfaces.
- Packages create a namespace for your classes and interfaces.

The Application Programming Interface (API) for the Java Platform, Standard Edition (Java SE) contains hundreds of packages that you can use in any Java SE application. As a Java programmer, you will create your own packages for the classes that you develop. Packages are often drawn as tabbed folders, as shown in Figure 1.1.

FIGURE 1.1   When designing a Java application, packages are drawn as tabbed folders.

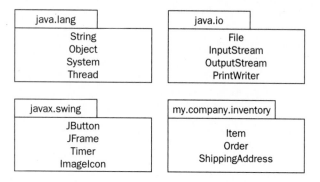

To view all of the packages in the Java SE API, visit the API documentation at http://java.sun.com/javase/6/docs/api/. This web page contains three frames. The upper-left frame is a list of all the packages. Clicking a package displays its classes and interfaces in the lower-left frame. Clicking a class or interface in the lower-left frame displays its documentation page in the main frame. You should spend time browsing the Java API documentation! I find it extremely useful, especially when using a Java class or interface for the first time.

If you are developing a Java program with hundreds of classes and interfaces, grouping related types into packages provides a much-needed organization to the project. In addition, the namespace provided by a package is useful for avoiding naming conflicts.

This section discusses these two benefits of packages in detail. I will start with a discussion on the package keyword and then cover the details of imports, the CLASSPATH environment variable, and the directory structure required for packages.

The *package* Keyword

The package keyword puts a class or interface in a package, and it must be the first line of code in your source file (aside from comments, which can appear anywhere within a source file). For example, the following Employee class is declared in the com.sybex.payroll package:

```
package com.sybex.payroll;

public class Employee {
  public Employee() {
      System.out.println(
          "Constructing a com.sybex.payroll.Employee");
  }
}
```

Putting a class in a package has two important side effects that you need to know for the exam:

1. The fully qualified name of a class or interface changes when it is in a package. The package name becomes a prefix for the class name. For example, the fully qualified name of the Employee class shown earlier is com.sybex.payroll.Employee.

2. The compiled bytecode file must appear in a directory structure on your file system that matches the package name. For example, a .class file for any class or interface in the com.sybex.payroll package must appear in a directory structure matching \com\sybex\payroll\. You can either create this directory structure yourself or use the -d flag during compilation and the compiler will create the necessary directory structure for you. We discuss the -d flag in detail later in this section.

The fully qualified name of the Employee class is com.sybex.payroll.Employee. Other classes that want to use the Employee class need to refer to it by its fully qualified name. For example, the following program creates an instance of the Employee class:

```
public class CreateEmployee {
  public static void main(String [] args) {
      com.sybex.payroll.Employee e =
          new com.sybex.payroll.Employee();
  }
}
```

Here's the output of the CreateEmployee program:

```
Constructing a com.sybex.payroll.Employee
```

The Unnamed Package

If a class is not specifically declared in a package, then that class belongs to the *unnamed package*. Classes and interfaces in the unnamed package cannot be imported into a source file. You should only use the unnamed package when writing simple classes and interfaces that are not being used in a production application. In the real world, you will rarely write a Java class or interface that is not declared in a package. Your classes will appear in a package name that contains your company's Internet domain name, which the next section discusses.

The *import* Keyword

As you can see by the CreateEmployee program, using the fully qualified name of a class can be tedious and makes for a lot of typing! The import keyword makes your life as a coder easier by allowing you to refer to a class in a source file without using its fully qualified name.

The import keyword is used to import a single class or, when used with the wildcard (*), an entire package. A source file can have any number of import statements, and they must appear after the package declaration and before the class declaration. Importing classes and packages tells the compiler that you are not going to use fully qualified names for classes. The compiler searches your list of imports to determine the fully qualified names of the classes referenced in the source file.

Here is the CreateEmployee program again, except this time the com.sybex.payroll .Employee class is imported, allowing the Employee class to be referred to without using its fully qualified name:

```
import com.sybex.payroll.Employee;

public class CreateEmployee2 {
    public static void main(String [] args) {
        Employee e = new Employee();
    }
}
```

The output is the same as before:

```
Constructing a com.sybex.payroll.Employee
```

In fact, the compiled bytecode files CreateEmployee.class and CreateEmployee2.class are completely identical (except for the number 2 that appears in CreateEmployee2.class). The import statement does not affect the compiled code. Behind the scenes, the compiler removes the import statement and replaces each occurrence of Employee with com.sybex .payroll.Employee.

What Does Import Mean?

The term *import* sounds like something is being brought into your source file, but nothing is physically added to your source code by importing a class or package. An import statement is strictly to make your life as a programmer easier. The Java compiler removes all import statements and replaces all the class names in your source code with their fully qualified names. For this reason, you never need to use import statements. Instead, you can use fully qualified names throughout your source files. However, you will quickly discover the benefit of import statements, especially when you work with long package names.

The CreateEmployee and CreateEmployee2 programs both refer to the String class. String is defined in the java.lang package, but this package was not imported. The java .lang package is unique in that the compiler automatically imports all the public classes and interfaces of java.lang into every source file, so there is never any need to import types from java.lang (although it is perfectly valid to do so).

The following program demonstrates an import statement that uses the wildcard to import an entire package. The program uses the File, FileReader, BufferedReader, and IOException classes, all found in the java.io package. The program reads a line of text from a file named mydata.txt.

```
1.  import java.io.*;
2.
3.  public class ReadFromFile {
4.    public static void main(String [] args) {
5.        File file = new File("mydata.txt");
6.        FileReader fileReader = null;
7.        try {
8.            fileReader = new FileReader(file);
9.            BufferedReader in = new BufferedReader(fileReader);
10.            System.out.println(in.readLine());
11.        }catch(IOException e) {
12.            e.printStackTrace();
13.        }
14.    }
15. }
```

Because nothing is actually included into your source file by the import keyword, using the wildcard does not impact the size of your bytecode files. However, common practice in Java is to avoid using the wildcard because it may lead to ambiguity when two packages are imported that share a common class name. For example, the following code does not compile because there is a class called AttributeList in both the javax.swing.text.html .parser package and the javax.management package:

```
1. import javax.swing.text.html.parser.*;
2. import javax.management.*;
3.
4. public class ImportDemo {
5.    public AttributeList a;
6. }
```

The ImportDemo class generates the following compiler error:

```
reference to AttributeList is ambiguous, both class
  javax.management.AttributeList in javax.management and class
  javax.swing.text.html.parser.AttributeList in
  javax.swing.text.html.parser match
    public AttributeList a;
```

If you ever are in a situation where you need to use two classes with the same name but in different packages, then using imports does not work. You will need to refer to each class by their fully qualified name in your source file. The following code compiles successfully:

```
1. public class FullyQualifiedDemo {
2.     public javax.management.AttributeList a1;
3.     public javax.swing.text.html.parser.AttributeList a2;
4. }
```

The `FullyQualifiedDemo` program demonstrates why packages are often referred to as namespaces because package names are used to avoid naming conflicts. Without packages, there is no way for the compiler or the JVM to distinguish between the two `AttributeList` classes. However, because the two `AttributeList` classes are declared in different packages, they can be referred to by their fully qualified names to avoid any ambiguity.

Naming Convention for Packages

The namespace ambiguity situation can still occur if programmers happen to use the same package names in different programs. If you and I both write a class called Dog and we both define Dog in a package named pets, then a naming conflict still occurs. However, the standard Java naming convention for a package name is to use your company's domain name (in reverse) as a prefix to your package names. For example, a class written by an employee of Sybex uses a package name that starts with com.sybex.

Subsequent components of the package name may include your department and project name, followed by a descriptive name for the package. For example, com.sybex .scjpbook.pets is a good package name for a class named Dog that appears in this book. It is extremely unlikely that someone else would use this package name, although I am sure there are other Dog classes in the world.

If everyone who writes Java code follows this naming convention for package names, then naming conflicts can only occur within a single company or project, making it easier to resolve the naming conflict.

Package Directory Structure

The exam objectives state that "given the fully-qualified name of a class that is deployed inside and/or outside a JAR file," you need to be able to "construct the appropriate directory structure for that class." This objective refers to the required directory structure that results from using packages. In addition to creating a namespace, packages organize your programs by grouping related classes and interfaces together. One result of using packages is that the bytecode of a class or interface must appear in a directory structure that matches its package name. If you do not put your bytecode in the proper directory structure, the compiler or the JVM will be unable to find your classes.

Suppose we have the following class definition:

```
package com.sybex.payroll;

public class Employee {
    public Employee() {
        System.out.println(
            "Constructing a com.sybex.payroll.Employee");
    }
}
```

This `Employee` class is in the `com.sybex.payroll` package, so its compiled file `Employee` `.class` must be in a directory with a pathname `\com\sybex\payroll`. This requires a directory named `\com`, which can appear anywhere on your file system. Inside `\com` you must have a `\sybex` subdirectory, which must contain a `\payroll` subdirectory.

The `\com` directory can appear anywhere on your file system. A common technique is to put your source files in a directory named `\src` and your bytecode files in a directory named `\build`. For example, suppose the `Employee` source file is in the following directory:

```
c:\myproject\src\com\sybex\payroll\Employee.java
```

Suppose you want the compiled code to be in the `c:\myproject\build` directory. You can use the `-d` flag of the compiler to achieve this. The `-d` flag has two effects:

- The compiled code will be output in the directory specified by the `-d` flag.
- The appropriate directory structure that matches the package names of the classes is created automatically in the output directory.

Consider the following compiler command, executed from the `c:\myproject\src` directory:

```
javac -d c:\myproject\build .\com\sybex\payroll\Employee.java
```

The `-d` flag specifies the output directory as `c:\myproject\build`. Assuming the class compiles successfully, the compiler creates the file `Employee.class` in the following directory:

```
c:\myproject\build\com\sybex\payroll\Employee.class
```

Keep in mind the directory `c:\myproject\build` is arbitrary; we could have output the bytecode into the directory of our choosing. After you start putting bytecode in arbitrary directories on your file system, the compiler and the JVM need to know where to look to find it. They look for the bytecode files in your classpath, an important concept that the next section discusses in detail.

The *CLASSPATH* Environment Variable

The exam objectives state that "given a code example and a classpath," you need to be able to "determine whether the classpath will allow the code to compile successfully." The *classpath* refers to the path on your file system where your .class files are saved, and the classpath is defined by the CLASSPATH environment variable. The CLASSPATH environment variable specifies the directories and JAR files where you want the compiler and the JVM to search for bytecode. Using CLASSPATH allows your bytecode to be stored in the directory of your choosing, as well as in multiple directories or Java archive (JAR) files.

For example, suppose you have a class named com.sybex.payroll.Employee. The compiler and the JVM look for the \com\sybex\payroll directory structure by searching your CLASSPATH environment variable. For example, if Employee.class is in the following directory:

```
c:\Documents and Settings\Rich\workspaces\build\com\sybex\payroll
```

then your CLASSPATH needs to include the directory:

```
c:\Documents and Settings\Rich\workspaces\build
```

The CLASSPATH environment variable can contain any number of directories and JAR files. Setting CLASSPATH on Windows can be done from a command prompt using a semicolon to separate multiple values:

```
set CLASSPATH="c:\Documents and Settings\Rich\workspaces\build";
 c:\myproject\build;c:\tomcat\lib\servlet.jar;.;
```

In this example, the compiler and the JVM look for bytecode files in the two \build directories specified, the servlet.jar file in c:\tomcat\lib, and the current working directory (represented by the dot). The double quotes are necessary in the first directory because of the spaces in the pathname.

On Unix, you use the setenv command and colons to separate multiple values. For example:

```
setenv CLASSPATH /usr/build:/myproject/build:/tomcat/lib/servlet.jar
```

A common mistake new Java programmers make is to include part of the package pathname in the CLASSPATH. If you are struggling with classes not being found, you might be tempted to try the following command line:

```
set CLASSPATH=c:\myproject\build\com\sybex\payroll;
```

Including \com\sybex\payroll in your CLASSPATH does not work! Do not add any of the package directories to your CLASSPATH, only the parent directory. The compiler and the JRE will look for the appropriate subdirectories.

CLASSPATH plays a key role in compiling and running your Java applications, which we discuss in the next section.

Running Java Applications

The SCJP certification exam tests your knowledge of running a Java program from the command line using an appropriate CLASSPATH. If you are using Sun's Java Development Kit (JDK), then java.exe in the \bin folder of the JDK directory is the executable used to run your Java applications. The sample commands in this book assume java.exe is in your path.

The entry point of a Java program is main, which you can define in any class. The signature of main must look like this:

```
public static void main(String [] args)
```

The only changes you can make to this signature are the name of the parameter args, which can be arbitrary, and the order of public and static. For example, the following declaration is a valid signature of main:

```
static public void main(String [] x)
```

In addition, you can specify the array of String objects using the syntax for variable-length arguments:

```
public static void main(String... args)
```

Variable-Length Arguments

As of Java 5.0, a method in Java can declare a variable-length argument list denoted by the ellipsis (. . .). Variable-length arguments are discussed in detail in Chapter 2.

The args array contains the command-line arguments, discussed in detail later in this section. The main method has to be public so that the JVM has access to it, and making it static allows the JVM to invoke this method without having to instantiate an instance of the containing class.

Let's start with a simple example. Suppose the following class is saved in the c:\myproject directory. First, does the following SaySomething class compile, and does it successfully declare the main method?

```
1. public class SaySomething {
2.     private static String message = "Hello!";
3.
4.     public static void main() {
5.         System.out.println(message);
6.     }
7. }
```

The answers are yes and no. Yes, this class compiles, but no, it does not define `main` properly. A `static` method can access a `static` field in the same class, so there is no problem with the `message` field. Also, you can write a method called `main` that does not have an array of `String` objects, so the compiler will not complain about the `main` method defined on line 4. However, this class cannot be executed as a Java application because it does not successfully declare the proper `main` method for a Java application.

Let's try it again, this time with the following `SayHello` class. Does this class compile and successfully declare the `main` method?

```
1. public class SayHello {
2.     private static String message = "Hello!";
3.
4.     public static void main(String [] args) {
5.         System.out.println(message);
6.     }
7. }
```

The answer is yes to both: `SayHello` compiles and declares the proper version of `main` so that it can be executed as a stand-alone Java application. The following command line runs the `SayHello` application:

```
java SayHello
```

This command line assumes that you run the command from the directory that contains the file `SayHello.class`, which in our case is `c:\myproject`. If you want to run this Java application from any directory (instead of just `c:\myproject`), you need to include `c:\myproject` in your CLASSPATH. Figure 1.2 shows `SayHello` being executed from `c:\myproject`, and then being executed from `c:\` after the CLASSPATH is correctly set.

FIGURE 1.2   Compiling and running the `SayHello` program from a command prompt

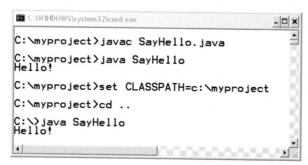

Specifying the Class Name

The command line for java.exe requires the name of the class that contains main. Notice that the name of the class is not the same as the name of the bytecode file, which in the SayHello example is SayHello.class. The following command line does not work:

```
java SayHello.class
```

The JVM looks for a class named class in the SayHello package (which it will not find) and throws a NoClassDefFoundError. The JVM only needs the name of the class; it will find the corresponding bytecode file by scanning all the directories and JAR files set in your CLASSPATH environment variable. If you do not set a CLASSPATH, the JVM looks in the current working directory.

The exam will likely test your knowledge with a more complex example where the class containing main is in a package. Let's look at another example, starting with a class called ColorChanger in the com.sybex.events package:

```
1.   package com.sybex.events;
2.
3.   import java.awt.Component;
4.   import java.awt.Color;
5.   import java.awt.event.*;
6.
7.   public class ColorChanger implements ActionListener {
8.      private Component container;
9.
10.     public ColorChanger(Component c) {
11.         container = c;
12.     }
13.
14.     public void actionPerformed(ActionEvent e) {
15.         String color = e.getActionCommand();
16.         if(color.equals("red")) {
17.             container.setBackground(Color.RED);
18.         } else if(color.equals("blue")) {
19.             container.setBackground(Color.BLUE);
20.         } else {
21.             container.setBackground(Color.WHITE);
22.         }
23.     }
24.  }
```

The source file ColorChanger.java is saved in c:\myproject\src\com\sybex\events and the class is compiled using the following command executed from c:\myproject\src:

```
javac -d c:\myproject\build .\com\sybex\events\ColorChanger.java
```

This command line creates ColorChanger.class in the c:\myproject\build\com\sybex\events directory. The following program contains main and tests the ColorChanger class:

```
1.   package com.sybex.demos;
2.
3.   import com.sybex.events.ColorChanger;
4.   import java.awt.Button;
5.   import java.awt.Color;
6.   import java.awt.event.ActionEvent;
7.
8.   public class TestColors {
9.
10.      public static void main(String [] args) {
11.          Button b = new Button("Testing...");
12.          b.setBackground(Color.GREEN);
13.          System.out.println("Color is " + b.getBackground());
14.
15.          ColorChanger cc = new ColorChanger(b);
16.          ActionEvent action = new ActionEvent(b,
17.                  ActionEvent.ACTION_PERFORMED,
18.                  "blue");
19.          cc.actionPerformed(action);
20.          System.out.println("Now the color is "
21.                  + b.getBackground());
22.      }
23. }
```

TestColors.java is saved in the c:\myproject\src\com\sybex\demos directory. Because TestColors is not in the same package as ColorChanger, it imports the ColorChanger class. TestColors is compiled using the following command executed from the c:\myproject\src directory:

```
javac -d c:\myproject\build .\com\sybex\demos\TestColors.java
```

This command line creates TestColors.class in the directory c:\myproject\build\com\sybex\demos. Figure 1.3 shows the directory structure after compiling the source files with -d.

FIGURE 1.3   The source code and bytecode are typically stored in separate folders.

```
c:\myproject\
    +src\
    | +com\
    |   +sybex\
    |     +demos\
    |     | +TestColors.java
    |     +events\
    |         +ColorChanger.java
    +build\
        +com\
          +sybex\
            +demos\
            | +TestColors.class
            +events\
                +ColorChanger.class
```

A typical exam question at this point is to ask what the CLASSPATH needs to be for you to run the TestColors program at the command prompt from any working directory. Do you know the answer? I will reveal it in a moment, but first here is the command prompt that runs the TestColors application if you execute it from the c:\myproject\build directory:

```
java com.sybex.demos.TestColors
```

Notice the fully qualified class name of TestColors must be specified to execute properly. Using the fully qualified name has nothing to do with CLASSPATH or the current working directory. The following command does not work and results in a java.lang .NoClassDefFoundError, no matter what directory you run it from or what your CLASSPATH is set to:

```
java TestColors
```

Why will this never work? Because there is no class called TestColors. Remember, putting a class in a package changes the name of the class. Because TestColors is in the com.sybex.demos package, the name of the class is com.sybex.demos.TestColors, and that name must be used on the command line.

By the way, the answer to the question earlier about CLASSPATH is it needs to contain c:\myproject\build:

```
set CLASSPATH=c:\myproject\build;
```

With this CLASSPATH, the command to run the TestColors program can be executed from any directory.

> ### Don't Panic During the Exam!
>
> The purpose of the ColorChanger and TestColors example is to demonstrate running a Java application from a command line, so what the code does is not relevant in this situation. If you are not familiar with the Container and ActionListener classes, a ColorChanger can listen to action events of a GUI component in Java because it implements ActionListener. When an action event occurs, the actionPerformed method is invoked, which changes the background color of the given GUI component.
>
> You might encounter a situation on the exam where you are not familiar with some of the classes in the given code. Don't panic! Focus on what the exam question is asking before trying to figure out what the code is doing. You might discover that the behavior of the code is irrelevant because the question is testing you on a different facet of the language.

You can also set the classpath for the JVM on the command line using the -classpath flag, which is discussed in the next section, followed by a discussion on running Java code stored in JAR files.

The *-classpath* Flag

The java command that starts the JVM has a -classpath flag that allows the classpath to be specified from the command line. This is a common technique for ensuring the classpath is pointing to the right directories and JAR files. Using the -classpath flag overrides the CLASSPATH environment variable.

For example, we could run the TestColors program using the following command prompt executed from any directory:

```
java -classpath c:\myproject\build com.sybex.demos.TestColors
```

If you have multiple directories or JAR files, use a semicolon on a Windows machine to separate them on the -classpath flag. For example, the following command line adds the current directory to the classpath:

```
java -classpath c:\myproject\build;. com.sybex.demos.TestColors
```

On a Unix machine, use a colon to separate multiple directories and JAR files:

```
java -classpath /myproject/build:. com.sybex.demos.TestColors
```

The java command can also define the classpath using the -cp flag, which is just a shortcut for the -classpath flag.

JAR Files

Bytecode can be stored in archived, compressed files known as *JAR files*. JAR is short for Java archive. The compiler and the JVM can find bytecode files in JAR files without needing to uncompress the files onto your file system. JAR files are the most common way to distribute Java code, and the exam tests your understanding of JAR files and how they relate to CLASSPATH.

The JDK comes with the tool jar.exe for creating and extracting JAR files. The following command adds the bytecode files of the c:\myproject\build directory to a new JAR file named myproject.jar:

```
C:\myproject\build>jar -cvf myproject.jar .
added manifest
adding: com/(in = 0) (out= 0)(stored 0%)
adding: com/sybex/(in = 0) (out= 0)(stored 0%)
adding: com/sybex/demos/(in = 0) (out= 0)(stored 0%)
adding: com/sybex/demos/TestColors.class(in = 1209) (out= 671)(deflated 44%)
adding: com/sybex/events/(in = 0) (out= 0)(stored 0%)
adding: com/sybex/events/ColorChanger.class(in = 883) (out= 545)(deflated 38%)
adding: com/sybex/payroll/(in = 0) (out= 0)(stored 0%)
adding: com/sybex/payroll/Employee.class(in = 402) (out= 292)(deflated 27%)
```

The -c flag is for creating a new JAR file. The -v flag tells the jar command to be verbose while it is processing files. The -f flag is for denoting the filename of the new JAR file, which in this example is myproject.jar. After the filename, you specify the files or directories to include in the JAR. In our example, because all of our bytecode was conveniently located in the \build directory, we simply added the entire contents of c:\myproject\build, using the dot to represent the current directory.

JAR Files and Package Names

If a class is in a package, then the JAR file must contain the appropriate directory structure when the .class file is included in the JAR. Notice in the verbose output of the jar command shown earlier, the necessary \com directory and subdirectories matching our package names are added to the JAR.

You can add a JAR file to your CLASSPATH. In fact, it is common to have lots of JAR files in your CLASSPATH. The following example demonstrates adding myproject.jar to the CLASSPATH of a Windows machine, then running the TestColors program (which is in myproject.jar):

```
C:\>set CLASSPATH=c:\myproject\build\myproject.jar;

C:\>java com.sybex.demos.TestColors
Color is java.awt.Color[r=0,g=255,b=0]
Now the color is java.awt.Color[r=0,g=0,b=255]
```

> ### 🌐 Real World Scenario
>
> #### Separating Source Code and Bytecode Files
>
> You might have been wondering why the examples in this chapter separated the source files from the bytecode files. In general, when you distribute your code you do not want the JAR files to include your source code. Having the bytecode separate makes it much easier to create JAR files that only contain your bytecode.
>
> You might have also noticed that the source code files in \src use the same directory structure as their package names. This is not a requirement for your .java files; they can be stored in any directory. In most development teams, you will be required to run the javadoc tool on your source files to generate the HTML documentation for your classes and interfaces. The javadoc tool requires that your source file directories match the package names. The exam does not contain any questions that involve the javadoc tool, but in the real world you will quickly learn to appreciate the benefits of javadoc documentation!
>
> In projects I work on, we put source code in the \src directory, using the package name subdirectory structure. Bytecode goes in a subdirectory of \build depending on whether or not the bytecode is in a JAR. JAR files appear in the \build\lib directory, and .class files appear in the \build\classes subdirectory that matches the package name structure.

Command-Line Arguments

The java.exe executable starts the JVM, and on the command line you provide the name of the class that contains the main method. The command-line arguments are passed into the main method as a single array of String objects. For example, suppose PrintGreetings is a class that contains main and it is executed with the command line in Figure 1.4.

FIGURE 1.4 This command line starts the JVM and invokes the main method in the PrintGreetings class.

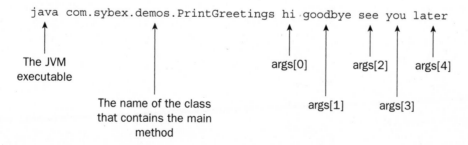

This command has five command-line arguments, so the first element in the String array is "hi", the second element in the array is "goodbye", and so on. The following PrintGreetings class contains a for loop that iterates through the command-line arguments and outputs them to the console:

```
1.  package com.sybex.demos;
2.  public class PrintGreetings {
3.      public static void main(String [] args) {
4.          for(int i = 0; i < args.length; i++) {
5.              System.out.println(args[i]);
6.          }
7.      }
8.  }
```

If PrintGreetings is executed with the command line in Figure 1.4, then the output looks like this:

```
hi
goodbye
see
you
later
```

Command-Line Arguments on the Exam

Notice that the first command-line argument in the array is args[0] because Java uses zero-based indexes for arrays. The exam creators seem to like questions about arrays and command-line arguments, so don't be surprised if you see a question that tests both topics at the same time. For example, what is the output of the DoSomething class when executed with the following command?

```
java DoSomething one two
```

```
1. public class DoSomething {
2.     public static void main(String args []) {
3.         System.out.print(args[1]);
4.         System.out.print(args[2]);
5.     }
6. }
```

By the way, the square brackets following args instead of preceding args are perfectly valid in Java, although not common practice. The output of this program is the string "two" followed by an ArrayIndexOutOfBoundsException on line 4, as shown here:

```
twoException in thread "main" java.lang.ArrayIndexOutOfBoundsException: 2
        at DoSomething.main(DoSomething.java:4)
```

The length of args is two, so args[2] is beyond the end of the array.

All command-line arguments are treated as String objects, even if they represent another data type. The wrapper classes in java.lang contain helpful methods for parsing strings into other data types. Consider the following ParseDemo program:

```
1.   public class ParseDemo {
2.     public static void main(String [] args) {
3.         System.out.println("Processing " + args.length +
4.                        " arguments");
5.         int x = Integer.parseInt(args[0]);
6.         System.out.println(x);
7.         boolean b = Boolean.parseBoolean(args[1]);
8.         System.out.println(b);
9.         float f = Float.parseFloat(args[2]);
10.        System.out.println(f);
11.        char c = args[3].charAt(0);
12.        System.out.println(c);
13.     }

14. }
```

Here is a command line that runs the ParseDemo program, followed by its output:

```
c:\myproject>java ParseDemo 34567 false 3.14159 R
Processing 4 arguments
34567
false
3.14159
R
```

There is no need to parse a String into a char because the String already is an array of characters. The ParseDemo program simply selects the first character in the String to "convert" it to a char.

We now turn our attention to a discussion on garbage collection, which first requires an understanding of the differences between reference types and primitive types.

Reference vs. Primitive Types

Java applications contain two types of data: *primitive types* and *reference types*. In this section, we will discuss the differences between a primitive type and a reference type. The differences are important when we discuss garbage collection later in this chapter.

Primitive Types

Java has eight built-in data types, referred to as the *Java primitive types*. These eight data types represent the building blocks for Java objects, because all Java objects are just a complex collection in memory of these primitive data types. The SCJP exam assumes you are well versed in the eight primitive data types, their size, and what can be stored in them. Table 1.1 shows the Java primitive types together with their size in bytes and the range of values that each holds.

TABLE 1.1   The Java Primitive Data Types

Primitive Type	Size	Range of Values (inclusive)
byte	8 bits	−128 to 127
short	16 bits	−32768 to 32767
int	32 bits	−2147483648 to 2147483647
long	64 bits	−9223372036854775808 to 9223372036854775807
float	32 bits	2^{-149} to $(2 - 2^{-23}) \cdot 2^{127}$
double	64 bits	2^{-1074} to $(2 - 2^{-52}) \cdot 2^{1023}$
char	16 bits	'\u0000' to '\uffff' (0 to 65535)
boolean	unspecified	true or false

Do I Need to Memorize These Sizes?

Not all of them. Don't try to memorize the range of values in a long, float, or double, but it is important to know their size in bits. However, you should be able to state the range of a byte exactly and recognize when a short or int has likely gone beyond its range. Expect a question involving the size of a char, especially because a char in C/C++ is only 8 bits and uses the ASCII format, while a Java char is 16 bits and uses the UNICODE format.

Primitive types are allocated in memory by declaring them in your code. For example, the following lines of code declare an int and a double:

```
int x;
double d;
```

In memory, the compiler allocates 32 bits for the variable x and 64 bits for the variable d. A primitive type can only store a value of that same type. For example, the variable x can only hold an int and d can only hold a double. Suppose we assign values to x and d:

```
x = 12345;
d = 2.7e45;
```

Figure 1.5 shows how these primitive types look in memory. The value 12345 is stored in the memory where x is allocated. Similarly, the value 2.7e45 is stored in the memory where d is allocated.

FIGURE 1.5   An int is 32 bits and a double is 64 bits.

32 bits of memory   64 bits of memory

Reference Types

Reference types are variables that are class types, interface types, and array types. A reference refers to an object (an instance of a class). Unlike primitive types that hold their values in the memory where the variable is allocated, references do not hold the value of the object they refer to. Instead, a reference "points" to an object by storing the memory address where the object is located, a concept referred to as a *pointer*. However, the Java language does not allow a programmer to access a physical memory address in any way, so even though a reference is similar to a pointer, you can only use a reference to gain access to the fields and methods of the object it refers to. It is impossible to determine the actual address stored in the memory of the reference variable.

Let's take a look at some examples that declare and initialize reference types. Suppose we declare a reference of type `java.util.Date` and a reference of type `String`:

```
java.util.Date today;
String greeting;
```

The `today` variable is a reference of type `Date` and can only point to a `Date` object. The `greeting` variable is a reference that can only point to a `String` object. A value is assigned to a reference in one of two ways:

- A reference can be assigned to another reference of the same type.
- A reference can be assigned to a new object using the new keyword.

For example, the following statements assign these references to new objects:

```
today = new java.util.Date();
greeting = "How are you?";
```

The `today` reference now points to a new `Date` object in memory, and `today` can be used to access the various fields and methods of this `Date` object. Similarly, the `greeting` reference points to a new `String` object, `"How are you?"` The `String` and `Date` objects do not have names and can only be accessed via their corresponding reference. Figure 1.6 shows how the reference types appear in memory.

FIGURE 1.6   An object in memory can only be accessed via a reference.

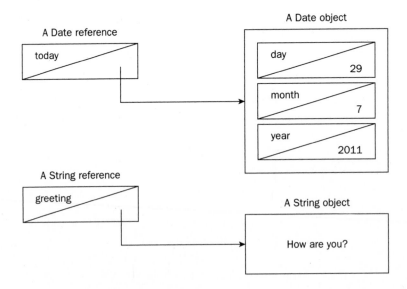

String Literals and the String Pool

The new keyword is not required for creating the String object "How are you?" because it is a string literal. String literals get special treatment by the JVM. Behind the scenes, the JVM instantiates a String object for "How are you?" and stores it in the *string pool*. The greeting reference refers to this String object in the pool. Because String objects in Java are *immutable* (which means they cannot be changed), the JVM can optimize the use of string literals by allowing only one instance of a string in the pool. For example, the following two String references actually point to the same string in the pool, as shown in the following diagram:

```
String s1 = "New York";
String s2 = "New York";
```

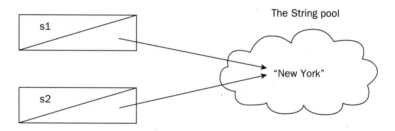

You might think if the two references point to the same object, then changing one object would inadvertently change the value of the other. But String objects are immutable, so the following statement only changes s2:

```
s2 = "New Jersey";
```

The reference s2 now points to "New Jersey", but s1 still points to "New York", as shown in the following diagram:

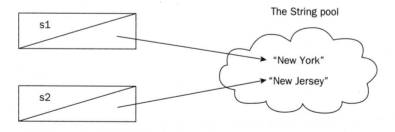

In addition, arrays in Java are objects and therefore have a reference type. The Java language implicitly defines a reference type for each possible array type: one for each of the eight primitive types and also an Object array. This allows for references of the following type:

```
int [] grades;
String [] args;
Runnable [] targets;
```

The null Type

There is a special data type in Java for null. The null type does not have a name, so it is not possible to declare a variable to be the null type. However, you can assign any reference to the null type:

```
String firstName = null;
Runnable [] targets = null;
```

Primitive types cannot be assigned to null, only references. The following statement is not valid:

```
int x= null;     //does not compile
```

We can also assign a reference to another reference as long as their data types are compatible. For example, the following code assigns two ArrayList references to each other:

```
java.util.ArrayList<Integer> a1 =
        new java.util.ArrayList<Integer>();
java.util.ArrayList<Integer> a2 = a1;
```

The references a1 and a2 both point to the same object, an ArrayList that contains Integer objects. (Two references pointing to the same object is a common occurrence in Java.) The ArrayList object can be accessed using either reference. Examine the following code and determine if it compiles successfully and, if so, what its output is:

```
a1.add(new Integer(12345));
a2.add(new Integer(54321));
for(int i = 0; i < a1.size(); i++) {
  System.out.println(a2.get(i));
}
```

The code adds an Integer to the ArrayList using a1, and then adds another Integer using a2. Because they point to the same ArrayList, the list now has two Integer objects in it, as shown in Figure 1.7.

FIGURE 1.7   The ArrayList object can be accessed using either a1 or a2.

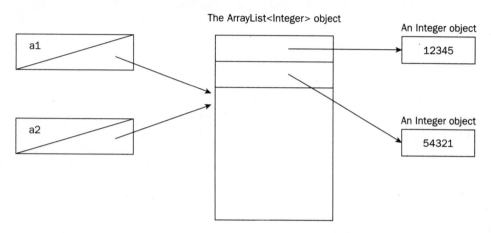

The for loop compiles successfully and the output looks like this:

```
12345
54321
```

Let's look at a different example. Examine the following code that assigns two references to each other and determine if it compiles successfully:

```
java.math.BigDecimal bd = new java.math.BigDecimal(2.75);
String s = bd;
```

The reference bd is of type BigDecimal, and s is of type String. These two classes are not compatible, so assigning s to bd generates the following compiler error:

```
incompatible types
found   : java.math.BigDecimal
required: java.lang.String
        String s = bd;
```

Even using the cast operator does not fix the problem. The following code generates a similar compiler error, except this time the compiler complains the types are inconvertible:

```
java.math.BigDecimal bd = new java.math.BigDecimal(2.75);
String s = (String) bd;
```

The compiler error looks like this:

```
inconvertible types
found   : java.math.BigDecimal
required: java.lang.String
        String s = (String) bd;
```

Even though s and bd are both references that behind the scenes are identical in terms of memory consumption (most likely they are 32-bit unsigned integers, but this is JVM-dependent), it is not possible to assign them to each other because there is no relationship between a String object and a BigDecimal object. Two references are compatible only when either the objects they point to are the same type or one of the objects is a child class of the other. String and BigDecimal have no inheritance relationship.

Hopefully you have a better understanding of the differences between references and primitive types. References play a key role in understanding garbage collection, our next topic.

Garbage Collection

All Java objects are stored in your program memory's *heap*. The heap, which is also referred to as the *free store,* represents a large pool of unused memory allocated to your Java application. The heap may be quite large, depending on your environment, but there is always a limit to its size. If your program keeps instantiating objects and leaving them on the heap, eventually it will run out of memory.

Garbage collection refers to the process of automatically freeing memory on the heap by deleting objects that are no longer reachable in your program. Every JVM has a garbage collector, and many different algorithms are used to determine the efficiency and timing of garbage collection. The SCJP exam does not test your knowledge of any individual garbage collection algorithm. However, you do need to know "what is and is not guaranteed by the garbage collection system," as well as "recognize the point when an object becomes eligible for garbage collection." This section discusses both of these objectives in detail.

The new keyword instantiates a new object on the heap and returns a reference to the object. Typically you will save that object's reference in a variable. An object will remain on the heap until it is no longer reachable. An object is no longer reachable when one of two situations occurs:

- The object no longer has any references pointing to it.
- All references to the object have gone out of scope.

Objects vs. References

Do not confuse a reference with the object that it refers to. They are two different enti-ties. The reference is a variable that has a name and can be used to access the contents of an object. A reference can be assigned to another reference, passed to a method, or returned from a method. All references are the same size, no matter what their type is. A reference is most likely 32 bits, but their actual size depends on your JVM.

An object sits on the heap and does not have a name. Therefore, you have no way to access an object except through a reference. Objects come in all different shapes and sizes and consume varying amounts of memory. An object cannot be assigned to another object, nor can an object be passed to a method or returned from a method. It is the object that gets garbage collected, not its reference.

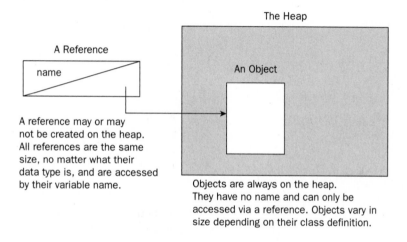

Realizing the difference between a reference and an object goes a long way toward understanding garbage collection, call by value, the new operator, and many other facets of the Java language.

Consider the following program that instantiates two GregorianCalendar objects and assigns them to various references. Study the code and see if you can determine when each of the two objects either goes out of scope or all references to it are lost.

```
1.    import java.util.GregorianCalendar;
2.
3.    public class GCDemo {
4.      public static void main(String [] args) {
5.          GregorianCalendar christmas, newyears;
```

```
6.          christmas = new GregorianCalendar(2009,12,25);
7.          newyears = new GregorianCalendar(2010,1,1);
8.
9.          christmas = newyears;
10.          GregorianCalendar d = christmas;
11.          christmas = null;
12.     }
13. }
```

The two GregorianCalendar objects are created on lines 6 and 7, resulting in the references and objects that Figure 1.8 shows.

FIGURE 1.8 Each GregorianCalendar object has a reference pointing to it.

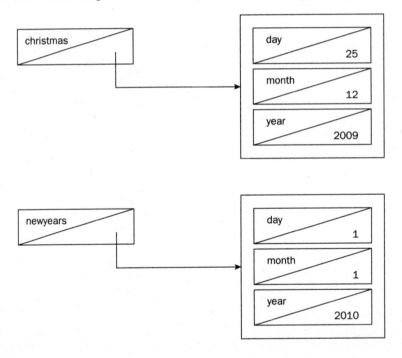

On line 9, the christmas reference is assigned to newyears, which results in no more references pointing to the object from line 6, so this object immediately becomes available for garbage collection after line 9. There is now only one GregorianCalendar object (from line 7) reachable in memory, and after line 10 there are three references pointing to it, as Figure 1.9 shows.

FIGURE 1.9 One GregorianCalendar object has no references to it and the other now has three.

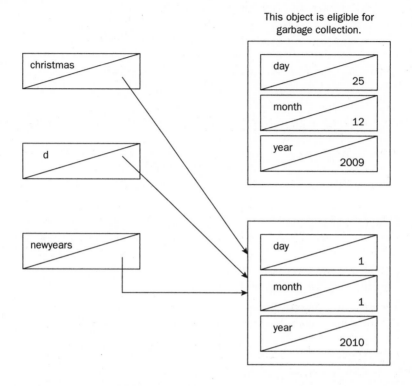

Setting christmas to null on line 11 does not cause the object from line 7 to become eligible for garbage collection because there are still two references pointing to it: d and newyears. However, after line 12 the main method ends and both d and newyears go out of scope. Therefore, the object instantiated on line 7 becomes eligible for garbage collection after line 12.

Know When an Object Is Eligible for Garbage Collection

The GCDemo program is typical of a question that you will encounter on the certification exam. Make sure you understand exactly when each of the two GregorianCalendar objects becomes eligible for garbage collection.

What does it mean to become eligible for garbage collection? Why not simply have the garbage collector immediately free the memory instead? The answer is that there is no guarantee in Java as to exactly when an object is actually garbage collected. The JVM specification does not define how a garbage collector accomplishes the task of freeing memory. The specification only states that when an object is eligible for garbage collection, the garbage collector must eventually free the memory.

As a Java coder, you cannot specifically free memory on the heap. You can only ensure that your objects that you no longer want in memory are no longer reachable. In other words, make sure you don't have any references to the object that are still in scope.

The following section discusses the System.gc method, which provides a small amount of control over freeing memory on the heap.

The *System.gc* Method

The java.lang.System class has a static method called gc that attempts to run the garbage collector. System.gc is the only method in the Java API that communicates with the garbage collector. Here is what the Java SE API documentation says about the System.gc method:

> Calling the gc method suggests that the Java Virtual Machine expend effort toward recycling unused objects in order to make the memory they currently occupy available for quick reuse. When control returns from the method call, the Java Virtual Machine has made a best effort to reclaim space from all discarded objects.

In other words, the gc method does not guarantee anything! The method might be useful if you are familiar with the intricate details of your JVM and how it implements this method. But the end result is that as a Java programmer you cannot free memory specifically in your code. You can only ensure that your objects are eligible for garbage collection, and then assume the garbage collector will do its job!

Let's look at another example typical of a question found on the exam. Examine the following code and determine when the String objects become eligible for garbage collection and when they actually get garbage collected:

```
1.  public class GCDemo2 {
2.    public static void main(String [] args) {
3.        String one = "Hello";
4.        String two = one;
5.        String three = "Goodbye";
6.
7.        three = null;
8.        System.gc();
9.        one = null;
10.       System.gc();
11.       two = null;
12.    }
13. }
```

The "Goodbye" object is created on line 5 and assigned to the reference three. Then three is set to null and the gc method is invoked. After line 7 the "Goodbye" object is definitely eligible for garbage collection, but if the exam question asks you when the object is garbage collected, the answer can only be "unknown." The call to gc on line 8 might have caused "Goodbye" to get garbage collected, but that is not guaranteed at all.

Line 9 does not cause "Hello" to become eligible because the reference two points to "Hello" also. Only after line 11 does "Hello" become eligible for garbage collection, and as already discussed we cannot know when the objects are actually garbage collected.

The *finalize* Method

According to the exam objectives, you need to be able to "recognize the behaviors of the Object.finalize() method." The garbage collector invokes the finalize method of an object right before the object is actually garbage collected. The finalize method is declared in Object, and any subclass can override finalize to perform any necessary cleanup or dispose of system resources. The finalize method is only invoked on an object once by the garbage collector.

There won't be any trick questions about finalize. Just remember it gets invoked once and only when the object is in the process of being removed from memory. Be sure not to do anything in the finalize method that might somehow cause the object's reference to come back into scope. It is also a good idea to call super.finalize because you are overriding the behavior of finalize in the parent classes.

Calling super.finalize

If you do call super.finalize, which is recommended, you need to declare the java.lang.Throwable exception thrown by the parent class's finalize method:

```
public class A extends Object {
    public void finalize() throws Throwable {
        System.out.println("Finalizing A");
    }
}
```

Let's look at an example. It is difficult to simulate garbage collection because you have little control over the garbage collector, but I came up with an example that demonstrates when the finalize method is called and also provides an extra level of complexity in determining when an object is eligible for garbage collection. Consider the following class named Dog that contains a `finalize` method that prints out a simple message:

```
1.  public class Dog {
2.     private String name;
3.     private int age;
4.
5.     public Dog(String name, int age) {
6.         this.name = name;
7.         this.age = age;
8.     }
9.
10.    public void finalize() {
11.        System.out.println(name + " is being garbage collected");
12.    }
13. }
```

The following program instantiates two Dog objects and stores them in a `java.util` `.Vector`. Examine this program and see if you can determine when the two Dog objects become eligible for garbage collection:

```
1.  import java.util.Vector;
2.  public class GCDemo3 {
3.     public static void main(String [] args) {
4.         Vector<Dog> vector = new Vector<Dog>();
5.         Dog one = new Dog("Snoopy", 10);
6.         Dog two = new Dog("Lassie", 12);
7.
8.         vector.add(one);
9.         vector.add(two);
10.
11.        one = null;
12.        System.out.println("Calling gc once...");
13.        System.gc();
14.
15.        vector = null;
16.        System.out.println("Calling gc twice...");
17.        System.gc();
18.
19.        two = null;
20.        System.out.println("Calling gc again...");
```

```
21.        System.gc();
22.        System.out.println("End of main...");
23.
24.    }
25. }
```

The calls to gc are an attempt to force garbage collection so we can see when finalize is invoked on the Dog objects. The first step is determining when the objects are eligible for garbage collection. Adding the two Dog objects to the Vector creates additional references to the objects. On line 11 the reference one is set to null, but Snoopy is not eligible yet for garbage collection because of line 8. The Vector still has a reference to the Snoopy object, as shown in Figure 1.10.

FIGURE 1.10 The Vector still has a reference to the Snoopy object.

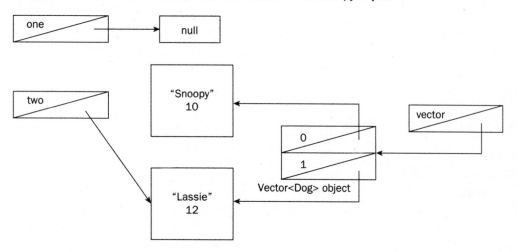

However, when you set vector to null on line 15, it causes the Snoopy object to immediately become eligible for garbage collection. The Lassie object still has the reference two pointing to it, so it does not become eligible until after line 19. Here is a sample output of the GCDemo3 program. (I use the term "sample output" because the output can change each time the program is executed depending on when the garbage collector actually invokes the finalize method.)

```
Calling gc once...
Calling gc twice...
Snoopy is being garbage collected
Calling gc again...
Lassie is being garbage collected
End of main...
```

No objects are freed after the first call to gc because no objects are eligible at that time. After the second call to gc, the Snoopy object is eligible, but the call to finalize happens in the thread of the garbage collector, so the output of Snoopy's finalize method may or may not appear before the third call to gc. The exact output of running the GCDemo3 program is indeterminate. The previous output is just one possible result.

The finalize Method Is Only Invoked Once

Expect at least one question on the exam about the finalize method. Keep in mind that it can only be called once on an object, and it only gets called by the garbage collector after an object is eligible for garbage collection but before the object is actually garbage collected.

This ends our discussion on garbage collection, an important topic not just for the SCJP exam but in our everyday programming of Java. Now we discuss another important topic in Java: the concept of call by value.

Call by Value

The exam objectives state that you need to know "the effect upon object references and primitive values when they are passed into methods that perform assignments or other modifying operations on the parameters." A variable that is passed into a method is called an *argument*. Java simplifies the concept of passing arguments into methods by providing only one way to pass arguments: by value. Passing arguments *by value* means that a copy of the argument is passed to the method. Method return values are also returned by value, meaning a copy of the variable is returned. The SCJP exam requires an understanding of what call by value means, and we will discuss the details now.

An argument is passed into a corresponding method parameter. A *parameter* is the name of the variable in the method signature that gets assigned the value of the argument. Let's look at an example. Suppose we have the following method definition:

```
21. public long cubic(int y) {
22.    long longValue = (long) y;
23.    y = -1;
24.    return longValue * longValue * longValue;
25. }
```

To invoke this method, you must pass in an int argument. For example, the following code invokes the cubic method:

```
31. int x = 11;
32. long result = cubic(x);
```

The value of x is copied into the parameter y. We now have two ints in memory that have the value 11: x and y. Changing y to –1 in cubic has no effect on x. In fact, it is impossible to change x within the cubic function.

Passing Primitives vs. Passing References

Sun seems to enjoy questions on the exam regarding call by value and methods that attempt to change the value of the argument. If the argument passed into a method parameter is a primitive type, it is impossible in Java for the method to alter the value of the original primitive.

If the argument passed into a method parameter is a reference type, the same rule applies: it is impossible for a method to alter the original *reference*. However, because the method now has a reference to the same object that the argument points to, the method *can* change the object. This is an important difference to understand. Study the upcoming StackDemo program for an example of this situation.

The following example of call by value uses references. Suppose we have the following method signature:

```
5. public int findByName(String lastName, String firstName) {
6.     lastName = "Doe";
7.     firstName = "Jane";
8.     return -1;
9. }
```

This method has two parameters, lastName and firstName. To invoke this method, two String objects must be passed in as arguments. For example, the following code invokes the findByName method. What is the output of this code?

```
14. String first = "Albert";
15. String last = "Einstein";
16. int result = findByName(last, first);
17. System.out.println(first + " " + last);
```

The argument `last` is copied into the parameter `lastName`. The argument `first` is copied into the parameter `firstName`. What gets copied? Well, because `last` and `first` are references, they contain memory addresses, and that is what gets copied. The result is that `lastName` points to the same `String` object as `last`, which in this example is `"Einstein"`. Similarly, `firstName` points to `"Albert"`, as shown in Figure 1.11. The objects did not get copied! There is still only one `String` object with the value `"Einstein"` in memory and only one `String` object with the value `"Albert"` in memory.

FIGURE 1.11   The arguments from `main` are copied into the parameters of `findByName`.

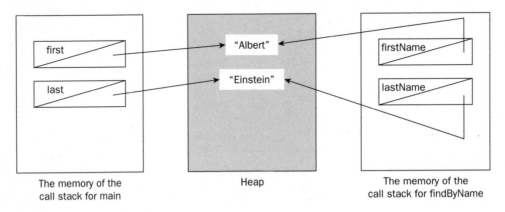

first   "Albert"   firstName

last   "Einstein"   lastName

The memory of the   Heap   The memory of the
call stack for main   call stack for findByName

Because `String` objects are immutable, the parameters `lastName` and `firstName` cannot change the objects `"Albert"` or `"Einstein"`. Setting the parameters equals to `"Jane"` and `"Doe"` has no effect on `first` and `last`, as Figure 1.12 shows. Therefore, the output of that code is

```
Albert Einstein
```

FIGURE 1.12   `String` objects are immutable, so `findByName` cannot change `first` and `last`.

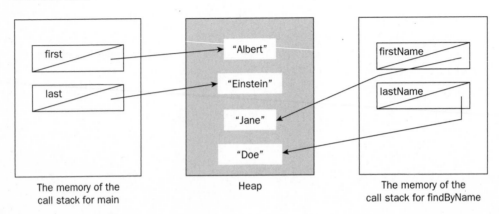

first   "Albert"   firstName

last   "Einstein"   lastName

"Jane"

"Doe"

The memory of the   Heap   The memory of the
call stack for main   call stack for findByName

The only reason firstName and lastName could not change the objects is because the example uses String types and String objects are immutable. Let's look at an example where the arguments passed in refer to objects that *can* be altered by the method. Examine the following program and try to determine its output. If you are not familiar with the java.util.Stack class, the push method adds an element to the top of the stack and the pop method removes the top element from the stack.

```
1.    import java.util.Stack;
2.
3.    public class StackDemo {
4.
5.       public static void modifyStacks(Stack<String> one,
6.                              Stack<Integer> two) {
7.          two.push(50);
8.          one.pop();
9.          one = new Stack<String>();
10.      }
11.
12.      public static void main(String [] args) {
13.         Stack<String> names = new Stack<String>();
14.         names.push("Kim");
15.         names.push("Edward");
16.         names.push("Jane");
17.
18.         Stack<Integer> grades = new Stack<Integer>();
19.         grades.push(95);
20.         grades.push(87);
21.
22.         modifyStacks(names, grades);
23.
24.         for(String name : names) {
25.            System.out.println(name);
26.         }
27.
28.         for(int grade : grades) {
29.            System.out.println(grade);
30.         }
31.      }
32. }
```

Within main, two Stack objects are instantiated. The reference names refers to a Stack that contains String objects, and the reference grades refers to a Stack containing Integer objects. Three strings are pushed onto the names stack, and two ints are pushed onto grades. Then names and grades are passed into modifyStacks. The parameter one points to the stack of Strings and two points to the stack of grades, as Figure 1.13 shows.

FIGURE 1.13 The references from main are copied into the parameters of modifyStacks.

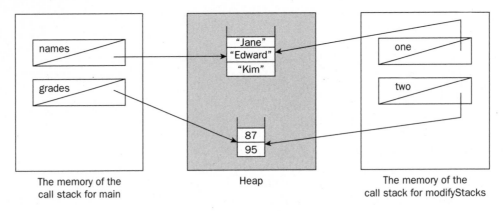

The memory of the call stack for main   Heap   The memory of the call stack for modifyStacks

Pushing 50 onto two is the same as pushing it onto grades because the two references point to the same stack. Similarly, popping a value off one removes "Jane" from the names stack.

Note that setting one equal to a new Stack does not affect the Stack that names points to. We cannot modify the reference names within modifyStacks. Figure 1.14 shows the references and objects just before the modifyStacks method returns.

FIGURE 1.14 Assigning the one reference to a new Stack does not affect the names stack.

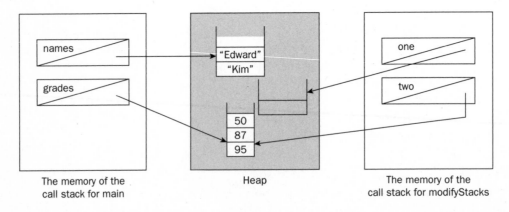

The memory of the call stack for main   Heap   The memory of the call stack for modifyStacks

When modifyStacks returns, names still points to the Stack containing "Kim" and "Edward", and grades now points to a Stack containing 95, 87, and 50. The output of StackDemo is

```
Kim
Edward
95
87
50
```

Changing the reference one does not change the reference names. Although it is impossible for the modifyStacks method to alter the names reference, it was quite easy for the method to modify the object that names points to.

The concept of call by value also applies to values returned by a method, as we will see in the next section. As discussed earlier in this chapter, you need to be able to view code and determine when an object becomes eligible for garbage collection. When does the object on line 9 of StackDemo become eligible for garbage collection? Because the variable one is a parameter, it goes out of scope when the modifyStacks method returns on line 10. Because one is the only reference pointing to the Stack object from line 9, the object is eligible for garbage collection after line 10.

Passing References vs. Passing Objects

You need to be able to distinguish the difference between a reference and an object. When passing arguments to a method, it is the reference that gets passed, not the object. It is impossible to pass an object to a method. In fact, the largest amount of data that can be copied into a parameter (or returned from a method) is a long or a double, both of which are 64 bits.

Return values are also passed by value, meaning a copy of the data is sent to the calling method. A method can return void, one of the eight primitive types, or a reference: there are no other possibilities. (Of course, the reference can be of any class or interface type, so the possible values you can return are actually endless, as long as you realize that a reference is getting returned, never an actual object!)

Let's look at an example using primitive types. Suppose we have the following method definition:

```
31. public int max(int a, int b) {
32.    int response;
33.    if( a < b) {
34.        response = b;
35.    } else {
```

```
36.        response = a;
37.    }
38.    return response;
39. }
```

The max method returns a local variable named response. A copy of response is returned to the calling method. Consider the following invocation of max:

```
45. public void go() {
46.     int x = 20, y = 30;
47.     int biggest = max(20, 30);
48.     System.out.println(biggest);
49. }
```

In this case, the parameter a is 20 and b is 30, resulting in a response of 30. A copy of 30 is passed back to the go method and stored in biggest. Because max is done executing, its call-stack memory is freed and a, b, and response all get destroyed. It doesn't make sense to try to modify response in the go method because response no longer exists in memory.

The Call Stack

Every method that gets invoked in a Java thread is pushed onto the thread's method *call stack*. The method at the top of the call stack is the currently executing method. Each method on the call stack gets its own small amount of memory. When a method finishes executing (by running to completion, returning a value, or throwing an exception), the method gets popped off the call stack and its memory is freed. Any parameters and local variables are destroyed and no longer exist in the program's memory.

The next example shows a method that returns a reference to an object. Examine the code and see if you can determine when the File object instantiated on line 6 is eligible for garbage collection:

```
1.  import java.io.File;
2.
3.  public class ReturnDemo {
4.
5.      public File getFile(String fileName) {
6.          File f = new File(fileName);
7.          return f;
```

```
8.      }
9.
10.     public static void main(String [] args) {
11.         ReturnDemo demo = new ReturnDemo();
12.         File file = demo.getFile(args[0]);
13.
14.         if(file.exists()) {
15.             System.out.println(file.getName() + " file exists");
16.         } else {
17.             System.out.println(file.getName() + " doesn't exist");
18.         }
19.
20.         file = null;
21.     }
22. }
```

The getFile method returns the reference f, which points to a new File object. Keep in mind that this File object is on the heap, not in the method's call stack memory, so the File object is not destroyed when getFile returns. The local variable file in main gets a copy of f when getFile returns. The File object from line 6 does not become eligible for garbage collection until after line 20.

The ReturnDemo program demonstrates a method that instantiates an object and returns a reference to that object. This is a common occurrence in Java. Just remember that the object is on the heap (all objects are instantiated on the heap!) and a *copy* of the reference is returned to the calling method. As with method arguments, the largest piece of data that can be returned from any Java method is 64 bits (a long or double). The fact that Java only allows call by value is an attempt to simplify the language. There is never any confusion with arguments and parameters: the parameter is always a copy of the argument.

Now that we have discussed the details of call by value, we turn our attention to another objective in the "Fundamentals" section: the Java operators.

Java Operators

You need to be able to "write code that correctly applies the appropriate operators." This section discusses the Java operators that appear on the exam. Table 1.2 lists all of the 41 operators in Java 6.0, listed in their *order of precedence*. Order of operations in Java is well defined, and the operators are guaranteed to be evaluated in the order shown. If operators have the same level of precedence, Java guarantees evaluation in left-to-right order.

TABLE 1.2   The Java Operators

Operator	Symbol and Precedence
Post-increment/post-decrement	*expression++, expression--*
Pre-increment/pre-decrement	*++expression, --expression*
Unary operators	+, -, ~, !
Multiplication/division/modulus	*, /, %
Addition/subtraction	+, -
Shift operators	<<, >>, >>>
Relational operators	<, >, <=, >=, instanceof
Equal to/not equal to	==, !=
Bitwise AND, exclusive OR, inclusive OR	&, ^,	
Logical AND, OR	&&, ||
Ternary operator	? :
Assignment operators	= += -= *= /= %= &= ^= |= <<= >>= >>>=

The SCJP exam objectives specifically mention the following operators:

- Assignment operators: =, += and -=
- Arithmetic operators: +, -, *, /, %, ++, and --
- Relational operators: <, <=, >, >=, ==, and !=
- The instanceof operator
- Bitwise and logical operators: &, |, ^, !, &&, and ||
- The conditional operator (?:)

The upcoming sections discuss each of these categories of operators and the details that you need to know about the operators for the SCJP exam.

The Assignment Operators

Java has 12 *assignment operators*: the *simple assignment* = and 11 *compound assignment operators*: +=, -=, *=, and so on. An assignment stores the result of the right-hand side of the expression into the variable on the left-hand side. Here is an example using a simple assignment:

```
4. byte b = 120;
5. int x = b;
```

The byte b is assigned the literal value 120, and the int x is assigned the value of b, which is also 120. An assignment will not compile if the right-hand operand cannot be converted to the data type of the left-hand variable. For example, the following line of code does not compile:

```
7. int y = 12.5;    //does not compile
```

The literal 12.5 is a double, and a double cannot implicitly be converted to an int without loss of data. For this code to compile, you would need to cast the right-side to an int:

```
8. int y = (int) 12.5;    //compiles fine
```

The value of y is 12 after this line of code executes. The decimal value is simply truncated.

The compound assignment operators perform the given operator first between the left and right sides of the operand, and then the result is stored in the left-hand variable. What is the value of z after this line of code?

```
10. int x = 5;
11. int z = 10;
12. z *= x;
```

The compound assignment operator is multiplication, so z is multiplied by x, which evaluates to 50, and then z is assigned 50. The same result could have been evaluated using a simple assignment:

```
13. z = z * x;
```

However, sometimes the compound operator can save us from needing to cast a value before the assignment. For example, the following statements generate a compiler error. Do you see why?

```
15. long m = 1000;
16. int n = 5;
17. n = n * m; //compiler error here
```

The expression n * m is an int times a long. Before the multiplication can be evaluated, the int is promoted to a long. The result is therefore a long, so we need a cast to make the compiler happy:

```
18. n = (int) (n * m);
```

The result is n equal to 5000. However, using the compound operator avoids the cast. The following statements compile successfully and assign n to 5000:

```
19. long m = 1000;
20. int n = 5;
21. n *= m;
```

In this case, the value of m is implicitly cast to an int before the multiplication occurs. An int times an int results in an int, so no cast is needed.

The Assignment Operators

According to the SCJP exam objectives, knowledge of the assignment operators is limited to =, += and –=. Of course, if you understand how += and –= work, you understand how the other compound assignment operators work!

The Arithmetic Operators

The exam objectives specifically mention having working knowledge of the following *arithmetic operators*:

- + – : addition and subtraction
- * / : multiplication and division
- % : modulus
- ++ –– : increment and decrement

We will now discuss each of these operators in detail.

The Additive Operators

The operators + and – are referred to as *additive operators*. They can be evaluated on any of the primitive types except boolean. Additionally, the + operator can be applied to String objects, which results in string concatenation.

If the operands are of different types, the smaller operand is promoted to the larger. At a minimum, the operands are promoted to ints. For example, the following innocent-looking code does not compile. Can you see why?

```
short s1 = 10, s2 = 12;
short sum = s1 + s2;    //does not compile!
```

Because a short is smaller than an int, both s1 and s2 are promoted to ints before the addition. The result of s1 + s2 is an int, so you can only store the result in a short if you use the cast operator. The compiler complains about a possible loss of precision, but casting fixes the problem:

```
short s1 = 10, s2 = 12;
short sum = (short) (s1 + s2);
```

The value of sum is 22 after this code executes.

A Note about Casting

I want to take a moment to point out something subtle but important about the cast operator. The sole purpose of casting primitive types is to make the compiler happy. When you assign a larger data type to a smaller one, the compiler complains about a possible loss of precision.

However, if you are aware and comfortable with the possible loss of precision at runtime, then you simply cast the result, which tells the compiler you know what you are doing. At runtime, the data may very well be invalid. For example, the following code compiles and runs, but you might be surprised by the output:

```
byte b1 = 60, b2 = 60;
byte product = (byte) (b1 * b2);
System.out.println(product);
```

This code outputs the number 16, clearly not the result of 60 times 60. The mistake lies in the limitations of a byte, which can only store values up to 127. Because 60 * 60 = 3600, the value of 16 is the lower 8 bits of the binary representation of 3600. The significant bits were lost in the runtime assignment of 3600 to the byte product.

We will revisit this discussion of casting again when we talk about inheritance and casting references in Chapter 6, "OO Concepts," because casting reference types is a different story altogether!

The JVM ensures order of operations is evaluated left-to-right when operators share the same precedence. For example, what is the value of x after this line of code executes?

```
String x = 12 - 6 + "Hello" + 7 + 5;
```

Following the order from left to right, 12 – 6 is evaluated first and results in 6. The next + operator is not addition but string concatenation, so the 6 is promoted to a String and the result is "6Hello". Following left to right, the next + is also string concatenation, resulting in "6Hello7", and finally the value of x after the last string concatenation is "6Hello75".

The Multiplicative Operators

The operators *, /, and % are referred to as the *multiplicative operators*. They have a higher precedence of operation than additive operators. The multiplicative operators can only be performed on the numeric primitive types; otherwise, a compiler error occurs.

As with + and –, the multiplicative operators promote both operands to the data type of the larger operand. If both operands are smaller than an int, both operands are converted to ints before the multiplication occurs. For example, what is the result of the following statements?

```
4. int a = 26, b = 5;
5. double d = a / b;
```

The expression a / b is integer division, which results in the int 5. Therefore, the value of d is 5.0. The fact that we store the result in a double does not affect the arithmetic because the assignment takes place after the arithmetic is already performed.

If one of the operands is a float or double, the expression is evaluated using floating-point arithmetic and the result will be a float or double depending on the operand types. For example, what is the result of the following statements?

```
8. int a = 26;
9. float f = a / 5.0F;
```

Because 5.0 is a float (by virtue of the "F" appended to it), the int a is promoted to a float and floating-point division is performed. The value of f is 5.2 after this code executes.

The MODULUS Operator

The modulus operator, also known as the remainder operator, evaluates the remainder of two numbers when they are divided. For example, what is the result of the following expression?

```
int x = 12 % 5;
```

The remainder of 12 divided by 5 is 2, so x is 2.

If the first operand is negative, so is the result of the modulus. The value of y after the following statement is –1:

```
int y = -17 % 4;
```

In Java you can evaluate the remainder of floating-point numbers as well. While not as intuitive as integer modulus, there is still a remainder in floating-point division. For example, what is the output of the following code?

```
System.out.println(12.4 % 3.2);
```

The answer is 2.8. A calculator won't help you on this one. You need to perform the division longhand to see where the remainder of 2.8 comes from.

The multiplication operators are evaluated left-to-right if the expression does not contain parentheses. What is the value of `result` after this statement?

```
int result = 12 + 2 * 5 % 3 - 15 / 4;
```

The expression evaluates to an `int` because all the literal values are `int`s. Here is how the expression is evaluated one level of precedence at a time. The parentheses are added for clarification.

```
12 + (2 * 5) % 3 - (15 / 4)
    12 + (10 % 3) - 3
       (12 + 1) - 3
           13 - 3
              10
```

Therefore the value of `result` is 10 after the statement executes.

The Increment and Decrement Operators

The operators ++ and – – are referred to as the increment and decrement operators because they increment and decrement (respectively) a numeric type by 1. The operators can be applied to an expression either prefix or postfix. These operators have the highest level of precedence of all the Java operators. They can only be applied to numeric operands, and the result is the same data type as the operand.

For example, the following statements create an `int` and increment it using ++. What is the output of this code?

```
3. int x = 6;
4. System.out.println(x++);
5. System.out.println(x);
```

Adding or subtracting 1 seems simple enough, but these operators can be confusing because of *when* they are evaluated! The output of the previous statements is

```
6
7
```

When the operator appears after the operand, the increment or decrement does not occur until after the operand is used in the current expression. On line 3, x is printed out as 6, then incremented to 7, which is demonstrated by the output of line 5.

When the increment operator appears before the operand, the operand is incremented first, and then the result is used in the current expression. The same is true for the decrement operator.

Examine the following code and try to determine its output:

```
10. char c = 'A';
11. for(int i = 1; i <= 10; i++) {
12.     System.out.print(c++ + " ");
13. }
14. System.out.print(c);
```

The first value printed is `'A'`, then c is incremented, which results in `'B'` printed on the second iteration of the loop. In total, 11 chars are printed and the output is

```
A B C D E F G H I J K
```

The following code demonstrates use of the decrement operator. Examine the code and try to determine its output:

```
16. int y = 5;
17. int result = y-- * 3 / --y;
18. System.out.println("y = " + y);
19. System.out.println("result = " + result);
```

I have to admit this is a tricky question! (I hope you never see code like this in the real world.) Notice y is decremented twice, so the output of y is 3. The value of `result` is not as obvious. Order of operations dictates that the multiplication is evaluated first. The value of y is 5, so 5 * 3 is 15. The multiplication is done, so the post-decrement occurs and y becomes 4. Now the division is evaluated and y is pre-decremented to 3 before the division, resulting in 15 / 3, which is 5. The output of this code is

```
y = 3
result = 5
```

Make Sure You Understand the Increment and Decrement Operators

The exam has plenty of questions that use the prefix and postfix increment and decrement operators. In many situations, the exam question is testing a different Java concept, not the incrementing or decrementing of variables. Make sure you have a good understanding of these fundamental (and sometimes tricky) operators.

The Relational Operators

The following operators are referred to as the *relational operators*:

- `<` : less than
- `<=` : less than or equal

- \> : greater than
- \>= : greater than or equal

The relational operators can only be performed on numeric primitive types, and the result of each relational operator is always a `boolean`. If the operands are not the same primitive type, the smaller operand is promoted to the larger operand's type before the comparison is made.

To demonstrate the relational operators, let's take a look at some examples. What is the result of the following statements?

```
5. int x = 10, y = 20, z = 10;
6. System.out.println(x < y);
7. System.out.println(x <= y);
8. System.out.println(x > z);
9. System.out.println(x >= z);
```

Because x and z are the same value, x > z is `false`. The other statements evaluate to `true`. Therefore, the output of this code is

```
true
true
false
true
```

The `boolean` Primitive Type

The result of a relational operator is a `boolean`, which can only be the values `true` or `false`. The following line of code does not compile:

```
int result = x < y;
```

The `boolean` primitive type in Java is not compatible with the `int` type. In other languages like C and C++, numeric types are often used for Boolean expressions, where 0 is false and non-zero is true. In Java, a `boolean` can never be treated as a numeric type, nor can a numeric type ever be treated as a `true` or `false` value.

The *instanceof* Operator

The `instanceof` operator compares a reference to a class or interface data type. The result is `true` if the reference is an instance of the data type; otherwise, the result is `false`. The syntax for the `instanceof` operator looks like this:

```
reference instanceof ClassOrInterfaceName
```

Let's take a look at an example. See if you can determine the output of the following statements:

```
3.  String s = "Hello, World";
4.  if(s instanceof String) {
5.      System.out.print("one");
6.  }
7.  if(s instanceof Object) {
8.      System.out.print("two");
9.  }
10. if(s instanceof java.io.Serializable) {
11.     System.out.print("three");
12. }
```

The reference s points to a String object, so line 4 is true and "one" is printed on line 5. Every object in Java is of type Object, so line 7 is true for any reference; therefore, "two" is printed. The String class implements the Serializable interface, which makes String objects Serializable objects as well. Therefore, line 10 is also true and the output of the previous code is

onetwothree

One of the main usages of the instanceof operator is when you cast a reference to a subclass type. If you cast a reference to an invalid data type, a ClassCastException is thrown by the JVM. For example, the following statements compile, but at runtime an exception is thrown:

```
Object x = new String("a String object");
Date d = (Date) x;
```

The output of this code is

```
Exception in thread "main" java.lang.ClassCastException:
 java.lang.String cannot be cast to java.util.Date
```

Using the instanceof operator, you can avoid this situation:

```
17. Object x = new String("a String object");
18. if(x instanceof Date) {
19.     Date d = (Date) x;
20. }
```

Because x points to a String object and not a Date object, line 18 is false and the invalid cast does not occur, avoiding the uncaught ClassCastException. We will see the instanceof operator again in Chapter 6.

The Bitwise and Logical Operators

The following operators are referred to as the *bitwise and logical operators*:

- & : the AND operator
- ^ : the exclusive OR operator
- | : the inclusive OR operator
- && : the conditional AND operator
- || : the conditional OR operator

The &, ^, and | operate on expressions where both operands are either primitive numeric types or both are `boolean` expressions. When operating on numeric types, they are bitwise operators. When operating on `boolean` types, they are logical operators. The && and || operators require both operands to be `boolean` expressions, so they are strictly logical operators.

The term *bitwise* refers to the &, ^, and | operators performing a bitwise AND or OR of the two operands. Table 1.3 shows the result of the possible outcomes for each of these three operators.

TABLE 1.3　The Bitwise Operators

& (AND)	^ (exclusive OR)		(inclusive OR)
0 & 0 is 0	0 ^ 0 is 0	0 | 0 is 0
0 & 1 is 0	0 ^ 1 is 1	0 | 1 is 1
1 & 0 is 0	1 ^ 0 is 1	1 | 0 is 1
1 & 1 is 1	1 ^ 1 is 0	1 | 1 is 1

Notice the & operator results in 1 only when both operands are 1, while the | operator results in 0 only when both operators are 0. The exclusive OR ^ is 1 when the two operands are different; otherwise it is 0.

The bitwise operators are evaluated on integer types. To compute the result, you need to know the binary representation of the values. For example, what is the result of the following expression?

```
int result = 12 ^ 45;
```

Begin by converting the 12 and 45 to binary numbers and align them vertically. Then perform the exclusive OR on each column, as Figure 1.15 shows.

FIGURE 1.15   Computing the exclusive or expression12^45

```
     12   =     0000 1100
     45   =     0010 1101
  12^45  =     0010 0001
```

The result is 00100001 in binary, which is 33 in decimal. Therefore, the value of `result` is 33.

The &, ^, and | are also logical operators, meaning they can operate on `boolean` types. The result of each operator is identical to Table 1.2 if you were to replace each 0 with `false` and each 1 with `true`. For example, the AND operator & is only `true` when both operands are `true`. The inclusive OR operator | is only `false` when both operands are `false`. The exclusive OR is only `true` when the two operands are different.

What is the output of the following logical statements?

```
3.  int a = 5, b = 10, c = 0;
4.  boolean one = a < b & c != 0;
5.  System.out.println(one);
6.  boolean two = true | true & false;
7.  System.out.println(two);
8.  boolean three = (c != 0) & (a / c > 1);
9.  System.out.println(three);
```

The variable one on line 4 is the result of `true & false`, which is `false`. The result of two on line 6 might surprise you. The & operator has a higher precedence than |, so the `true & false` is evaluated first, which results in `false`. Then `true | false` is evaluated, which is `true`, so two evaluates to `true`.

You might think that the Boolean on line 8 evaluates to `false`, but that line of code actually throws an `ArithmeticException` when attempting to compute a / c. The value of c is 0 and integer division by 0 is undefined in Java. Therefore, the last `println` never executes.

The example of a / c is a typical situation where a conditional operator comes in handy. The conditional operators && and || short-circuit, meaning the right operand may not get evaluated if the left hand operand can determine the result.

For example, when using &&, if the left operand is `false`, there is no need to check the right operand. False AND anything is `false`. In this case, the right-hand expression is not evaluated. Similarly, when using ||, if the left operand is `true`, there is no need to check the right operand because true OR anything is `true`.

The following statements are a modification of the previous example, except this time the logical expression short-circuits. What is the value of `three` after the following statements?

```
21.  int a = 5, b = 10, c = 0;
22.  boolean three = (c != 0) && (a / c > 1);
```

Because c is 0, the expression c != 0 is false and evaluation stops. The variable three is false and this code does not throw an exception at runtime.

Short-Circuit Behavior

Watch for the short-circuit behavior on the exam. The exam question might alter a variable in the right operand. For example, what is the output of the following code?

```
int x = 6;
boolean answer = (x >= 6) || (++x <= 7);
System.out.println(x);
```

Because x >= 6 is true, the incrementing of x does not occur in the right operand, so the output of this code is 6.

The Conditional Operator

Java contains a *conditional operator* ? :, often referred to as the *ternary operator* because it is the only operator in Java that has three operands. The syntax for the conditional operator is

```
boolean_expression ? true_expression : false_expression
```

The first operand must be a boolean expression. If this boolean expression is true, then the second operand is chosen; otherwise, the third operand is chosen. The second and third operands can be any expressions that evaluate to a value, or any method calls that return a value.

The conditional operator is a condensed version of an if/else statement that can be handy in a lot of different situations, especially when outputting or displaying data. For example, what is the output of the following statements?

```
int x = 6;
System.out.println( x != 0 ? 10/x : 0);
```

Because x is not 0, the output is the result of 10 / 6, which is 1.

Let's look at another example. What is the output of the following statements?

```
double d = 0.36;
System.out.println( d > 0 && d < 1 ? d *= 100 : "not a percent");
```

Because d is between 0 and 1, the output is 36.0. There is no requirement that the second and third operands be the same data types (or even compatible types).

The Equality Operators

The == (equal to) and != (not equal to) operators are referred to as the equality operators. The equality operators can be used in the following three situations, all of which return a boolean:

- The two operands are numerical primitive types.
- The two operands are boolean types.
- The two operands are references types or null types.

This implies that you cannot compare a byte to a boolean, or an int to a reference type. The two operands must be compatible. If one operand is a larger type, then the smaller type is promoted before the comparison. For example, you can compare an int to a float; the int is promoted to a float and a floating-point comparison is made. You can compare a char to an int: the char is promoted to an int and integer equality is performed.

Let's look at some uses of the equality operators. Examine the following code and try to determine its output:

```
6.   int x = 57;
7.   float f = 57.0F;
8.   double d = 5.70;
9.   boolean b = false;
10.
11.  boolean one = x == 57;
12.  System.out.println(one);
13.  boolean two = (f != d);
14.  System.out.println(two);
15.  boolean three = (b = true);
16.  System.out.println(three);
```

Lines 12 and 14 both print out true. The order of operations on line 11 ensures that x is compared to 57 before the assignment to one, even though parentheses would have made that statement easier to read (as in line 13). If you glanced over this code too quickly, you may think that line 16 prints out false, but the actual output is true. On line 15, (b = true) is an assignment, not a test for equality. Following the order of parentheses, b is set to true first, then three = b is evaluated, which sets three equal to true. The output of these statements is

```
true
true
true
```

The equality operators can also be evaluated on reference types. It is important to understand that evaluating == and != on two references compares the references, not the objects they point to. Two references are equal if and only if they point to the same object (or both point to null); otherwise, the two references are not equal.

The following `ReferenceDemo` program demonstrates comparing references. Examine the code and try to determine its output.

```
1.   import java.io.File;
2.   import java.util.Date;
3.
4.   public class ReferenceDemo {
5.     public static void main(String [] args) {
6.         File f1 = new File("mydata.txt");
7.         File f2 = new File("mydata.txt");
8.         if(f1 != f2) {
9.             System.out.println("f1 != f210.
11.        }
12.        Date today = new Date();
13.        Date now = today;
14.        if(today == now) {
15.            System.out.println("today == now");
16.        }
17.
18.        String s1 = "Hello";
19.        String s2 = "Hello";
20.        if(s1 == s2) {
21.            System.out.println("s1 == s2");
22.        }
23.
24.        String x1 = new String("Goodbye");
25.        String x2 = new String("Goodbye");
26.        if(x1 == x2) {
27.            System.out.println("x1 == x2");
28.        }
29.     }
30. }
```

Let's study this program. The references f1 and f2 point to two different `File` objects, so the two references cannot be equal. It is irrelevant that the two `File` objects look the same in memory; they are clearly two different objects so their references are not equal. On the other hand, there is only one `Date` object in memory and today and now both point to it, so today == now is true.

Comparing `String` references in Java tends to be confusing because of how the JVM treats string literals. Because `String` objects are immutable, the JVM can reuse string literals for efficiency and to save memory. Because `"Hello"` is a `String` literal known at compile time, the JVM only creates one `"Hello"` object in memory, and s1 and s2 both refer to it. Therefore, s1 == s2 evaluates to true. On the other hand, x1 and x2 are not literals but actual String objects created dynamically at runtime, making them distinct objects. Therefore, x1 and x2 point to different objects and cannot be equal. The output of the ReferenceDemo program is

```
f1 != f2
today == now
s1 == s2
```

The important point to take from this discussion is that evaluating == and != on reference types only compares whether or not the two references point to the same object. If you want to compare the actual contents of two objects, the equals method is used, which we discuss next.

Equality of Objects

The exam objectives address the ability to "determine the equality of two objects or two primitives." As we saw in the previous section, you use the == operator to determine if two primitives are equal. We also saw that two references are equal if and only if they point to the same object. But what does it mean for two *objects* to be equal? (Don't forget: references and objects are different entities!) As a Java programmer, you get to decide what it means for two objects to be equal. The java.lang.Object class contains an equals method with the following signature:

```
public boolean equals (Object obj)
```

The default implementation in Object tests for reference equality, which we can already perform with ==. The general rule of thumb is to override equals in all your classes to define what it means for two objects of your class type to be equal. Equality should be based on the business logic of your application.

The equals Method

Because the equals method is defined in Object, you can invoke equals on any object, passing in any other object. For example, the following statements are valid:

```
String s = "Hello";
java.util.Date d = new java.util.Date();
boolean b = s.equals(d);
```

The value of b is false. Logic would tell us that a String object and a Date object should never be equal, and that is the case. Typically two objects have to be of the same class type for them to be equal. However, that doesn't stop you from comparing two objects of different types, because the equals method can be invoked with any two objects.

Let's look at an example. Suppose we have the following class named Dog:

```
1.  public class Dog {
2.     private String name;
3.     private int age;
4.
5.     public Dog(String name, int age) {
6.         this.name = name;
7.         this.age = age;
8.     }
9.  }
```

What does it mean for two Dog objects to be equal? Suppose in our application two Dog objects are equal if they have the same name and age. Then Dog can override equals and implement this business logic:

```
1.  public class Dog {
2.     private String name;
3.     private int age;
4.
5.     public Dog(String name, int age) {
6.         this.name = name;
7.         this.age = age;
8.     }
9.
10.    public boolean equals(Object obj) {
11.        if(!(obj instanceof Dog))
12.            return false;
13.        Dog other = (Dog) obj;
14.        if(this.name.equals(other.name) &&
15.          (this.age == other.age)) {
16.            return true;
17.        } else {
18.            return false;
19.        }
20.    }
21. }
```

Within equals, we first test to see if the class type of the other object is Dog. If the other object is not a Dog object, we can quickly deduce the two objects are not equal. Otherwise, the incoming reference is cast to a Dog reference and the name and age are checked for equality. Because the name is a String object, we use the equals method of the String class to compare the two name objects.

The following DogTest program creates three Dog objects and test them for equality. Examine the code and try to determine its output:

```
1.  public class DogTest {
2.    public static void main(String [] args) {
3.        Dog one = new Dog("Fido", 3);
4.        Dog two = new Dog("Fido", 3);
5.        Dog three = new Dog("Lassie", 3);
6.
7.        if(one.equals(two)) {
8.            System.out.println("Fido");
9.        }
10.
11.        if(one.equals(three)) {
12.            System.out.println("Lassie");
13.        }
14.
15.        if(one == two) {
16.            System.out.println("one == two");
17.        }
18.    }
19. }
```

Because the Dog objects referred to by one and two have the same name and age, one.equals(two) is true and "Fido" is displayed. The "Lassie" object has a different name, so one.equals(three) is false. The test for one == two is false because one and two point to different (but equal) objects.

The hashCode Method

The Object class contains a method named hashCode with the following signature:

`public int hashCode()`

This method is used by hash table data structures. The hashCode and equals methods are related in the sense that two objects that are equal should generate the same hash code. Therefore, any time you override equals in a class, you should also override hashCode. In the Dog class, the following hashCode method maintains this required relationship of equals and hashCode:

```
public int hashCode() {
    return age;
}
```

If two Dog objects are equal in our example, they have the same age and therefore will have the same hash code.

Summary

This chapter covered the "Fundamentals" objectives of the SCJP exam. Sun lists these topics last in their official list of objectives, but we needed to discuss these fundamentals first before tackling the more advanced topics of the exam.

The goal of this chapter was to discuss the details of running Java applications, including working with packages and using an appropriate classpath. You should also have a good understanding of garbage collection and when an object becomes eligible for garbage collection.

We also discussed the details of using the many operators in Java. As the title of the chapter suggests, these topics are the "fundamentals" of Java that provide the building blocks for the remainder of this book.

Be sure to test your knowledge of these fundamentals by answering the Review Questions that follow. I tried to write questions that reflect the style and difficulty level of questions on the SCJP exam, so attempt to answer the questions seriously without looking back at the pages of this chapter and do your best. Make sure you have a good understanding of the following Exam Essentials before attempting the Review Questions, and good luck!

Exam Essentials

Understand the effect of putting a class in a package.   In the real world, all classes are declared within a package. Know how to run a Java class from a command prompt when the class is in a package, and be sure to recognize what the CLASSPATH environment variable needs to be.

Get comfortable with looking at code and determining its output.   Many of the exam questions provide either a small program or a snippet of code and ask what the output is. Practice reading code and determining what it does, including whether or not the given code compiles successfully.

Understand call by value.   I can guarantee at least two or three questions on the exam that have an argument passed into a method and the method alters the parameter. Understand that a method cannot change the argument. The only effect a method can have on an argument is when the argument is a reference, in which case the method can alter the object that the reference points to.

Be able to determine when an object becomes eligible for garbage collection.   Knowing when an object is eligible for garbage collection demonstrates an important understanding of Java and how it creates and destroys objects. You will see at least one question on the exam that asks you when an object is eligible for garbage collection, and also at least one question involving the `Object.finalize()` method.

Understand the difference between == and the `equals` method.   Use the == comparison operator to determine if two primitive types are equal and also to determine if two references point to the same object. Use the `equals` method to determine if two objects are "equal," which is whatever equality means in the business logic of the class.

Familiarize yourself with the Java operators.   The Java operators are a fundamental aspect of the language, and almost all of the exam questions that contain sample code use one or more of the Java operators.

Review Questions

1. The following code appears in a file named `Plant.java`. What is the result of compiling this source file? (Select one answer.)

```
1.   public class Plant {
2.      public boolean flowering;
3.      public Leaf [] leaves;
4.   }
5.
6.   class Leaf {
7.      public String color;
8.      public int length;
9.   }
```

   A. The code compiles successfully and two bytecode files are generated: `Plant.class` and `Leaf.class`

   B. The code compiles successfully and one bytecode file is generated: `Plant.class`.

   C. A compiler error occurs on line 1.

   D. A compiler error occurs on line 3.

   E. A compiler error occurs on line 6.

2. Suppose a class named `com.mycompany.Main` is a Java application, and `Main.class` is in the following directory:

   `\projects\build\com\mycompany`

   Which of the following commands successfully executes `Main`? (Select two answers.)

   A. `java -classpath=\projects\build com.mycompany.Main`

   B. `java -classpath \projects\build\com\mycompany Main`

   C. `java -classpath \projects\build com.mycompany.Main`

   D. `java -classpath \projects\build\com mycompany.Main`

   E. `java -cp \projects\build com.mycompany.Main`

3. A class named `Test` is in the `a.b.c` package, defined in a file named `Test.java` and saved in the following directory:

   `c:\abcproject\src\Test.java`

   Assuming the code in `Test.java` uses only classes from `java.lang` and contains no compiler errors, what is the result of the following command line? (Select one answer).

   `c:\abcproject\src>javac -d c:\abcproject\deploy Test.java`

A. A NoClassDefFoundError occurs.

B. A ClassNotFoundException occurs.

C. Test.class is generated in the c:\abcproject\deploy directory.

D. Test.class is generated in the c:\abcproject\deploy\abc directory.

E. Test.class is generated in the c:\abcproject\deploy\a\b\c directory.

4. What is the outcome of the following code?

```
1.   public class Employee {
2.      public int employeeId;
3.      public String firstName, lastName;
4.      public java.util.GregorianCalendar hireDate;
5.
6.      public int hashCode() {
7.          return employeeId;
8.      }
9.
10.     public boolean equals(Employee e) {
11.         return this.employeeId == e.employeeId;
12.     }
13.
14.     public static void main(String [] args) {
15.         Employee one = new Employee();
16.         one.employeeId = 101;
17.
18.         Employee two = new Employee();
19.         two.employeeId = 101;
20.
21.         if(one.equals(two)) {
22.             System.out.println("Success");
23.         } else {
24.             System.out.println("Failure");
25.         }
26.     }
27. }
```

A. Success

B. Failure

C. Line 6 causes a compiler error.

D. Line 10 causes a compiler error.

E. Line 10 causes a runtime exception to occur.

5. What is the result of compiling the following class?

```
1.  public class Book {
2.      private int ISBN;
3.      private String title, author;
4.      private int pageCount;
5.
6.      public int hashCode() {
7.          return ISBN;
8.      }
9.
10.     public boolean equals(Object obj) {
11.         if(!(obj instanceof Book)) {
12.             return false;
13.         }
14.         Book other = (Book) obj;
15.         return this.ISBN == other.ISBN;
16.     }
17. }
```

A. The class compiles successfully.

B. Line 6 causes a compiler error because hashCode does not return a unique value.

C. Line 10 causes a compiler error because the equals method does not override the parent method correctly.

D. Line 14 does not compile because the ClassCastException is not handled or declared.

E. Line 15 does not compile because other.ISBN is a private field.

6. What is the outcome of the following statements? (Select one answer.)

```
6.  String s1 = "Canada";
7.  String s2 = new String(s1);
8.  if(s1 == s2) {
9.    System.out.println("s1 == s2");
10. }
11. if(s1.equals(s2)) {
12.     System.out.println("s1.equals(s2)");
13. }
```

A. There is no output.

B. s1 == s2

C. s1.equals(s2)

D. Both B and C

7.   Suppose we have the following class named GC:

```
1.   import java.util.Date;
2.
3.   public class GC {
4.     public static void main(String [] args) {
5.         Date one = new Date();
6.         Date two = new Date();
7.         Date three = one;
8.         one = null;
9.         Date four = one;
10.        three = null;
11.        two = null;
12.        two = new Date();
13.    }
14. }
```

Which of the following statements are true? (Select two answers.)

A. The Date object from line 5 is eligible for garbage collection immediately following line 8.

B. The Date object from line 5 is eligible for garbage collection immediately following line 10.

C. The Date object from line 5 is eligible for garbage collection immediately following line 13.

D. The Date object from line 6 is eligible for garbage collection immediately following line 11.

E. The Date object from line 6 is eligible for garbage collection immediately following line 13.

8.   What is the output of the following code?

```
1.   private class Squares {
2.     public static long square(int x) {
3.         long y = x * (long) x;
4.         x = -1;
5.         return y;
6.     }
7.
8.     public static void main(String [] args) {
9.         int value = 9;
10.        long result = square(value);
11.        System.out.println(value);
12.    }
13. }
```

A. This code does not compile.

B. 9

C. -1

D. 81

9. What is the output of the following code?

```
1.  public class TestDrive {
2.
3.     public static void go(Car c) {
4.         c.velocity += 10;
5.     }
6.
7.     public static void main(String [] args) {
8.         Car porsche = new Car();
9.         go(porsche);
10.
11.        Car stolen = porsche;
12.        go(stolen);
13.
14.        System.out.println(porsche.velocity);
15.     }
16. }
17.
18. class Car {
19.    public int velocity = 10;
20. }
```

A. 0

B. 10

C. 20

D. 30

E. This code does not compile.

10. What is the output of the following code?

```
1.  import java.util.*;
2.
3.  public class DateSwap {
4.
```

```
5.     public static void swap(GregorianCalendar a, GregorianCalendar b)
6.     {
7.         GregorianCalendar temp = a;
8.         a = new GregorianCalendar(2012, 1, 1);
9.         b = temp;
10.    }
11.
12.    public static void main(String [] args) {
13.        GregorianCalendar one = new GregorianCalendar(2010, 1, 1);
14.        GregorianCalendar two = new GregorianCalendar(2011, 1, 1);
15.
16.        swap(one, two);
17.
18.        System.out.print(one.get(Calendar.YEAR));
19.        System.out.println(two.get(Calendar.YEAR));
20.    }
21. }
```

A. 20112010

B. 20102011

C. 20122011

D. 20122010

E. 20102012

F. This code does not compile.

11. When does the `String` object instantiated on line 4 become eligible for garbage collection?

```
1.   public class ReturnDemo {
2.
3.       public static String getName() {
4.           String temp = new String("Jane Doe");
5.           return temp;
6.       }
7.
8.       public static void main(String [] args) {
9.           String result;
10.          result = getName();
11.          System.out.println(result);
12.          result = null;
13.          System.gc();
14.      }
15. }
```

A. Immediately after line 4

B. Immediately after line 5

C. Immediately after line 10

D. Immediately after line 12

E. Immediately after line 13

F. Immediately after line 14

12. What is the output of the following code?

```
4. byte a = 40, b = 50;
5. byte sum = (byte) a + b;
6. System.out.println(sum);
```

A. Line 5 generates a compiler error.

B. 40

C. 50

D. 90

E. An undefined value

13. What is the output of the following code?

```
5. int x = 5 * 4 % 3;
6. System.out.println(x);
```

A. Line 5 generates a compiler error.

B. 2

C. 3

D. 5

E. 6

14. What is the output of the following code?

```
3. byte y = 14 & 9;
4. System.out.println(y);
```

A. Line 3 generates a compiler error.

B. 15

C. 14

D. 9

E. 8

15. What is the output of the following code?

```
1.  public class FinalTest {
2.
3.    public static void main(String [] args) {
4.         House h = new House();
5.         h.address = "123 Main Street";
6.         h = null;
7.         System.gc();
8.    }
9.  }
10.
11. class House {
12.    public String address;
13.
14.    public void finalize() {
15.        System.out.println("Inside House");
16.        address = null;
17.    }
18. }
```

A. There is no output.

B. `Inside House`

C. The output cannot be determined.

D. The code generates a compiler error.

16. Given the following class named House, which of the following statements is true? (Select two answers.)

```
1.  public class House {
2.    public String address = new String();
3.
4.    public void finalize() {
5.        System.out.println("Inside House");
6.        address = null;
7.    }
8.  }
```

A. `"Inside House"` is displayed just before a House object is garbage collected.

B. `"Inside House"` is displayed twice just before a House object is garbage collected.

C. The `finalize` method on line 4 never actually gets called.

D. There is no need to assign `address` to `null` on line 6.

E. The `String` object from line 2 is guaranteed to be garbage collected after its corresponding House object is garbage collected.

17. Which of the following statements is true about the following `BaseballTeam` class?

```
1.  public class BaseballTeam {
2.      private String city, mascot;
3.      private int numberOfPlayers;
4.
5.      public boolean equals(Object obj) {
6.          if(!(obj instanceof BaseballTeam)) {
7.              return false;
8.          }
9.          BaseballTeam other = (BaseballTeam) obj;
10.         return (city.equals(other.city)
11.                 && mascot.equals(other.mascot));
12.     }
13.
14.     public int hashCode() {
15.         return numberOfPlayers;
16.     }
17. }
```

A. The class does not compile.

B. The class compiles but contains an improper `equals` method.

C. The class compiles but contains an improper `hashCode` method.

D. The class compiles and has proper `equals` and `hashCode` methods.

18. What is the output of the following code?

```
3. int x = 0;
4. String s = null;
5. if(x == s) {
6.     System.out.println("Success");
7. } else {
8.     System.out.println("Failure");
9. }
```

A. Success

B. Failure

C. Line 4 generates a compiler error.

D. Line 5 generates a compiler error.

19. What is the output of the following code?

```
3. int x1 = 50, x2 = 75;
4. boolean b = x1 >= x2;
5. if(b = true) {
```

```
6.    System.out.println("Success");
7. } else {
8.    System.out.println("Failure");
9. }
```

A. Success

B. Failure

C. Line 4 generates a compiler error.

D. Line 5 generates a compiler error.

20. What is the output of the following code?

```
5. int c = 7;
6. int result = 4;
7. result += ++c;
8. System.out.print(result);
```

A. 8

B. 11

C. 12

D. 15

E. 16

F. Line 7 generates a compiler error.

21. Determine the output of the following code when executed with the command:

```
java HelloWorld hello world goodbye
```

```
1.    public static class HelloWorld {
2.      public static void main(String [] args) {
3.           System.out.println(args[1] + args[2]);
4.      }
5.    }
```

A. hello world

B. world goodbye

C. null null

D. An ArrayIndexOutOfBoundsException occurs at runtime.

E. The code does not compile.

Answers to Review Questions

1.   A. The code does not contain any compiler errors. It is valid to define multiple classes in a single file as long as only one of them is `public` and the others have the default access.

2.   C and E. C assigns the `-classpath` flag to the appropriate directory. E also set the class path correctly except `-cp` is used. The `-cp` and `-classpath` flags are identical. A uses an equals sign `=` with the `-classpath` flag, which is not the correct syntax. B and D set the class path to the wrong directory and also incorrectly refer to the `Main` class without its fully qualified name, which is `com.mycompany.Main`.

3.   E. The `-d` flag creates the appropriate directory structure that matches the package name. In this case, that directory created is `c:\abcproject\deploy\a\b\c`. Therefore, C and D are wrong. A `NoClassDefFoundError` occurs if the compiler cannot find the source file, but in this example the `javac` command is executed from the same directory that contains the source file, so this error does not occur. A `ClassNotFoundException` is a runtime exception that is not thrown by a compiler, so B is incorrect.

4.   A. Based on the definition of the `equals` method, two `Employee` objects are equal if they have the same `employeeId` field, so line 21 evaluates to `true` and `"Success"` is output, so B is incorrect. Line 6 successfully overrides `hashCode`, so C is incorrect. Line 10 is a valid overriding of `equals`, so D and E are incorrect.

5.   A. B is incorrect because `hashCode` does not have to return a unique value (not that the compiler could determine if the value was unique anyway). C is incorrect because the `equals` method correctly overrides `equals` in `Object`. D is incorrect because a `ClassCast-Exception` does not need to be handled or declared. E is incorrect because although ISBN is a `private` field, the `equals` method is within the class and therefore has access to the `private` field. Therefore, the code compiles successfully and the answer is A.

6.   C. The reference s1 points to a `String` object in the string pool because `"Canada"` is a literal string known at compile time. The reference s2 points to a `String` object created dynamically at runtime, so this object is created on the heap. Therefore B is incorrect because s1 and s2 point to different objects. However, C is correct because s1 and s2 are both `String` objects that equal "Canada", so `s1.equals(s2)` evaluates to `true`. Because C is correct, A and D must be incorrect.

7.   B and D. The `Date` object from line 5 has two references to it — one and `three` — and becomes eligible for garbage collection after line 10, so B is a true statement. The reference `four` is set to `null` on line 9, which does not affect the object from line 5. The `Date` object from line 6 only has a single reference to it — `two` — and therefore becomes eligible for garbage collection after line 11 when `two` is set to `null`, so D is a true statement.

8.   A. A top-level class cannot be declared `private`, so line 1 causes a compiler error. This is one of those exam questions where you might waste a couple of minutes if you do not notice the compiler error right away. Don't forget to keep an eye out for these subtle types of compiler errors.

9. D. The code compiles, so E is incorrect. The Car object on line 8 has an initial velocity of 10 from line 19. The call to go on line 9 changes its velocity to 20. The stolen reference points to the same Car object, so calling go with the stolen argument changes the Car object's velocity to 30, so the correct answer is D.

10. B. The code compiles successfully, so F is incorrect. The two GregorianCalendar references are passed to the swap method, which does not change either object. In fact, the only thing swapped in the swap method is b getting assigned to a, but these changes do not affect the references one and two. Because the objects that one and two refer to are not changed in the swap method, the output is 20102011 and B is the correct answer.

11. D. The object on line 4 is referred to by the temp reference, which goes out of scope after line 5. However, the result reference gets a copy of temp, so it refers to the "Jane Doe" object until line 12 when result is set to null, at which point "Jane Doe" is no longer reachable and becomes immediately eligible for garbage collection. Therefore, the answer is D.

12. A. Line 5 generates a possible loss of precision compiler error. The cast operator has the highest precedence, so it is evaluated first, casting a to a byte (which is fine). Then the addition is evaluated, causing both a and b to be promoted to ints. The value 90, stored as an int, is assigned to sum, which is a byte. This requires a cast, so the code does not compile and therefore the correct answer is A. (This code would compile if parentheses were used around (a + b).)

13. B. The * and % operators have the same level or precedence and are therefore evaluated left-to-right. The result of 5 * 4 is 20 and 20 % 3 is 2 (20 divided by 3 is 18; the remainder is 2). Therefore, the answer is B.

14. E. To evaluate the & operator, you need to express the numbers in binary and evaluate & on each column, as shown here:

14	=	0000 1110
9	=	0000 1001
14&9	=	0000 1000

The resulting binary number 00001000 is 8 in decimal, so the answer is E.

15. C. The code compiles successfully, so D is incorrect. Due to the unpredictable behavior of System.gc, the output cannot be determined. The House object from line 4 is eligible for garbage collection after line 6, and the call to System.gc may free its memory and cause "Inside House" to be displayed from the finalize method. However, the System.gc method may not free the memory of the House object, in which case there would be no output. Because A or B may occur, the answer is C.

16. A and D. Just before an object is garbage collected, its finalize method is invoked once, so A is true but B is incorrect. C is incorrect because it is just not a true statement. D is correct; there is no need to assign address to null because it is about to be deleted from memory. E is incorrect, though, because address may not be the only reference to the String object that address refers to.

17. C. The class compiles successfully, so A is incorrect. B is incorrect because an `equals` method can use any business logic you want to determine if two objects are equal. However, the rule for proper overriding of `equals` and `hashCode` is that if two objects are equal, they should generate the same hash code. The `hashCode` method does not properly follow this rule. Two teams with the same `city` and `mascot` but different `numberOfPlayers` would be equal but would generate different hash codes. Therefore, D is incorrect and the answer is C.

18. D. The variable `x` is an `int` and `s` is a reference. These two data types are incomparable because neither variable can be converted to the other variable's type. The compiler error occurs on line 5 when the comparison is attempted, so the answer is D.

19. A. The code compiles successfully, so C and D are incorrect. The value of `b` after line 4 is `false`. However, the `if` statement on line 5 contains an assignment, not a comparison. The value of `b` is assigned to true on line 5, and the assignment operator returns `true`, so line 6 executes and displays `"Success"`.

20. C. The code compiles successfully, so F is incorrect. On line 7, `c` is incremented to 8 before being used in the expression because it is a pre-increment. The 8 is added to `result`, which is 4, and the resulting 12 is assigned to `result` and displayed on line 8. Therefore, the answer is C.

21. E. The class declaration on line 1 contains the `static` modifier, which is not a valid modifier for a top-level class. This causes a compiler error, so the correct answer is E.

Chapter 2

Declarations, Initialization, and Scoping

SCJP EXAM OBJECTIVES COVERED IN THIS CHAPTER:

✓ Develop code that declares classes (including abstract and all forms of nested classes), interfaces, and enums, and includes the appropriate use of package and import statements (including static imports).

✓ Develop code that declares an interface. Develop code that implements or extends one or more interfaces. Develop code that declares an abstract class. Develop code that extends an abstract class.

✓ Develop code that declares, initializes, and uses primitives, arrays, enums, and objects as static, instance, and local variables. Also, use legal identifiers for variable names.

✓ Develop code that declares both static and non-static methods, and — if appropriate — use method names that adhere to the JavaBeans naming standards. Also develop code that declares and uses a variable-length argument list.

✓ Given a code example, determine if a method is correctly overriding or overloading another method, and identify legal return values (including covariant returns), for the method.

✓ Given a set of classes and superclasses, develop constructors for one or more of the classes. Given a class declaration, determine if a default constructor will be created, and if so, determine the behavior of that constructor. Given a nested or non-nested class listing, write code to instantiate the class.

These objectives are Section 1 of the SCJP exam objectives. The exam tests your knowledge of all aspects of declaring a Java class, including the details of declaring fields, methods, and constructors. The exam also tests your knowledge of declaring interfaces, enums, arrays, and nested classes. This chapter covers all of these topics in detail.

Declaring Variables

The exam objectives state that you need to be able to "develop code that declares, initializes, and uses primitives, arrays, enums, and objects." Declaring these various data types involves creating a variable. A *variable* represents an allocated piece of memory for storing data. Java is a strongly typed programming language, meaning every variable must be declared with a specific data type before it can be used. Declaring a variable involves stating the data type and giving the variable a name. For example, the following statements declare three variables; an int named channel, a double named diagonal, and a String reference named brand:

```
int channel;
double diagonal;
String brand;
```

A variable is initialized when it is first assigned a value. For example, the following statements initialize our three variables:

```
channel = 32;
diagonal = 53.0;
brand = "Acme";
```

In Java, a variable must be initialized before you can use it. Variables that represent fields in a class are automatically initialized to their corresponding "zero" value during object instantiation. Local variables must be specifically initialized. The next section, "Scoping," discusses the initializing of variables in detail.

The name of a variable is referred to as its *identifier*. (The names of your fields, classes, methods, interfaces, and enums are also identifiers.) The exam objectives include knowing the "legal identifiers for variable names." Here are the rules for legal identifiers:

- An identifier is a Unicode character sequence of Java letters and Java digits. These include the ASCII characters A–Z and a–z, the digits 0–9, the underscore character (_), and the dollar sign ($).

- The first character of an identifier must be a Java letter, underscore, or dollar sign. (In other words, the first character cannot be a digit.)

- An identifier must not be a Java keyword, `true`, `false`, or `null`.

Table 2.1 contains a list of valid and invalid identifiers to demonstrate these rules. Let's take a look at the invalid identifiers:

TABLE 2.1   Java Identifiers

Valid Identifiers	Invalid Identifiers
x1	x 1
True	true
_7_	me@company
_firstName	1stName
car$model	x*y
$color	seven#

- `x 1` has a space in it, which is not allowed.
- `true` is a reserved word.
- `me@company` contains the @ symbol, which is not a Java letter or digit.
- `1stName` does not start with a Java letter. Identifiers cannot start with a digit.
- `x*y` contains the multiplication operator. Identifiers cannot contain any of the Java operators.
- `seven#` contains the # symbol, which is also not a Java letter or digit.

Java Tokens

When your source code is compiled, the compiler breaks down your code into *tokens* based on the spaces, line feeds, tabs and other separators in your code. There are five types of tokens in Java:

- Separators
- Keywords
- Literals
- Operators
- Identifiers

Because identifiers are the names you come up with for your variables, classes, fields, methods, interfaces (and so on), the compiler needs to be able to recognize them easily. This is why Java needs a specific set of rules that must be followed for creating legal identifiers.

Scoping

As mentioned previously, the exam objectives state that you need to be able to develop code that uses "static, instance, and local variables." Each of these three types of variables has a different scope. *Scope* refers to that portion of code where a variable can be accessed. There are three kinds of variables in Java, depending on their scope:

Instance variables   These variables represent the nonstatic fields of a class.

Class variables   These variables represent the static fields of a class.

Local variables   These variables are defined inside a method. Local variables are only accessible within the method in which they are declared.

This section discusses these three types of variables in detail, starting with a discussion of instance variables.

Instance Variables

Instance variables are the nonstatic fields of your class, often referred to simply as *fields*. These variables get allocated in memory when a new object is instantiated. Because the new operator zeroes the memory for an object, all fields initially have their corresponding zero value, which are as follows:

- Primitive numeric fields initialize to 0. This includes byte, short, int, long, float and double.
- boolean types initialize to false.
- char types initialize to the null character '\u0000'.
- Reference types initialize to null.

Instance variables are always initialized during object instantiation, so you can use an instance variable even if you do not specifically assign it a value.

Let's take a look at an example. Suppose we have the following class named Television:

```
1.  public class Television {
2.    public int channel;
3.    public double diagonal;
4.      public String brand;
5.
6.      public Television() {
7.              channel = 4;
8.    }
9.  }
```

Examine the following statements and try to determine the output:

```
3. Television tv = new Television();
4. System.out.println(tv.channel + " " + tv.diagonal + " " + tv.brand);
```

The preceding code compiles fine. The channel field is initially 0 but is set to 4 in the constructor. The diagonal field is a double so its initial value is 0.0. The brand field is a reference so its value is null. The output is

```
4 0.0 null
```

Figure 2.1 shows what this Television object looks like in memory.

FIGURE 2.1   A Television object has three fields in memory.

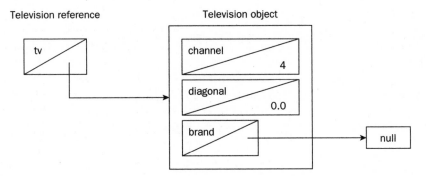

The Lifetime of Instance Variables

An instance variable does not exist in memory until an instance of the class is instantiated. When an object is instantiated, its instance variables exist in memory until the object is garbage collected.

Explicit Initialization

Java allows for the explicit initialization of instance variables. *Explicit initialization* is when a field is assigned a value at the same time that the field is declared. The field therefore gets initialized before the constructor executes.

For example, the following `Apple` class uses explicit initialization to initialize its `variety` field:

```
1.  public class Apple extends Fruit {
2.     public String variety = "McIntosh";
3.
4.     public Apple(String variety) {
5.         System.out.println("Constructing an Apple");
6.         this.variety = variety;
7.     }
8.  }
```

The `variety` field is assigned the value `"McIntosh"` after the memory is zeroed by the new operator. That means that `variety` was actually `null` for a brief moment before it was assigned `"McIntosh"`.

Explicit initialization allows you to initialize a field before a constructor is executed. However, the most common reason for using explicit initialization is simply that sometimes it is just easier to initialize a field when you declare it, especially if the initialization is the same for every instance of the class.

In the previous example, setting the `variety` field of all `Apple` objects to initially be `"McIntosh"` probably does not make sense in a real-world application. However, there are plenty of situations where explicit initialization comes in handy. For example, the following `Movie` class has a `Vector` field that contains Fan objects:

```
1.  import java.util.Vector;
2.
3.  public class Movie {
4.     public Vector<Fan> fans = new Vector<Fan>();
5.     public String title;
6.     public double boxOfficeTotal;
7.
8.     public Movie(String title) {
9.         this.title = title;
10.    }
11.
12.    public void addFan(Fan f) {
13.        fans.add(f);
14.    }
15. }
```

Because the `Vector` has the same initial value for all instances of the `Movie` class, using explicit initialization makes sense and simplifies the constructor code. If the `Movie` class had multiple constructors, we would have to make sure that the `Vector` gets instantiated in each constructor. By using explicit initialization, we are ensured that the `fans` field is properly initialized for all instances of Movie, and the initialization takes place in a single location (instead of in multiple constructors).

 The code on the exam uses a lot of explicit initialization. This is probably because it makes the code shorter and simpler. Often the exam question will likely be testing your knowledge of a topic not specifically related to explicit initialization, so explicit initialization is one of those fundamental concepts you are just expected to know.

Class Variables

A *class variable* is a field within a class declared as static, often referred to as a *static variable* or *static field*. A static field is unique in that the memory is allocated for the field when the class is loaded by the JVM's class loader, and the variable remains in memory until the class loader unloads the class. Because a program typically terminates before a class is unloaded, the lifetime of a static field is often the lifetime of the application.

Static fields do not belong to instances of a class. You can access a static field before any instances of the class are created, and if you have 100 instances of the class, you still only have one instance of the static field.

Global Variables in Java

Java does not support the concept of global variables. All variables in Java appear within a class or interface. Static fields are the closest thing you have in Java to global variables, because a static field has a lifetime beyond the life of the instances of the class and a static field can be accessed from any other class or object (depending on the access specifier).

Consider the following class named House with a static int field named counter:

```
1.  package my.blueprints;
2.  public class House {
3.     private Room kitchen;     //instance variable
4.     public static int counter = 0;     //class variable
5.
6.     public House() {
7.         kitchen = new Room();
8.     }
```

```
9.
10.    public Room getKitchen() {
11.         counter++;
12.         return kitchen;
13.    }
14. }
```

The counter field is a class variable. There is only one instance of counter in memory, and it exists in memory before any House objects are instantiated.

Access a class variable using the name of the class. For example, to access counter you use the following syntax:

```
House.counter
```

Notice on line 11 that counter was incremented and we did not use the name of the class to reference it. Code within the class that contains the static field does not need to use the class name.

Examine the following HouseTest program. Does it compile, and if so, what is its output?

```
1.   import my.blueprints.House;
2.
3.   public class HouseTest {
4.     public static void main(String [] args) {
5.          System.out.println("counter = " + House.counter);
6.          House one = new House();
7.          House two = new House();
8.          one.getKitchen();
9.          two.getKitchen();
10.         one.getKitchen();
11.         System.out.println("counter = " + House.counter);
12.     }
13. }
```

On line 5 the counter variable displays before any House objects are created. This is a valid statement and the value of counter is 0 at line 5. Two House objects are instantiated, and calling getKitchen three times on the two House objects increments counter to 3. The code compiles successfully and the output is

```
counter = 0
counter = 3
```

Even though the HouseTest class creates two House objects (which in turn causes two Room objects to be instantiated for the kitchen field), there is still only one counter in memory and it exists until the program terminates.

Understanding Static Fields

I often refer to static fields as breaking the rules of object-oriented programming. I am not implying that static should be avoided, because static fields are an important part of the Java language and I use them all the time. However, it is important to understand what it means for a field to be static. It might seem odd that a field of a class can exist before the class is ever instantiated. Recall my analogy of a class being the blueprint of a house, and an object being the house. If we make the kitchen static, that means we have a kitchen before we ever build the house! In addition, if we build 100 houses from our blueprint, we still only have one kitchen! Obviously a kitchen is not a good candidate for static when it comes to building houses.

We use static fields when the field is shared among all classes and the field is not unique to any particular instance. For example, the House class can keep track of how many times a particular method is invoked on all House objects. Because counter is shared among all House objects, this is a perfect situation for using a static field.

Global variables are another common example of when to use static. For example, there is only one standard input and standard output. Making them global variables allows all objects in your program to access the standard input and output, so System.in and System.out are good candidates for static fields.

Static Imports

As of Java 5.0, a static variable can be imported into a source file, which allows the static variable to be accessible without being prefixed with its corresponding class or interface name. Importing a static member is referred to as a *static import* and uses the following syntax:

```
import static packagenames.classname.variablename;
```

You can also use the asterisk as a wildcard, which allows you to import all of the static variables from a class or interface. Static imports appear in the same location of a source file as regular imports: after the package declaration and before the class declaration.

The following program is the same code as the HouseTest program in the previous example, except the static field counter from House is imported on line 3. The class also imports all static fields in java.lang.System on line 4, which includes the out field.

```
1.   import my.blueprints.House;
2.
3.   import static my.blueprints.House.counter;
4.   import static java.lang.System.*;
5.
6.   public class StaticImportDemo {
```

```
7.     public static void main(String [] args) {
8.         out.println("counter = " + counter);
9.         House one = new House();
10.        House two = new House();
11.        one.getKitchen();
12.        two.getKitchen();
13.        one.getKitchen();
14.        out.println("counter = " + counter);
15.    }
16.}
```

This code compiles successfully and has the same output as HouseTest. Notice the static imports allow counter and out to be referenced by their simple names and not prefixed with their corresponding class name.

> Because static imports are a fairly new concept in Java, expect at least one question on the exam to test your knowledge of how to properly declare and use a static import.

Local Variables

A *local variable* is a variable defined within a method, which includes any method parameters. A local variable gets created in memory on the call stack when the method executes, and is deleted from memory when the method returns and the call stack memory is destroyed. Local variables never appear on the heap, although a local variable that is a reference can certainly refer to an object on the heap.

Local variables must be initialized before use. They do not have a default value and contain garbage data until initialized. The compiler enforces this rule. For example, the following code generates a compiler error:

```
4. public int notValid() {
5.     int y = 10;
6.     int x;
7.     int reply = x + y;
8.     return reply;
9. }
```

The ints y and x are local variables and y is initialized to 10. However, because x is not initialized before it is used in the expression on line 7, the compiler generates the following error:

```
Test.java:5: variable x might not have been initialized
        int reply = x + y;
              ^
```

Until x is assigned a value, it cannot appear within an expression, and the compiler will gladly remind you of this rule.

The following `Mouse` class is another example of using local variables. Examine the code and see if you can distinguish the local variables from the instance variables. Does the Mouse class compile successfully?

```
1.   public class Mouse {
2.      public boolean hasWheel;
3.      private int clickCount;
4.
5.      public int rightClick(double d) {
6.         int response = (int) d;
7.         return response;
8.      }
9.
10.     public String wheelClick() {
11.        if(hasWheel) {
12.           double pi = 3.14159;
13.           String greeting = "The mouse ate the " + pi;
14.           return greeting;
15.        } else {
16.           String error = "No wheel found";
17.           return error;
18.        }
19.     }
20.
21.     public void leftClick(int clickCount) {
22.        System.out.println("Left click " + clickCount + " times");
23.        this.clickCount = clickCount;
24.     }
25.}
```

Although there may be some confusion about `clickCount` in the `leftClick` method, this class compiles fine. The `Mouse` class has two instance variables: `hasWheel` and `clickCount`.

The `rightClick` method has two local variables: `d` and `response`. When the `rightClick` method is invoked, `d` and `response` get allocated in memory. When `response` is returned on line 7, a copy of `response` is sent to the calling method and both `d` and `response` go out of scope.

The `wheelClick` method has three local variables: `pi`, `greeting`, and `error`. If `hasWheel` is true, this method returns `greeting`, at which point `pi` and `greeting` go out of scope. The `String` object "The mouse ate the 3.14159" is on the heap, as shown in Figure 2.2, so it is not destroyed when the method returns. The same scenario happens when `error` is returned: `error` goes out of scope but the `String` "No wheel found" is on the heap and still exists (for as long as it is reachable by a reference).

FIGURE 2.2   The local variable greeting points to an object on the heap.

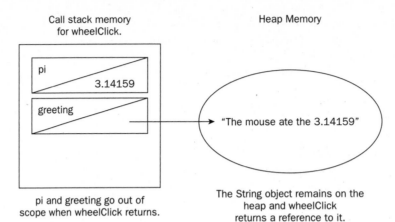

On line 21, the leftClick method has one local variable: clickCount. The clickCount parameter just happens to match the identifier of the clickCount field. In these situations, the local variable is seen first by the method and you must use the this reference to distinguish between the instance and local variable. The clickCount displayed on line 22 is the value of the parameter. To assign the clickCount parameter to the clickCount field, we must use this.clickCount on line 23 to refer to the field.

Examine the following statements and try to determine the output:

```
4. Mouse m = new Mouse();
5. m.clickCount = 2;
6. System.out.println(m.wheelClick());
7. m.leftClick(1);
8. System.out.println(m.clickCount);
```

The field hasWheel initializes to false, so calling wheelClick on line 6 causes "No wheel found" to be returned. Calling leftClick with 1 as the argument causes the 1 to be displayed and also assigned to the field clickCount. Therefore, the output is

```
No wheel found
Left click 1 times
1
```

Declaring Arrays

The exam objectives state that you should be able to "develop code that declares, initializes, and uses arrays." An *array* is a contiguous chunk of memory on the heap representing a fixed-size collection of values that all have the same data type. An array in Java is an object, so you can instantiate an array using the new keyword and assigning a reference to it, just like any other object. Arrays are fixed in size and cannot dynamically grow or shrink. (If you need a dynamically sized data structure, use one of the classes in the Java Collections API found in the java.util package discussed in Chapter 7, "Collections and Generics.") This section discusses the details of declaring array references and instantiating array objects, including the following topics:

- How to declare array references
- How to instantiate array objects
- How to access the elements of an array
- Multidimensional arrays
- Array initializers
- What arrays look like in memory

Array References

An *array reference* is a reference that denotes the data type of the values to be stored in the array, using square brackets to denote the array reference. For example, the following code declares three array references:

```
4. int [] finishTimes;
5. String lastNames [];
6. GregorianCalendar [] july;
```

Notice lastNames demonstrates how the square brackets can appear after the identifier. This technique is not recommended, though, because the code is more readable when the square brackets appear before the identifier.

The finishTimes reference can point to any array of ints. Similarly, lastNames can point to any array of String references and july can point to any array of GregorianCalendar references. Notice I didn't use the term "objects" when referring to the elements of the array. The array is the object, but the contents of the array are either primitive types or references, as we will see next.

Declaring an Array Reference

In Java it is not valid to declare a size for the array when declaring a reference. An array reference can point to arrays of any length. The following code is not valid:

```
int [20] finishTimes;      //not valid
String lastNames [100];   //not valid
```

When declaring an array reference, we are only specifying the data type of the elements of the array. The size of the array is determined only when the array object is instantiated.

Array Objects

Because a Java array is an object, it should be no surprise that you use the new keyword to instantiate an array. The new keyword requires the type of array being instantiated along with the size of the array. For example, the following code instantiates three array objects:

```
5. int [] finishTimes = new int[20];
6. String lastNames [] = new String[100];
7. GregorianCalendar [] july;
8. july = new GregorianCalendar[31];
```

The finishTimes reference now points to an array of 20 ints. Because this array of ints is a new object, its memory is zeroed on the heap, so all 20 ints are initially 0. The lastNames reference points to an array of 100 String references (not String objects!). Each of the 100 String references is null. Similarly, july points to an array of 31 null GregorianCalendar references. Arrays in Java are zero-based indexed, meaning the first element in the array is index 0, the second element is index 1, and so on. For example, the following code is valid and initializes some of the values in the arrays:

```
10. finishTimes[0] = 1002892;
11. finishTimes[1] = 1004830;
12. lastNames[99] = "Washington";
13. july[0] = new GregorianCalendar(2010, 7, 1);
```

Figure 2.3 shows what the finishTimes and lastNames arrays look like in memory; Figure 2.4 shows what the july array looks like in memory.

FIGURE 2.3 Examples of array references pointing to array objects.

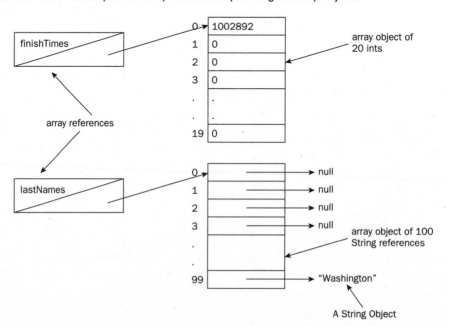

FIGURE 2.4   The july reference points to array of 31 GregorianCalendar references.

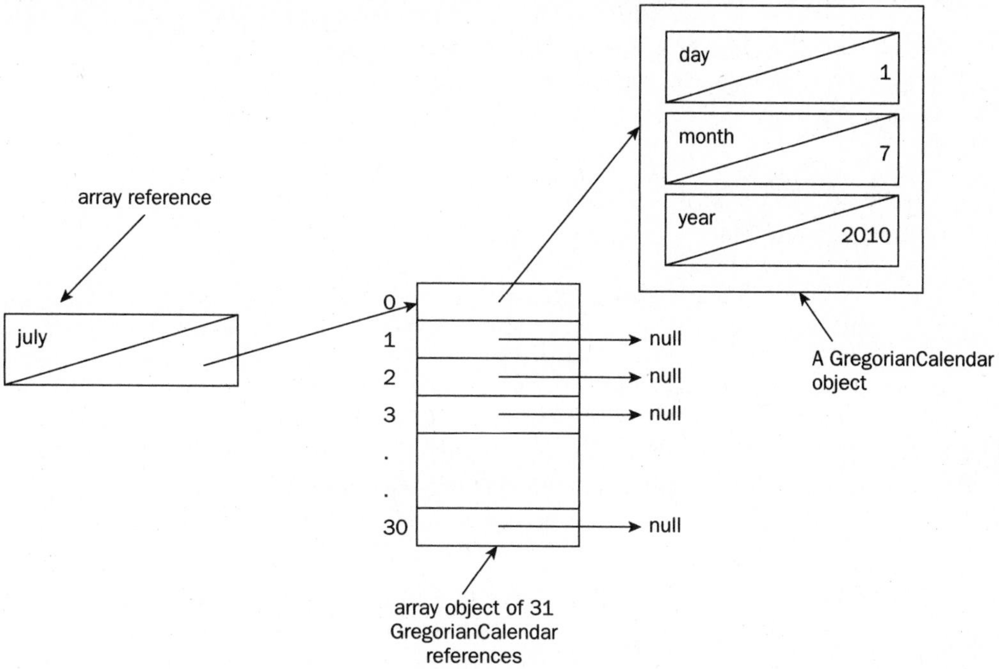

Using Arrays

Every array has an attribute named length that is the size of the array. The length attribute is particularly useful when using a for loop to iterate through the elements of the array. For example, the following for loop initializes the 31 GregorianCalendar references in the july array:

```
13. GregorianCalendar [] july;
14. july = new GregorianCalendar[31];
15. int year = 2010, month = 7;
16. for(int i = 0; i < july.length; i++) {
17.    july[i] = new GregorianCalendar(year, month, i+1);
18. }
```

The Enhanced for Loop

In Java 5.0, a new for loop was introduced called the *enhanced* for loop (also called a for-each *loop*). The following code demonstrates the syntax of a for-each loop by iterating through the july array and displaying each of the 31 GregorianCalendar objects:

```
for(GregorianCalendar day : july) {
    System.out.print(day.get(Calendar.MONTH) + "/"
                    + day.get(Calendar.DAY_OF_MONTH) + "/"
                    + day.get(Calendar.YEAR) + " ");
}
```

This enhanced for loop is read "for each day in july", where day is of type GregorianCalendar. The enhanced for loop can also be used for iterating through many of the data structures found in the java.util package. We discuss these data structures along with the enhanced for loop in more detail in Chapter 3, "Flow Control."

Let's look at an example to demonstrate some of the details of working with arrays. Study the following ArrayDemo program and determine if it compiles and what its output is. In addition, try to determine when the array object on line 3 becomes eligible for garbage collection.

```
1.   public class ArrayDemo {
2.     public static void main(String [] args) {
3.         double [] cubics = new double[10];
4.         for(int i = 0; i < cubics.length; i++) {
5.             int value = i + 1;
6.             cubics[i] = value * value * value;
7.         }
8.
9.         double [] temp = cubics;
10.        temp[5] = -1;
11.        System.out.println(cubics[5]);
12.        cubics = null;
13.        for(double a : temp) {
14.            System.out.print(a + " ");
15.        }
16.
17.        temp = new double[20];
18.     }
19. }
```

While perhaps confusing, this code compiles successfully. The cubics and temp references are of the same type (a reference to an array of doubles), so they can be assigned to each other as on line 9. There is still only one array object in memory, so setting temp[5] to -1 is the equivalent of setting cubics[5] to -1. Figure 2.5 shows the state of the array before line 12.

FIGURE 2.5   The array of cubic values has two references to it: cubics and temp.

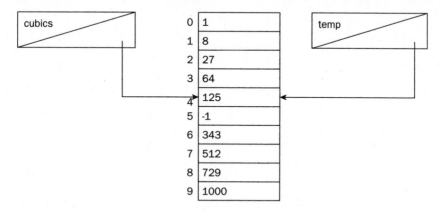

Here is the output of the ArrayDemo program:

```
-1.0
1.0 8.0 27.0 64.0 125.0 -1.0 343.0 512.0 729.0 1000.0
```

Setting cubics to null on line 12 still leaves temp pointing to the array. The array object is not eligible for garbage collection until immediately after line 17 when temp is assigned to a different array. By the way, the cubic values are lost at this point and temp refers to an array with 20 new doubles, each of value 0.0.

Multidimensional Arrays

Java allows for multidimensional arrays, up to as many dimensions as you require. Declaring a reference to a multidimensional array consists of denoting a set of square brackets for each dimension of the array. For example, the following values reference can point to any two-dimensional array of chars, and names can refer to any three-dimensional array of String references:

```
5. char [][] values;
6. String [][][] names;
```

To instantiate a multidimensional array, you denote the size of each dimension in the new statement. For example:

```
7. values = new char[4][3];
8. names = new String[10][5][20];
```

To access an element in a multidimensional array, specify an index for each dimension. For example, the following statement stores an 'A' in the first column of the first row of values, and "George Washington" in the twentieth level of the second column of the first row of names:

```
9.  values[0][0] = 'A';
10. names[0][1][19] = "George Washington";
```

The following nested for loops are typical when working with two-dimensional arrays. These particular nested loops fill the values array with chars starting with 'A'. (Similarly, you could use three nested loops to iterate through the names array.)

```
11. char current = 'A';
12. for(int row = 0; row < values.length; row++) {
13.     for(int col = 0; col < values[row].length; col++) {
14.         values[row][col] = current++;
15.     }
16. }
```

Figure 2.6 shows what the values array looks like in memory. The values array consists of 4 arrays, each containing 3 chars for a total of 12 chars.

FIGURE 2.6   The values array is a double array of chars.

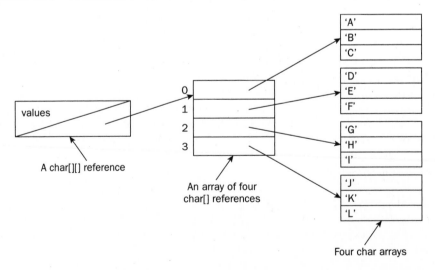

Figure 2.7 shows the memory of the names array. The names array consists of 10 array references, each pointing to an array of 5 array references, each pointing to an array of 20 String references for a total of 1,000 String references.

FIGURE 2.7   Multidimensional arrays in Java.

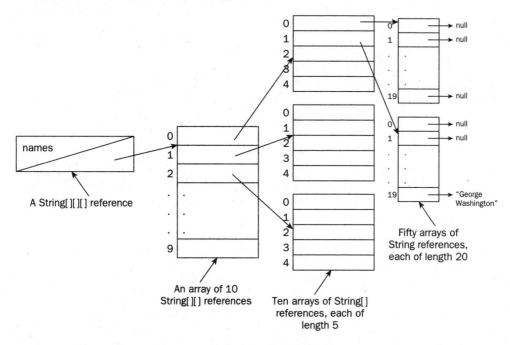

As you can see in Figure 2.7, the structure of multidimensional arrays in Java allows for various column lengths. For example, the following statements are valid:

```
4. GregorianCalendar [][] months = new GregorianCalendar[12][];
5. months[0] = new GregorianCalendar[31];
6. months[1] = new GregorianCalendar[29];
7. months[3] = new GregorianCalendar[30];
```

The months array has 12 rows, the first row is length 31, the second row is length 29, and the fourth row is length 30. The rest of the rows could be initialized in this same fashion.

Array Initializers

An *array initializer* is a shorthand notation for declaring an array and filling it with values, all in a single statement. Array initializers are convenient for quickly creating smaller arrays. Instead of using the new keyword, you list the elements of the array in curly braces separated by commas.

The following statement uses an array initializer to create a new array of length 5 and initializes the `ints` with the values listed:

```
int [] amps = {5, 10, 20, 30, 50};
```

The value of `amps[0]` is 5, `amps[1]` is 10, and so on. Notice the semicolon at the end of the line. It's a common mistake to forget it, but the compiler will gladly remind you if it is missing!

 You will definitely see array initializers on the exam, probably in several questions. Some of the questions will be testing your knowledge of array initializers, but expect to see array initializers on questions that are testing your knowledge of some other exam objective.

If the array contains objects instead of primitives, you can use the new keyword in the list of array elements. For example, the following statement creates an array referencing three `File` objects:

```
File [] files = {new File("input.txt"),
           new File("output.txt"),
           new File("error.txt")};
```

The `files` array consists of three `File` references, with `files[0]` pointing to `"input.txt"`, `files[1]` pointing to `"output.txt"`, and `files[2]` pointing to `"error.txt"`.

Notes on Array Initializers

To use the array initializer syntax, the array must be declared in the same statement that declares the reference. For example, the following code generates a compiler error:

```
int [] amps;
amps = {5, 10, 20, 30, 50};
```

An array initializer can also be used to create a multidimensional array. For example, the following statements create a two-dimensional array of floats:

```
float [][] results = {{2.0F, 1.5F},{-5.1F, 9.2F, 6.7F}};
```

The value of `results[0][0]` is 2.0, `results[1][0]` is −5.1, `results[1][2]` is 6.7, and so on.

Declaring Classes

According to the exam objectives, you need to be able to "develop code that declares classes." A class is a description of an object and is one of the fundamental building blocks of object-oriented programming. A Java class is defined in a `.java` source file and its corresponding compiled bytecode is in a `.class` file. The name of the `.class` file matches the name of the class, and the `.class` file must be saved in a directory structure that matches the package name of the class. In this section, we discuss the elements that make up a Java class.

A Java class can contain the following elements:

Instance variables Also referred to as fields, instance variables represent the attributes of the object being described and are used to store the state of the object.

Class variables These are the static fields of the class and represent global variables and data that is shared among instances of the class.

Methods The methods of a class represent the behaviors of the object being described. We will discuss methods in detail later in this chapter.

Constructors These are special methods that get invoked during the instantiation process and allow for the object to initialize its state.

Nested classes A Java class can contain within it the definition of another class. We will discuss nested classes in detail later in this chapter.

Instance initializers These are blocks of code that execute during the instantiation process.

Static initializers These are blocks of code that execute when the class is loaded by the class loader.

We have already discussed instance and class variables earlier in this chapter and we will see an example of the other elements now. Examine the `ColorChanger` class in Listing 2.1 and see if you can determine its instance and class variables, methods, constructors, nested classes and instance and static initializers. The class displays a window with three buttons in it, and clicking a button changes the background color of the window.

Listing 2.1: The ColorChanger Class

```
1.   package com.sybex.demos;
2.
3.   import java.awt.*;
4.   import java.awt.event.*;
5.   import static java.awt.BorderLayout.*;
6.
7.   public class ColorChanger extends Frame {
```

```
8.     private Button redBtn, whiteBtn, blueBtn;
9.     {
10.        redBtn = new Button("Red");
11.        whiteBtn = new Button("White");
12.        blueBtn = new Button("Blue");
13.     }
14.
15.    private static final Color RED, WHITE, BLUE;
16.
17.    static {
18.        RED = new Color(255,0,0);
19.        WHITE = new Color(255,255,255);
20.        BLUE = new Color(0,0,255);
21.     }
22.
23.    private class MyButtonListener implements ActionListener {
24.        public void actionPerformed(ActionEvent e) {
25.            String label = e.getActionCommand();
26.            if(label.equals(redBtn.getLabel())) {
27.                ColorChanger.this.setBackground(RED);
28.            } else if(label.equals(whiteBtn.getLabel())) {
29.                ColorChanger.this.setBackground(WHITE);
30.            } else if(label.equals(blueBtn.getLabel())) {
31.                ColorChanger.this.setBackground(BLUE);
32.            }
33.        }
34.     }
35.
36.    public static Color [] getColors() {
37.        Color [] colors = {RED, WHITE, BLUE};
38.        return colors;
39.     }
40.
41.    public Button [] getButtons() {
42.        Button [] buttons = {redBtn, whiteBtn, blueBtn};
43.        return buttons;
44.     }
45.
46.    public ColorChanger(String title) {
47.        super(title);
```

```
48.        layoutButtons();
49.        initializeEvents();
50.        this.setSize(200, 200);
51.        this.setVisible(true);
52.    }
53.
54.    private void initializeEvents() {
55.        MyButtonListener m = new MyButtonListener();
56.        redBtn.addActionListener(m);
57.        whiteBtn.addActionListener(m);
58.        blueBtn.addActionListener(m);
59.    }
60.
61.    protected void layoutButtons() {
62.        this.setLayout(new BorderLayout());
63.        this.add(redBtn, NORTH);
64.        this.add(whiteBtn, SOUTH);
65.        this.add(blueBtn, WEST);
66.    }
67.
68.    public static void main(String [] args) {
69.        new ColorChanger("Click a button");
70.    }
71.}
```

Here is a breakdown of each of the elements within the ColorChanger class:

- Line 8 declares three instance variables, each of type java.awt.Button: redBtn, whiteBtn, and blueBtn.

- Line 15 declares three class variables, each of type java.awt.Color: RED, WHITE, and BLUE.

- The class has five methods. The main method is static and the other methods are instance methods: getColors, getButtons, initializeEvents, and layoutButtons.

- This class has one constructor defined on line 46. It takes in a single argument of type String that appears in the title bar of the window.

- The ColorChanger class declares one nested class, MyButtonListener, on line 23. This nested class contains one method, actionPerformed, which gets invoked whenever one of the three buttons is clicked.

- The class declares one instance initializer, which is the block of code on lines 9 to 13.

- The class declares one static initializer, which is the block of code on lines 17 to 21.

Notice ColorChanger contains the main method, so it can be executed as a Java program. Figure 2.8 shows what the ColorChanger program looks like when it is executed.

FIGURE 2.8   The ColorChanger program.

 Do not get hung up on the details of the graphical user interface (GUI) code in the ColorChanger example. The SCJP exam no longer requires knowledge of GUI programming. However, whether or not you understand what the code does, you should definitely be able to identify the various elements of the ColorChanger class.

All of these different elements of a class are listed in the exam objectives. If you have not seen some of these concepts before, do not worry as I cover all of these topics in detail. We start with a discussion on object initialization, which covers the details of constructors and the instance and static initializers. Then we discuss the details of writing Java methods and nested classes.

The Instantiation Process

Initialization is one of the main exam objectives and refers to the details of initializing the various data types of Java. We have discussed the initialization of primitive types and arrays. This section discusses the initialization of objects and the instantiation process.

As a Java programmer, you write classes and instantiate them to create objects. The new operator is the typical way to instantiate a class. For example, the following line of code instantiates a new java.text.DecimalFormat object:

```
DecimalFormat df = new DecimalFormat("#,###.00");
```

This is a fairly straightforward statement, as you have seen the new operator countless times before. The new operator instantiates the DecimalFormat object on the heap and returns a reference to the object. The assignment operator = stores this reference in the variable df. The new operator also has to specify which constructor is invoked on the class. In the previous statement, a String is passed in, so the DecimalFormat constructor that takes in a String is invoked.

Behind the scenes, the instantiation of an object is a fairly involved process that involves several steps that occur in a well-defined order. The events that occur during the creation of a new object are referred to as the *instantiation process*. The following list of events takes place when a new object is instantiated:

1. The JVM determines the amount of memory needed for the new object, allocates the memory on the heap, and zeroes the memory so that it does not contain any garbage data.

2. Explicit initialization of instance variables is performed.

3. The appropriate constructor is invoked, depending on the arguments specified in the new statement.

4. Before the constructor executes, one of the immediate parent class constructors is executed.

5. Any instance initializers are executed. If a class has multiple instance initializers, they are executed in the order they appear in the source file.

6. The body of the constructor executes.

7. The new operator returns a reference to the new object.

Even though the new operator looks like it directly invokes a constructor, the execution of that constructor occurs at the end of the instantiation process.

Let's look at an example. Examine the following Fruit and Apple class definitions (defined in separate source files) and see if you can determine the output of executing main in Apple.

```
1.  public class Fruit {
2.    public String color;
3.
4.    public Fruit() {
5.        System.out.println("Constructing a Fruit");
6.    }
7.  }


8.  public class Apple extends Fruit {
9.    public String variety = "McIntosh";
10.
11.    public Apple(String variety) {
12.        System.out.println("Constructing an Apple");
13.        this.variety = variety;
14.    }
15.
16.    {
17.        System.out.println("Inside the instance initializer");
```

```
18.        System.out.println("The variety is " + variety);
19.    }
20.
21.    public static void main(String [] args) {
22.        Apple apple = new Apple("Granny Smith");
23.        System.out.println("Variety is " + apple.variety);
24.    }
25.}
```

The main method instantiates a new Apple object, passing in "Granny Smith". The JVM allocates memory for an Apple (which includes the memory for the Fruit parent object) and zeroes the memory. Then explicit initialization occurs, which in this example assigns variety to "McIntosh" on line 9. Then the Apple constructor on line 11 is invoked, but before it executes the Fruit constructor on line 4 is invoked and executes. After the Fruit constructor completes, the instance initializer on lines 16 to 19 is invoked, then the body of the Apple constructor on line 11 executes. The output of running main looks like this:

```
Constructing a Fruit
Inside the instance initializer
The variety is McIntosh
Constructing an Apple
Variety is Granny Smith
```

Now that you have seen the order of events that occur when a new object is instantiated, we will next look at the details of declaring and using constructors in Java.

Constructors

The exam objectives state that "given a set of classes and superclasses," you should be able to "develop constructors for one or more of the classes. Given a class declaration, determine if a default constructor will be created, and if so, determine the behavior of that constructor." This section discusses these topics in detail.

A *constructor* is a special method within a class that gets invoked during the instantiation process. The purpose of a constructor is to allow you to "construct" your object, ensuring that all of the fields are properly initialized. Constructors also can take in arguments, allowing you to initialize the state of the object.

A constructor has the following properties:

- The name of a constructor must match the name of the class.

- A constructor does not declare a return value.

- A constructor is only invoked one time during the instantiation process.

- A constructor can have any of four levels of access: public, private, protected, or the default.

- A constructor can throw any number of exceptions.

The following Camera class has two constructors: one that takes in an int and one that takes in no arguments.

```
1.  public class Camera {
2.    public int imageCount;
3.
4.    public Camera() {
5.        System.out.println("Inside no-arg constructor");
6.    }
7.
8.    public Camera(int imageCount) {
9.        this.imageCount = imageCount;
10.   }
11.}
```

Each constructor introduces a different way to invoke new on the class. For example, because the Camera class has two constructors, we can instantiate Camera objects two different ways, either passing in an int or passing in no arguments:

```
Camera one = new Camera(1024); //invokes the constructor on line 8
Camera two = new Camera();   //invokes the constructor on line 4
```

A constructor does not declare a return value. If it did, it would just be a method in the class. For example, the following code contains a compiler error. Can you see what the problem is?

```
1.  public class Camera {
2.    public int imageCount;
3.
4.    public Camera() {
5.        System.out.println("Inside no-arg constructor");
6.    }
7.    //The following is not a constructor. It is a method.
8.    public void Camera(int imageCount) {
9.        this.imageCount = imageCount;
10.   }
11.
12.   public static void main(String [] args) {
13.       Camera c = new Camera(60);
14.   }
15.}
```

You might think the compiler error is on line 8, but line 8 compiles fine because it is valid for a class to have a method named Camera. However, because it declares void for a return value, it is not a constructor. This Camera class does not have a constructor that takes in an int, so the compiler generates the following error:

```
Camera.java:13: cannot find symbol
symbol   : constructor Camera(int)
location: class Camera
          Camera c = new Camera(60);
                         ^
```

```
1 error
```

The Default Constructor

Every class has a constructor. If you do not explicitly define a constructor for a class, then the Java compiler inserts a *default constructor* for you. The default constructor takes in no arguments and has an empty method body.

For example, suppose we have a class named Tomato with the following definition:

```
1.  public class Tomato extends Fruit {
2.      private double weight;
3.      private boolean ripe;
4.
5.      public void setWeight(double w) {
6.          weight = w;
7.      }
8.
9.      public double getWeight() {
10.         return weight;
11.     }
12.
13.     public void setRipe(boolean b) {
14.         ripe = b;
15.     }
16.
17.     public boolean isRipe() {
18.         return ripe;
19.     }
20. }
```

Because the Tomato class does not explicitly define a constructor, the compiler generates one that looks like the following:

```
public Tomato() {
}
```

Notice the default constructor does not do anything at all. However, it does allow us to instantiate Tomato objects using new with empty parentheses:

```
Tomato roma = new Tomato();
```

Because the Tomato class does not contain any explicit initialization and the default constructor does not do anything, the values of the fields will be their corresponding default value, which is 0.0 for the double weight and false for the boolean ripe.

Know When a Class Gets a Default Constructor

Keep in mind that you only get a default constructor if you do not explicitly include one in your class. Suppose we modify the Tomato class and explicitly declare a constructor:

```
public class Tomato extends Fruit {
    public Tomato(double weight, boolean ripe) {
        this.weight = weight;
        this.ripe = ripe;
    }
    //The remainder of the class definition remains the same
}
```

Because this Tomato class has a constructor, the compiler does not add a default constructor. With only one constructor, that means there is only one way to instantiate a new Tomato, and that is by passing in a double and a boolean. For example:

```
Tomato beefsteak = new Tomato(10.45, false);
```

The following line of code will not compile with this Tomato class:

```
Tomato t = new Tomato();   //Generates a compiler error
```

Because knowing when a class gets a default constructor is a specific exam objective, expect at least one question to test your knowledge of this topic.

Using *this* in Constructors

The this keyword in Java represents the reference that every object has to itself. The this keyword also has another use within constructors that is unrelated to the this reference. You can use the this keyword to invoke another constructor in the same class, allowing you to avoid repeating code in multiple constructors.

For example, the following `Employee` class has two constructors that perform similar tasks. Line 10 sets the `hireDate` field to the current date, while line 16 sets `hireDate` to a supplied `Date`. Otherwise, the two constructors are identical.

```
1.   import java.util.Date;
2.
3.   public class Employee {
4.       private String firstName, lastName;
5.       private Date hireDate;
6.
7.       public Employee(String fn, String ln) {
8.           firstName = fn;
9.           lastName = ln;
10.          hireDate = new Date();
11.      }
12.
13.      public Employee(String fn, String ln, Date hd) {
14.          firstName = fn;
15.          lastName = ln;
16.          hireDate = hd;
17.      }
18.}
```

There are many good reasons to avoid repeating code like these two `Employee` constructors do. It would be nice if we could pass the arguments from one constructor to another and perform all the necessary initialization in one place. By using the `this` keyword, we can invoke another constructor in the same class. You use `this` like a method call, passing in the arguments to the other constructor.

Let's look at an example that fixes our issue of repeated code in the `Employee` class. The following modification has one `Employee` constructor invoking the other constructor:

```
1.   import java.util.Date;
2.
3.   public class Employee {
4.       private String firstName, lastName;
5.       private Date hireDate;
6.
7.       public Employee(String fn, String ln) {
8.           this(fn, ln, new Date());
9.           System.out.println("Inside first constructor");
10.      }
11.
```

```
12.    public Employee(String fn, String ln, Date hd) {
13.        System.out.println("Inside second constructor");
14.        firstName = fn;
15.        lastName = ln;
16.        hireDate = hd;
17.    }
18.}
```

Notice how there is no repetition of code in the constructors. Study this Employee class and try to determine the output of the following statement:

```
Employee e = new Employee("Beetle", "Bailey");
```

This statement results in the following sequence of events:

1. The Employee constructor on line 7 is invoked because we are passing in two String objects.

2. Line 8 invokes the constructor on line 12.

3. This second constructor actually executes first, and when it is finished, control jumps back to line 9.

Therefore, the output of instantiating this new "Beetle Bailey" Employee is

```
Inside second constructor
Inside first constructor
```

Invoking Another Constructor Using this

The call to this must be the first line of code in the constructor or a compiler error occurs. For example, the following Employee constructor does not compile:

```
public Employee(String fn, String ln) {
    System.out.println("Inside first constructor");
    this(fn, ln, new Date());
}
```

The compiler generates the following error:

```
Employee.java:9: call to this must be first statement in constructor
        this(fn, ln, new Date());
            ^
```

We will revisit this rule in the next section on using the super keyword in constructors.

Using *super* in Constructors

Similar to how you can use the this keyword to invoke another constructor in the same class, you can use the super keyword to invoke a constructor in the parent class. Using super allows the child class to choose which parent class constructor gets executed. As with the this keyword, any calls to super must be the first line of code in your constructor or the code will not compile.

The super Keyword

Don't confuse the use of super in a constructor with the super keyword that represents the reference to an object's parent. Using super in a constructor is a different, unrelated use of the super keyword.

Let's look at an example. The following NonFictionBook class is a child of the Book class and invokes one of the constructors in Book using the super keyword on line 6:

```
1.  //Book.java
2.  public class Book {
3.    public String title;
4.    public Person author;
5.    public String ISBN;
6.
7.    public Book(String ISBN) {
8.        this.ISBN = ISBN;
9.    }
10.
11.   public Book() {
12.       title = "Unknown";
13.       author = null;
14.       ISBN = "-1";
15.   }
16.}
```

```
1.  //NonFictionBook.java
2.  public class NonFictionBook extends Book {
3.    public String subject;
4.
```

```
5.     public NonFictionBook(String subject, String ISBN) {
6.          super(ISBN);
7.          this.subject = subject;
8.     }
9.
10.    public NonFictionBook(String subject) {
11.         this.subject = subject;
12.     }
13. }
```

 WARNING   These two class definitions are not numbered sequentially because they cannot be defined in the same source file.

The call to super on line 6 of NonFictionBook.java invokes the Book constructor on line 7 of Book.java, passing in a String that gets stored in a field of Book. Study the following code and try to determine its output:

```
4. NonFictionBook x = new NonFictionBook("American History", "123-45");
5. NonFictionBook y = new NonFictionBook("Greek Mythology");
6. System.out.println(x.ISBN);
7. System.out.println(y.ISBN);
```

Executing this code results in the following sequence of events:

1. The string "123-45" in the new statement is passed into the constructor on line 5 of NonFictionBook.

2. On line 6 of NonFictionBook, the call to super passes the String to line 7 of Book.

3. On line 8 of Book, the String is assigned to the ISBN field declared on line 5. Therefore, x.ISBN is "123-45".

4. The new statement for y invokes the NonFictionBook constructor on line 10 of NonFictionBook.

5. Because no explicit call to super appears in that constructor, the no-argument constructor of Book on line 11 is invoked, which assigns the ISBN field to "-1". Therefore, y.ISBN is "-1".

6. The println statements output the following:

```
123-45
-1
```

Why does the no-argument constructor get invoked on `Book` within the `NonFictionBook` constructor declared on line 10? The instantiation process requires that the parent class constructor execute before any child class constructor executes. There are two important rules of using `super` in a constructor that enforce this behavior:

- Any call to `super` must be the first line of code in a constructor or the code will not compile.

- If a constructor does not explicitly have a call to `super` or `this` as its first line of code, the compiler inserts the statement `super();` as the first line of code in the constructor.

In other words, if you write a constructor and do not call `super`, the compiler does it for you. In the `NonFictionBook` constructor on line 10, the constructor actually looks like the following:

```
public NonFictionBook(String subject) {
super(); //Compiler adds this statement
    this.subject = subject;

}
```

If you want, you can explicitly add the call to `super` to make your code more readable. The behavior of your code does not change by adding `super();` because the compiler adds it for you anyway. With the call to `super` explicitly declared, it becomes clear which constructor in the parent is being invoked.

Default Constructors and super

Watch out on the exam for a question that tests your knowledge of the default call to super. It is an important concept in Java and this default line of code (that you don't even write) generates a compiler error if the parent class does not have a no-argument constructor. For example, suppose we have the following Book class:

```
public class Book {
    public String ISBN;

    public Book(String ISBN) {
        this.ISBN = ISBN;
    }
}
```

This version of Book only has one constructor. A String must be passed into any new Book being instantiated. (Recall that you do not get a default constructor in a class that explicitly defines its own constructor.) Using this version of the Book class, the following FictionBook class does not compile:

```java
public class FictionBook extends Book {
    public String mainCharacter;

    public FictionBook(String m) {
        mainCharacter = m;
    }
}
```

The following compiler error is generated:

```
FictionBook.java:4: cannot find symbol
symbol  : constructor Book()
location: class Book
    public FictionBook(String m) {
                      ^
```

To fix this compiler error, a call to super that passes in a String must explicitly appear on the first line of code in the constructor of FictionBook, even if it is not clear what value to pass to the Book constructor. The following constructor in FictionBook compiles successfully:

```java
    public FictionBook(String m) {
        super("-1");
        mainCharacter = m;
    }
```

Instance Initializers

An *instance initializer* is a block of code declared in a class that executes for each new instance of the class. An instance initializer executes immediately after the parent class constructor finishes and before the body of the class constructor executes. A class can have multiple instance initializers and they are executed in the order they appear in the source file. Instance initializers are not members of a class like fields and methods are. You cannot explicitly invoke an instance initializer because it does not have a name.

The following Book class contains an instance initializer on lines 11 to 15:

```
1.   public class Book {
2.      public String title;
3.      public Person author;
```

```
4.    public String ISBN;
5.
6.    public Book(String ISBN) {
7.        System.out.println("Inside Book constructor");
8.        this.ISBN = ISBN;
9.    }
10.
11.   {
12.        System.out.println("Inside instance initializer");
13.        title = "Unknown";
14.        author = null;
15.   }
16.}
```

The only syntax for an instance initializer is the curly braces. It is simply a block of code located in a class definition with no name or special keyword to declare it. What is the output of the following statement that instantiates a new **Book** object?

```
Book b = new Book("888-999-7777");
```

Because the instance initializer is invoked before the constructor, line 12 is displayed before line 7 and the output is

```
Inside instance initializer
Inside Book constructor
```

Let's look at another example of an instance initializer. Study the following **Vehicle** and **Car** class and try to determine the output of **main** in **Car**:

```
1.   //Vehicle.java
2.   public class Vehicle {
3.     public int numOfWheels;
4.
5.     public Vehicle(int n) {
6.         System.out.println("Inside Vehicle constructor");
7.         numOfWheels = n;
8.     }
9.   }
```

```
1.   //Car.java
2.   public class Car extends Vehicle {
```

```
3.     public String make, model, color;
4.
5.     {
6.         System.out.println("Inside Car instance initializer");
7.         color = "Red";
8.     }
9.
10.    public Car(String make, String model) {
11.        super(4);
12.        System.out.println("Inside Car constructor");
13.        this.make = make;
14.        this.model = model;
15.    }
16.
17.    public String toString() {
18.        return make + " " + model + " " + color;
19.    }
20.
21.    public static void main(String [] args) {
22.        Car ford = new Car("Ford", "Mustang");
23.    }
24. }
```

Running the Car program results in the following sequence of events:

1. The new Car statement executes on line 22 of Car.java, which invokes the constructor on line 10 of Car.

2. The call to super(4) on line 11 passes control to the Vehicle constructor on line 5, which displays the message "Inside Vehicle constructor".

3. After the Vehicle constructor returns, the instance initializer in Car on line 5 is invoked, displaying the message "Inside Car instance initializer".

4. The body of the Car constructor executes last, displaying "Inside Car constructor".

Therefore, the output of main is

```
Inside Vehicle constructor
Inside Car instance initializer
Inside Car constructor
```

Why Use an Instance Initializer?

You can write lots of Java classes that do not use instance initializers. A constructor can always be used to initialize any fields of an object. Some developers like to use instance initializers for code readability, because you can put an instance initializer in the vicinity of your field declarations. For example, the following Button objects in the ColorChanger class do not rely on constructor arguments to be initialized:

```
7.   public class ColorChanger extends Frame {
8.      private Button redBtn, whiteBtn, blueBtn;
9.      {
10.         redBtn = new Button("Red");
11.         whiteBtn = new Button("White");
12.         blueBtn = new Button("Blue");
13.      }
```

In this scenario, it really does not matter if the Button objects are instantiated in a constructor or an instance initializer, so using an instance initializer might make the code more readable, especially if this is a large source file with multiple constructors.

Static Initializers

A *static initializer* is a block of code that executes once when a class is loaded by the class loader. The syntax for a static initializer is the static keyword followed by a set of curly braces:

```
static {
    //a static initializer
}
```

A class can contain multiple static initializers. They are executed in the order they appear in the source file. The purpose of a static initializer is to perform any complex initialization of static fields in the class or to perform any tasks that need to be performed only once. For example, a common use of static initializers is to load system libraries:

```
1.   public class MyLibrary {
2.      static {
3.         System.loadLibrary("mylibrary");
4.      }
5.
6.      //remainder of class definition
7.   }
```

If a system library is loaded more than once by a class loader, an exception occurs. Therefore, calling loadLibrary for "mylibrary" is something you only want to perform once during the lifetime of this class, and a static initializer is the perfect place for such a task.

What Is a Class Loader?

Every JVM has a built-in class loader object of type java.lang.ClassLoader that is responsible for the loading of classes into the memory of a Java program. When you refer to a class in your Java program, the class loader searches the class path for the appropriate .class file and loads the bytecode into memory. For each class that is loaded, the class loader instantiates a java.lang.Class object.

The class loader loads a class only once, so there is only one Class object for each class that your program uses. It is here in a Class object that the static fields and methods of your class are stored in memory. The class loader also invokes any static initializers in a class after the class is loaded. These static initializers allow you to initialize any static fields or perform any onetime tasks for the class.

You can write your own class loader, but the built-in class loader is sufficient for most Java applications.

The following MyNumberFormatter class demonstrates a static field getting initialized in a static initializer. The initialization of the static field involves more than a single statement, so this is another good example of when to use a static initializer.

```
1.   import java.text.NumberFormat;
2.   import java.text.DecimalFormat;
3.   import java.util.Locale;
4.
5.   public class MyNumberFormatter {
6.       public static DecimalFormat df;
7.
8.       static {
9.           Locale locale = new Locale("de"); //German
10.          NumberFormat nf = NumberFormat.getInstance(locale);
11.          df = new DecimalFormat("#,###.00");
12.      }
13.}
```

Now that we have seen how static initializers work, we will change topics and discuss one of the most important elements of a class: methods.

Declaring Methods

A Java class contains fields that represent the attributes of the object and methods that represent the behaviors of the object. We have already discussed fields in detail. The exam objectives state that you should be able to "develop code that declares both static and non-static methods, and — if appropriate — use method names that adhere to the JavaBeans naming standards. Also develop code that declares and uses a variable-length argument list." This section discusses everything you need to know about declaring and using Java methods, including the JavaBeans naming convention, static methods, variable-length arguments, method overloading, method overriding, and covariant return types.

Method Declarations

The definition of a method in Java is referred to as a *method declaration*. A method declaration in Java has the following syntax:

```
accessspecifier otherspecifier returnvalue methodName(parameterlist) throws
exceptionlist {
    methodbody
}
```

Figure 2.9 shows the elements of the `sleep` method declared in the `Thread` class.

FIGURE 2.9 The elements that comprise a method declaration.

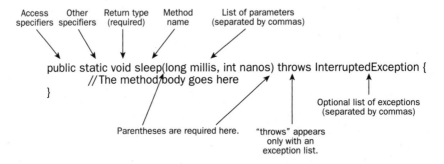

Like any member of a class, a method has an access specifier, which is one of the following four values:

public   The method is accessible to any other class.

private   The method is only accessible from within the class.

protected   Only classes in the same package and child classes can access the method.

Default access   Only classes in the same package can access the method.

The other specifiers are Java keywords from the following list:

static   This modifier declares a static method, also known as a class method.

final   The method cannot be overridden by a child class.

abstract   This modifier declares an abstract method that must be overridden by any non-abstract child classes.

native   The Java method maps to a method written in a different language, usually C or C++. The SCJP exam does not require knowledge of the native keyword.

synchronized   The calling thread must obtain the object's lock before the method executes. We will discuss synchronized methods in Chapter 5, "Concurrency."

A method might not declare any of these modifiers, or a method might declare more than one of these. For example, you can have a final synchronized method.

A Java method must declare a return value. (A method declares void if it does not actually return anything.) A list of the possible return values of a method follows:

void   The method does not return anything.

Primitive type   A method can return a byte, short, int, long, float, double, boolean, or char.

Reference type   A method can return any reference, meaning a method can return any data type.

The name of a method must be a valid Java identifier. The name of a method should be a verb starting with a lowercase letter using the mixed uppercase notation. For example, the following list of method names is found in the Java API:

- toString

- run

- getStackTrace

- isEmpty

- setTimeZone

The parameter list is a comma-separated list of variable declarations placed within the parentheses. Use empty parentheses for a method that does not take in any arguments. Here are some sample parameter lists:

- yield(): No parameters.

- read(byte [] b, int off, int len): Three parameters — an array of bytes and two ints.

- connect(SocketAddress endpoint, int timeout): Two parameters — a SocketAddress and an int.

- displayErrors(OutputStream out, String... errors): An OutputStream followed by any number of String references.

Variable-Length Argument List

As of Java 5.0, a method in Java can declare a variable-length argument list by using the ellipsis (. . .) after the data type of the variable-length parameter. For example, the following method can take in any number of `String` references:

```
public void displayErrors(OutputStream out, String... errors)
```

Behind the scenes, the `errors` variable is actually implemented as an array of `String` references. We will discuss the details of variable-length arguments later in this section.

The exception list is a `throws` clause that lists the exceptions the method declares. Separate multiple exceptions by commas. The `throws` clause is not needed if the method does not throw any checked exceptions. Here are some examples of methods with a `throws` clause:

- `readLine() throws IOException`
- `forName(String n) throws ClassNotFoundException`
- `clone() throws CloneNotSupportedException`
- `getResponse(int x) throws IOException, RMIException`

We will discuss exceptions in detail in Chapter 3, "Flow Control."

Method Signatures

A *method signature* consists only of a method's name and parameter types. The modifiers, return type, exception list, and method body are not considered a part of a method's signature. The concept of a method signature is important in method overriding, which we discuss later in this chapter.

JavaBeans Naming Convention

JavaBeans is a technology for developing software components in Java. Knowledge of developing JavaBeans is not required for the SCJP exam. However, the exam objectives specifically state knowledge of the JavaBeans naming convention for methods. The methods in the Java API use this naming convention, as do most Java developers.

JavaBeans have properties that are determined by the `public` methods in the class. These special methods have the following properties:

- The property methods begin with "set" and "get," or "set" and "is" for `boolean` data types. The set methods are referred to as *mutator methods* because they change the property, and get methods are referred to as *accessor methods* because they return a property.

- The letter following the set or get is capitalized.

- The property name is the name of method minus the set or get, with the first letter in lowercase.

For example, suppose a class contains the following two methods:

```
public void setLastName(String s)
public String getLastName()
```

The name of the JavaBean property resulting from these two methods is `lastName`, and the data type of the property is `String`. The parameter of the set method has to be the same data type as the return value of the get method.

Let's take a look at the following `Employee` class example and see if you can determine its JavaBeans properties:

```
1.   import java.util.GregorianCalendar;
2.
3.   public class Employee implements java.io.Serializable {
4.      private String first, last;
5.      private GregorianCalendar hireDate;
6.      public double salary;
7.      private boolean fullTime;
8.
9.      public String getFirstName() {
10.         return first;
11.     }
12.
13.     public void setLastName(String s) {
14.         last = s;
15.     }
16.
17.     public String getLastName() {
18.         return last;
19.     }
20.
21.     public GregorianCalendar getHireDate() {
22.         return hireDate;
```

```
23.    }
24.
25.    public void setHireDate(GregorianCalendar hd) {
26.        hireDate = hd;
27.    }
28.
29.    public void setFullTime(boolean fullTime) {
30.        this.fullTime = fullTime;
31.    }
32.
33.    public boolean isFullTime() {
34.        return fullTime;
35.    }
36.}
```

Read and Write JavaBeans Properties

A class does not need to contain matching set and get methods for each property. A read-only property would only have a get method and a write-only property would only have a set method.

I should also point out that the names of the fields in a class have nothing to do with JavaBean properties. For example, line 6 of the Employee class declares a public field named salary, but salary is not a JavaBean property of the Employee class.

Here are the JavaBean properties that the Employee class does have:

- firstName: A read-only String property
- lastName: A String property
- hireDate: A GregorianCalendar property
- fullTime: A boolean property

JavaBean Event Methods

The JavaBean specification also defines event handler methods that have the following naming convention:

```
public void addXxxxListener(XxxxListener a)
public void removeXxxxListener(XxxxListener a)
```

For example, the java.awt.Button class declares the following methods:

```
public void addActionListener(ActionListener a)
public void removeActionListener(ActionListener a)
```

According to the JavaBeans method naming convention, the Button class is therefore a source of events of type ActionEvent, and another object can register and unregister itself with the Button to listen to the ActionEvent by calling the appropriate add and remove method.

The exam objectives do not specifically state that you need to know the event listener methods, so you may or may not see this topic on the exam. However, it is useful information that is worth knowing as a Java developer because JavaBeans show up in all sorts of Java technologies.

Instance Methods

An *instance method* is a nonstatic method of a class. They are referred to as instance methods because they represent the behaviors of each instance of the class. Instance methods are also referred to as member methods, member functions, or simply methods.

An instance method can only be invoked on an instance of the class. Without an instance of the class, the method does not exist and it does not make sense to attempt to invoke it. You can't drive a car until you manufacture the car. You can't cook in the kitchen until you build the house. Methods are behaviors of the objects, so the objects need to exist before they can perform their desired behaviors.

You use the dot operator on a reference to invoke an instance method. Let's look at an example. The following Customer class contains one constructor and five instance methods:

```
1.  public class Customer {
2.     private String name;
3.     private int id;
4.
5.     public Customer(int id, String name) {
6.         setId(id);
7.         this.setName(name);
8.     }
9.
10.    public void setName(String name) {
11.        this.name = name;
12.    }
13.
```

```
14.    public String getName() {
15.        return name;
16.    }
17.
18.    public int getId() {
19.        return id;
20.    }
21.
22.    private void setId(int id) {
23.        if(id > 0) {
24.            this.id = id;
25.        }
26.    }
27.
28.    public void processOrder(String itemName) {
29.        System.out.println(this.getName() + " is ordering a "
30.                        + itemName);
31.    }
32.}
```

Invoking an Instance Method Requires a Reference

Notice that every instance method call in Java requires a reference. Even within a class we have to use the this reference to invoke another method in the same class, although the this reference is not required because the compiler adds it implicitly when you leave it off. For example, in the Customer class the this reference is explicitly denoted on lines 7 and 29, while on line 6 the this reference is implied and the compiler adds it behind the scenes, resulting in this.setId(id).

Examine the following statements. Do they compile and, if yes, what is the result?

```
41. Customer c = null;
42. c.setName("Sherlock Holmes");
43. System.out.println(c.getName());
```

You might be surprised to find out that this code compiles fine, even though it does not make sense to invoke setName and getName because no Customer objects have been instantiated yet. Without any Customer objects in memory, there are no setName and getName methods to invoke. Because c is null and does not point to an actual Customer object, the statement on line 42 generates a NullPointerException.

Now look at the following statements and determine if they compile and what their result is:

```
45. Customer y = new Customer(101, "Dr. Watson");
46. System.out.println(y.getName());
47. Customer z = new Customer(202, "Mr. Rattigan");
48. z.processOrder("Widget #4");
49. System.out.println(z.getName());
```

The code compiles fine. Two `Customer` objects are instantiated in memory, as shown in Figure 2.10. The output of the code is

```
Dr. Watson
Mr. Rattigan is ordering a Widget #4
Mr. Rattigan
```

FIGURE 2.10   Each `Customer` object has its own instance fields and methods in memory.

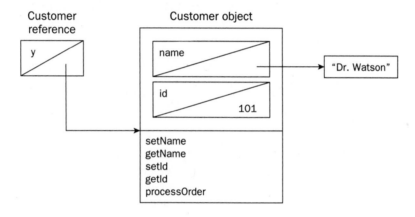

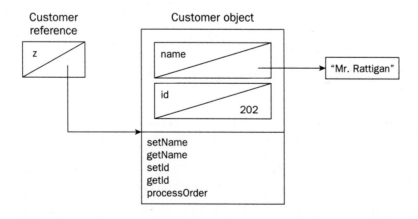

Methods Behind the Scenes

From an object-oriented point of view, each instance of a class gets each field and method of the class in memory when the object is instantiated. For fields, this is exactly what happens on the heap. Every object must have its own memory for each nonstatic field of the class because the values of the fields are unique for each object.

However, from a practical point of view, each object does not need its own copy of the methods because methods do not have any state and the implementation of each method is the exact same for every instance. To save memory, the JVM instead stores the method implementations in the Class object of the class, and each object accesses these implementations by storing a corresponding function pointer for each method in the class. In other words, instance methods are actually shared among all instances.

However, it is important to understand that from a theoretical point of view every object has its own copy of each field and each method in memory. If no Customer objects exist in memory, then neither do any fields or methods of the Customer class. If there are 100 Customer objects in memory, then there are 100 name references and 100 ints named id. In theory, there are also 100 setName methods, 100 getName methods, 100 processOrder methods, and so on.

These behind-the-scenes details of how Java stores instance methods in the Class object to save memory are not a topic on the SCJP exam.

Static Methods

A *static method*, also referred to as a *class method*, is declared using the static keyword. A static method is just like a static field in that it belongs to the class, not the instances. A static method is invoked without any instances of the class. Instead, use the name of the class to invoke one of its static methods.

For example, the java.lang.Math class has a static method named sqrt that computes the square root of a double:

```
public static double sqrt(double a)
```

To invoke sqrt, you prefix it with the class name Math:

```
double x = 49.0;
double response = Math.sqrt(x);
```

Compare Static to Global

Java does not allow global methods; all methods must be defined within a class.
A static method is the closest thing we have in Java to creating a global function. They
are utility methods that perform their task only with the arguments passed in or with
other "global" data like static fields.

The following class contains a static method. Examine the code and see if it compiles
and what its output is when incrementCounter is invoked:

```
1.  public class StaticProblem {
2.     public static int counter = 0;
3.     public String message;
4.
5.     public static void incrementCounter() {
6.         counter++;
7.         System.out.println(message + counter);
8.     }
9.  }
```

There is a problem with this class. Keep in mind that incrementCounter can be invoked
with or without any instances of StaticProblem. Let's assume there are no instances of
StaticProblem in memory when incrementCounter is invoked. That means there are no
message references in memory, so displaying message on line 7 does not make any sense.
Suppose we have 10 instances in memory. Then we would have 10 different message
references in memory, and it is totally unclear which message we are attempting to display.

The StaticProblem class generates a compiler error on line 7. A static method does not
have access to the nonstatic fields in a class because a static method does not have a this
reference. Remember, accessing a field in a class implicitly uses the this reference if you do
not explicitly denote it. Line 7 actually looks like:

```
7.         System.out.println(this.message + counter);
```

Because a static method does not have an object associated with it, using the this
reference does not make sense and causes the following compiler error:

```
StaticProblem.java:7: non-static variable message cannot be
referenced from a static context
        System.out.println(message + counter);
                           ^
```

NOTE

I can safely bet that you will be asked a question on the exam regarding a static method attempting to access a nonstatic field. Static methods cannot reference the nonstatic fields of the class and do not have access to a this reference. Understanding this rule implies your understanding of static methods, and static methods are a fundamental aspect of the Java language, so expect your knowledge of this subject to be tested on the exam.

Variable-Length Arguments

As of Java 5.0, a method can allow for a variable-length list of arguments to be passed in to the method. The syntax for declaring a *variable-length argument list* is to use three dots, referred to as an ellipsis, following the data type of the parameter. A method can only declare one parameter as variable length, and it must appear at the end of the list of parameters.

For example, the following method declaration allows for a variable number of String references to be passed in:

```
public void logErrors(Date timeStamp, String... errors)
```

To invoke logErrors, the first argument must be a java.util.Date object followed by any number of String objects. Examine the following statements and determine if they are valid method invocations of logErrors:

```
31.  Date now = new Date();
32.  m.logErrors(now);
33.  m.logErrors(now, "Problem #1");
34.  m.logErrors(now, "a", "b", "c", "d", "e", "f");
35.  String [] array = {"does", "this", "work?"};
36.  m.logErrors(now, array);
```

Java treats a variable-length parameter as an array whose elements are the data type of the parameter. The errors parameter in logErrors is actually an array of String references, so each of the previous calls to logErrors is valid. The array is empty with the method call on line 32. Line 33 creates an array with one String: "Problem #1", and line 34 creates a String array containing six String objects. Line 36 already passes in an array, so the compiler does not need to create a new one.

The following example shows the logErrors method in a class named MyErrorLog. Notice on line 18 the logErrors method uses a for-each loop to iterate through the variable-length parameter errors and write each one to a text file. Examine the code and see if you can determine its result.

```
1.  import java.io.*;
2.  import java.util.Date;
3.
4.  public class MyErrorLog {
```

```
5.
6.      private PrintWriter out;
7.
8.      public MyErrorLog(String fileName) {
9.          try {
10.             out = new PrintWriter(new FileWriter(fileName));
11.         }catch(IOException e) {
12.             e.printStackTrace();
13.         }
14.     }
15.
16.     public void logErrors(Date timeStamp, String... errors) {
17.         out.print(timeStamp + ":");
18.         for(String error : errors) {
19.             out.print(error + ", ");
20.         }
21.         out.println();
22.          out.flush();
23.     }
24.
25.     public void finalize() {
26.         out.close();
27.     }
28.
29.     public static void main(String [] args) {
30.         Date now = new Date();
31.         MyErrorLog m = new MyErrorLog("errors.txt");
32.         m.logErrors(now);
33.         m.logErrors(now, "Problem #1");
34.         m.logErrors(now, "a", "b", "c", "d", "e", "f");
35.         String [] array = {"does", "this", "work?"};
36.         m.logErrors(now, array);
37.     }
38.}
```

The new MyErrorLog statement on line 31 invokes the constructor on line 8, which creates a new text file named errors.txt for writing to. The logErrors method is invoked four times, and after running this program the errors.txt file looks something like this:

```
Tue Aug 04 14:32:56 MDT 2009:
Tue Aug 04 14:32:56 MDT 2009:Problem #1,
Tue Aug 04 14:32:56 MDT 2009:a, b, c, d, e, f,
Tue Aug 04 14:32:56 MDT 2009:does, this, work?,
```

NOTE As with any new feature of the language, expect variable-length arguments to be on the exam. Remember that a method can only declare one parameter as variable-length, and it must appear at the end of the parameter list.

Variable-length arguments can sometimes lead to ambiguities in method overloading when the compiler cannot determine which method to invoke. For example, a class could legally declare the following two methods named `average`:

```
public static int average(int... values)
public static double average(double... values)
```

Invoking `average` with a list of `doubles` works fine:

```
average(12.5, -4.78, 39.04);    //works fine
```

However, any attempt to invoke the `average` method with a list of `ints` generates a compiler error:

```
average(6, 10, 14, 20);    //does not compile
```

Here is the compiler error from this statement:

```
MyMath.java:12: reference to average is ambiguous, both method average(int...)
in MyMath and method average(double...) in MyMath match
        average(6, 10, 14, 20);
```

The same compiler error occurs when you attempt to invoke `average` with no arguments:

```
average();    //ambiguous!
```

When using variable-length arguments and method overloading, you need to ensure that the data types of your parameter lists are unique enough to avoid any ambiguities.

Method Overloading

Method overloading is when a class contains multiple methods with the same name but different parameter lists. Constructors can also be overloaded. We use method overloading all the time in Java. It is easier than trying to come up with different names for methods that perform similar tasks but require different types of data to be passed in. This section discusses the details of method overloading.

The rules that apply to method overloading follow:

- The parameter lists must be unique, either in the number of parameters or their data type.
- The return value can be different (as long as the parameter lists are unique).
- The list of declared exceptions can be different (as long as the parameter lists are unique).

For example, suppose a class has the following methods. Do these method declarations follow the rules for valid method overloading?

```
public void send(String recipient, String message)
public boolean send(String recipient, StringBuffer message)
public void send(int id) throws UnknownHostException
public void send(float f)
public int send(String [] headers)
```

Because the parameter lists for these five send methods are unique and unambiguous, these methods do follow the rules for proper method overloading and could appear in the same class. The key in overloading is that the parameter lists are unique enough that the compiler can resolve the appropriate method.

The method signatures must be different for valid method overloading. The return values and declared exceptions are irrelevant if the method signatures are unique. For example, the following two method declarations are not valid method overloading because they have the same signature:

```
public boolean send(String name, String address)
public void send(String recipient, String message)
```

Changing the return type is not sufficient, and the names of the parameter does not help the compiler resolve anything, so these two send methods could not appear in the same class.

Method Overloading and Data Type Promotion

There can be some confusion when the parameter types of overloaded methods are related either by inheritance or promotion. For example, suppose we have the following overloaded methods:

```
12. public String convert(int x) {
13.     return "int";
14. }
15. public String convert(short b) {
16.     return "short";
17. }
```

> Now consider the following statements and try to determine which convert method is invoked at runtime:
>
> ```
> byte b = -41;
> System.out.println(convert(b));
> ```
>
> The compiler looks for a convert method with a byte parameter. Because one doesn't exist, it looks for a convert method with a compatible parameter that a byte can be promoted to, starting with the smallest promotion, which in this example is a short. Therefore, the convert method on line 15 is invoked when a byte is the argument. The output of the previous two lines of code is "short".

Let's look at an example. The following Email class has four overloaded send methods. Study the code carefully and try to determine its output.

```
1.  public class Email {
2.     public void send(float f) {
3.         System.out.println("float parameter");
4.     }
5.
6.     public void send(Object x) {
7.         System.out.println("Object parameter");
8.     }
9.
10.    public void send(String s) {
11.        System.out.println("String parameter");
12.    }
13.
14.    public void send(int id) {
15.        System.out.println("int parameter");
16.
17.    }
18.
19.    public static void main(String [] args) {
20.        Email email = new Email();
21.        email.send(12.5);
22.        email.send(123456);
23.        email.send(new String("Hello"));
24.        email.send(new java.util.Date());
25.    }
26. }
```

Within main, the following sequence of events occurs:

1. The call to send on line 21 has a double argument, so the next largest compatible data type of send parameters is Object on line 6. (Note that as of Java 5.0, primitive types are autoboxed into their equivalent Object type, which for the literal 12.5 is java.lang.Double.)

2. Line 22 invokes the send method on line 14 because 123456 is an int.

3. Line 23 invokes the send method on line 10 because the argument is a String.

4. Line 24 invokes the send method on line 6 because Date is a child of Object.

Therefore, the output of running main in the Email class is

```
Object parameter
int parameter
String parameter
Object parameter
```

Autoboxing of Primitive Types

Primitive types are automatically boxed into their corresponding wrapper class object whenever necessary, and they are also unboxed automatically whenever necessary. We discuss the wrapper classes and autoboxing and unboxing in Chapter 4, "API Contents."

Method Overriding

The exam objectives state that you should be able to "determine if a method is correctly overriding another method, and identify legal return values (including covariant returns), for the method." *Method overriding* means writing a child class that contains the same method signature as its parent class. At runtime the child method executes, not the parent method. The child method takes the place of the parent method, thereby overriding the behavior of the parent. Method overriding is an important capability of object-oriented programming, and this section discusses the details of overriding methods in Java.

The rules for overriding an instance method follow:

- The method in the child has to have the same signature (name and parameter list) as the method in the parent.

- The access to the child method has to be at least the same or more accessible than the parent method. For example, if the method is public in the parent class, then it has to be public in the child class. A method with default access in the parent could be public or protected, or have the default access in the child class.

- The child method cannot throw a greater exception than the parent. In other words, any exception thrown by the child method must be a subclass of one of the exceptions thrown by the parent method.

- The return type of the method in the child class has to be the same or a subclass of the parent method's return type.

Private Methods and Overriding

Method overriding refers to a child class overriding an instance method that it inherits from its parent. A private method is not accessible outside of the class it is defined in, and private methods are not inherited by child classes. Therefore, any discussion on method overriding implies we are talking about the nonprivate instance methods of a class. (We discuss overriding nonprivate static methods in the upcoming section on method hiding.)

The following example demonstrates a child class Lion overriding the eat method in its parent class Mammal:

```
//Mammal.java
public class Mammal {
    protected int eat(String something) {
        System.out.println("Inside Mammal");
        return -1;
    }
}
```

```
//Lion.java
public class Lion extends Mammal {
    public int eat(String something) {
        System.out.println("Inside Lion");
        return something.length();
    }
}
```

Notice the eat method in Lion has the same name and parameter type as eat in Mammal. The eat method is protected in Mammal and public in Lion, which is valid because public is more accessible than protected, so Lion successfully overrides the eat method in Mammal. What is the output of the following statements?

```
20. Mammal mammal = new Mammal();
21. Lion lion = new Lion();
22. mammal.eat("food");
23. lion.eat("warthog");
```

Because the eat method in Lion hides the eat method in Mammal, calling eat on line 23 results in only the eat method of the Lion class executing. The output of these four lines of code is

```
Inside Mammal
Inside Lion
```

There are situations in method overriding where you might not want to hide the parent class method, but just add some behavior to it in the child class. You can use the super keyword to invoke the parent method from the child method, as shown in Figure 2.11 and demonstrated in the following modified Lion class:

```
1.  public class Lion extends Mammal {
2.    public int eat(String something) {
3.        System.out.println("Inside Lion");
4.        return super.eat(something);
5.    }
6.  }
```

FIGURE 2.11 A child can invoke a parent's overridden method using the super keyword.

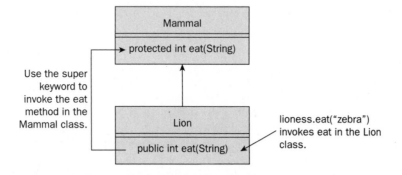

Using the same Mammal class from the previous example, what would be the output of the following statements?

```
29. Lion lioness = new Lion();
30. lioness.eat("zebra");
```

The following sequence of events occurs:

1. The eat method in Lion is invoked, which prints "Inside Lion".

2. The eat method in Mammal is called on line 4 using the super reference, which causes "Inside Mammal" to be displayed.

    Therefore, the output is

```
Inside Lion
Inside Mammal
```

The super Reference

Just like every object has a reference to itself via the this keyword, every object has a reference to its parent object via the super keyword. A child object can actually use the this reference to access parent class members, but there are situations where the child class must use super to access a parent field or method.

For example, suppose in the Lion class we had the following eat method:

```
10. public class Lion extends Mammal {
11.     public int eat(String something) {
12.         System.out.println("Inside Lion");
13.         return this.eat(something);
14.     }
15. }
```

The call to this.eat on line 13 is a recursive call that causes control to jump to line 11, which creates an infinite recursion eventually resulting in a stack overflow error. In this example, if the Lion wants to call eat in Mammal, it must use the super reference.

Covariant Return Types

Before Java 5.0, it was required that the overriding method in the child have the same return type as the overridden method in the parent. Java 5.0 introduced *covariant return types*, which allows the overriding method to return a data type that is a child of the return type in the parent class.

For example, the following Child class successfully overrides the doSomething method in Parent because FileOutputStream is a child of OutputStream:

```
//Parent.java
public class Parent {
    public OutputStream doSomething(int x, String s) {
        //do something
    }
```

```
    }
//Child.java
public class Child extends Parent {
    public FileOutputStream doSomething(int y, String s) {
        //do something else
    }
}
```

Covariant return types are not allowed for primitive types, only Object types. The following code does not compile:

```
//Parent.java
public class Parent {
    public int doNothing() {
        return 0;
    }
}
//Child.java
public class Child extends Parent {
    public short doNothing() {  //not valid!
        return 1;
    }
}
```

The following compiler error is generated:

```
Child.java:2: doNothing() in Child cannot override doNothing() in
 Parent; attempting to use incompatible return type
found    : short
required: int
    public short doNothing() {
                 ^
```

Covariant return types are yet another new concept introduced in Java 5.0, so expect at least one question on the exam that involves understanding how they work.

Method Hiding

Method hiding occurs when a child class contains a static method that is also defined in its parent, using the same rules of instance method overriding discussed earlier. If a static method in a child class contains the same static method as its parent class, then the method in the child class *hides* the method in the parent class but does not override it.

Method hiding is subtly different than method overriding. When a method is overridden, the child version of the method always executes at runtime. Technically, a static method cannot be overridden because you can still invoke the static method in the parent class.

For example, the following FictionBook class contains the same static method getCounter that is declared in its parent class Book:

```
1.  //Book.java
2.  public class Book {
3.     private static int counter = 0;
4.     public static int getCounter() {
5.        System.out.println("Inside Book");
6.        return ++ counter;
7.     }
8.  }
```

```
1.  //FictionBook.java
2.  public class FictionBook extends Book {
3.     public static int getCounter() {
4.        System.out.println("Inside FictionBook");
5.        return -1;
6.     }
7.
8.     public static void main(String [] args) {
9.        System.out.println(Book.getCounter());
10.       System.out.println(FictionBook.getCounter());
11.    }
12. }
```

Inside main, getCounter is invoked using both Book and FictionBook. If getCounter was truly overridden, then the output would be "Inside FictionBook" for both method calls. However, as you can see by the output here, the getCounter method in Book executes from line 9:

```
Inside Book
1
Inside FictionBook
-1
```

The getCounter method in Book is referred to as a hidden method, which is probably not the best term to use because the method is not really hidden at all. You can invoke getCounter in Book at any time using the syntax Book.getCounter, as shown in Figure 2.12.

FIGURE 2.12   The static getCounter method in FictionBook does not override getCounter in Book.

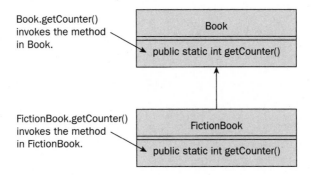

Book.getCounter()
invokes the method
in Book.

Book
public static int getCounter()

FictionBook.getCounter()
invokes the method
in FictionBook.

FictionBook
public static int getCounter()

Nonetheless, method hiding is the term used to describe this situation.

Overridden vs. Hidden

When a child class contains the same instance method as a parent class instance method (assuming all the rules of method overriding are followed), the child class method *overrides* the parent class method. When a child class contains a static method that is the same as a static method in the parent, this child method *hides* the parent class method.

In simpler terms, instance methods are overridden and static methods are hidden.

A child class cannot contain a nonstatic version of a static method in its parent class. Neither can a child class contain a static method with the same version of a nonstatic method in the parent. Either of these situations generates a compiler error.

Final Methods

A method in Java can be declared final using the final keyword. A *final method* cannot be overridden. You might make a method final if it has a critical implementation that should not be changed, or you might just want a child class not to have the option of overriding a particular method. Whatever the motivation, an attempt to override a final method generates a compiler error.

The following Lion class has a final method named breathe:

```
1.  public class Lion {
2.    public void eat(String something) {
3.        System.out.println("Lion is eating");
4.    }
```

```
5.
6.    public final void breathe() {
7.        System.out.println("Lion is breathing");
8.    }
9.  }
```

No subclass of Lion can override the breathe method, but let's try it anyway and see what happens. The following MountainLion class extends Lion and declares a breathe method:

```
1.  public class MountainLion extends Lion {
2.    public void breathe() {
3.        System.out.println("MountainLion is breathing");
4.    }
5.  }
```

As expected, this does not compile. Here is the compiler error that it generates:

```
MountainLion.java:2: breathe() in MountainLion cannot override breathe() in
Lion; overridden method is final
    public void breathe() {
              ^
```

Declaring Abstract Classes

The exam objectives state that you should be able to "develop code that declares classes (including abstract classes)." An *abstract class* is a class that cannot be instantiated. Use the abstract keyword to declare a class as abstract, as demonstrated by the following Mammal class:

```
1.  public abstract class Mammal {
2.    public boolean hasFur;
3.
4.    public Mammal() {
5.        hasFur = false;
6.    }
7.
8.    public Mammal(boolean hasFur) {
9.        this.hasFur = hasFur;
10.   }
11.
12.   public void breathe() {
13.       System.out.println("Mammal is breathing");
14.   }
15.
```

```
16.    public void eat(String something) {
17.        System.out.println("Mammal is eating " + something);
18.    }
19. }
```

The `Mammal` class seems like a typical class with one field, two constructors, and two public methods. However, adding the `abstract` keyword to line 1 makes the `Mammal` class abstract and it cannot be instantiated. The following line of code does not compile:

```
21.  Mammal m = new Mammal();
```

This statement generates the following compiler error:

```
Mammal.java:21: Mammal is abstract; cannot be instantiated
        Mammal m = new Mammal();
            ^
```

So how do we take advantage of this abstract class if we cannot instantiate it? The answer is to subclass it! A child class of `Mammal` will inherit all the public fields and methods of `Mammal`, as well as the ability to invoke its constructors. The `Mammal` class is still very useful; we just can't create any instances of it. From a design point of view, this actually makes sense because no animal is just a mammal. The concept of mammal is abstract in the real world, so making it abstract in a Java application seems like a good design.

Why Use Abstraction?

The objective of this section is to discuss the details of declaring abstract classes and abstract methods. The reason for using abstraction is discussed in detail in Chapter 6, "OO Concepts," where we revisit our discussion on abstract classes and explain the benefits and usefulness of abstraction in object-oriented programming.

The following `Platypus` class extends `Mammal`. Examine the code, determine if it compiles successfully, and try to figure out the output of running the `main` method:

```
1.   public class Platypus extends Mammal {
2.     public int eggCount;
3.
4.     public void layEggs() {
5.         System.out.println("Platypus is laying eggs");
6.     }
7.
8.     public void eat(String something) {
9.         System.out.println("Platypus is eating " + something);
10.    }
11.
```

```
12.    public Platypus(boolean hasFur) {
13.        super(hasFur);
14.        eggCount = 1;
15.    }
16.
17.    public static void main(String [] args) {
18.        Platypus p = new Platypus(false);
19.        p.eat("leaves");
20.        p.breathe();
21.        p.layEggs();
22.
23.    }
24.}
```

The code compiles fine. The Platypus class correctly overrides the eat method in Mammal and also declares a new method, layEggs, and a field, eggCount. Inside main, the following sequence of events occurs:

1. A new Platypus is instantiated on line 18, which is valid because Platypus is not abstract. The constructor on line 12 is invoked.

2. Line 13 passes the hasFur boolean up to the Mammal constructor. Line 14 sets the eggCount field to 1.

3. Invoking the eat method on line 19 executes the overridden eat method on line 8.

4. Invoking breathe on line 20 executes the breathe method in Mammal.

5. Invoking layEggs on line 21 invokes the layEggs method on line 4.

    Therefore, the output is

```
Platypus is eating leaves
Mammal is breathing
Platypus is laying eggs
```

We use abstract parent classes all the time in Java to represent the common attributes and behaviors of child objects. Now that you have seen how to declare an abstract class, we can discuss the concept of an abstract method in Java.

Abstract Methods

An *abstract method* is an instance method of a class that does not contain a method body and must be overridden by any nonabstract child classes. Use the abstract keyword to declare a method as abstract. Instead of a method body, an abstract method simply has a semicolon at the end of its declaration. For example, the java.io.InputStream declares the following method:

```
public abstract int read() throws IOException;
```

Notice there are no curly braces—not even empty braces. An abstract method does not contain a method body. Declaring a method as `abstract` in a class has the following consequences:

- The enclosing class must be declared `abstract`.

- Any concrete subclass must override all the abstract methods inherited from the parent class.

- If a subclass does not override its parent's abstract methods, the subclass must also be declared `abstract`.

Concrete Subclasses

Because an abstract method does not have any implementation, its class must be abstract. Otherwise, instances of the class could attempt to invoke the abstract method, which doesn't make sense because the abstract method does not contain any code. The term *concrete subclass* refers to a subclass that is not abstract. Child classes that do not want to be abstract must override the abstract methods in the parent or be abstract classes themselves.

Let's look at an example. The following `Mammal` class is similar to the previous version, with the addition of an abstract method named `walk`:

```
1.  public abstract class Mammal {
2.     public boolean hasFur;
3.
4.     public Mammal() {
5.         hasFur = false;
6.     }
7.
8.     public Mammal(boolean hasFur) {
9.         this.hasFur = hasFur;
10.    }
11.
12.    public void breathe() {
13.        System.out.println("Mammal is breathing");
14.    }
15.
16.    public void eat(String something) {
17.        System.out.println("Mammal is eating " + something);
18.    }
19.
20.    public abstract void walk();
21. }
```

All the other methods of the class have not changed and can still be called just like before. However, this time `Mammal` must be declared `abstract` because of the `walk` method on line 20. Without the `abstract` keyword on line 1, the `Mammal` class would not compile.

The following two classes shown in Figure 2.13 are valid child classes of `Mammal`. The `Buffalo` class successfully overrides the `walk` method. The `Feline` class does not override `walk`, but it is declared abstract.

```
1.  //Buffalo.java
2.  public class Buffalo extends Mammal {
3.    public void walk() {
4.        System.out.println("Buffalo is walking");
5.    }
6.  }
7.  //Feline.java
8.  public abstract class Feline extends Mammal {
9.    public void sleep() {
10.       System.out.println("Feline is sleeping");
11.   }
12. }
```

FIGURE 2.13 `Buffalo` is a concrete subclass and `Feline` is an abstract subclass of `Mammal`.

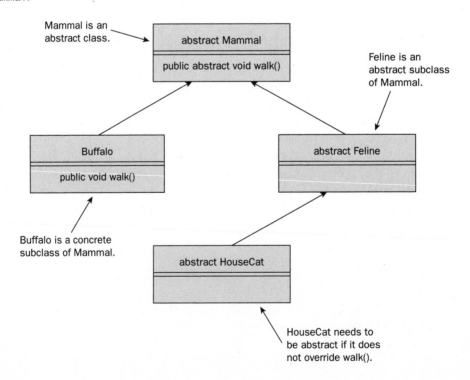

Does the following `HouseCat` class compile?

```
1.  public class HouseCat extends Feline {
2.     public void eat() {
3.         System.out.println("HouseCat is eating");
4.     }
5.
6.     public void breathe() {
7.         System.out.println("HouseCat is breathing");
8.     }
9.  }
```

Because `HouseCat` extends from `Feline` and `Feline` inherits the abstract `walk` method from `Mammal`, `HouseCat` must either override `walk` or declare itself `abstract`. Because it does neither, the class does not compile and generates the following error:

```
HouseCat.java:1: HouseCat is not abstract and does not override
 abstract method walk() in Mammal
public class HouseCat extends Feline {
       ^
```

Declaring Interfaces

An *interface* is a collection of abstract methods. A class implements an interface, inheriting all the abstract methods declared in the interface. Therefore, a class that implements an interface must either override the interface methods or the class must be declared `abstract`.

An interface has the following properties:

- An interface is defined in a `.java` file. If the interface is `public`, the name of the file must match the name of the class. If the interface has the default access, it is only accessible from within its package.

- The bytecode file for a compiled interface is a `.class` file that matches the name of the interface. All the rules of package names and subdirectories that apply to classes also apply to interfaces.

- All the methods in an interface are abstract, whether or not the `abstract` keyword is explicitly denoted.

- All the methods in an interface are public, whether or not they are explicitly declared `public`.

- The fields of an interface are `public`, `static`, and `final`.

- An interface cannot declare static methods.

An interface has some similarities to a class, but an interface is not a class. For example, an interface cannot be instantiated, and it cannot contain any instance fields.

Let's look at an example. Suppose we have the following interface named `Drawable`:

```
1.   import java.awt.Rectangle;
2.
3.   public interface Drawable {
4.     int MAX_WIDTH = 1024;
5.
6.     public void draw();
7.     abstract Rectangle getDimensions();
8.     void resize(int w, int h);
9.   }
```

The `Drawable` interface declares one field, `MAX_WIDTH`, and three methods. Note that `MAX_WIDTH` is `public`, `static`, and `final`, even though these specifiers were omitted. Similarly, the draw method is `abstract`, the `getDimensions` method is `public`, and the `resize` method is both `public` and `abstract`.

Implementing Interfaces

A class implements an interface using the `implements` keyword in the declaration of the class. A class can implement multiple interfaces by separating the interface names with commas. For example,

```
public class Picture implements Drawable
public class Flower implements Plant, Drawable
```

A class that implements an interface must do one of the following:

- Override all the methods of the interface.
- Declare itself as abstract.

Let's look at an example. The following `Picture` class implements the `Drawable` interface. Study the code and determine if it compiles successfully.

```
1.   import java.awt.Rectangle;
2.
3.   public class Picture implements Drawable {
4.     private Rectangle dimensions;
5.     private String artist;
6.
7.     public Picture(String artist, int width, int height) {
8.         this.artist = artist;
9.         dimensions = new Rectangle(width, height);
10.    }
11.
12.    public void draw() {
```

```
13.          System.out.println("Drawing a Picture");
14.      }
15.
16.      public Rectangle getDimensions() {
17.          return dimensions;
18.      }
19.
20.      public String getArtist() {
21.          return artist;
22.      }
23.
24.      public void resize(int width, int height) {
25.          if(width < Drawable.MAX_WIDTH) {
26.              dimensions = new Rectangle(width, height);
27.          }
28.      }
29. }
```

Because Picture is not declared asbstract, Picture must implement all the methods of Drawable for it to compile, which it does. Notice the Picture class can have any number of fields and methods in addition to the methods of Drawable. But one thing is certain: if you have an instance of Picture, then you can invoke draw, resize, and getDimensions on it because Picture implements Drawable.

What Is the Purpose of Interfaces?

An interface can contain abstract method declarations but no method implementations. Why would we create such an entity? Well, one of the main uses of interfaces is to provide a communication contract between two objects. In other words, two objects that need to "interface" with each other use an interface. If you know a class implements an interface, then you know that class contains concrete implementations of the methods in that interface, and you are guaranteed to be able to invoke those methods safely and know the object has implemented them.

For example, the java.lang.Runnable interface contains a single method:

```
public void run();
```

If you give me an object whose class implements Runnable, then I can invoke run(); on that object, even though I might not know or care about any other methods and fields of the object.

This is a very powerful feature of the Java language used throughout the Java API, and any well-designed application will use interfaces extensively.

If a class implements multiple interfaces, then an implementing class must override the methods of all the interfaces it implements. Suppose we have the following interface named Plant:

```
1.  public interface Plant {
2.      public void photosynthesize();
3.  }
```

The following Flower plant successfully implements both Plant and Drawable:

```
1.  import java.awt.Rectangle;
2.
3.  public class Flower implements Plant, Drawable {
4.         public int numOfLeaves;
5.
6.      public void photosynthesize() {
7.          System.out.println("Plant is photosynthesizing");
8.      }
9.
10.     public void draw() {
11.         System.out.println("Drawing a Plant");
12.     }
13.
14.     public Rectangle getDimensions() {
15.         return new Rectangle(0,0);
16.     }
17.
18.     public void resize(int w, int h) {
19.         System.out.println("Resizing a Plant?");
20.     }
21. }
```

I can understand drawing a flower, but resizing a flower probably doesn't make any sense. There are definitely situations in Java where I have implemented an interface and have been forced to write methods that I did not want to implement. It is not unusual to have empty method bodies in these situations, which might apply here to the resize and getDimension methods of Flower.

Interfaces and Data Types

If a class implements an interface, objects from that class are also the data type of the interface. For example, the Picture and Flower classes, which seem like two totally unrelated classes, actually share a common data type because both classes implement Drawable. Objects of type Picture and Flower are also objects of type Drawable. An object taking on the form of different data types is referred to as polymorphism, and we discuss the effects of interfaces on polymorphism in detail in Chapter 6.

Extending Interfaces

An interface can extend another interface. In fact, an interface can extend multiple interfaces. (Don't accuse Java of not allowing multiple inheritance!) Use the `extends` keyword to declare that an interface extends another interface. For example, the following interface extends the `Drawable` interface:

```
1.  public interface Paintable extends Drawable {
2.    public void paint();
3.  }
```

A class that implements `Paintable` must override `paint` and also the three methods in `Drawable`.

Let's look at an example of multiple interface inheritance. The following `Image` interface extends both `java.lang.Runnable` and `Drawable`:

```
1.  public interface Image extends Runnable, Drawable {
2.    public String getFormat();
3.  }
```

A class that implements `Image` must implement the `getFormat` method, as well as the `run` method from `Runnable` and the three methods from `Drawable`.

Multiple Inheritance with Interfaces

While valid, writing an interface that extends multiple interfaces is not a common occurrence in Java. There are situations where the multiple inheritance makes sense, but this is not something you will do every day.

Declaring Enumerations

Java 5.0 introduced the concept of enumerations to the Java language, along with a new keyword: enum. An *enumeration* is a fixed set of constants. An *enum* is a Java class that represents an enumeration. You use enumerations whenever you have a set of items whose values are known at compile time. Common uses of enumerations include days of the week, months of the year, the planets in the solar system, the directions on a compass, or your favorite flavors of ice cream. The possibilities for enums are endless, and you should use them in your Java applications whenever applicable because they provide a type-safe representation of constant data in your application.

Use the enum keyword to declare an enumeration. Just like classes, an enum is defined in a source file with a `.java` extension, and all the rules of package names and directory structures apply. For example, the following enumeration represents the four seasons:

```
1.   public enum Season {
2.     WINTER, SPRING, SUMMER, FALL
3.   }
```

The `Season` enum is saved in a source file named `Season.java`, and the compiled bytecode is in a file named `Season.class`. Enumerations have the following properties:

- The enum keyword actually defines a class behind the scenes that extends `java.lang.Enum`. Therefore, an enum cannot extend any other class or enum.

- You do not instantiate an enum. The constants defined in an enum are all implicitly `public`, `final`, and `static`, so there is no reason to create instances of the enum class.

- The enum can declare methods and additional fields. These additional fields and methods must appear after the enum list, and the enum list must end with a semicolon in this situation.

Because the elements of an enum are static, you can access them using the name of the enum. Behind the scenes, the compiler writes a class that extends Enum and creates an instance of the class for each element in the enum. This generated class contains a static field for each element in the enum.

The following code demonstrates the syntax for accessing enum elements. Study the code and try to determine its output:

```
5.   Season now = Season.WINTER;
6.   switch(now) {
7.      case WINTER :
8.         System.out.println("It is cold now");
9.         break;
10.     case SUMMER :
11.        System.out.println("It is hot now");
12.        break;
13.     default:
14.        System.out.println("It is nice now");
15.   }
```

You can declare variables of an enum type. The now variable on line 5 is of type `Season` and is assigned to `Season.WINTER`. The case on line 7 is true, so the output of the preceding code is

```
It is cold now
```

Using enums in a `switch` Statement

A unique feature of enums is that when you `switch` on a variable of an enum type, you do not prefix the case statements with the enum type and the case statements must be values from the enum. For example, the following `switch` statement does not compile if now is of type Season:

```
switch(now) {
    case 0 :
        System.out.println("It is cold now");
        break;
    case 1 :
        System.out.println("It is hot now");
        break;
    default:
        System.out.println("It is nice now");
}
```

This code generates the following compiler error:

```
EnumTest.java:5: an enum switch case label must be the unqualified
 name of an enumeration constant
            case 0 :
                ^
```

Using enums

The compiler generates a special method named `values` when it generates the class for your enum declaration. The `values` method returns an array of the enum values. For example, suppose we have the following `Direction` enum:

```
1.  public enum Direction {
2.    NORTH, SOUTH, EAST, WEST
3.  }
```

The following `for-each` loop iterates through the array returned by the `values` method and displays each value using the `toString` method of the enum:

```
10. for(Direction d : Direction.values()) {
11.    System.out.print(d.toString() + " ");
12. }
```

The output of this loop is

```
NORTH SOUTH EAST WEST
```

If you ever need the integer value of an enum element, you can use the static method ordinal inherited from java.lang.Enum. Can you determine the output of the following for-each loop?

```
14. for(Direction d : Direction.values()) {
15.     System.out.print(d.ordinal() + " ");
16. }
```

The integer values of an enum start at 0 and Direction has four values, so the output is

```
0 1 2 3
```

The static valueOf method, inherited from java.lang.Enum, is used to convert a String value to its corresponding enum value. Examine the following statements and try to determine the output:

```
23. Direction home = Direction.valueOf("SOUTH");
24. System.out.println("Heading " + home);
25. Direction nowhere = Direction.valueOf("NORTHWEST");
26. System.out.println("Going " + nowhere);
```

The home variable equals Direction.SOUTH, so line 24 displays

```
Heading SOUTH
```

However, line 25 throws an exception at runtime because NORTHWEST is not an element of Direction. The stack trace looks like this:

```
Exception in thread "main" java.lang.IllegalArgumentException:
No enum const class Direction.NORTHWEST
        at java.lang.Enum.valueOf(Enum.java:192)
        at Direction.valueOf(Direction.java:1)
        at EnumTest.main(EnumTest.java:25)
```

Declaring enum Methods

An enum can declare methods and constructors, as well as other fields that are not a part of the enumerated list of elements. The enumeration list must be declared first in the enum, followed by a semicolon.

Let's look at an example. The following version of the `Direction` enum overrides the `toString` method, converting the uppercase enum name to lowercase:

```
1.  public enum Direction {
2.     NORTH, SOUTH, EAST, WEST;
3.
4.     public String toString() {
5.         return this.name().toLowerCase();
6.     }
7.  }
```

The `name` method is inherited from `Enum` and returns the corresponding element name. Try to determine the output of the following statements:

```
10. for(Direction d : Direction.values()) {
11.    System.out.print(d + " ");
12. }
```

Printing the `Direction` variable d invokes `toString` behind the scenes, and the output of this for-each loop is

```
north south east west
```

Declaring enum Constructors

An enum can also define constructors, useful for enums that contain additional fields. For example, suppose the following enum represents the types of ice cream cones a store sells, and the number of scoops for each cone is also a constant. Because all of this information regarding ice cream cones is known at compile time, this is a good scenario for using an enum.

```
1.  public enum IceCream {
2.     PLAIN(2),
3.     SUGAR(3),
4.     WAFFLE(5);
5.
6.     private IceCream(int scoops) {
7.         this.scoops = scoops;
8.     }
9.
10.     public final int scoops;
11. }
```

When each element of the enum is declared, you have to denote the argument for the constructor within parentheses. This invokes the constructor on line 6, which stores the value in the scoops field of each element in the IceCream enum.

Study the following code and determine its output:

```
IceCream cone1 = IceCream.PLAIN;
IceCream cone2 = IceCream.WAFFLE;
System.out.println(cone1 + " needs " + cone1.scoops + " scoops.");
System.out.println(cone2 + " needs " + cone2.scoops + " scoops.");
```

The output is shown here:

```
PLAIN needs 2 scoops.
WAFFLE needs 5 scoops.
```

Declaring Nested Classes

The exam objectives state that you need to be able to "develop code that declares classes (including all forms of nested classes)." A *nested class* is a class defined within another class. A nested class that is nonstatic is referred to as an *inner class*. There are four types of nested classes in Java:

- A member inner class is a nonstatic nested class that is declared at the member level of a class.

- A local inner class is defined within a method. Because it appears within a method, making it static does not make sense.

- An anonymous inner class is a special case of a local inner class that does not have a name.

- Top-level inner classes are static inner classes that are nested at the member level of a class.

The concept of inner classes was introduced in Java 1.1. There are several benefits of using inner classes, including making your code more readable, allowing for utility classes to be encapsulated within the class using it, and simplifying the process of writing a class, thereby actually encouraging developers to be more object oriented. (The easier it is to write a class, the more likely you are to use classes!) This section discusses the details of declaring and using the four different types of nested classes.

Member Inner Classes

A *member inner class* is defined at the member level of a class (the same level as fields, methods and constructors). Member inner classes have the following properties:

- A member inner class can be declared `public`, `private`, `protected` or have the default access.

- A member inner class can extend any class and implement any number of interfaces.

- A member inner class can be `abstract` or `final`.

- An inner class cannot declare static fields or methods.

- Most importantly, a member inner class has access to the members of the outer class, even the private members.

That last property is what makes inner classes so useful and beneficial. A member inner class has access to its outer class members without using any special syntax.

Let's look at a simple example to get started. Here is a class named `Outer` that contains a protected member inner class named `Inner`:

```
1.  public class Outer {
2.     private String greeting;
3.
4.     protected class Inner {
5.         public int repeat = 3;
6.         public void go() {
7.             for(int i = 1; i <= repeat; i++) {
8.                 System.out.println(greeting);
9.             }
10.        }
11.     }
12. }
```

An inner class declaration is like any other top-level class. It can declare fields, methods, constructors, and so on. The `Inner` class has a field named `repeat` and a method named `go`. However, what makes `Inner` unique is it can access the members of `Outer`.

The important line of code here to focus on is line 8 when the `Inner` class displays the private `greeting` field of the `Outer` class. For line 8 to make sense, there has to be a unique `greeting` associated with the instance of `Inner`. Otherwise, it is not clear which `greeting` reference to display. What makes this possible are the following properties of inner classes:

- An inner class object is associated with exactly one outer class object. This association is made when the inner object is instantiated with the `new` keyword.

- You cannot instantiate an instance of an inner class without a corresponding outer class instance.

The syntax for instantiating an inner class is to use a reference with the `new` operator. For example:

```
Outer a = new Outer();
Outer.Inner b = a.new Inner();
```

Notice the data type of the `Inner` reference is `Outer.Inner`. You only use this syntax in situations where you are instantiating an inner class from somewhere else other than inside its outer class, something not commonly done. Typically you instantiate inner objects from within the enclosing class, using the `this` reference with the new operator:

```
Inner x = this.new Inner();
```

The `Inner` object that x refers to is associated with the `Outer` object that the `this` reference refers to. The `this` reference is implied and can be omitted, but your code might be clearer if you explicitly denote it.

Study the following `Outer` class and see if you can determine the output of its `main` method:

```
1.   public class Outer {
2.       private String greeting;
3.
4.       protected class Inner {
5.           public int repeat = 3;
6.           public void go() {
7.               for(int i = 1; i <= repeat; i++) {
8.                   System.out.println(greeting);
9.               }
10.          }
11.      }
12.
13.      public void displayGreeting() {
14.          Inner x = this.new Inner();
15.          x.repeat = 2;
16.          x.go();
17.      }
18.
19.      public static void main(String [] args) {
20.          Outer y = new Outer();
21.          y.greeting = "Hello, Outer";
22.          y.displayGreeting();
23.      }
24.}
```

Running `main` causes the following sequence of events to occur:

1. An `Outer` object is instantiated within `main` and its `displayGreeting` method is invoked from line 22.

2. One line 14, an `Inner` object is instantiated that is associated with the `Outer` object from line 20.

3. The repeat field of x is set to 2 on line 15.

4. Line 16 invokes the Inner object's go method, which prints out the greeting field of y twice.

Therefore, the output is

```
Hello, Outer
Hello, Outer
```

Inner Classes Behind the Scenes

Something interesting to know about inner classes is that a JVM does not have a concept of inner classes. They are a compile-time feature, and the compiler actually writes a top-level class for every inner class that you declare. This new top-level class needs some special fields and methods so that it can access all the members of its enclosing class. For example, the inner class contains an implicit reference to its outer class object.

When the Outer class example from this section is compiled, two bytecode files are created: Outer.class and Outer$Inner.class. (Inner classes are one of the only times you will ever see a dollar sign in an identifier.) The compiler wrote a class named Outer$Inner to represent our inner class. You cannot instantiate an Outer$Inner object explicitly. You have to use the appropriate inner class syntax.

Inner classes also have a special syntax for accessing a field in the outer class that you need to use if the outer class shares a name with a field or method from the inner class. The following contrived example demonstrates this syntax. Study the code carefully and see if you can determine the output:

```
1.   public class A {
2.      private int x = 10;
3.
4.      public class B {
5.         private int x = 15;
6.
7.         public class C {
8.            private int x = 20;
9.
10.           public void go() {
11.              System.out.println(x);
12.              System.out.println(this.x);
```

```
13.              System.out.println(B.this.x);
14.              System.out.println(A.this.x);
15.          }
16.       }
17.    }
18.
19.    public static void main(String [] args) {
20.        A a = new A();
21.        A.B b =a.new B();
22.        A.B.C c = b.new C();
23.        c.go();
24.    }
25.}
```

Nested Inner Classes

Notice in the A class it has a nested class B that also has a nested class C. This is perfectly valid but probably not something you will ever see in the real world.

A breakdown of the code in the A class follows:

1. An object of type C is instantiated using an instance of A and B, and its go method is invoked.

2. The x on line 11 is implicitly referring to this.x, so 11 and 12 display the same value, which is 20. (The this reference inside the C class refers to the C object.)

3. To access the x field of the B object, prefix the this keyword with the B class name: B.this.x. Line 13 displays 15.

4. Similarly, the x in A is A.this.x, which is displayed on line 14.

Keep in mind the syntax A.this and B.this is unique to inner classes only. The output of running main is

```
20
20
15
10
```

Inner Classes as Event Handlers

A common use of inner classes is for event handlers. An event handler is the type of object that often needs access to the members of its outer class but likely won't be reused by another class, making it a good candidate for an inner class. The ColorChanger class discussed in Listing 2.1 earlier in this chapter declared a member inner class named MyButtonListener:

```
7.   public class ColorChanger extends Frame {
8.       private Button redBtn, whiteBtn, blueBtn;

23.      private class MyButtonListener implements ActionListener {
24.          public void actionPerformed(ActionEvent e) {
25.              String label = e.getActionCommand();
26.              if(label.equals(redBtn.getLabel())) {
27.                  ColorChanger.this.setBackground(RED);
28.              } else if(label.equals(whiteBtn.getLabel())) {
29.                  ColorChanger.this.setBackground(WHITE);
30.              } else if(label.equals(blueBtn.getLabel())) {
31.                  ColorChanger.this.setBackground(BLUE);
32.              }
33.          }
34.      }

54.      private void initializeEvents() {
55.          MyButtonListener m = new MyButtonListener();
56.          redBtn.addActionListener(m);
57.          whiteBtn.addActionListener(m);
58.          blueBtn.addActionListener(m);
59.      }
60.      //Remainder of class definition...

71. }
```

Notice the MyButtonListener class uses the special this syntax for accessing the setBackground method that ColorChanger inherits from Frame. The inner class also references the three private Button fields of the outer class.

Local Inner Classes

A *local inner class* is a nested class defined within a method. Like local variables, a local inner class declaration does not exist until the method is invoked, and it goes out of scope when the method returns. That means if you define an inner class locally, you can only create instances from within the method. Local inner classes have the following properties:

- Local inner classes do not have an access specifier.

- Local inner classes cannot be declared static, nor can they declare static fields or methods.

- Local inner classes have access to all the fields and methods of its enclosing class.

- A local inner class does not have access to the local variables of method unless those variables are final.

It might seem odd that a local inner class cannot access a local variable, but recall that the compiler generates a top-level class from your inner class declaration. It is not possible for a top-level class to have access to a local variable from a method in another class. However, if the local variable is final, then a copy of the local variable can be stored in the generated top-level class, which is exactly what the compiler does behind the scenes.

The following class demonstrates a local inner class. Examine the code and see if you can determine what its output is:

```
1.   public class LocalInner {
2.
3.       public double radius;
4.
5.       public void doSomething() {
6.           final double pi = 3.1415;
7.
8.           class Circle {
9.               public double area() {
10.                  return pi * radius * radius;
11.              }
12.          }
13.
14.          Circle c = new Circle();
15.          System.out.println(c.area());
16.      }
17.
18.      public static void main(String [] args) {
19.          LocalInner x = new LocalInner();
```

```
20.        x.radius = 10;
21.        x.doSomething();
22.    }
23.}
```

The doSomething method contains a local inner class named Circle. The Circle class declares a method named area that refers to the pi variable from line 6, which is only valid because pi is final. Circle also refers to radius on line 10, which is valid because radius is a field of the outer class. The code compiles fine, the value of radius is 10, so the output is

314.15000000000003

By the way, compiling LocalInner.java creates two bytecode files: LocalInner.class and LocalInner$1Circle.class. The compiler adds a 1 to the name of the Circle class because it is possible that a different method in the class defines another local class named Circle.

Precision of Doubles

I didn't mean for the local inner class example to demonstrate an issue with the precision of doubles, but because the output of LocalInner is slightly unusual, I probably should clarify the result. The product of 3.1415 * 10 * 10 is 314.15, but the output is 314.15000000000003. This is because double values are not exact. They are stored in 64 bits using the IEEE standard 754, which is an accurate technique for representing a floating-point number as a sequence of 1s and 0s, but the values are not entirely exact. You won't see a question about this on the exam, but it is good information to know. Visit the IEEE website at www.ieee.org if you are interested in delving into this topic further.

Anonymous Inner Classes

An *anonymous inner class* is a local inner class that does not have a name. It is declared and instantiated all in one statement using the new keyword. Anonymous inner classes either extend an existing class or implement an existing interface.

For example, the following statement declares and instantiates a new class that is a child of Thread. The anonymous inner class definition starts on line 6 and ends with the right curly brace on line 12. The semicolon on line 12 denotes the end of the new statement.

Notice that the anonymous inner class has access to the field x and also the final local variable s. Study the code and try to determine its output.

```
1.   public class AnonInner {
2.      public int x = 10;
3.
4.      public void printX() {
5.          final String s = "x = ";
6.          Thread t = new Thread() {
7.              public void run() {
8.                  while(true) {
9.                      System.out.println(s + x);
10.                 }
11.             }
12.         };
13.         t.start();
14.     }
15.
16.     public static void main(String [] args) {
17.         new AnonInner().printX();
18.     }
19. }
```

You might not be familiar with threads in Java, but invoking start on a Thread object causes its run method to execute in a new thread of the process. Here is the sequence of events that occurs within main:

1. A new outer object is instantiated on line 17 and its printX method on line 4 is invoked.

2. An anonymous inner class that extends Thread is declared and instantiated on lines 6 to 12.

3. The start method is invoked on this Thread object on line 13, which causes the run method on line 7 to execute.

4. The run method contains an infinite loop and prints out "x=10" until the JVM is terminated manually (press Ctrl+C in Windows).

Because the anonymous inner class does not have a name, the compiler assigns it a number. When AnonInner is compiled, two bytecode files are generated: AnonInner.class and AnonInner$1.class.

Anonymous Inner Classes and Interfaces

An anonymous inner class must either extend an existing class or implement an existing interface. When implementing an interface, the syntax almost looks like you are attempting to instantiate an interface, which of course would not be valid. For example, the following anonymous inner class implements the java.awt.event.ActionListener interface:

```
ActionListener x = new ActionListener() {
    public void actionPerformed(ActionEvent e) {
        System.out.println("Action occurred");
    }
};
```

The above inner class declaration is valid because we are not instantiating a new ActionListener interface (which wouldn't be valid), but instead we are instantiating an anonymous class that implements ActionListener.

Because anonymous inner classes are also local inner classes, all the same rules apply to both. The difference with anonymous inner classes is that you can create multiple instances of a local inner class within the method, but an anonymous inner class can only be instantiated one time.

Inner Classes as Event Handlers

Inner classes were introduced to the Java language in JDK 1.1, which coincided with the Java language introducing the delegation model for event handling. In the real world, an inner class is an easy option for handling simple events.

To demonstrate, the following SimpleWindow class defines two inner classes: an anonymous WindowAdapter that terminates the JVM when a user closes the window, and an ActionListener that changes the background color of the window to red:

```
import java.awt.*;
import java.awt.event.*;

public class SimpleWindow {
    private Frame frame;

    public SimpleWindow() {
        frame = new Frame("Click the button");
```

```
        frame.setSize(250,200);
        frame.setLayout(new FlowLayout());

        frame.addWindowListener(new WindowAdapter() {
            public void windowClosing(WindowEvent e) {
                System.exit(0);
            }
        });

        Button red = new Button("Red");
        red.addActionListener(new RedHandler());

        frame.add(red);
        frame.setVisible(true);
    }

    private class RedHandler implements ActionListener {
        public void actionPerformed(ActionEvent e) {
            frame.setBackground(Color.RED);
        }
    }

    public static void main(String [] args) {
        new SimpleWindow();
    }
}
```

Notice both of the inner classes perform simple tasks that require the private frame field, making them good candidates for inner classes.

You should be aware, however, that inner classes go against some of the fundamental OOP concepts, such as reuse of classes and high cohesion (discussed in Chapter 6). Therefore, make sure inner classes make sense in your program's design and do not unnecessarily add complexity to your top-level classes.

Static Nested Classes

A *static nested class* is a static class defined at the member level of an enclosing class. Static nested classes are not inner classes. They do not have access to the fields and methods of the enclosing class, and they can be instantiated without a corresponding instance of the outer class.

In other words, a static nested class is not really much different than a top-level class except for a few subtle benefits:

- The nesting creates a type of namespace. To denote a nested class from outside its enclosing class, the nested class is prefixed with the name of the enclosing class (similar to how static fields and methods are accessed).

- Access to the nested class can be controlled by an access specifier. For example, a nested class declared as `private` can only be used within its enclosing class, in effect hiding it from any other classes.

- The enclosing class has access to the fields and methods of the nested class, even the `private` ones.

Let's look at an example. The following `Box` class is nested within `Shipment`:

```
1.  import java.awt.Dimension;
2.
3.  public class Shipment {
4.    public static class Box {
5.        public Dimension dimension;
6.        public int depth;
7.
8.        public Box(Dimension d, int x) {
9.            dimension = d;
10.           depth = x;
11.       }
12.
13.       public int getVolume() {
14.           return dimension.height * dimension.width * depth;
15.       }
16.   }
17.
18.   public Box box;
19. }
```

Even though `Box` is defined inside `Shipment`, because `Box` is `static` it can be used like any other top-level class. The syntax for referring to `Box` outside of `Shipment` is `Shipment .Box`. The following `Shoe` class declares a field of type `Shipment.Box` and initializes the field in its constructor. See if you can determine the output of running the `main` method in `Shoe`:

```
1.  import java.awt.Dimension;
2.
3.  public class Shoe {
4.    public Shipment.Box box;
5.
```

```
6.    public Shoe() {
7.        Dimension dim = new Dimension(6, 10);
8.        box = new Shipment.Box(dim, 4);
9.    }
10.
11.   public static void main(String [] args) {
12.       Shoe sandal = new Shoe();
13.       System.out.println("Volume = "
14.               + sandal.box.getVolume());
15.   }
16.}
```

Here is a breakdown of main:

1. A Shoe object is instantiated on line 12, invoking the constructor on line 6.

2. A new Box is instantiated on line 8 with dimensions 6 by 10 by 4, which has a volume of 240.

3. The volume is printed out on line 14.

Therefore, the output of this program is

```
Volume = 240
```

Importing a Nested Class

Because a static nested class is a `static` member of a class, it can be imported using a static import. For example, suppose Shipment is in the com.sybex.demos package. Then we can import the Box class using the following static import:

```
import static com.sybex.demos.Shipment.Box;
```

You might be surprised to find out that you can also import the Box class using a regular import statement. For example, the following Cereal class is valid and compiles successfully:

```
import com.sybex.demos.Shipment.Box;

public class Cereal {
    Box box;
}
```

Being able to use an import statement like the one in Cereal is an example of how declaring a static nested class is like creating a namespace.

Summary

This chapter covered the "Declarations, Initialization, and Scoping" section of the SCJP exam objectives. Topics discussed include declaring variables, methods, classes, nested classes, interfaces and enums, as well as the initialization and scoping of variables and objects.

Declaring a variable involves stating the data type and giving the variable a name. Variables that represent fields in a class are automatically initialized to their corresponding "zero" value during object instantiation. Local variables must be specifically initialized. Make sure you know the rules for declaring a valid identifier in Java.

Scope refers to that portion of code where a variable can be accessed. There are three kinds of variables in Java, depending on their scope: instance variables, class variables and local variables. Instance variables are the nonstatic fields of your class. Class variables are the static fields within a class. Local variables are declared within a method.

An array is a contiguous chunk of memory on the heap representing a fixed-size collection of values that all have the same data type. Arrays are `Object` types in Java instantiated using the `new` keyword or with an array initializer. Java allows for multidimensional arrays.

A Java class is defined in a `.java` source file and its corresponding compiled bytecode is in a `.class` file. A class contains instance variables, class variables, methods, constructors, nested classes, and instance and static initializers. We discussed the events that occur during the creation of a new object, referred to as the instantiation process, which is memory allocation, explicit initialization, parent class construction, instance initializers, then the class constructor executes.

A constructor is a special method within a class that gets invoked during the instantiation process. Every class has a constructor: the compiler adds a default constructor if you do not explicitly define one. Use the `this` keyword to invoke another constructor in the same class and the `super` keyword to invoke a parent class constructor.

An instance initializer is a block of code declared in a class that executes for each new instance of the class. An instance initializer executes immediately after the parent class constructor finishes and before the body of the class constructor executes. A static initializer is a block of code that executes once when a class is loaded by the class loader.

A method declaration contains an access specifier, return value, method name, parameter list, and a `throws` clause. A method can also be declared static, final, abstract, native, or synchronized. Use the ellipsis (...) to declare a variable-length argument list. Classes typically use the JavaBeans naming convention for declaring a property's accessor and mutator methods. A static method belongs to the class and is invoked using the name of the class.

Method overloading is when a class contains multiple methods with the same name but different parameter lists. Method overriding means writing a child class that contains the same method signature as its parent class. At runtime the child method executes, not the parent method. Covariant return types allow the overriding method to return a data type that is a child of the return type in the parent class. A final method cannot be overridden. Method hiding occurs when a child class contains a static method that is also defined in its parent.

An abstract class is a class that cannot be instantiated. An abstract method is an instance method of a class that does not contain a method body and must be overridden by any nonabstract child classes. An interface is a collection of abstract methods. A class implements an interface, inheriting all the abstract methods declared in the interface.

An enum is a Java class that represents an enumeration. Use the enum keyword to declare an enumeration. The constants defined in an enum are all implicitly public, final, and static. The compiler generates a special method named values that returns an array of the enum values.

A nested class is a class defined within another class. A nested class that is nonstatic is referred to as an inner class. A member inner class is defined at the member level of a class. A local inner class is a nested class defined within a method. An anonymous inner class is a local inner class that does not have a name. It is declared and instantiated all in one statement using the new keyword. A static nested class is a static class defined at the member level of an enclosing class.

Be sure to test your knowledge of declarations, initialization, and scoping by answering the Review Questions that follow. Make sure you have a good understanding of the following Exam Essentials before attempting the Review Questions.

Exam Essentials

Be able to read and understand a class definition.   A large percentage of questions on the exam show you a class definition or a snippet of a class and ask you to determine the result of the code. You need to understand the concepts of instance variable, static variables, methods, constructors, nested classes.

Recognize the difference between method overloading and method overriding.   A method is overloaded when the class contains two methods with the same name but different parameter lists. A child class can overload a method that is defined in the parent, but that is not the same as method overriding. A child class overrides a parent class method when it contains a method with the same signature as a parent method.

Understand the difference between static and instance.   An instance variable or method is associated with the instances (objects) of the class. They do not exist in memory until an object is instantiated, and each object has its own instance members in memory. A static variable belongs to the class and is accessed using the class name. A static variable or method exists when the class is loaded and there is only one instance of the variable or method in memory.

Understand the use of this and super in constructors.   The this keyword is used to invoke another constructor in the same class. The super keyword invokes a parent class constructor. A constructor must contain either a call to this or a call to super on the first line of the constructor. If you write a constructor and do not explicitly call this or super on the first line, the compiler inserts super().

Know how to declare and use an enumeration.   An enumeration is declared using the enum keyword. Expect a question on the exam that uses an enum in a switch statement.

Recognize the different types of nested classes.   There are four types of nested classes: member, local, anonymous and static. Member, local and anonymous nested classes are referred to as inner classes because they have access to all the fields and methods of their corresponding outer class. Local inner classes can only access local variables that are final.

Understand how to instantiate and use arrays.   Arrays are a common occurrence in the exam questions. Remember that an array is fixed in size and accessing an index outside of the array's range results in an ArrayIndexOutOfBoundsException. All array objects have a length attribute. Arrays can be in a single statement using an array initializer.

Review Questions

1. What is the result of the following code?

```
1.  public class Shape {
2.      private String color;
3.
4.      public Shape(String color) {
5.          System.out.print("Shape");
6.          this.color = color;
7.      }
8.
9.      public static void main(String [] args) {
10.         new Rectangle();
11.     }
12. }
13.
14. class Rectangle extends Shape {
15.     public Rectangle() {
16.         System.out.print("Rectangle");
17.     }
18. }
```

A. ShapeRectangle

B. RectangleShape

C. Rectangle

D. Line 4 generates a compiler error.

E. Line 15 generates a compiler error.

2. Given the following class definitions:

```
1.  public class Parent {
2.      public Parent() {
3.          System.out.print("A");
4.      }
5.  }
6.
7.  class Child extends Parent {
8.      public Child(int x) {
9.          System.out.print("B");
10.     }
11.
```

```
12.    public Child() {
13.         this(123);
14.         System.out.print("C");
15.    }
16.}
```

what is the output of the following statement?

```
new Child();
```

A. ABC

B. ACB

C. AB

D. AC

E. This code does not compile.

3. Which of the following identifiers are valid Java identifiers? (Select three.)

A. A$B

B. _helloWorld

C. transient

D. java.lang

E. Public

F. 1980_s

4. What is the output of the following program?

```
1.    public class WaterBottle {
2.        private String brand;
3.        private boolean empty;
4.
5.        public static void main(String [] args ) {
6.            WaterBottle wb = new WaterBottle();
7.            if(!wb.empty) {
8.                System.out.println("Brand = " + wb.brand);
9.            }
10.       }
11.}
```

A. Line 6 generates a compiler error.

B. Line 7 generates a compiler error.

C. Line 8 generates a compiler error.

D. There is no output.

E. Brand = null

5.   Given the following class definition:

```
1.  public class Television {
2.     private int channel = setChannel(7);
3.
4.     public Television(int channel) {
5.          this.channel = channel;
6.          System.out.print(channel + " ");
7.     }
8.
9.     public int setChannel(int channel) {
10.         this.channel = channel;
11.         System.out.print(channel + " ");
12.         return channel;
13.    }
14.}
```

what is the output of the following statement?

```
new Television(12);
```

A. 12

B. 12 7

C. 7 12

D. 7

E. The code does not compile.

6.   Given the following my.school.ClassRoom and my.city.School class definitions:

```
1.  //ClassRoom.java
2.  package my.school;
3.  public class ClassRoom {
4.     private int roomNumber;
5.     protected String teacherName;
6.     static int globalKey = 54321;
7.
8.     ClassRoom(int r, String t) {
9.          roomNumber = r;
10.          teacherName = t;
11.    }
12. }
```

```
//School.java
```

```
1.  package my.city;
2.  import my.school.ClassRoom;
3.  public class School {
4.    public static void main(String [] args) {
5.        System.out.println(ClassRoom.globalKey);
6.        ClassRoom room = new ClassRoom(101, "Mrs. Anderson");
7.        System.out.println(room.roomNumber);
8.        System.out.println(room.teacherName);
9.    }
10. }
```

which of the following line numbers in `main` generate a compiler error? (Select all that apply.)

A. None; the code compiles fine.

B. Line 5

C. Line 6

D. Line 7

E. Line 8

7. Suppose we have the following class named `ClassRoom`:

```
1.  package my.school;
2.  public class ClassRoom {
3.    public static int globalKey = 54321;
4.  }
```

Now suppose we have the following class named Administrator:

```
1.  package my.city;
2.
3.  public class Administrator {
4.    public int getKey() {
5.        return globalKey;
6.    }
7.  }
```

Which one of the following statements inserted at line 2 of the `Administrator` class will make the `Administrator` class compile successfully?

A. `import my.school.ClassRoom;`

B. `import static my.school.ClassRoom.*;`

C. `import static my.school.ClassRoom;`

D. `import static my.school.*;`

E. Nothing — the class compiles.

8. What is the output of the following program?

```
1.  public class ScorePrinter {
2.     public static void printScores(int... scores) {
3.        for(int x : scores) {
4.           System.out.print(x + ",");
5.        }
6.     }
7.
8.     public static void main(String [] args) {
9.        int [] x = {198, 247, 152, 207};
10.       printScores(x);
11.    }
12.}
```

A. Compiler error on line 2

B. Compiler error on line 9

C. Compiler error on line 10

D. 198,247,152,207

E. 198,247,152,207,

9. Given the following class definition:

```
1.  public class Test {
2.     public void print(byte x) {
3.        System.out.print("byte");
4.     }
5.     public void print(int x) {
6.        System.out.print("int");
7.     }
8.     public void print(float x) {
9.        System.out.print("float");
10.    }
11.    public void print(Object x) {
12.       System.out.print("Object");
13.    }
14.}
```

what is the result of the following statements?

```
20. Test t = new Test();
21. short s = 123;
22. t.print(s);
```

```
23. t.print(12345L);
24. t.print(6.789);
```

A. bytefloatObject

B. intfloatObject

C. byteObjectfloat

D. intObjectfloat

E. intObjectObject

F. byteObjectObject

10. Given the following interface and class defined in a file named Traceable.java, what is the result of compiling this code?

```
1.  public interface Traceable {
2.     public static int MAX_TRACE;
3.     public void trace();
4.  }
5.
6.  class Picture implements Traceable {
7.     public void trace() {
8.         System.out.println("Tracing a picture");
9.     }
10. }
```

A. Two bytecode files: Traceable.class and Picture.class

B. One bytecode file: Traceable.class

C. Compiler error on line 2

D. Compiler error on line 3

E. Compiler error on line 6

F. Compiler error on line 7

11. Given the following class definition:

```
1.  public class Browser {
2.     public static void addToFavorites(int id, String... urls) {
3.         for(String url : urls) {
4.             System.out.println(url);
5.         }
6.     }
7.  }
```

which of the following statements are valid method calls to addToFavorites?

A. Browser.addToFavorites(101);

B. Browser.addToFavorites();

C. `Browser.addToFavorites(102, "a");`

D. `Browser.addToFavorites(103, 104, 105);`

E. `Browser.addToFavorites(106, "x", "y", "z");`

12. Suppose we have the following class definition:

```
1.  public class Outer {
2.     private int x = 5;
3.
4.     protected class Inner {
5.         public static int x = 10;
6.
7.         public void go() {
8.             System.out.println(x);
9.         }
10.    }
11.}
```

Given the following code:

```
15. Outer out = new Outer();
16. Outer.Inner in = out.new Inner();
17. in.go();
```

which of the following statements are true?

A. The output is 10.

B. The output is 5.

C. Line 16 generates a compiler error.

D. Line 5 generates a compiler error.

13. Given the following class definitions:

```
1.  class Parent {
2.     public void printResults(String... results) {
3.         System.out.println("In Parent");
4.     }
5.  }
6.
7.  class Child extends Parent {
8.     public int printResults(int id) {
9.         System.out.println("In Child");
10.        return 0;
11.    }
12.}
```

what is the result of the following statement?

```
new Child().printResults(0);
```

A. In Parent

B. In Child

C. 0

D. Line 2 generates a compiler error.

E. Line 8 generates a compiler error.

14. Given the following enum declaration:

```
1.  public enum Flavors {
2.      VANILLA, CHOCOLATE, STRAWBERRY
3.  }
```

what is the result of the following statement?

```
System.out.println(Flavors.CHOCOLATE.ordinal());
```

A. 0

B. 1

C. CHOCOLATE

D. 9

E. The statement will not compile.

15. What is the result of the following program?

```
1.  class Parent {
2.      public float computePay(double d) {
3.          System.out.println("In Parent");
4.          return 0.0F;
5.      }
6.  }
7.
8.  public class Child extends Parent {
9.      public double computePay(double d) {
10.         System.out.println("In Child");
11.         return 0.0;
12.     }
13.
14.     public static void main(String [] args) {
15.         new Child().computePay(0.0);
16.     }
17. }
```

A. In Parent

B. In Child

C. 0.0

D. null

E. The code does not compile.

16. Given the following class definition:

```
1.   import java.awt.Dimension;
2.   public class Shipment {
3.     public static class Box {
4.           public Dimension dimension;
5.           public int depth;
6.
7.           public Box(Dimension d, int x) {
8.               dimension = d;
9.               depth = x;
10.          }
11.
12.          private int getVolume() {
13.              return dimension.height * dimension.width * depth;
14.          }
15.    }
16.
17.    public Box box;
18.
19.    public void go() {
20.          System.out.println(box.getVolume());
21.    }
22.}
```

what is the result of the following code (assuming all types are properly imported)?

```
Dimension dim = new Dimension(10,10);
Box b = new Box(dim, 10);
Shipment s = new Shipment();
s.box = b;
s.go();
```

A. 1000

B. Compiler error on line 3

C. Compiler error on line 13

D. Compiler error on line 17

E. Compiler error on line 20

17. Given the following enum definition:

```
1.  public enum Flavors {
2.      VANILLA, CHOCOLATE, STRAWBERRY
3.  }
```

what is the output from the following code?

```
9.  Flavors f = Flavors.STRAWBERRY;
10. switch(f) {
11.    case 0:
12.        System.out.println("vanilla");
13.    case 1:
14.        System.out.println("chocolate");
15.    case 2:
16.        System.out.println("strawberry");
17.        break;
18.    default:
19.        System.out.println("missing flavor");
20. }
```

A. vanilla

B. chocolate

C. strawberry

D. missing flavor

E. The code does not compile.

18. Given the following class definition:

```
1.  import java.awt.*;
2.  import java.awt.event.*;
3.
4.  public class MyWindow {
5.     private Frame frame = new Frame();
6.
7.     public void registerEvents() {
8.         WindowAdapter wa = new WindowAdapter() {
9.             public void windowClosing(WindowEvent e) {
10.                frame.setVisible(false);
11.                frame.dispose();
12.            }
13.        };
14.        frame.addWindowListener(wa);
15.    }
16.}
```

which of the following statements are true? (Select two.)

A. Lines 10 and 11 generate a compiler error.

B. Lines 8 to 13 are an anonymous inner class declaration.

C. The object instantiated on line 8 does not have access to the `frame` field on line 5 because `frame` is `private`.

D. The method on line 9 never executes because its definition goes out of scope after line 15.

E. The anonymous inner class on line 8 is a child of `WindowAdapter`.

19. Suppose a method in a class has the following method declaration:

```
public java.io.OutputStream createStream(String fileName) {
    //method body here...
}
```

Which of the following methods could appear in a child class and override `createStream`? (Select two.)

A. `public java.io.OutputStream createStream(String f)`

B. `public java.io.OutputStream createStream(char c)`

C. `public java.io.FileOutputStream createStream(String f)`

D. `public void createStream(String c)`

E. `public java.io.OutputStream createStream(StringBuffer fileName)`

F. `protected java.io.OutputStream createStream(String fileName)`

20. Given the following class definitions, what is the output of the statement `new Child();`?

```
1.  class Parent {
2.      {
3.          System.out.print("1");
4.      }
5.
6.      public Parent(String greeting) {
7.          System.out.print("2");
8.      }
9.  }
10.
11. class Child extends Parent {
12.     static {
13.         System.out.print("3");
14.     }
15.
16.     {
17.         System.out.print("4");
18.     }
19. }
```

A. 1234

B. 3123

C. 3142

D. 3124

E. The code does not compile.

21. Given the following enum declaration:

```
1.  public enum Fruit {
2.     APPLE("red"),
3.     BANANA("yellow"),
4.     ORANGE("orange"),
5.     PLUM("purple");
6.
7.     private Fruit(String color) {
8.         this.color = color;
9.     }
10.
11.    public String color;
12. }
```

what is the result of the following program?

```
15.  public class FruitStore {
16.     public static void main(String [] args) {
17.        Fruit one = Fruit.PLUM;
18.        System.out.println("a " + one.name() + " is " + one.color);
19.     }
20. }
```

A. a PLUM is purple

B. a Fruit.PLUM is purple

C. The Fruit enum does not compile.

D. Compiler error on line 17

E. Compiler error on line 18

22. Given the following class definition:

```
1.  class Outer {
2.     private int x = 24;
3.
4.     public int getX() {
5.         String message = "x is ";
6.         class Inner {
7.             private int x = Outer.this.x;
8.             public void printX() {
```

```
9.                    System.out.println(message + x);
10.            }
11.          }
12.        Inner in = new Inner();
13.        in.printX();
14.        return x;
15.    }
16.}
```

what is the result of the following statement?

```
new Outer().getX();
```

A. x is 24

B. x is 0

C. Compiler error on line 7

D. Compiler error on line 9

E. Compiler error on line 12

23. Given the following class definitions:

```
1.  class Parent {
2.    public void print(double d) {
3.        System.out.print("Parent");
4.    }
5.  }
6.
7.  class Child extends Parent {
8.    public void print(int i) {
9.        System.out.print("Child");
10.   }
11.}
```

what is the result of the following code?

```
15. Child child = new Child();
16. child.print(10);
17. child.print(3.14);
```

A. ChildParent

B. ChildChild

C. ParentParent

D. Line 8 generates a compiler error.

E. Line 17 generates a compiler error.

24. Given the following interface definitions:

```
1.  //Readable.java
2.  public interface Readable {
3.    public abstract void read();
4.  }
```

```
1.  //SpellCheck.java
2.  public interface SpellCheck extends Readable {
3.      public void checkSpelling();
4.  }
```

which of the following statements are true? (Select all that apply.)

A. The SpellCheck interface does not compile.

B. A class that implements Readable must override the read method.

C. A class that implements SpellCheck inherits both the checkSpelling and read methods.

D. A class that implements SpellCheck only inherits the checkSpelling method.

E. An interface cannot extend another interface.

25. Given the following class definitions:

```
1.  class Pet {
2.    {
3.        System.out.print("A");
4.    }
5.    public Pet() {
6.        System.out.print("B");
7.    }
8.    {
9.        System.out.print("C");
10.   }
11.
12. }
13.
14. class Cat extends Pet {
15.   public Cat() {
16.       System.out.print("D");
17.   }
18.   static {
19.       System.out.print("E");
20.   }
21. }
```

what is the result of the following statement?

```
new Cat();
```

A. ABCDE

B. ACBED

C. EACBD

D. EBACD

E. The output may vary.

Answers to Review Questions

1. E. If a constructor does not call `this` or `super` on its first line of code, the compiler inserts the statement `super();`, which occurs in the `Rectangle` class just after line 15. A call to `super()` in `Rectangle` invokes a no-argument constructor in `Shape`, but `Shape` does not have a no-argument constructor. The compiler error occurs at line 15, so the answer is E.

2. A. The statement `new Child()` invokes the constructor on line 12. The call to `this(123)` invokes the constructor on line 8, which calls `super()` implicitly before line 9. The call to `super()` invokes the constructor on line 3, where A is printed. Control jumps back to line 9 and B is printed. Control jumps back to line 14 and C is printed.

3. A, B, and E. A is valid because you can use the dollar sign in identifiers. B is valid because the underscore is a valid Java character. C is not a valid identifier because `transient` is a Java keyword. D is not valid because the dot (.) is not allowed in identifiers. E is valid because Java is case sensitive, so `Public` is not a keyword and therefore a valid identifier. F is not valid because the first character is not a letter.

4. E. The code compiles fine, so A, B, and C are incorrect. Boolean fields initialize to `false` and references initialize to `null`, so `empty` is `false` and `brand` is `null`. Therefore, line 7 is `true` and `Brand = null` is output. Therefore, D is incorrect and the answer is E.

5. C. The code compiles fine, so E is incorrect. Because explicit initialization occurs before a constructor is invoked, line 2 executes before the `Television` constructor on line 4 is executed. The `7` is output on line 11, then the constructor is invoked and `12` is output. Therefore, the output is `7  12`, so the answer is C.

6. B, C, D, and E. The code does not compile, so A is incorrect. Line 5 is not valid because `globalKey` has the default access and `School` is in a different package than `ClassRoom`. Line 6 is not valid for the same reason: the `ClassRoom` constructor has default access so `School` does not have access to it. Line 7 is not valid because `roomNumber` is `private` and therefore not accessible outside of `ClassRoom`. Line 8 is not valid because `teacherName` is `protected` and `School` is neither in the same package nor a subclass of `ClassRoom`. Therefore, the answers are B, C, D, and E.

7. B. E is incorrect. Without any imports, the `Administrator` class will not compile because line 5 of `Administrator` refers to `globalKey`, a static field in `ClassRoom`. A imports the `ClassRoom` class, which is a valid import but does not import `globalKey`. B imports all static fields of `ClassRoom`, so B is a correct answer. C and D are not valid statements and generate compiler errors. Therefore, the only correct answer is B.

8. E. The `printScores` method takes in a variable-length argument on line 2 and it is correctly declared, so A is incorrect. Line 9 is a valid array initializer statement, so B is incorrect. A variable-length parameter is an array behind the scenes and can accept an array argument, so line 10 is valid and C is incorrect. The code compiles and the `for-each` loop displays each number in the array followed by a comma, so D is incorrect and E is the correct answer.

9. B. The argument on line 22 is a `short`. It can be promoted to an `int`, so `print` on line 5 is invoked. The argument on line 23 is a `long`. It can be promoted to a `float`, so `print` on line 8 is invoked. The argument on line 24 is a `double`. It can be promoted to a `java.lang.Double`, so `print` on line 11 is invoked. Therefore, the output is `intfloatObject` and the correct answer is B.

10. C. This is a tricky question. The code does not compile, so A and B are incorrect. All fields in an interface are implicitly final, and static final fields must be initialized. Line 3 compiles fine, as do lines 6 and 7, so D, E, and F are incorrect. Because `MAX_TRACE` is not initialized, line 2 generates a compiler error. Therefore, the answer is C.

11. A, C, and E. The `urls` parameter is variable length, so any number of `Strings` can be passed in after the `int` argument. A has no `Strings`, C has one `String`, and E has three `Strings`, so these answers are correct. B does not pass in the required `int` and generates a compiler error. D passes in three `ints`, which also generates a compiler error.

12. D. The class does not compile, so A and B are incorrect. Line 16 compiles and is the proper syntax for instantiating a new `Inner` object outside of the `Outer` class, so C is incorrect. An inner class cannot declare static fields or methods, so line 5 generates a compiler error and the answer is D.

13. B. The code compiles fine, so D and E are incorrect. The `printResults` method in `Child` is overloading `printResults` in `Parent`, not overriding. In method overloading, the return type can be any data type, so `printResults` in `Child` returning an `int` is not a problem. Invoking `printResults` with an `int` argument calls the method on line 8, which displays `In Child`. Therefore, the answer is B.

14. B. The `ordinal` method of an enum element returns its corresponding `int` value. Enums are zero-based, so `VANILLA` is 0, `CHOCOLATE` is 1, and `STRAWBERRY` is 2. Therefore, the answer is B.

15. E. The return type of an overridden method must either be the same or a child class of the return type of the parent method. Because `double` is not a child class of `float` (they are primitive types), line 8 generates a compiler error. Therefore, the answer is E.

16. A. The code compiles fine. A class can contain a static nested class, so B is incorrect. Line 13 can access only fields of `Box` which it does, so C is incorrect. `Shipment` can use the `Box` class without any special syntax or prefixes, so line 17 is valid and D is incorrect. `Shipment` has access to the private methods of `Box`, so line 20 is valid and E is incorrect. The volume of the `Box` is 10*10*10 = 1000, so the output is 1000 and the answer is A.

17. E. A `case` statement on an enum data type must be the unqualified name of an enumeration constant. You cannot use their ordinal values in a `case`. Therefore, a compiler error occurs on lines 11, 13, and 15, so the answer is E.

18. B and E. The code compiles fine, so A is incorrect. B is a true statement. C is incorrect because inner classes have access to all private fields of the enclosing class. D is incorrect because the scope of a method declaration is really not relevant. (The method can still be invoked at any time.) E is a true statement. Therefore, the correct answers are B and E.

19. A and C. A has the same signature and return type, and C has the same signature and a covariant return type, so A and C are valid overriding declarations. B and E are valid methods for a child class, but they are examples of method overloading, not overriding. D has an incompatible return type. F is a weaker access than public, which is not allowed.

20. E. The Child class gets the default constructor because it does not define a constructor explicitly. The default constructor contains the line super(); which does not compile because Parent does not have a no-argument constructor. Therefore, the correct answer is E.

21. A. All the code compiles fine, so C, D, and E are incorrect. The name method of an enum element returns its unqualified name, which for the one reference is PLUM. The color field for PLUM is purple, so the output is a PLUM is purple. Therefore, the answer is A.

22. D. The code does not compile, so A and B are incorrect. Line 7 uses the proper syntax for an inner class accessing a field in the enclosing class, so C is incorrect. Line 12 is fine, so E is incorrect. On line 9, the local inner class Inner is attempting to access a non-final local variable, which generates a compiler error. Therefore, the answer is D.

23. A. The code compiles fine, so D and E are incorrect. The child class is overloading print, not overriding it. The method call on line 16 invokes print in the child, and the method call on line 17 invokes print in the parent, so the output is ChildParent. Therefore, the answer is A.

24. C. The SpellCheck interface compiles fine, so A is false. B is false; a class that implements Readable can be declared abstract and not override read. C is a true statement; a class that implements SpellCheck must either override both checkSpelling and read or declare itself as abstract. Because C is true, D must be false. E is false; an interface can actually extend multiple interfaces. Therefore, the only answer is C.

25. C. Executing new Cat() means the Cat class must be loaded first by the class loader, which causes its static initializer on line 18 to execute first, displaying E. The Pet instance initializers are next, in the order they appear, so A and C are displayed. Then the Pet constructor is invoked, displaying B, and finally the Cat constructor is invoked, displaying D. The output is EACBD, so the answer is C.

Flow Control

SCJP EXAM OBJECTIVES COVERED IN THIS CHAPTER:

✓ Develop code that implements an if or switch statement; and identify legal argument types for these statements.

✓ Develop code that implements all forms of loops and iterators, including the use of for, the enhanced for loop (for-each), do, while, labels, break, and continue; and explain the values taken by loop counter variables during and after loop execution.

✓ Develop code that makes use of assertions, and distinguish appropriate from inappropriate uses of assertions.

✓ Develop code that makes use of exceptions and exception handling clauses (try, catch, finally), and declares methods and overriding methods that throw exceptions.

✓ Recognize the effect of an exception arising at a specified point in a code fragment. Note that the exception may be a runtime exception, a checked exception, or an error.

✓ Recognize situations that will result in any of the following being thrown: ArrayIndexOutOfBoundsException, ClassCastException, IllegalArgumentException, IllegalStateException, NullPointerException, NumberFormatException, AssertionError, ExceptionInInitializerError, StackOverflowError or NoClassDefFoundError. Understand which of these are thrown by the virtual machine and recognize situations in which others should be thrown programmatically.

The exam tests your knowledge of all aspects of flow control, including decision making, loop control structures, assertions, and exception handling. This chapter covers all of these topics in detail.

Overview of Flow Control

Flow control refers to the order in which the statements in your Java program execute. The starting point of a Java program is the main method, and the statements of your Java program generally execute in the order they appear. However, we often need to alter this flow of control by making decisions or looping through statements to repeat a task. Problems might arise at runtime that might justify a method immediately terminating, or you might have trouble finding a bug so you make various assertions in your code. Each of these situations changes the order of execution (and therefore the flow of control) of the statements in your program.

Section 2 of the SCJP exam tests your knowledge of the various aspects of Java that affect the flow of control of a Java program. For example, Java contains the following typical control structures that most programming languages define for making decisions and repetition:

- Decision Making: The if-else and switch statements are the two control structures in Java for making decisions.

- Repetition: for loops, enhanced for loops, while loops, and do-while loops are the control structure for performing repetition.

This chapter discusses the proper syntax and usage of these control structures. We also examine the details of Java assertions, which are helpful in detecting and fixing bugs in your Java programs. In addition, we cover exception handling in detail, including when exceptions need to be caught and when they can be ignored. We start with the control structures, beginning with the most basic of decision-making structures: the if-else statement.

The *if* Statement

The exam objectives state that you should be able to "develop code that implements an if statement and identify legal argument types." An *if statement*, also referred to as an if-else or if-then-else statement, is the most basic of decision-making control structures in Java. Figure 3.1 shows the syntax of an if statement.

FIGURE 3.1   The syntax of an if statement

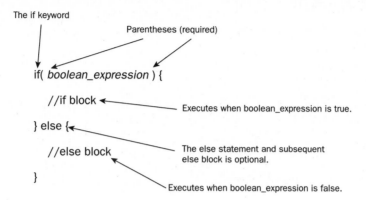

The following rules apply to an if-else statement:

- The expression in parentheses must evaluate to a boolean. Otherwise, a compiler error is generated.
- If the boolean expression evaluates to true, the block of code following the if executes.
- If the boolean expression evaluates to false, the else block executes.
- The else block is optional.
- The curly braces are not required in either the if or else block if the block of code is a single statement. However, for readability it is a good idea to always use the curly braces.
- An else block can contain an additional if statement.

The following simple example of an if statement demonstrates the syntax:

```
8.  int x = (int) (Math.random() * 10 + 1);
9.  if(x <= 5) {
10.        System.out.println("Under five");
11. }
```

The value of x is assigned a random number between 1 and 10. If the value of x is less than or equal to 5, then Under five displays on line 10. If x is greater than 5, the block of code that contains line 10 is skipped.

An else can be added to any if statement. The following if-then-else statement outputs either Under five or Over five:

```
8.  int x = (int) (Math.random() * 10 + 1);
9.  if(x <= 5) {
10.    System.out.println("Under five");

11. } else {
12.    System.out.println("Over five");
13. }
```

if Statements and boolean Expressions

The expression in parentheses of an if statement must evaluate to a boolean expression. The following code does not compile:

```
int y = 12;
if(y) {
    //This does not work
}
```

The following compiler error occurs:

```
If Then.java:11: incompatible types
found   : int
required: boolean
        if(y) {
```

In other languages like C and C++ that do not have primitive Boolean types, any non-zero value is considered true and any zero value is false. This concept does not translate in Java. All the control structures that we discuss in this chapter require boolean expressions that evaluate to either true or false.

An if-then-else statement can contain any number of else if blocks. For example, study the following code and see if you can determine its output:

```
1.  public class Grades {
2.    public static void showGrade(int grade) {
3.        if(grade >= 90) {
4.            System.out.print("A");
5.        } else if(grade >= 80) {
6.            System.out.print("B");
7.        } else if(grade >= 70) {
8.            System.out.print("C");
9.        } else if(grade >= 60) {
10.           System.out.print("D");
11.       } else {
12.           System.out.print("F");
13.       }
14.       System.out.println(" is your grade");
15.   }
16.
```

```
17.    public static void main(String [] args) {
18.        showGrade(77);
19.        showGrade(54);
20.    }
21.}
```

After an `if` expression evaluates to `true` and its corresponding block of code executes, control leaves the if-then-else statement. For example, when grade equals 77, line 7 is true and line 8 executes, printing C. Line 9 is also `true`, but it is not evaluated because control jumps out of the `if` statement to line 14.

When grade equals 54, none of the `if` statements are `true`, so the `else` on line 11 executes and an F displays. The output of the Grades program is

```
C is your grade
F is your grade
```

Note that at most one block of code in an `if-then-else` control structure executes. The last `else` block is always optional. When no else block appears, no block of code executes if all the `boolean` expressions are `false`. Otherwise, when an `if-then-else` does contain an ending `else` block, exactly one block of code in the control structure executes: either the first `if` condition to evaluate to `true`, or the `else` block if all `if` conditions are `false`.

Be Careful with `boolean` Comparisons

Watch out for assignment statements that look like `boolean` expressions. For example, look at the following code and see if you can determine its output:

```
12. boolean b = false;
13. if(b = true) {
14.     System.out.println("true");
15. } else {
16.     System.out.println("false");
17. }
```

This code compiles fine. On line 13, b = true is an assignment, not a comparison. The result of this `boolean` assignment is the value of b after the assignment, which is `true`. Therefore, the output of this code is

```
true
```

Keep an eye out for this type of question on the exam.

Next we discuss the other decision-making control structure in Java: the `switch` statement.

The *switch* Statement

The exam objectives state that you should be able to "develop code that implements a `switch` statement and identify legal argument types." A *switch statement* is a decision-making control structure based on testing an integer value for equality to a list of `case` statements. A `switch` is similar to an `if-then-else` statement, except that a `switch` statement can only test for equality and it is possible for multiple blocks of code in a `switch` to execute. Figure 3.2 shows the syntax of a `switch` statement.

FIGURE 3.2   The syntax of a `switch` statement

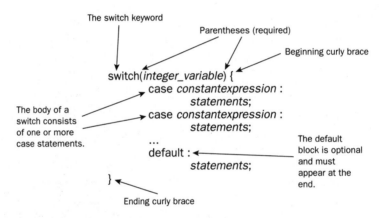

The following rules apply to using `switch` statements:

- The *integer_variable* must be compatible with an `int`, which means you can only switch on a `byte`, `short`, `char`, `int`, `Byte`, `Short`, `Character`, `Integer`, or an enum type.

- Any number of `case` statements can appear.

- The *constantexpression* of a `case` must be a literal value or a `final` variable.

- The `default` block is optional and must appear at the end of all the `case` statements. If none of the `case` statements equal the expression, the `default` block executes.

- When a `case` is true, no other `case` statements are tested for equality, and all statements following the `case` execute until a `break` occurs or the end of the `switch` statement is reached.

The last rule is what makes a switch statement unique. The value being switched on is compared for equality to each case statement in the order that they appear. Once a case statement is true, no subsequent case statements are tested. All statements following a true case execute, even if control "falls through" other case statements, until a break occurs.

Let's look at an example. The following code switches on an int. See if you can determine the output:

```
6.  int x = 0;
7.  switch(x) {
8.    case 0 :
9.    case 1 :
10.       System.out.println("0 or 1");
11.       break;
12.    case 2 :
13.       System.out.println("2");
14.    case 3 :
15.       System.out.println("2 or 3");
16.       break;
17.   default :
18.       System.out.println("default");
19.}
20.System.out.println("After switch");
```

Here is the flow of control that occurs when this code executes:

1. The int x is declared and assigned the value 0.
2. The case 0 is true on line 8, so no more cases are tested for equality.
3. x does not equal 1 on line 9, but x is not compared to 1 on line 9. Instead, control just falls through to line 10.
4. 0 or 1 is printed on line 10.
5. The break is hit on line 11, causing control to jump out of the switch statement down to line 20 and After switch is printed.

Therefore, the output of this switch is

```
0 or 1
After switch
```

Using the same switch statement, the following output displays when x equals 2:

```
2
2 or 3
After switch
```

Notice if x is 2, the case on line 12 is true, so all statements after line 12 execute until the break on line 16. Therefore, lines 13 and 15 both execute, resulting in the preceding output.

Switching on a Reference

Because Java autoboxes and unboxes the primitive types, you can switch on a reference of type Byte, Short, Character, or Integer. For example, the following switch variable is a Character reference:

```
Character value = 'C';
switch(value) {
    case 'A' :
    case 'B' :
        System.out.println("Nice job!");
        break;
    case 'C' :
        System.out.println("Not bad.");
        break;
    default :
        System.out.println("Not good.");
}
```

The wrapped Character value is unboxed to a char in the switch statement. If the reference happens to be null at runtime, a NullPointerException is thrown.

Switching on an Enum

A switch statement can be executed on integer-compatible types, which includes enums. When the variable being switched on is an enum, the following rules apply:

- The case statements must be one of the elements of the enumeration. A compiler error occurs if one of the case statements is not one of the values in the enum.

- You cannot use an enum value's ordinal value for a case; you can only use the name of the enum element.

- The enum element in the case is not prefixed with the enum name.

The following class contains a `switch` statement on an enum named `Console`. Study the code and see if you can determine its output:

```
1.  public class EnumSwitch {
2.    public enum Console {
3.        XBOX, WII, PLAYSTATION
4.    }
5.
6.    public static void main(String [] args) {
7.        Console myConsole = Console.WII;
8.        switch(myConsole) {
9.            case XBOX :
10.               System.out.println("XBox console");
11.               break;
12.            case WII :
13.               System.out.println("WII console");
14.               break;
15.            case PLAYSTATION :
16.               System.out.println("PlayStation console");
17.               break;
18.            default :
19.               System.out.println("Not here");
20.        }
21.    }
22.}
```

The `switch` variable on line 8 is a `Console` reference, so the only valid `case` statements are elements of the `Console` enum. The `myConsole` reference points to `WII`, so line 12 is true and the output is

```
WII console
```

Because the three `case` statements are every possible value of `myConsole` and each `case` contains a break, the `default` block of code in this example should never execute. Even though it appears to be unreachable, the compiler does not complain. (This is a good place for an assertion, discussed later in the section "Overview of Assertions.")

The following `switch` statement would not be valid:

```
25. Console yourConsole = Console.XBOX;
26. switch(yourConsole) {
27.    case 0 :  //not valid
28.        System.out.println("XBox console");
29.        break;
```

```
30.    case Console.WII :  //not valid
31.        System.out.println("WII console");
32.        break;
33. }
```

Line 27 attempts to use the ordinal value of XBOX, which is not allowed. Line 30 uses the fully qualified name of the WII element, which is also not allowed. The following compiler errors occur:

```
EnumSwitch.java:27: an enum switch case label must be the unqualified
 name of an enumeration constant
    case 0 :
        ^

EnumSwitch.java:30: an enum switch case label must be the unqualified
 name of an enumeration constant
    case Console.WII :
             ^
```

Final *case* Values

A case value must be a constant expression. The examples in this chapter have been either literals or enum constants, but you can also use final variables. Examine the following code and try to determine its output:

```
public class FinalSwitch {

    public static final char UPPER_A = 'A';
    public static final char UPPER_B = 'B';
    public static final char UPPER_C = 'C';

    public static String convertGrade(char grade) {
        String response = "";
        switch(grade) {
            case UPPER_A :
            case UPPER_B :
                System.out.println("Nice job!");
                break;
            case UPPER_C :
                System.out.println("Not bad.");
                break;
            default :
                System.out.println("Not good.");
        }
```

```
        return response;
    }

    public static void main(String [] args) {
        System.out.println(convertGrade('C'));
    }
}
```

The value being switched on is the parameter `grade`. Because each `case` statement uses a `final` variable, the code compiles fine and the output is

```
Not bad.
```

The *for* Statement

The exam objectives state that you should be able to "develop code that implements all forms of loops and iterators, including the use of for and the enhanced for loop (for-each), and explain the values taken by loop counter variables during and after loop execution." This section discusses these details of `for` and `for-each` loops. A *for statement* is a repetition control structure that is useful for repeating a block of code a fixed number of times. There are two types of `for` statements in Java:

- The basic `for` statement
- The enhanced `for` statement

This section discusses the details of both types of `for` statements, starting with the basic `for` statement.

The Basic *for* Statement

A basic `for` statement has the following properties:

- The two semicolons are required and create three sections: an `initialization` statement, a `boolean` expression, and an update statement.
- The *initialization* step occurs once at the beginning of the loop.
- The *boolean_expression* must evaluate to `true` or `false`.
- The *initialization* and *update_statement* sections can contain multiple statements, separated by commas.

Figure 3.3 shows the syntax and order of execution of the basic `for` statement.

FIGURE 3.3   The syntax of a basic `for` statement

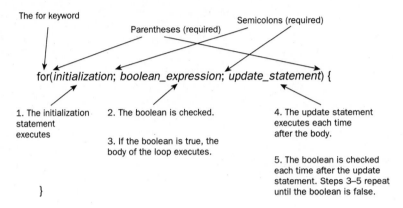

Let's look at an example. The following `for` loop displays the numbers 1 to 10:

```
for(int x = 1; x <= 10; x++) {
    System.out.print(x + " ");
}
```

The following sequence of events occurs during this loop:

1. The `int` x is allocated in memory and initialized to 1.

2. The `boolean` expression is evaluated. x is less than or equal to 10 so the body of the loop executes.

3. The print statement displays 1 and a space.

4. The end of the `for` loop is reached on line 7, so control jumps to the update statement x++, incrementing x to 2.

5. The `boolean` is checked again. x is still less than or equal to 10, so steps 3 and 4 repeat until x is the value 11.

6. The `boolean` is now false, so the `for` loop terminates and x goes out of scope.

   The output of this loop is

```
1 2 3 4 5 6 7 8 9 10
```

The Scope of for Loop Variables

Any variables declared in the initialization step are local variables in the for loop and go out of scope when the loop finishes. For example, the following code attempts to display k after it goes out of scope:

```
for(int k = 10; k >= 1; k--) {
    System.out.print(k);
}
System.out.print(k);
```

The following compiler error occurs:

```
For.java:19: cannot find symbol
symbol  : variable k
location: class For
System.out.println(k);
                  ^
```

Watch for a question that tests your knowledge of this subject. By the way, if you need to use k outside the loop, declare it outside the loop. For example, the following code is valid:

```
int k = 10;
for(k = 10; k >= 1; k--) {
    System.out.print(k);
}
System.out.print(k);
```

The output of this code is

109876543210

There will be questions on the SCJP exam that test your knowledge of the syntax and behavior of basic for statements. The exam seems to favor nested for statements, something along the lines of the following example:

```
4. for(char one = 'a'; one <= 'f'; one++) {
5.    for(int i = 1; i <= 3; i++) {
6.        System.out.print(" " + one + i);
7.    }
8.    System.out.println();
9. }
```

Be sure to check the syntax first to make sure the code compiles, which it does in this example. The outer loop has a char loop control variable that goes from 'a' to 'f', totaling six iterations. The inner loop has an int loop control variable that goes from 1 to 3 and prints something, so the output will be 6 * 3 = 18 values. The println call on line 8 occurs after the inner loop, so a line break occurs after every three values are printed. If you carefully go through the steps of displaying the first couple of rows, you will quickly deduce the remaining rows. The output of these nested loops is

```
a1 a2 a3
b1 b2 b3
c1 c2 c3
d1 d2 d3
e1 e2 e3
f1 f2 f3
```

Let's look at another example. Examine the following code and determine if it compiles and what the output is:

```
12. for(int a = 1, b = 10; a < b; a++, b = b - 2) {
13.     System.out.println(a + b);
14. }
```

Again, be sure to look for compiler errors first. This code compiles fine. You can initialize two variables in the initialization step, and you can have multiple update statements as long as they are separated by commas. If you see a loop like this on the exam, my advice is to carefully step through each iteration. This example might look confusing, but it actually only iterates three times:

1. a is 1 and b is 10: Because 1 < 10 is true, 11 displays and the update statement executes, incrementing a to 2 and decrementing b to 8.

2. a is 2 and b is 8: Because 2 < 8 is true, 10 displays and we go back to the update statement.

3. a is 3 and b is 6: Because 3 < 6 is true, 9 displays and the updates execute again.

4. a is 4 and b is 4: Because 4 < 4 is false, we are finished.

Therefore, the output of this example is

```
11
10
9
```

Some for Statement Notes

All of the three sections of a for statement are optional. If you don't need to initialize a variable or update anything, you can leave those sections blank. For example, the following for loop does not contain an update statement:

```
for(int i = 1; i <= 10; ) {
    System.out.print(i++ + ",");
}
```

The output of this loop is

```
1,2,3,4,5,6,7,8,9,10,
```

Updating the loop control variable within the loop defeats the purpose of the update statement and makes your code more difficult to read, so this example is not something I recommend using in the real world.

Also, the boolean expression of a for statement defaults to true if it is left blank. For example, the following for statement is an infinite loop:

```
for( ; ; ) {
    System.out.print("Hi");
}
```

This particular loop will run until the JVM is terminated.

The Enhanced *for* Statement

Java 5.0 introduced a new looping control structure called the *enhanced for statement,* also referred to as a *for-each loop.* An enhanced for statement is designed for iterating through arrays and collections. The syntax is simpler than a basic for loop and makes your code more readable. Figure 3.4 shows the syntax of an enhanced for statement.

FIGURE 3.4   The syntax of an enhanced for statement

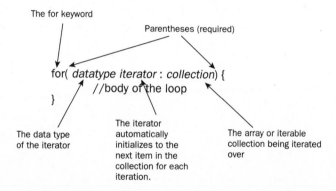

An enhanced for statement has the following properties:

- The data type of the iterator must be compatible with the data type of the collection.

- The scope of the iterator is the body of the loop.

- The number of iterations of the loop equals the size of the collection. If the collection is empty, the body of the loop does not execute.

- The collection must be an array or an object of type java.lang.Iterable, an interface introduced in Java 5.0 exclusively for for-each loops.

Let's start with a simple example to demonstrate how it looks. Examine the following enhanced for statement and try to determine its output:

```
3.  char [] grades = {'A', 'B', 'C', 'D', 'F'};
4.  for(char grade : grades) {
5.      System.out.print(grade + " ");
6.  }
```

The collection in this example has five elements, so the loop executes five times. The grade iterator is initially 'A', then 'B', and so on. The output is

```
A B C D F
```

You must declare the iterator within the enhanced for statement; it cannot be a variable that is already declared. For example, the following code does not compile:

```
9.   char grade;
10. for(grade : grades) { //does not compile!
11.     System.out.print(grade + " ");
12. }
```

The compiler complains that grade on line 10 is not a statement and that a semicolon is expected. The compiler thinks I am trying to declare a basic for loop on line 10 because the declaration of the iterator does not include a data type.

The Scope of Enhanced for Loop Variables

The scope of the iterator in an enhanced for loop is only within the body of the loop. To demonstrate, study the following code and see if you can determine its result:

```
15. String [] replies = {"Hello", "Hi", "How are you?"};
16. String s = "Bye";
17. for(String reply : replies) {
18.     s = reply;
19. }
20. System.out.println(s);
21. System.out.println(reply);
```

The variable `reply` is out of scope at line 21, so the following compiler error occurs:

```
EnhancedFor.java:21: cannot find symbol
symbol  : variable reply
location: class EnhancedFor
System.out.println(reply);
                 ^
```

By the way, if we comment out line 21 and run this code, what is the output of s on line 20? If you are unsure, try typing in this code and running it yourself to verify the result.

I will now discuss two common uses of the nested `for` statements: iterating over collections and nesting enhanced `for` statements.

Enhanced *for* Loops and Collections

Let's look at an example of an enhanced for loop that iterates over a collection. The collection must be an object whose class implements `java.lang.Iterable`, which includes most of the Collections API classes in the `java.util` package. The following code iterates through a `java.util.ArrayList`. Examine the code and see if you can determine its output:

```
1.    import java.util.ArrayList;
2.
3.    public class Favorites {
4.        private ArrayList<String> urls = new ArrayList<String>();
5.
6.        public void showFavorites() {
7.            for(String url : urls) {
8.                if(url.startsWith("http://")) {
9.                    System.out.println(url);
10.               } else {
11.                   System.out.println("http://" + url);
12.               }
13.           }
14.       }
15.
16.       public void addFavorite(String url) {
17.           urls.add(url);
18.       }
19.
20.       public static void main(String [] args) {
21.           Favorites f = new Favorites();
```

```
22.          f.addFavorite("sybex.com");
23.          f.addFavorite("wiley.com");
24.          f.addFavorite("http://google.com");
25.          f.addFavorite("yahoo.com");
26.          f.showFavorites();
27.    }
28.}
```

The sequence of events of the Favorites program follows:

1. A Favorites object is instantiated in main and four String objects are added to the urls field.

2. The showFavorites method is invoked, which executes the enhanced for loop on line 7.

3. The first time through the loop the iterator url is "sybex.com" and "http://sybex.com" displays.

4. The loop iterates three more times until all four String objects are output.

The output of main in Favorites is

```
http://sybex.com
http://wiley.com
http://google.com
http://yahoo.com
```

 Real World Scenario

When to Use—or Not Use—Enhanced for Loops

The enhanced for statement was added to the Java language to simplify your code in those common situations where you need to iterate over an array or collection of objects. You will use enhanced for loops all the time when iterating over arrays and collections.

Notice that the enhanced for loop hides the index variable when iterating over arrays, and it hides the actual iterator when iterating over collections. For example, suppose you need to iterate over an array and change each element. You won't be able to do that with an enhanced for loop because you won't have the index variable of the array. Similarly, suppose you want to delete the element in a collection represented by the current iterator. You may not be able to do this (depending on the collection) because the iterator does not know of its location in the collection. In these situations, you can simply use a basic for loop for iterating over the array or collection.

However, this situation does not diminish the usefulness of enhanced for statements. In many programming situations, you iterate over a collection of data and do not need to modify or delete elements in the collection, making an enhanced for loop the preferred solution. They can also make your code more readable when iterating over nested collections, as shown in the next section. The general rule of thumb is to use enhanced for loops whenever you can!

Nested Enhanced *for* Loops

You really start to see the benefit of the enhanced for syntax when iterating over tabular data (with rows and columns) using nested loops. The following example uses nested enhanced for loops to display a multiplication table of the numbers 1 to 9. Examine the code and see if you can determine its output:

```
3. int [] digits = {1,2,3,4,5,6,7,8,9};
4.  for(int x : digits) {
5.    for(int y : digits) {
6.        System.out.print(x * y + "\t");
7.    }
8.    System.out.println();
9.  }
```

The digits array has nine elements, so the outer loop on line 4 iterates nine times and so does the inner loop on line 5. Therefore, line 6 executes 9 * 9 = 81 times. The first time through the outer loop, x is 1 and y goes from 1 to 9, printing 1*1, 1*2, 1*3, and so on up to 1*9. This process repeats for x equal to 2, printing 2*1, 2*2, 2*3, and so on up to 2*9. The process keeps repeating until the following multiplication table displays:

1	2	3	4	5	6	7	8	9
2	4	6	8	10	12	14	16	18
3	6	9	12	15	18	21	24	27
4	8	12	16	20	24	28	32	36
5	10	15	20	25	30	35	40	45
6	12	18	24	30	36	42	48	54
7	14	21	28	35	42	49	56	63
8	16	24	32	40	48	56	64	72
9	18	27	36	45	54	63	72	81

I could have just as easily written this example using basic for loops, and before Java 5.0 it would have been the only option! But I like the enhanced for loop for its simplicity and readability. Make sure you understand the details of the enhanced for statement. As I have mentioned before, the newer Java topics tend to be emphasized on the SCJP exam.

Next we discuss another popular looping control structure: the while statement.

The *while* Statement

The exam objectives state that you should be able to "develop code that implements all forms of loops and iterators, including while". A *while statement* is a repetition control structure that is useful for repeating a block of code an indeterminate number of times. Figure 3.5 shows the syntax of a while statement.

FIGURE 3.5   The syntax of a while loop

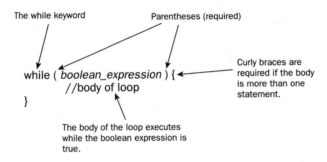

The following rules apply to a while statement:

- The value in parentheses must evaluate to a boolean expression, either true or false.
- If the boolean expression is true, the body of the loop executes and the boolean is checked again.
- If the boolean expression is false, the loop does not execute and control jumps to the next statement following the end of the loop.
- The body of the loop executes until the boolean expression is false.

Let's start with a simple example. The following while statement prints the chars 'A' to 'H' on the same line:

```
3. char c = 'A';
4. while(c <= 'H') {
5.    System.out.print(c++);
6. }
```

The loop executes eight times, and the output is

```
ABCDEFGH
```

The following program demonstrates a better example of when to use a `while` loop because it executes an indeterminate number of times. Examine the code and see if you can determine the result:

```
1.  public class RollDice {
2.    public static int rollDice() {
3.        return ((int) (Math.random() * 6)) + 1;
4.    }
5.
6.    public static void main(String [] args) {
7.        int one = rollDice();
8.        int two = rollDice();
9.        System.out.print("You rolled a " + (one + two));
10.       while(one + two != 11) {
11.           one = rollDice();
12.           two = rollDice();
13.           System.out.print(", " + (one + two));
14.       }
15.   }
16.}
```

The `while` loop on line 10 executes until the two variables one and two add up to 11. Because they are randomly generated, this could happen right away or it could take a while. A sample output follows:

```
You rolled a 7, 8, 9, 6, 11
```

The output changes every time you run `RollDice` because it uses randomly generated numbers.

You can easily write an infinite loop with a `while` statement:

```
13. while(true) {
14.     System.out.println("This could take a while.");
15. }
```

In this example, line 14 will print `This could take a while.` until the user terminates the JVM.

A Note on Unreachable Code

It is possible to have a while loop whose body never gets executed:

```
8.   int x = 0;
9.   while(x > 0) {
10.      System.out.println("Not here");
11.  }
```

However, you cannot write code that is unreachable or a compiler error is generated. For example, the following code does not compile:

```
17.  while(false) {
18.      System.out.println("Not here.");
19.  }
```

The difference between these two while loops is that the compiler knows on line 17 that line 18 will never execute. The compiler cannot make the same assumption about the while loop on line 9 because x is a variable. Line 17 generates the following compiler error:

```
WhileLoop.java:17: unreachable statement
while(false) {
          ^
```

While we are on the subject, an if-then statement *can* contain unreachable code. For example, the following statements compile fine:

```
21.  if(false) {
22.      System.out.println("Unreachable");
23.  }
```

Java allows you to write unreachable if statements to simplify debugging code. I could easily change the statement on line 21 to if(true) to test something and then change it back to if(false) in production. Better yet, I could use a static final boolean that could be defined in one place and used anywhere in my program.

You can write infinite while loops and while loops that never execute.

Next we discuss do statements, which are similar to while loops except the body of a do-while loop is guaranteed to execute at least one time.

The *do* Statement

The exam objectives state that you should be able to "develop code that implements all forms of loops and iterators, including do." A *do statement*, also referred to as a do-while loop, is a repetition control structure that is useful for repeating a block of code an indeterminate number of times, but at least once. A do-while loop is declared using the do keyword. Figure 3.6 shows the syntax of a do statement.

FIGURE 3.6   The syntax of a do statement

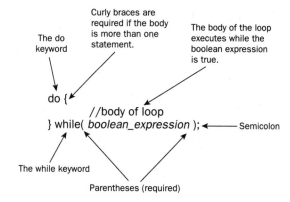

The following rules apply to a do statement:

- The body of the loop executes once before the boolean expression is tested.
- The value in parentheses must evaluate to a boolean expression, either true or false.
- If the boolean expression is true, the body of the loop executes again, and then the boolean is checked again.
- If the boolean expression is false, the loop does not execute again and control jumps to the next statement following the end of the loop.
- Just like a while loop, the body of the do loop executes until the boolean expression is false.
- Don't forget the semicolon after the boolean expression — it's easy to miss!

The following simple example prints out the numbers 1 to 10:

```
3.  int y = 1;
4.  do {
5.    System.out.print(y++ + " ");
6.  }while(y <= 10);
```

The output is

1 2 3 4 5 6 7 8 9 10

You cannot write a do-while loop whose body never executes because the body executes before the boolean expression is tested. For example, try to determine the output of the following example:

```
8.   char c = 'a';
9.   do {
10.      System.out.println(c++);
11.  }while(false);
12.  System.out.println(c);
```

An 'a' is printed on line 10, and then the boolean expression on line 11 is tested. Because it is false, the loop terminates. Line 12 prints out a 'b', so the output is

a

b

In the section on the while statement, I wrote a program that simulated the rolling of two dice until an 11 is rolled. That example is actually better suited for a do-while loop because we have to roll the dice at least once. The same loop rewritten using a do statement follows:

```
7.   int one = 0, two = 0;
8.   System.out.print("You rolled a ");
9.   do {
10.      one = rollDice();
11.      two = rollDice();
12.      System.out.print(one + two + " ");
13.  }while(one + two != 11);
```

The two dice are rolled first, and then we check to see if an 11 was rolled. If not, the dice are rolled again and again until they add up to 11. The output looks something like the following:

You rolled a 7 2 8 5 8 7 5 9 10 10 9 7 8 8 5 11

The output is different each time you run the program because of the use of random numbers, but the dice are always rolled at least once.

Scope of do Variables

A variable declared within the block of a do statement only has scope within that block. Be aware that the boolean expression of a do statement is outside the block, so the following code does not compile:

```
17. do {
18.     int one = rollDice();
19.     int two = rollDice();
20.     System.out.println("You rolled a " + (one + two));
21. }while(one + two != 11);
```

The variables one and two are out of scope on line 21. For this loop to work, one and two need to be declared outside of the do statement.

Now that we have discussed the various looping control structures in Java, I want to discuss two important keywords that affect the flow of control of loops: break and continue. Let's start with a discussion of the break statement.

The *break* Statement

The exam objectives state that you should be able to "develop code that implements all forms of loops and iterators, including the use of break." A *break statement* transfers flow of control out of an enclosing statement. A break statement can appear within the following control structures:

- switch
- for
- while
- do

Figure 3.7 shows the syntax for a break statement within a while statement. (The syntax is similar for the other control structures.)

FIGURE 3.7   The syntax of a break statement.

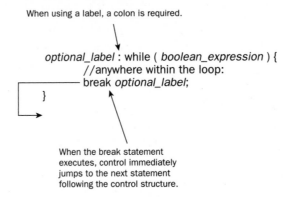

When using a label, a colon is required.

optional_label : while (*boolean_expression*) {
    //anywhere within the loop:
    break *optional_label*;
}

When the break statement
executes, control immediately
jumps to the next statement
following the control structure.

We saw an example of using an unlabeled `break` in the earlier section on `switch` statements. A break statement within one of the repetition control structures causes the loop to immediately complete. For example, see if you can determine the effect of the `break` in this loop:

```
3.  for(int k = 1; k < 10; k++) {
4.      System.out.print(k + " ");
5.      if(k % 3 == 0)
6.          break;
7.  }
```

If the loop control variable k is divisible by 3 on line 5, then the break executes on line 6 and flow of control jumps down to the next statement after line 7. The output of this loop is

1 2 3

Let's look at a more complex example. The following `Vacation` class uses an enhanced `for` loop to iterate over an enum named `Days`. Examine the code and see if you can determine the output of running `main`:

```
1.  public class Vacation {
2.      public enum Days {
3.          SUNDAY, MONDAY, TUESDAY, WEDNESDAY,
4.          THURSDAY, FRIDAY, SATURDAY
5.      }
6.
7.      public void workUntil(Days dayOff) {
8.          for(Days day : Days.values()) {
9.              if(day != dayOff) {
```

```
10.                    System.out.println("Working on " + day);
11.            } else {
12.                break;
13.            }
14.        }
15.    }
16.
17.    public static void main(String [] args) {
18.        Vacation v = new Vacation();
19.        v.workUntil(Days.THURSDAY);
20.    }
21.}
```

The enhanced for loop on line 8 iterates through the values of the enum and displays a message on line 10 if the dayOff argument doesn't match the current day. Once line 9 is false, the break occurs on line 12 and the loop terminates. The number of times this loop iterates varies depending on the value of dayOff. The main method invokes workUntil with Days.THURSDAY as the argument, so the output of main is

```
Working on SUNDAY
Working on MONDAY
Working on TUESDAY
Working on WEDNESDAY
```

A break statement can contain a label denoting which control structure to break out of. An unlabeled break statement terminates the immediately enclosing control structure. If you need to break out of an outer loop or switch, you need to use a *labeled break*.

A label is a prefix that appears before a statement and is followed by a colon:

label_name : statement

A label can be any valid identifier, as long as it is does not hide a label being used by an enclosing statement. The following while loop contains a label named myloop and a break statement that refers to the myloop label. See if you can determine the output:

```
4.  int count = 1;
5.  int sum = 0;
6.  myloop : while(count <= 100) {
7.    sum += count++;
8.    if(sum > 10) {
9.        break myloop;
10.   }
11.}
12.System.out.println("sum = " + sum);
13.System.out.println("count = " + count);
```

Here is the sequence of events for this `while` loop:

1. `count` is 1 and `sum` is 0, so the first time through the loop `sum` is 0 + 1 = 1 and `count` gets incremented to 2.

2. Line 8 is `false`, the body of the loop is complete, and control jumps back up to the `boolean` expression on line 6.

3. The loop executes again, `sum` is now 1 + 2 = 3, and `count` is now 3, so the loop executes again.

4. `sum` is 3 + 3 = 6, `count` is 4, and the loop executes again.

5. `sum` is 6 + 4 = 10, `count` is 5, and the loop executes again.

6. `sum` is 10 + 5 = 15, `count` is 6, and line 8 is finally `true`.

7. Line 9 executes, causing `myloop` to terminate and control jumps to line 12.

Therefore, the output of this code is

```
sum = 15
count = 6
```

Using Labels

Note that the `myloop` label is not required in the previous example, but you can still use a label even when it is unnecessary. You might use a label for clarification if a loop is long and it is unclear what is being affected by a break statement. You might also use a label to ensure that modifications to the code later do not affect your use of the break statement.

There are also situations where a label is required, as we will see in the next example.

The `myloop` label is not needed in the previous example, but there are situations where a label is necessary (especially in nested loops) to obtain the desired behavior of a break. To demonstrate this type of situation, let's start with a nested loop that does not use labels. See if you can determine the behavior of the following loops:

```
15. int x = 1;
16. while(x <= 10) {
17.     System.out.print(x++ + " ");
18.     for(int y = 10; y >= 1; y--) {
19.         System.out.print(y + " ");
20.         if(y == 8)
21.             break;
22.     }
23. }
```

The break on line 21 refers to its enclosing loop, which is the for loop on line 18. The while loop executes 10 times, and for each value of x the for loop executes three times (when y is 10, 9, and 8). The output is

1 10 9 8 2 10 9 8 3 10 9 8 4 10 9 8 5 10 9 8 6 10 9 8 7 10 9 8 8 10 9
 8 9 10 9 8 10 10 9 8

If we want the outer while loop to break on line 21 instead of the inner for loop, we need to use a label as shown here:

```
25. int x = 1, y = 10;
26. loopx : while(x <= 10) {
27.    System.out.print(x++ + " ");
28.    for( ; y >= 1; y--) {
29.        System.out.print(y + " ");
30.        if(y == 8)
31.            break loopx;
32.    }
33. }
```

The break statement on line 31 refers to the while loop on line 26. The while loop terminates during its first iteration when y becomes 8, so the output of this code is

1 10 9 8

You can also use labels with the continue keyword, which we discuss next.

The *continue* Statement

The exam objectives state that you should be able to "develop code that implements all forms of loops and iterators, including the use of continue." A *continue statement* within a repetition control structure transfers flow of control to the loop-continuation point of the loop. The control structures that can contain a continue statement together with their corresponding continuation point follow:

- for: Control transfers to the update expression of the for statement.
- while: Control transfers to the boolean expression.
- do: Control transfers to the boolean expression.

Figure 3.8 shows the syntax for the continue statement within a for loop.

FIGURE 3.8   The syntax of the `continue` statement

When using a label, a colon is required.

```
optional_label : for ( initialization; booleanexpression; update_statement ) {
        //anywhere within the loop:
        continue optional_label;
}
```

When the continue statement
executes, control immediately
jumps to the *update_statement.*

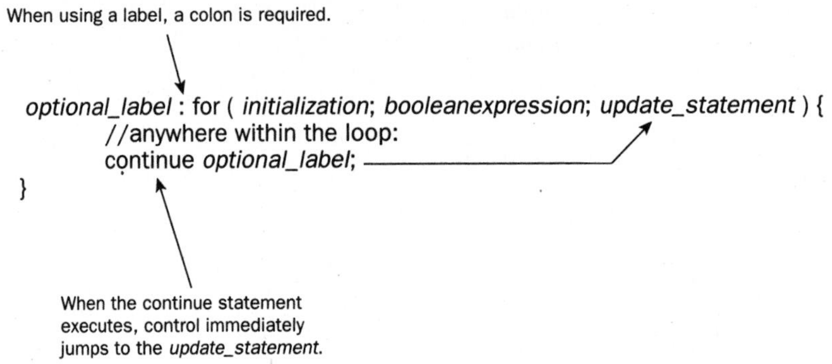

Here's a simple `for` loop with an unlabeled `continue` statement. See if you can determine its output:

```
3. for(char c = 'm'; c <= 'p'; c++) {
4.    if(c == 'n') {
5.        continue;
6.    }
7.    System.out.print(c);
8. }
```

The sequence of events for this loop follows:

1. `c` is initialized to `'m'`, which is less than `'p'`, so the loop body executes.

2. Line 4 is `false` and `'m'` displays on line 7. The loop body is done, so control jumps to the update statement and `c` is incremented to `'n'`.

3. The loop body executes again, but this time line 4 is `true` so the `continue` executes on line 5, causing control to jump immediately to the update statement c++. No output displays because line 7 is skipped.

4. The loop body executes two more times with `c` equal to `'o'` and `c` equal to `'p'`.

    Therefore, the output is

mop

Let's look at an example with a nested loop. Study the following code and see if you can determine what the output is:

```
10. for(int a = 1; a <= 4; a++) {
11.    for(char x = 'a'; x <= 'c'; x++) {
12.        if(a == 2 || x == 'b')
13.            continue;
14.        System.out.print(" " + a + x);
15.    }
16. }
```

The previous nested for loop is obviously a contrived example, but it is the type of example you will find on the exam. My advice is to write down the values of each variable through each iteration of the loop. Take your time and step through the loops carefully.

Here is a breakdown of each iteration through the loop:

1. a equals 1 the first time through the outer loop, and x equals 'a' the first time through the inner loop, so 'la' is output on line 14. Then x equals 'b', so the continue executes and control jumps to the x++ update statement on line 11. x equals 'c' and 'lc' displays.

2. a equals 2 the second time through the outer loop. The inner loop executes three times, but line 12 is true on each iteration so the continue executes each time and the print statement is skipped. No output occurs when a equals 2.

3. a equals 3 on the next iteration, which is similar to the case when a was 1. The continue executes when x is 'b', so the output is '3a' and '3c'.

4. Similarly, when a equals 4 the output is '4a' and '4c'.

Therefore, the output of the code is

```
1a 1c 3a 3c 4a 4c
```

As with break statements, a continue statement can declare a label denoting the loop to continue on. The following nested loops demonstrate a labeled continue statement. Examine the code and see if you can determine its output:

```
19. char row = 'A';
20. rowlabel : while(row <= 'D') {
21.     System.out.print(row++);
22.     for(int i = 1; i <= 5; i++) {
23.         if(i%2 == 0)
24.             continue;
25.         if(i%3 == 0) {
26.             System.out.println();
27.             continue rowlabel;
28.         }
29.         System.out.print(i);
30.     }
31. }
```

Here is a breakdown of what this code does:

1. The first time through the outer `while` loop on line 20, row equals `'A'` and it is printed on line 21 and incremented to `'B'`. `i` equals 1 during the first iteration of the inner loop. Line 23 and 25 are false, so line 29 executes and `'1'` is printed.

2. When `i` equals 2, line 23 is `true` and the `continue` statement on line 24 executes. Because it is an unlabeled `continue`, it applies to the `for` loop, so control jumps to the update statement `i++` and `i` now equals 3.

3. When `i` equals 3, line 25 is true, a newline is printed and the `continue` statement on line 27 executes. This `continue` refers to the `while` loop, so control jumps to the boolean expression on line 20.

4. `row` equals `'B'` the second time through the outer loop and is printed on line 21. The inner loop behaves the same, printing only `'1'` because of the `continue` statements.

5. When `row` equals `'C'` and `row` equals `'D'`, the result is similar.

Therefore, the output of this code is

```
A1
B1
C1
D1
```

Line 24 of this example could have been clearer if we had used a label on the `for` loop on line 22, but I wanted to demonstrate that it wasn't required.

We now turn our attention to two other aspects of Java that affect flow control: assertions and exceptions.

Overview of Assertions

The exam objectives state that you should be able to "develop code that makes use of assertions, and distinguish appropriate from inappropriate uses of assertions." This section addresses these objectives. An *assertion* in Java is a `boolean` expression placed at particular points in your code where you think something should always be true. (The definition of the word "assert" is to insist that something is true and to affirm your claim with certainty.) For example, I am certain that in the following code, the value of x is greater than 0:

```
int a = 3, b = 5;
int x = a * b;
assert x > 0;
```

An assertion allows me to check for bugs in my code that might otherwise go unnoticed. You can place assertions throughout your code, turn them on for testing and debugging purposes, and then turn them off when your program is in production.

Why assert something if you are sure it is true? Well, in the world of computer programming, asserting that something is true and verifying it at runtime are two different things. During the coding phase, I might be certain that a value is positive, but it would be nice to verify at runtime that the value actually is positive, and the assertion allows me to do that.

In the next section, we discuss the details of writing and using assertions in Java and how they affect the flow of control of your application.

The *assert* Statement

An *assert statement* inserts an assertion at a particular point in your code. The syntax for an assert statement has two forms:

```
assert boolean_expression;
assert boolean_expression : error_message;
```

The boolean expression must evaluate to true or false. The optional error message is a String used as the message for the AssertionError that is thrown. The two possible outcomes of an assert statement are

- If the boolean expression is true, then our assertion has been validated and nothing happens. The program continues to execute in its normal manner.

- If the boolean expression is false, then our assertion was invalid and a java.lang .AssertionError is thrown, causing our program to terminate at this line of code.

The AssertionError is typically not handled by your code, so your program terminates and the stack trace displays at the standard output. For example, the following assertion fails:

```
1. public class Asserts {
2.    public static void main(String [] args) {
3.        int x = 10;
4.        assert x < 0;
5.        System.out.println("x = " + x);
6.    }
7. }
```

Because the assert statement on line 4 is false, line 5 does not execute. Assuming assertions are enabled, the program terminates at line 4 and the following stack trace displays:

```
Exception in thread "main" java.lang.AssertionError
        at Asserts.main(Asserts.java:4)
```

The next section discusses how to enable assertions in your Java programs.

Enabling Assertions

By default, `assert` statements are ignored by the JVM at runtime. To enable assertions, use the `-enableassertions` flag on the command line:

```
java -enableassertions Rectangle
```

You can also use the shortcut `-ea` flag:

```
java -ea Rectangle
```

Using the `-enableassertions` flag without any arguments enables assertions in all classes except system classes. You can also enable assertions for a specific class or package. For example, the following command enables assertions only for classes in the `com.sybex.demos` package and any subpackages:

```
java -ea:com.sybex.demos... my.programs.Main
```

If the classes are in the unnamed packaged, then simply use the three dots:

```
java -ea:... Rectangle
```

You can also enable assertions for a specific class:

```
java -ea:com.sybex.demos.TestColors my.programs.Main
```

You can disable assertions using the `-disableassertions` (or `-da`) for a specific class or package that was previously enabled. For example, the following command enables assertions for the `com.sybex.demos` package, but disables assertions for the `TestColors` class:

```
java -ea:com.sybex.demos... -da:com.sybex.demos.TestColors my.programs.Main
```

Enabling assertions is an important aspect of using them, because if assertions are not enabled, assert statements are ignored at runtime. Assertions were added to the Java language in the J2SE 1.4 release, as was the new assert keyword. This was a fairly major addition to the Java language, and you can expect at least one question on the syntax and flow of control of an assertion, as well as at least one question on how to enable assertions at runtime. Keep an eye out for a question that contains an assert statement but that is not executed with assertions enabled; the assert statement is ignored in that situation.

Using Assertions

We use assertions for many reasons, including the following:

Internal invariants   You assert that a value is within a certain constraint. `assert x < 0` is an example of an internal invariant.

Class invariants   You assert the validity of an object's state. Class invariants are typically private methods within the class that return a `boolean`. The upcoming `Rectangle` class demonstrates a class invariant.

Control flow invariants   You assert that a line of code you assume is unreachable is never reached. The upcoming `TestColors` class demonstrates a control flow invariant.

Preconditions   You assert that certain conditions are met before a method is invoked.

Post conditions   You assert that certain conditions are met after a method executes successfully.

The following example demonstrates a control flow invariant. Suppose we have the following enum declaration:

```
1. public enum Colors {
2.     RED, GREEN, BLUE
3. }
```

The following `TestColors` class contains a `switch` statement that switches on a `Colors` object. Because there are only three possible outcomes, the `default` statement on line 11 should never execute:

```
1.  public class TestColors {
2.    public static void testColor(Colors c) {
3.        switch(c) {
4.            case RED :
5.            case GREEN :
6.                System.out.println("Red or green");
7.                break;
8.            case BLUE :
9.                System.out.println("Blue");
10.               break;
11.           default :
12.               assert false : "Invalid color";
13.        }
14.    }
15. }
```

Because the value of c on line 2 can only be RED, GREEN, or BLUE and the switch statement has a case for all three of these outcomes, you can assert that line 12 is not reachable. This example is typical of when to use an assertion. I insist with all certainty that line 12 will not execute. Notice that if it does, an AssertionError is thrown because the boolean is false.

The only way this assertion would fail is if somehow the enum is modified. Suppose you are working on a project that uses the Colors enum, and during the development phase it is discovered that yellow needs to be added to the list of colors. The assertion can help uncover the ripple effect of such a change. Suppose the new version of Colors looks like this:

```
1. public enum Colors {
2.     RED, GREEN, BLUE, YELLOW
3. }
```

See if you can determine the output of the following main method added to the TestColors class:

```
public static void main(String [] args) {
    Colors c = Colors.YELLOW;
    testColor(c);
}
```

Because YELLOW is a new color and not one of the cases, the default block executes and the assert fails. (It has to fail because it uses false for the boolean expression.) Assuming assertions are enabled, an AssertionError is thrown and the following stack trace displays:

```
Exception in thread "main" java.lang.AssertionError: Invalid color
        at TestColors.testColor(TestColors.java:12)
        at TestColors.main(TestColors.java:18)
```

A control flow assertion is a common use of assert statements. When possible, place an assert statement at any location in your code that you assume will not be reached.

Assertions Should Not Alter Outcomes

Because assertions can and probably will be turned off in a production environment, your assertions should not contain any business logic that affects the outcome of your code. For example, the following assertion is not a good design because it alters the value of a variable:

```
int x = 10;
assert ++x > 10;   //Not a good design!
```

When assertions are turned on, x is incremented to 11, but when assertions are turned off, the value of x is 10. Therefore, the outcome of the code will be different, and assert statements should have no effect on your application if they are turned off, so this is not a good use of assertions.

The following example demonstrates a class invariant. A Rectangle object is not considered valid if either its width or height is negative. Examine the following Rectangle class, and assuming assertions are turned on, determine the output of running the main method:

```
1.  public class Rectangle {
2.     private int width, height;
3.
4.     public Rectangle(int width, int height) {
5.         this.width = width;
6.         this.height = height;
7.     }
8.
9.     public int getArea() {
10.        assert isValid() : "Not a valid Rectangle";
11.        return width * height;
12.     }
13.
14.     private boolean isValid() {
15.        return (width >= 0 && height >= 0);
16.     }
17.
18.     public static void main(String [] args) {
19.        Rectangle one = new Rectangle(5,12);
20.        Rectangle two = new Rectangle(-4,10);
21.        System.out.println("Area one = " + one.getArea());
22.        System.out.println("Area two = " + two.getArea());
23.     }
24. }
```

The isValid method is an example of a class invariant. It is a private method that tests the state of the object. Line 10 invokes isValid in an assertion statement before computing the area. Within main, Rectangle one is valid and its area is output. Rectangle two has a negative width so the assertion fails on line 10. The output is shown here:

```
Area one = 60
Exception in thread "main" java.lang.AssertionError: Not a valid Rectangle
        at Rectangle.getArea(Rectangle.java:10)
        at Rectangle.main(Rectangle.java:22)
```

Validating Method Parameters

Do not use assertions to check for valid arguments passed in to a method. Use an IllegalArgumentException instead. For example, the constructor of Rectangle should throw an IllegalArgumentException when either the width or height is negative:

```java
public Rectangle(int width, int height) {
    if(width < 0 || height < 0) {
        throw new IllegalArgumentException();
    }
    this.width = width;
    this.height = height;
}
```

This constructor greatly improves the reliability of the Rectangle class because there is no way to change the field's width and height except in the constructor. Remember, assertions are for situations where you are certain of something and you just want to verify it. You cannot be certain that someone instantiating a Rectangle will pass in positive values. However, with the Rectangle constructor defined here, I should be able to assert with a great deal of certainty that invoking isValid on any Rectangle object will return true.

Assertions are used for debugging purposes, allowing you to verify that something you think is true during the coding phase is actually true at runtime. The next section covers exceptions, which affect the flow of control of your application similar to failed assertions. Unlike assertions, exceptions are situations that arise at runtime that cannot be predicted during the coding phase.

Overview of Exceptions

This section addresses the exam objectives that state you should be able to "develop code that makes use of exception handling clauses (try, catch, finally), and declares methods and overriding methods that throw exceptions," as well as "recognize the effect of an exception arising at a specified point in a code fragment." An *exception* is an event that occurs during the execution of a program that disrupts the normal flow of control. In Java, an exception is an object that a method "throws" down the method call stack by handing it to the JVM and letting the JVM search for a handler. As the exception object travels down the methods on the call stack, any method along the way has the opportunity to catch the exception. Once caught, the method can obtain information about the problem and attempt to fix it, log the error in a file, or simply ignore the exception altogether. A caught exception can also be rethrown, or a method can throw a different type of exception.

I want to start with a simple example to demonstrate how an exception affects the flow of control of an application. The following ExceptionDemo class generates an ArithmeticException on line 15 when 5 is divided by 0. Study the code and see if you can determine its output.

```
1.   public class ExceptionDemo {
2.      public void method1() {
3.          System.out.println("Inside method1");
4.          method2();
5.      }
6.
7.      public void method2() {
8.          System.out.println("Inside method2");
9.          method3();
10.     }
11.
12.     public void method3() {
13.         System.out.println("Inside method3");
14.         int x = 5, y = 0;
15.         int z = x/y;     //throws an ArithmeticException
16.         System.out.println("z = " + z);
17.     }
18.
19.     public static void main(String [] args) {
20.         System.out.println("Inside main");
21.         new ExceptionDemo().method1();
22.         System.out.println("End of main");
23.     }
24.}
```

Here is the sequence of events that occurs in this program:

1. Running the program puts the main method on the bottom of the call stack. (Figure 3.7 shows the method call stack.) Inside main displays on line 19 and method1 is invoked on a new ExceptionDemo object.

2. method1 is pushed on the call stack. Inside method1 displays on line 3 and method2 is called.

3. method2 is pushed on the call stack. Inside method2 displays on line 8 and method3 is called.

4. method3 is pushed on the call stack. Inside method3 displays, and then line 15 causes an ArithmeticException to be thrown.

5. Because `method3` does not catch the exception, it is immediately popped off the call stack. Notice that line 16 does not execute.

6. Because `method2` does not catch the exception, it also pops off the call stack. The same happens with `method1` and `main`.

7. Because the exception was not caught, the program terminates and the JVM dumps the following stack trace:

```
Inside main
Inside method1
Inside method2
Inside method3
Exception in thread "main" java.lang.ArithmeticException: / by zero
        at ExceptionDemo.method3(ExceptionDemo.java:15)
        at ExceptionDemo.method2(ExceptionDemo.java:9)
        at ExceptionDemo.method1(ExceptionDemo.java:4)
        at ExceptionDemo.main(ExceptionDemo.java:21)
```

Figure 3.9 shows the exception being thrown down the method call stack of `ExceptionDemo`.

FIGURE 3.9   The `ArithmeticException` is thrown down the call stack.

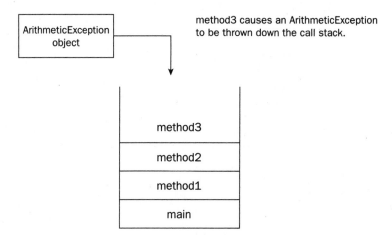

Notice that an unhandled exception terminates your program, which obviously is not good if you don't want your program terminating every time an exception occurs.

We now look at how to catch an exception so it does not terminate the application using a `try` statement.

The *try* Statement

A *try statement* is a block of code that contains one or more statements that may throw an exception. A `try` statement can be followed by one or more *catch clauses*, also called exception handlers. Figure 3.10 shows the syntax of a try statement.

FIGURE 3.10   The syntax of a try statement

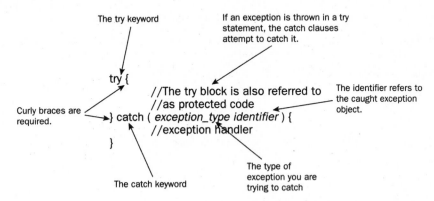

A `try` statement can declare any number of `catch` clauses. A `catch` clause must have exactly one parameter: the data type of the exception trying to be caught. If an exception is thrown within a `try` block, the JVM searches for a handler by checking the exception types of its `catch` clauses in the order they appear. If the exception type of a `catch` clause matches the data type of the thrown exception, flow of control jumps to that `catch` block and the catch's identifier receives a copy of the reference to the exception object (similar to an argument copied into a method parameter).

For example, the following `try` statement catches the `ArithmeticException` thrown in `method3` of the `ExceptionDemo` class from the previous section. See if you can determine the output of running `main` in `ExceptionDemo` if `method3` is modified as follows:

```
12. public void method3() {
13.     System.out.println("Inside method3");
14.     int x = 5, y = 0;
15.     try {
16.         int z = x/y;    //throws an ArithmeticException
17.         System.out.println("z = " + z);
18.     }catch(ArithmeticException e) {
19.         System.out.println("Something went wrong: "
20.                             + e.getMessage());
21.     }
23. }
```

Here is the sequence of events that occurs when method3 executes:

1. "Inside method3" displays and x and y are initialized.

2. Flow of control enters the try block on line 15, and line 16 causes an ArithmeticException to be thrown.

3. The JVM searches the associated catch clauses for one that catches an ArithmeticException, which line 18 does. Flow of control jumps to line 18. (Line 17 does not execute.)

4. The catch block executes, displaying an error message.

5. Because the exception was handled, execution resumes as normal. method3 finishes successfully and is popped off the method call stack. The remaining methods complete successfully, and the output is

```
Inside main
Inside method1
Inside method2
Inside method3
Something went wrong: / by zero
End of main
```

Because the exception was handled, the program did not terminate prematurely, as shown by the display of End of main.

The Throwable Class

The java.lang.Throwable class is the parent class of all objects that can be thrown (either by the JVM or by using the throw keyword). Only objects of type Throwable or subclasses of Throwable can appear in a catch clause.

When you catch an exception, a common task is to display the stack trace or log it to a file. The following methods defined in Throwable provide information about the stack trace and the exception thrown:

public void printStackTrace()

This method prints the stack trace to System.err.

public void printStackTrace(PrintStream s)

This method prints the stack trace to the specified PrintStream.

public void printStackTrace(PrintWriter s)

This method prints the stack trace to the specified PrintWriter.

public String getMessage()

This method returns the detail message of the Throwable object. The message is set in the Throwable constructor.

public String toString()

This method returns a short description of the Throwable object that includes the type of exception and its message.

You can find examples of printing the stack trace throughout this section. Here is a simple example to demonstrate the difference between getMessage and toString:

```
try {
    throw new NullPointerException("Be careful!");
}catch(NullPointerException e) {
    System.out.println("getMessage: " + e.getMessage());
    System.out.println("toString: " + e.toString());
}
```

The output of this code is

```
getMessage: Be careful!
toString: java.lang.NullPointerException: Be careful!
```

Multiple *catch* Clauses

Let's look at a more realistic example and one that contains multiple catch clauses. The following MyFileReader class opens a file for reading and reads in a single character. The FileReader constructor invoked on line 6 throws a FileNotFoundException if the specified file cannot be found. Study the code and see if you can determine the output when the file is not found on line 6.

```
1.  import java.io.*;
2.
3.  public class MyFileReader {
4.    public void readFromFile(String fileName) {
5.        try {
6.            FileReader fis = new FileReader(fileName);
7.            System.out.println(fileName + " was found");
```

```
8.              char data = (char) fis.read();
9.              System.out.println("Just read: " + data);
10.         } catch(FileNotFoundException e) {
11.             System.out.println("Oops - file not found: " +
12.                     e.getMessage());
13.         } catch(IOException e) {
14.             System.out.println("Something went wrong");
15.             e.printStackTrace();
16.         }
17.         System.out.println("End of readFromFile");
18.     }
19.
20.     public static void main(String [] args) {
21.         MyFileReader reader = new MyFileReader();
22.         reader.readFromFile("mydata.txt");
23.         System.out.println("End of main");
24.     }
25.}
```

Here is the flow of control of main when no file is found:

1. Line 21 instantiates a new MyFileReader object and its readFromFile method is invoked on line 22 with the filename mydata.txt.

2. The try block is entered on line 5.

3. The FileReader constructor invoked on line 6 throws a java.io .FileNotFoundException.

4. Flow of control jumps to the first catch block on line 10. The FileNotFoundException is caught and e refers to it. Line 11 displays a message.

5. The catch on line 13 is skipped because the exception has already been caught. Line 17 executes and the readFromFile method completes its execution.

6. Control jumps to line 23. End of main displays and the program finishes successfully.

    The output of running MyFileReader is

```
Oops - file not found: mydata.txt (The system cannot find the file specified)
End of readFromFile
End of main
```

The Order of catch **Clauses**

catch clauses are checked in the order they appear. If an exception is caught in a catch clause, any subsequent catch blocks are ignored. Watch for invalid try-catch statements that contain unreachable code and therefore do not compile. For example, do you see what is wrong with the following try-catch statement?

```
5.  try {
6.      FileReader fis = new FileReader(fileName);
7.      System.out.println(fileName + " was found");
8.      char data = (char) fis.read();
9.      System.out.println("Just read: " + data);
10. } catch(IOException e) {
11.     System.out.println("Something went wrong");
12.     e.printStackTrace();
13. } catch(FileNotFoundException e) {
14.     System.out.println("Oops - file not found: " +
15.                         e.getMessage());
16. }
```

FileNotFoundException is a child class of IOException. If a FileNotFoundException is thrown within this try block, it will be caught on line 10. Therefore, it is not possible for the catch block on line 13 to ever execute. This code does not compile and generates the following compiler error:

```
MyFileReader.java:13: exception java.io.FileNotFoundException has
 already been caught
        } catch(FileNotFoundException e) {
          ^
```

A catch clause of a try statement cannot catch an exception that is a child class of an earlier catch clause.

The Handle or Declare Rule

According to the exam objectives, you should know "that the exception may be a runtime exception, a checked exception, or an error." These different types of exceptions are important because of the Handle or Declare Rule, which this section discusses. Exceptions fit into three categories:

Runtime exceptions   An exception is referred to as a *runtime exception* if its data type is java.lang.RuntimeException or a subclass of RuntimeException.

Checked exceptions An exception is referred to as a *checked exception* if its data type is a child class of java.lang.Exception, but not a child class of RuntimeException.

Errors An exception is referred to as an *error* if its data type is a child class of java .lang.Error. An error is associated with problems that arise outside of your application, and you typically do not attempt to recover from errors.

Figure 3.11 shows the class hierarchy of the three types of exceptions along with some examples of errors, checked exceptions, and runtime exceptions. You can always determine what category an exception fits into by whether it subclasses RuntimeException, Exception, or Error.

FIGURE 3.11 The three categories of exceptions.

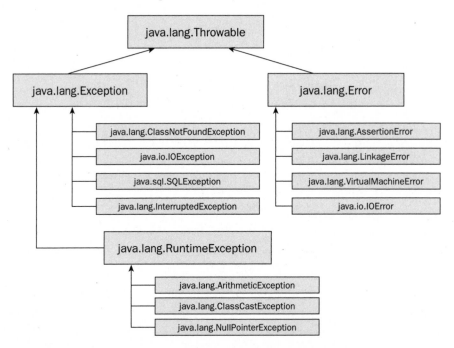

You might wonder why there is such a distinct categorizing of exceptions. The categories are important because the compiler enforces a rule known as the *Handle or Declare Rule* that only applies to checked exceptions. The Handle or Declare Rule states that if any statement might throw a checked exception, it must do one of the following:

- Handle the exception by enclosing the statement in a try block that provides a corresponding handler for the exception.

- The method that contains the statement must declare the checked exception in the throws clause of the method declaration.

In other words, checked exceptions cannot be ignored. You must write code to either catch and handle a checked exception, or declare that you are not catching the exception, which means it must be handled by some other method down the call stack. Either way, eventually a checked exception must be handled.

The throws Keyword

A method uses the throws keyword to declare that it might throw an exception. For example, the following method named readFromFile declares that it might throw a java.io.IOException:

```
public void readFromFile(String fileName) throws IOException {
    FileReader fis = new FileReader(fileName);
    System.out.println(fileName + " was found");
    char data = (char) fis.read();
    System.out.println("Just read: " + data);
    System.out.println("End of readFromFile");
}
```

Because IOException is a checked exception, any method that invokes readFromFile must either handle or declare the IOException.

Why Not Catch Errors or Runtime Exceptions?

Checked exceptions must be handled or declared, while errors and runtime exceptions can be ignored. This does not imply that you cannot try to catch an error or exception. You can try to catch any object of type Throwable, which includes errors and runtime exceptions.

However, catching an error is often pointless because recovering from an error is difficult and often impossible. On the other hand, you could catch a runtime exception and recover from the problem, but in general this is considered poor programming design. Believe it or not, the preferred technique for runtime exceptions is to let them crash your program, because, in general, runtime exceptions can be avoided with better code. For example, if a NullPointerException occurs at runtime, modify your code so that it tests the corresponding reference for null before trying to use it.

Be glad that errors and runtime exceptions do not need to handled or declared. They can occur in so many situations that if you had to handle or declare them, you would quickly become irritated with Java!

To demonstrate the Handle or Declare Rule, let's look at an example similar to the ExceptionDemo earlier in this section. (By the way, ExceptionDemo threw an ArithmeticException, which is a runtime exception, so the Handle or Declare Rule did not apply to its method3.) In the following CheckedDemo class, line 14 calls the static method Class.forName, which declares the checked exception ClassNotFoundException. Study the following code and see if it compiles:

```
1.   public class CheckedDemo {
2.     public void method1() {
3.         System.out.println("Inside method1");
4.         method2();
5.     }
6.
7.     public void method2() {
8.         System.out.println("Inside method2");
9.         method3();
10.    }
11.
12.    public void method3() {
13.        System.out.println("Inside method3");
14.        Class c = Class.forName("java.lang.String");
15.        System.out.println("class name: " + c.getName());
16.    }
17. }
```

Because line 14 invokes a method that declares a checked exception, the Handle or Declare Rule applies. Because the ClassNotFoundException is neither handled nor declared, *this code does not compile* and the following compiler error is generated:

```
CheckedDemo.java:14: unreported exception java.lang.ClassNotFoundException; must
be caught or declared to
be thrown
        Class c = Class.forName("java.lang.String");
                    ^
```

There are two options for method3: either include a try-catch statement around line 14 that catches a ClassNotFoundException, or declare the exception using the throws keyword. Let's have method3 declare the exception instead of handling it:

```
12.    public void method3() throws ClassNotFoundException {
13.        System.out.println("Inside method3");
14.        Class c = Class.forName("java.lang.String");
15.        System.out.println("class name: " + c.getName());
16.    }
```

Declaring the exception fixes the compiler error on line 14, but the CheckedDemo class still does not compile. We have simply moved the compiler error up to line 9:

```
CheckedDemo.java:9: unreported exception java.lang.ClassNotFoundException; must
be caught or declared to be thrown
        method3();
          ^
```

Because method3 now declares a checked exception, method2 needs to handle or declare the ClassNotFoundException. Notice how declaring a checked exception does not mean we can ignore that exception; it simply pushes the responsibility to the calling method. method2 now has two options: catch the ClassNotFoundException or declare it. Let's declare it again:

```
7.    public void method2() throws ClassNotFoundException {
8.        System.out.println("Inside method2");
9.        method3();
10.   }
```

Again, this fixes the compiler error on line 9, but the CheckedDemo class still does not compile. Now the error message is on line 4:

```
CheckedDemo.java:4: unreported exception java.lang.ClassNotFoundException; must
be caught or declared to be thrown
        method2();
          ^
```

method1 must either handle or declare the ClassNotFoundException. Let's handle it this time, which should take care of the compiler error. See if you can determine the output of the following version of CheckedDemo:

```
1.  public class CheckedDemo {
2.    public void method1() {
3.        System.out.println("Inside method1");
4.        try {
5.            method2();
6.        }catch(ClassNotFoundException e) {
7.            e.printStackTrace();
8.        }
9.    }
10.
11.   public void method2() throws ClassNotFoundException {
12.       System.out.println("Inside method2");
```

```
13.          method3();
14.      }
15.
16.      public void method3() throws ClassNotFoundException {
17.          System.out.println("Inside method3");
18.          Class c = Class.forName("java.lang.String");
19.          System.out.println("class name: " + c.getName());
20.      }
21.
22.      public static void main(String [] args) {
23.          System.out.println("Inside main");
24.          new CheckedDemo().method1();
25.          System.out.println("End of main");
26.      }
27.}
```

I should point out that although the Class.forName method might throw a ClassNotFoundException, it is not thrown in this example on line 18 because the String class is found by the JVM's class loader. The output of running this program is

```
Inside main
Inside method1
Inside method2
Inside method3
class name: java.lang.String
End of main
```

Suppose we modify line 18 so that it attempts to load a class that is not found. A simple typo can cause the exception to be thrown. Try and determine the output of CheckedDemo if line 18 is the following:

```
18. Class c = Class.forName("java.lang.string");
```

Here is the sequence of events that occurs in this case:

1. main is called, which invokes method1.

2. method1 invokes method2.

3. method2 invokes method3.

4. Line 18 throws a ClassNotFoundException, which is not caught in method3. method3 is immediately popped off the call stack and the exception is thrown to method2.

5. method2 does not catch the exception, so it is immediately popped off the call stack and the exception is thrown to method1.

6. method1 catches the exception on line 6. The catch block executes and the stack trace is printed. Flow of control now continues normally for the remainder of this program.

7. method1 finishes executing normally, so control jumps back to main and End of main displays. The program successfully runs to completion.

Here is the output of CheckedDemo when a ClassNotFoundException occurs:

```
Inside main
Inside method1
Inside method2
Inside method3
java.lang.ClassNotFoundException: java.lang.string
        at java.net.URLClassLoader$1.run(URLClassLoader.java:200)
        at java.security.AccessController.doPrivileged(Native Method)
        at java.net.URLClassLoader.findClass(URLClassLoader.java:188)
        at java.lang.ClassLoader.loadClass(ClassLoader.java:306)
        at sun.misc.Launcher$AppClassLoader.loadClass(Launcher.java:276)
        at java.lang.ClassLoader.loadClass(ClassLoader.java:251)
        at java.lang.ClassLoader.loadClassInternal(ClassLoader.java:319)
        at java.lang.Class.forName0(Native Method)
        at java.lang.Class.forName(Class.java:169)
        at CheckedDemo.method3(CheckedDemo.java:18)
        at CheckedDemo.method2(CheckedDemo.java:13)
        at CheckedDemo.method1(CheckedDemo.java:5)
        at CheckedDemo.main(CheckedDemo.java:24)
End of main
```

Exceptions on the Exam

Watch for questions on the exam that specifically test your knowledge of the Handle or Declare Rule. Remember that declaring a checked exception does not magically take care of the exception. It simply pushes the responsibility of handling that exception to some other method, which means somewhere down the call stack a try statement is needed to handle the exception and the compiler enforces this rule.

You should also know which common exceptions are runtime or checked exceptions. For example, you should know that ArithmeticException and NullPointerException are runtime exceptions, while IOException, ClassNotFoundException, and InterruptedException are checked exceptions.

Now that we have discussed the details of the `try` statement, we can discuss the `finally` keyword, which we use to create an optional block of code at the end of a `try` statement that always executes after the code in the `try` block.

The *finally* Block

A `try` statement can be followed by a *finally block*. A `finally` block is a unique feature of Java: it executes after a `try` statement, regardless of whether an exception occurs within the `try` block. A `finally` block can only appear after a `try` statement and must appear at the end of the `catch` clauses. Figure 3.12 shows the syntax for a `finally` block.

FIGURE 3.12 The syntax of a `finally` block

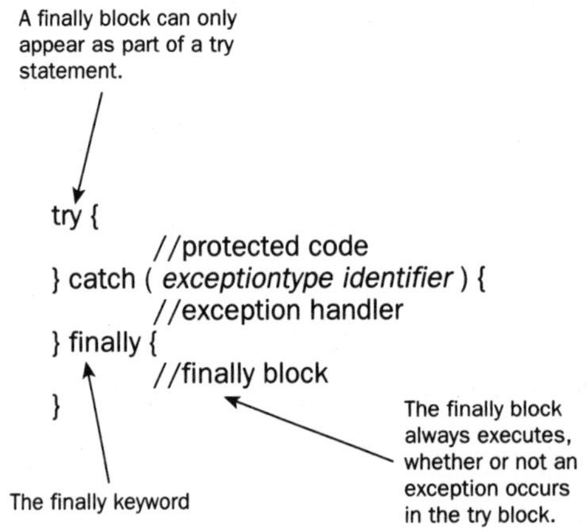

A `finally` block allows you to perform any cleanup tasks that need to execute regardless of what happens during the `try` block. For example, the following code closes a file after attempting to read from it, whether or not the read is successful. Study the code carefully and see if you can determine the output when no exception occurs:

```
1.  import java.io.*;
2.
3.  public class FinallyDemo {
4.      public void readFromFile(String fileName) {
5.          System.out.println("Inside readFromFile");
6.          FileReader fis = null;
7.          try {
8.              fis = new FileReader(fileName);
9.              char data = (char) fis.read();
10.             System.out.println("Just read: " + data);
```

```
11.            }catch(IOException e) {
12.                System.out.println("Handler for IOException");
13.                System.out.println(e.getMessage());
14.                return;
15.            }finally {
16.                System.out.println("Inside finally block");
17.                try {
18.                    if(fis != null) {
19.                        fis.close();
20.                    }
21.                }catch(IOException e) {}
22.            }
23.            System.out.println("End of readFromFile");
24.        }
25.
26.        public static void main(String [] args) {
27.            FinallyDemo reader = new FinallyDemo();
28.            reader.readFromFile("mydata.txt");
29.            System.out.println("End of main");
30.        }
31.    }
```

Here is the sequence of events when main executes:

1. A new FinallyDemo object is instantiated and its readFromFile is invoked on line 28.

2. Line 5 displays Inside readFromFile, then line 6 declares a FileReader reference named fis. Notice that the finally block uses the fis reference, so it must be declared outside the try block. This situation is common when writing try statements.

3. We are assuming the try block executes successfully, so line 10 displays the first character from the file mydata.txt.

4. Control jumps to the finally block on line 15. Inside finally block displays and the file is closed on line 19. Notice the close method declares an IOException, so our finally block contains another try statement, a common situation in Java.

5. Line 23 executes and readFromFile is popped off the method call stack.

6. Control returns to main and End of main displays.

When no exceptions occur, the output of the FinallyDemo program is

```
Inside readFromFile
Just read: H
Inside finally block
End of readFromFile
End of main
```

Suppose we change line 28 to the following statement:

```
28.  reader.readFromFile("mydat.txt");
```

Note that the filename is changed to mydat.txt. Assuming this file does not exist, a FileNotFoundException is thrown on line 8. Study the FinallyDemo program carefully and try to determine its output when a FileNotFoundException is thrown on line 8. This scenario is exactly the type of question that you will see on the certification exam, and here is the sequence of events that occurs:

1. Line 5 displays Inside readFromFile.
2. Line 8 throws a FileNotFoundException. Lines 9 and 10 do not execute.
3. The exception is caught on line 11. Lines 12 and 13 execute. Line 14 also executes, but the method does not immediately return.
4. Control jumps to line 15 and the finally block executes.
5. The return from line 14 now executes and the readFromFile method is popped off the method call stack. Notice that line 23 does not execute.
6. Control returns to main and line 28 executes.

Here is the output of the FinallyDemo program when a FileNotFoundException occurs:

```
Inside readFromFile
Handler for IOException
mydat.txt (The system cannot find the file specified)
Inside finally block
End of main
```

As you can see, a finally block is an interesting feature of Java. Typically, a return like the one on line 14 of the FinallyDemo causes a method to immediately get popped off the method call stack. However, because a finally block always executes, the return gets put on hold until the finally block finishes.

A try-finally Statement

A try statement can contain a finally block without any catch clauses, as the following class demonstrates. See if you can determine its output:

```java
public class TryFinally {

    public String go() {
        System.out.println("Inside go");
        String message = null;
        try {
```

```
            message.toUpperCase();
            System.out.println("End of try");
        }finally {
            System.out.println("Inside finally");
        }
        System.out.println("End of go");
        return message;
    }

    public static void main(String [] args) {
        System.out.println("Inside main");
        TryFinally test = new TryFinally();
        System.out.println(test.go());
        System.out.println("End of main");
    }
}
```

The statement message.toUpperCase() throws a NullPointerException. Here is the output of running the code:

```
Inside main
Inside go
Inside finally
Exception in thread "main" java.lang.NullPointerException
        at TryFinally.go(TryFinally.java:6)
        at TryFinally.main(TryFinally.java:18)
```

Even though an uncaught exception is thrown within the try block, the finally block still executes before the exception is actually thrown and go is popped off the method call stack.

There are situations where a finally block might not execute. For example, if an error is thrown and the JVM is no longer able to run properly, a finally block probably might not execute. Calling System.exit in a catch block terminates the JVM, which means the corresponding finally block cannot execute.

Now that we have discussed the details and syntax of handling and declaring exceptions, I want to go over some of the common types of exceptions and errors that arise in Java. The following section discusses the details of various exceptions and errors specifically listed in the certification exam objectives.

Java API Exceptions and Errors

The exam objectives state that you should be able to "recognize situations that will result in any of the following being thrown," and also "understand which of these are thrown by the virtual machine and recognize situations in which others should be thrown programmatically"

This section covers the details of each of the following Throwable types, all declared in the java.lang package:

ArrayIndexOutOfBoundsException   This exception is thrown by the JVM when your code uses an illegal index to access an array.

ClassCastException   This exception is thrown by the JVM when an attempt is made to cast an object reference to a subclass of which it is not an instance.

IllegalArgumentException   This exception is thrown programmatically to indicate that a method has been passed an illegal or inappropriate argument.

IllegalStateException   This exception is thrown programmatically when a method has been invoked while the program is in an inappropriate state.

NullPointerException   This exception is thrown by the JVM when an attempt is made to use a null reference where an object is required.

NumberFormatException   This exception is thrown programmatically when an attempt is made to convert a string to a numeric type, but the string does not have the appropriate format.

AssertionError   This exception is thrown by the JVM when an assert statement fails.

ExceptionInInitializerError   This exception is thrown by the JVM when an unexpected exception occurs in a static initializer.

StackOverflowError   This exception is thrown by the JVM when the method call stack overflows.

NoClassDefFoundError   This exception is thrown by the JVM or ClassLoader when a class needs to be loaded but no definition of the class can be found.

Note that you can programmatically throw any of these exceptions and errors, even if an exception is typically thrown by the JVM. For example, if your code is aware of a situation where an illegal array index is being used, you can instantiate a new ArrayIndexOutOfBoundsException object and throw it using the throw keyword. However, this is not something commonly done in Java.

The following section briefly discusses each of these types of exceptions and demonstrates situations where they might be thrown.

ArrayIndexOutOfBoundsException

Arrays have a fixed size in Java, and the JVM throws an `ArrayIndexOutOfBoundsException` when any attempt is made to access an array element outside of the bounds of the array. For example, the following statements compile but cause an exception at runtime. Do you see why?

```
3. int [] scores = {10, 21, 14, 35};
4. int total = 0;
5. for(int i = 0; i <= scores.length; i++) {
6.     total += scores[i];
7. }
8. System.out.println(total);
```

The problem is that the `for` loop executes five times with i incrementing from 0 to 4, but the array only contains 4 elements. When i equals 4, an `ArrayIndexOutOfBoundsException` occurs on line 6. Here is the output:

```
Exception in thread "main" java.lang.ArrayIndexOutOfBoundsException: 4
        at ApiExceptions.main(ApiExceptions.java:6)
```

As with most situations where this exception occurs, proper code can eliminate the exception from being thrown. With arrays, take advantage of the new `for-each` loop whenever possible to avoid accessing an illegal array element:

```
for(int score : scores ) {
    total += score;
}
```

Using the `length` Attribute Properly

A common mistake beginning Java programmers make is to write a for loop that steps off the end of the array:

```
for(int i = 0; i <= scores.length; i++)
```

The proper syntax is to use < instead of <= when using the `length` attribute of the array:

```
for(int i = 0; i < scores.length; i++)
```

This scenario makes a good exam question, so keep an eye out for loops that generate an `ArrayIndexOutOfBoundsException`.

ClassCastException

A ClassCastException is thrown by the JVM when an object is cast to a data type that the object is not an instance of. Note that the compiler often helps you avoid a ClassCastException because you cannot attempt to cast an object to an incompatible data type. For example, the following code does not compile:

```
Integer x = new Integer(10);
String y = (String) x;
```

The reference x is of type Integer and the compiler complains about x being inconvertible to a String. However, there are situations where the compiler is unable to determine whether or not a cast is convertible. For example, the following statements do compile:

```
Object x = new Integer(10);
String y = (String) x;
```

The difference here is that x is a reference of type Object, and an Object reference *can* be converted to a String reference. The code compiles, but at runtime you will have a problem because x is not a String. Here is the stack trace generated by the previous two lines of code:

```
Exception in thread "main" java.lang.ClassCastException: java.lang.Integer cannot
be cast to java.lang.String
        at ClassCastDemo.main(ClassCastDemo.java:6)
```

Avoiding a ClassCastException

You might wonder why you would ever cast a parent reference down to one of its child types, but this situation is actually quite common in the real world. A lot of the methods in the Java API return Object types that need to be cast to their appropriate child class type.

The instanceof operator is used in Java to avoid the ClassCastException, as demonstrated in the following code:

```
6.   Object x = new Integer(10);
7.   if(x instanceof String) {
8.       String y = (String) x;
9.   }
```

The cast on line 8 is avoided in this example because line 7 evaluates to false. We will see the instanceof operator again in Chapter 6, "OO Concepts."

IllegalArgumentException

An `IllegalArgumentException` is thrown programmatically if an argument passed into a method is not valid, where validity is based on the business logic of your application and the specific behavior of the method. For example, the following `HomeForSale` class declares a constructor with a parameter of type `double` that needs to be a percentage between 0 and 1. The constructor throws an `IllegalArgumentException` on line 7 when the argument is out of this range:

```
1.  public class HomeForSale {
2.      private String agent;
3.      private double commission;
4.
5.      public HomeForSale(String agent, double commission) {
6.          if(commission < 0.0 || commission > 1.0) {
7.              throw new IllegalArgumentException(
"commission must be between 0 and 1");
8.          }
9.          this.agent = agent;
10.         this.commission = commission;
11.     }
12. }
```

Be careful not to use an assertion in this situation. We may want the commission to be between 0 and 1, but we cannot assert this because the argument passed in can be any value. Throwing an `IllegalArgumentException` is a good way to communicate to the calling method that the data they provided is not valid.

IllegalStateException

An `IllegalStateException` is thrown programmatically when a method is invoked and the program is not in an appropriate state for that method to perform its task. This typically happens when a method is invoked out of sequence, or perhaps a method is only allowed to be invoked once and an attempt is made to invoke it again.

For example, suppose you develop an order processing system and an attempt is made to ship an order before the shipping address has been input. The `shipOrder` method could throw an `IllegalStateException`, as the following code demonstrates:

```
1.  public class CustomerOrder {
2.      private String address;
3.
4.      public void shipOrder() {
5.          if(address == null) {
6.              throw new IllegalStateException(
```

```
7.                       "address must be set first");
8.          }
9.          System.out.println("Shipping order...");
10.    }
11. }
```

Invoking shipOrder on a CustomerOrder object with a null address field results in the following exception:

```
Exception in thread "main" java.lang.IllegalStateException: address must be set
first
        at CustomerOrder.shipOrder(CustomerOrder.java:6)
        at CustomerOrder.main(CustomerOrder.java:12)
```

NullPointerException

A NullPointerException is thrown when a null reference is used in situations where an actual object is required. This exception is one that is thrown frequently by both the JVM and programmatically. For example, the JVM throws a NullPointerException in the following code:

```
3. Integer x = null;
4. System.out.println(x.intValue());
```

The reference x is null, so attempting to invoke any method on it results in a NullPointerException. The stack trace looks like:

```
Exception in thread "main" java.lang.NullPointerException
        at NullPointerDemo.main(NullPointerDemo.java:4)
```

Programmatically, you can throw a NullPointerException if you know a reference is null. For example, the following method throws a NullPointerException if the argument passed in is a null reference:

```
public void printMessage(String message) {
    if(message == null) {
        throw new NullPointerException("message cannot be null");
    }
    System.out.println(message);
}
```

NumberFormatException

A NumberFormatException is thrown when a string is parsed into a numeric value and the string does not have the appropriate format. The exception is thrown by the parsing and `valueOf` methods of all the wrapper classes in `java.lang`. For example, the following code generates a `NumberFormatException`:

```
3. String s = "hello";
4. int x = Integer.parseInt(s);
```

The string `"hello"` is clearly not an integer, so attempting to parse it into an `int` generates the following stack trace:

```
Exception in thread "main" java.lang.NumberFormatException: For input string:
"hello"
        at java.lang.NumberFormatException.forInputString(NumberFormatException.
java:48)
        at java.lang.Integer.parseInt(Integer.java:447)
        at java.lang.Integer.parseInt(Integer.java:497)
        at NumberFormatDemo.main(NumberFormatDemo.java:4)
```

AssertionError

An `AssertionError` is thrown to indicate an assertion has failed. You do not throw an `AssertionError` programmatically. The JVM throws one when assertions are enabled and the `boolean` expression of an `assert` statement is `false`.

ExceptionInInitializerError

An `ExceptionInInitializer` is thrown by the JVM when an unexpected exception occurs during a static initializer or the initializer of a static variable. Here is a simple example that demonstrates this exception:

```
1.  public class ExceptionInInitializerDemo {
2.      static {
3.          Integer x = null;
4.          x.intValue();
5.      }
6.
7.      public static void main(String [] args) {
8.          System.out.println("Inside main");
9.      }
10. }
```

A `NullPointerException` occurs on line 4, which causes an `ExceptionInInitializerError` to be thrown. Running this program generates the following stack trace:

```
Exception in thread "main" java.lang.ExceptionInInitializerError
Caused by: java.lang.NullPointerException
        at ExceptionInInitializerDemo.<clinit>(ExceptionInInitializerDemo.java:4)
```

As with most errors in Java, you cannot recover from an ExceptionInInitializerError because there is no way to catch it.

StackOverflowError

A StackOverflowError is thrown by the JVM when the method call stack overflows, typically due to method recursion that does not end. The following example causes a StackOverflowError due to its infinite recursion:

```
1.  public class StackOverflowDemo {
2.      private int x = 0;
3.
4.      public void go() {
5.          System.out.println(++x);
6.          go();
7.      }
8.      public static void main(String [] args) {
9.          new StackOverflowDemo().go();
10.     }
11. }
```

The go method invokes itself recursively on line 6, so eventually the method call stack will consume all of its allotted memory, causing a StackOverflowError. Running the previous program generates the following stack trace:

```
Exception in thread "main" java.lang.StackOverflowError
        at sun.nio.cs.SingleByteEncoder.encodeArrayLoop(SingleByteEncoder.
java:91)
        at sun.nio.cs.SingleByteEncoder.encodeLoop(SingleByteEncoder.java:130)
        at java.nio.charset.CharsetEncoder.encode(CharsetEncoder.java:544)
        at sun.nio.cs.StreamEncoder.implWrite(StreamEncoder.java:252)
        at sun.nio.cs.StreamEncoder.write(StreamEncoder.java:106)
        at java.io.OutputStreamWriter.write(OutputStreamWriter.java:190)
        at java.io.BufferedWriter.flushBuffer(BufferedWriter.java:111)
        at java.io.PrintStream.newLine(PrintStream.java:495)
        at java.io.PrintStream.println(PrintStream.java:687)
        at StackOverflowDemo.go(StackOverflowDemo.java:5)
        at StackOverflowDemo.go(StackOverflowDemo.java:6)
        at StackOverflowDemo.go(StackOverflowDemo.java:6)
```

The output actually displays the last line (the call to go on line 6) in the stack trace for each time the method is invoked, which is several thousand calls to go. You can catch a StackOverflowError and recover from it, but that would be an unusual situation because the error is typically avoided by using proper code.

NoClassDefFoundError

A `NoClassDefFoundError` is thrown by the JVM or class loader when the definition of a class cannot be found. You might have seen this error before when attempting to run a Java program and the JVM cannot find your class:

```
java NotThere
```

If there is no class named `NotThere` in the classpath, the following output displays:

```
Exception in thread "main" java.lang.NoClassDefFoundError: NotThere
Caused by: java.lang.ClassNotFoundException: NotThere
        at java.net.URLClassLoader$1.run(Unknown Source)
        at java.security.AccessController.doPrivileged(Native Method)
        at java.net.URLClassLoader.findClass(Unknown Source)
        at java.lang.ClassLoader.loadClass(Unknown Source)
        at sun.misc.Launcher$AppClassLoader.loadClass(Unknown Source)
        at java.lang.ClassLoader.loadClass(Unknown Source)
        at java.lang.ClassLoader.loadClassInternal(Unknown Source)
```

Summary

This chapter covered the "Flow Control" objectives of the SCJP exam. The goal of this chapter was to discuss the details of various entities in Java that alter the flow of control.

The decision-making control structures in Java are the `if` and `switch` statements. An `if` statement is the most basic of decision-making control structures in Java, and the `switch` statement is useful when comparing an integer value to a fixed number of cases.

The repetition control structures in Java are the `for`, enhanced `for`, `while`, and `do` loops. The `for` loop is useful for repeating something a fixed number of times. The enhanced `for` is designed for iterating through arrays and collections. The `while` and `do-while` loops are used when repeating a task an indeterminate number of times; the difference is that a do-while loop executes at least once. We also discussed the effect of the `break` and `continue` keywords on a loop.

This chapter discussed assertions in detail. An assertion is a `boolean` expression placed at particular points in your code where you think something should always be true. A failed assertion throws an `AssertionError`, and we explored how to enable assertions at runtime.

We also explained the details of exceptions in Java, including the differences between errors, runtime exceptions, and checked exceptions. We saw the effect the Handle or Declare Rule has on your code and the use of the `try`, `catch`, `finally`, `throw`, and `throws` keywords.

The SCJP exam objectives specifically list ten exceptions, and we examined the details of each one, including which ones are thrown by the JVM and which ones are thrown programmatically.

Be sure to test your knowledge of flow control by answering the Review Questions that follow. Make sure you have a good understanding of the following Exam Essentials before attempting the Review Questions, and good luck!

Exam Essentials

Understand the if and switch decision control structures.   The if and switch statements show up on a lot on the exam. The questions are usually testing your knowledge of some other aspect of Java, so it is important to be very familiar with if and switch.

Understand the looping control structures.   Make sure you know the syntax and behavior of for, while, and do loops, including the enhanced for loop. Expect at least one exam question testing your basic understanding of one of the loops, along with at least one question involving nested loops.

Know how to enable assertions.   Assertions are a new concept in Java, and they are enabled by default. Watch for a question that uses assertions but does not enable them, or a question that tests your knowledge of how assertions are enabled from the command line.

Understand the flow of control of a try-catch-finally block.   Exception handling is an important concept in Java programming. You need to understand the flow of control of all aspects of a try-catch-finally statement, whether or not an exception occurs.

Review Questions

1. What is the result of the following code?

```
3.   int x = 10, y = 3;
4.   if(x % y == 2)
5.       System.out.print("two");
6.       System.out.print(x%y);
7.   if(x%y == 1)
8.       System.out.print("one");
```

   A. two
   B. two1
   C. two2
   D. one
   E. 1one

2. What is the result of the following code?

```
4.   int x = 5, y = 10;
5.   boolean b = x < 0;
6.   if(b = true) {
7.       System.out.print(x);
8.   } else {
9.       System.out.print(y);
10. }
```

   A. Compiler error on line 5.
   B. Compiler error on line 6.
   C. 5
   D. 10
   E. The code compiles but there is no output.

3. What is the output of the following program?

```
1.   public class Question3 {
2.       public static void main(String [] args) {
3.           String year = "Senior";
4.           switch(year) {
5.               case "Freshman" :
6.               case "Sophomore" :
7.               case "Junior" :
8.                   System.out.print("See you next year");
9.                   break;
10.              case "Senior" :
```

```
11.                    System.out.print("Congratulations");
12.            default :
13.                    System.out.print("Invalid year");
14.        }
15.    }
16. }
```

A. See you next year

B. Congratulations

C. CongratulationsInvalid year

D. Invalid year

E. The code does not compile.

4. Given the following class definition:

```
1.  public class PickAColor {
2.      enum Color {RED, BLUE, GREEN}
3.
4.      public static void go(Color c) {
5.          switch(c) {
6.              case RED :
7.                  System.out.print("red");
8.              case BLUE :
9.                  System.out.print("blue");
10.                 break;
11.             case GREEN :
12.                 System.out.print("green");
13.             default :
14.                 assert false;
15.         }
16.     }
17.
18.     public static void main(String [] args) {
19.         go(Color.RED);
20.     }
21. }
```

what is the result of the following command line?

`java -ea PickAColor`

A. red

B. redblue

C. redblue, followed by an AssertionError

D. Compiler error on line 5

E. Compiler errors on line 6, 8, and 11

5. What is the result of the following code?

```
4.   final char a = 'A', d = 'D';
5.   char grade = 'B';
6.   switch(grade) {
7.      case a :
8.      case 'B' :
9.         System.out.print("great");
10.     case 'C' :
11.        System.out.print("passed");
12.        break;
13.     case d :
14.     case 'F' :
15.        System.out.print("not good");
16. }
```

A. great

B. greatpassed

C. Compiler error on line 4

D. Compiler error on line 7

E. Compiler errors on lines 7 and 13

6. What is the result of the following code?

```
4.   char c = a;
5.   for(int i = 1; i <= 3; i++) {
6.      for(int j = 0; j <= 2; j++) {
7.         System.out.print(c++);
8.      }
9.   }
```

A. abcdefghi

B. bcdefghij

C. abcdef

D. abcabcabc

E. The code does not compile.

7. What is the result of the following code?

```
10. String [] values = {"one", "two", "three"};
11. for(int index = 0; index < values.length; index++) {
12.    System.out.print(values[index]);
13. }
14. System.out.print(index);
```

   A. onetwothree

   B. onetwothree2

   C. onetwothree3

   D. onetwothree4

   E. The code does not compile.

8. What is the output of the following program?

```
1.  public class Average {
2.      public static void main(String [] args) {
3.          int [] scores = {2,4,5,5,6,8};
4.          int sum = 0;
5.          for(int x : scores) {
6.              sum += x;
7.          }
8.          System.out.println(sum / scores.length);
9.      }
10. }
```

   A. 30

   B. 6

   C. 4

   D. 5

   E. The code does not compile.

9. What is the output of the following code?

```
5.  int count = 0;
6.  rowloop : for(int row = 1; row <= 3; row++) {
7.      for(int col = 1; col <= 2; col++) {
8.          if(row * col % 2 == 0)
9.              continue rowloop;
10.         count++;
11.     }
12. }
13. System.out.println(count);
```

   A. 1

   B. 2

   C. 3

   D. 4

   E. 6

10. What is the result of the following code?

```
5.  int m = 9, n = 1;
6.  int x = 0;
7.  while(m > n) {
8.      m--;
9.      n += 2;
10.     x += m + n;
11. }
12. System.out.println(x);
```

A. 11

B. 13

C. 23

D. 36

E. 50

11. Given the following class definition:

```
1.  public class Forever {
2.      public void run() {
3.          while(true) {
4.              System.out.println("Hello");
5.          }
6.          System.out.println("Goodbye");
7.      }
8.  }
```

what is output of the following statement?

```
new Forever().run();
```

A. Prints Hello indefinitely

B. Prints Hello until an error occurs

C. Prints Hello until an error occurs, then prints Goodbye

D. Compiler error on line 3

E. Compiler error on line 6

12. What is the result of the following code?

```
7.  int y = 1;
8.  do {
9.      System.out.print(y + " ");
10. }while(y <= 10);
```

A. The code does not compile.

B. 1 2 3 4 5 6 7 8 9

C. 1 2 3 4 5 6 7 8 9 10

D. 1 2 3 4 5 6 7 8 9 10 11

E. '1' an infinite number of times

13. What is the result of the following code?

```
7.  do {
8.      int y = 1;
9.      System.out.print(y++ + " ");
10. }while(y <= 10);
```

A. The code does not compile.

B. 1 2 3 4 5 6 7 8 9

C. 1 2 3 4 5 6 7 8 9 10

D. 1 2 3 4 5 6 7 8 9 10 11

E. '1' an infinite number of times.

14. What is the result of the following code?

```
5.  Boolean keepGoing = true;
6.  int result = 1;
7.  int i = 10;
8.  do {
9.      i--;
10.     if(i == 5) {
11.         keepGoing = false;
12.     }
13.     result <<= 1;
14. }while(keepGoing);
15. System.out.println(result);
```

A. 8

B. 16

C. 32

D. 64

E. Line 14 generates a compiler error.

15. Given the following class definition:

```
1.  public class Question15 {
2.      public static void main(String [] args) {
```

```
3.          int x = 7;
4.          assert x >= 1 && x <= 6;
5.          System.out.println(x);
6.      }
7.  }
```

and given the following command line, which of the following statements are true? (Select two.)

```
java Question15
```

A. Line 4 generates a compiler error.

B. Line 4 throws an `AssertionError`.

C. The output is 7.

D. Line 5 does not execute.

E. The `assert` statement on line 4 is ignored.

16. Given the following class definition:

```
1.  public class PrintTen {
2.      private int x = 10;
3.
4.      public void go() {
5.          assert x == 10;
6.          System.out.println(x);
7.      }
8.
9.      public static void main(String [] args) {
10.         PrintTen pt = new PrintTen();
11.         pt.x = 5;
12.         pt.go();
13.     }
14. }
```

and given the following command line, which of the following statements are true? (Select two.)

```
java -ea PrintTen
```

A. Line 11 generates a compiler error.

B. The `assert` statement on line 5 throws an `AssertionError`.

C. The `assert` statement on line 5 is ignored.

D. The output is 5.

E. Line 6 does not execute.

17. Which of the following exceptions are thrown by the JVM? (Select three.)

A. `java.io.IOException`

B. `NullPointerException`

C. `ExceptionInInitializerError`

D. `NumberFormatException`

E. `ArrayIndexOutOfBoundsException`

18. Given the following class definition:

```
1.   import java.io.*;
2.
3.   public class MyFileReader2 {
4.       public void readFromFile(String fileName) throws IOException {
5.           FileReader fis = new FileReader(fileName);
6.           System.out.println(fileName + " was found");
7.           char data = (char) fis.read();
8.           System.out.println("Just read: " + data);
9.           System.out.println("End of readFromFile");
10.      }
11.
12.      public static void main(String [] args) {
13.          MyFileReader2 reader = new MyFileReader2();
14.          reader.readFromFile("greeting.txt");
15.          System.out.println("End of main");
16.      }
17. }
```

and given that the file `greeting.txt` has one line of text:

`Welcome`

which one of the following statements is true?

A. The code compiles and the output is `"W"`.

B. Line 4 generates a compiler error.

C. Line 5 generates a compiler error.

D. Line 7 generates a compiler error.

E. Line 14 generates a compiler error.

19. Given the following class definition:

```
1.   public class DoSomething {
2.       public void go() {
3.           System.out.print("A");
```

```
4.          try {
5.              stop();
6.          }catch(ArithmeticException e) {
7.              System.out.print("B");
8.          }finally {
9.              System.out.print("C");
10.         }
11.         System.out.print("D");
12.     }
13.
14.     public void stop() {
15.         System.out.print("E");
16.         Object x = null;
17.         x.toString();
18.         System.out.print("F");
19.     }
20.
21.     public static void main(String [] args) {
22.         new DoSomething().go();
23.     }
24. }
```

what is printed before the stack trace caused by the `NullPointerException` thrown on line 17 displays?

A. AE

B. AECD

C. AEC

D. AEBCD

E. No output appears before the stack trace displays.

20. What is the output of the following program?

```
1.  public class MathProblem {
2.      public static int divide(int a, int b) {
3.          try {
4.              return a / b;
5.          }catch(RuntimeException e) {
6.              return -1;
7.          }catch(ArithmeticException e) {
8.              return 0;
9.          }finally {
10.             System.out.print("done");
```

```
11.            }
12.        }
13.
14.     public static void main(String [] args) {
15.            System.out.print(divide(12, 0));
16.        }
17. }
```

A. -1

B. 0

C. done0

D. done-1

E. The code does not compile.

21. What is the output of the following program?

```
1.  public class Vowels {
2.      public static int countVowels(String input) {
3.          int count = 0;
4.          int length = input.length();
5.          int i = 0;
6.
7.          String lowercase = input.toLowerCase();
8.          while(i < length) {
9.              switch(lowercase.charAt(i)) {
10.                 case 'a':
11.                 case 'e':
12.                 case 'i':
13.                 case 'o':
14.                 case 'u':
15.                     count++;
16.             }
17.             i++;
18.         }
19.         return count;
20.     }
21.
22.     public static void main(String [] args) {
23.         int x = countVowels("Supercalifragilisticexpialidocious");
24.         System.out.print(x);
25.     }
26. }
```

A. 0

B. 16

C. 34

D. 35

E. The code does not compile.

22. What is the output of the following program?

```
1.  public class Laptop {
2.      public void start() {
3.          try {
4.              System.out.print("Starting up");
5.              throw new Exception();
6.          }catch(Exception e) {
7.              System.out.print("Problem");
8.              System.exit(0);
9.          }finally {
10.             System.out.print("Shutting down");
11.         }
12.     }
13.
14.     public static void main(String [] args) {
15.         new Laptop().start();
16.     }
17. }
```

A. Starting up

B. Starting upProblem

C. Starting upProblemShutting down

D. Starting upShutting down

E. The code does not compile.

23. What is the output of the following program?

```
1.  public class Dog {
2.      public String name;
3.
4.      public void parseName() {
5.          System.out.print("1");
6.          try {
7.              System.out.print("2");
8.              int x = Integer.parseInt(name);
9.              System.out.print("3");
```

```
10.              }catch(NumberFormatException e) {
11.                  System.out.print("4");
12.              }
13.          }
14.
15.     public static void main(String [] args) {
16.          Dog fido = new Dog();
17.          fido.name = "Fido";
18.          fido.parseName();
19.          System.out.print("5");
20.     }
21. }
```

A. 1235

B. 124

C. 1245

D. 1234

E. 12

24. What is the output of the following program?

```
1.  public class Cat {
2.      public String name;
3.
4.      public void parseName() {
5.          System.out.print("1");
6.          try {
7.              System.out.print("2");
8.              int x = Integer.parseInt(name);
9.              System.out.print("3");
10.          }catch(NullPointerException e) {
11.              System.out.print("4");
12.          }
13.          System.out.print("5");
14.      }
15.
16.     public static void main(String [] args) {
17.          Cat felix = new Cat();
18.          felix.name = "Felix";
19.          felix.parseName();
20.          System.out.print("6");
21.     }
22. }
```

A. 1256, followed by a stack trace for a `NumberFormatException`

B. 12456

C. 1256

D. 12, followed by a stack trace for a `NumberFormatException`

E. 124, followed by a stack trace for a `NumberFormatException`

25. What is the result of the following code?

```
3.  int x = 10;
4.  if(x < 0)
5.      System.out.print("anywhere");
6.      else if(x < 5)
7.          if(x == 10)
8.              System.out.print("here");
9.      else if(x >= 5)
10.         System.out.print("there");
11.         else
12.             System.out.print("somewhere");
13.             else
14.                 System.out.print("nowhere");
```

A. anywhere

B. here

C. there

D. somewhere

E. nowhere

F. The code does not compile.

26. What is the result of the following code?

```
String city = null;
if(city.equals("Boston")) {
    System.out.print("true");
}else {
    System.out.print("false");
}finally {
    System.out.print("finally");
}
```

A. false

B. falsefinally

C. finally

D. finally, followed by the stack trace from a `NullPointerException`

E. The code does not compile.

27. What gets printed in the following program? (Select four answers.)

```
1.   public class Mouse {
2.       public String name;
3.
4.       public void run() {
5.           System.out.print("1");
6.           try {
7.               System.out.print("2");
8.               name.toString();
9.               System.out.print("3");
10.          }catch(NullPointerException e) {
11.              System.out.print("4");
12.              throw e;
13.          }
14.          System.out.print("5");
15.      }
16.
17.      public static void main(String [] args) {
18.          Mouse jerry = new Mouse();
19.          jerry.run();
20.          System.out.print("6");
21.      }
22. }
```

A. 1

B. 2

C. 3

D. 4

E. 5

F. 6

G. Stack trace for a NullPointerException

Answers to Review Questions

1. E. 10%3 equals 1, so line 4 is `false`, which results in line 5 being skipped. I intentionally omitted the curly braces from the `if` on line 4 and indented line 6 to throw you off. Line 6 executes and 1 is printed regardless because it is not a part of the `if` statement. Line 7 is `true`, so one is also printed. Therefore, the answer is E.

2. C. The code compiles fine, so A and B are incorrect. In an `if-else` statement, either the true block or false block executes, so either x or y must be printed, which implies E is incorrect. On line 5, the `boolean` variable b is assigned to `false` because 5 is not less than 0. Line 6 is an assignment, not a comparison. b is assigned to `true` on line 6 and the result of the assignment is `true`, so line 7 executes and a 5 is printed. Therefore, the answer is C.

3. E. You cannot switch on a `String`. Line 4 generates a compiler error, so the correct answer is E.

4. B. The code compiles fine, so D and E are incorrect. Assertions are enabled, but the `default` case on line 13 does not execute, so C is incorrect. The `Color` is RED, so the `case` on line 6 is satisfied and red is printed on line 7. There is no `break`, so line 9 executes and `blue` is printed, so A is incorrect. Line 10 breaks out of the `switch` and the program is done. The output is `redblue`, so the answer is B.

5   B. The code compiles fine, so C, D, and E are incorrect. The `case` on line 8 is satisfied, so line 9 executes and `great` is printed. There is no `break`, so line 11 executes and `passed` is printed and therefore A is incorrect. The `switch` breaks at line 12, so the final output is `greatpassed` and the answer is B.

6. A. The outer loop executes 3 times and the inner loop executes 3 times, so 9 characters are printed starting with `'a'`, then `'b'` and so on up to `'i'`. Therefore, the output is `'abcdefghi'` and the answer is A.

7. E. The `int` variable `index` is declared within the `for` statement, so its scope is only within the `for` loop. Line 14 generates a compiler error because `index` is out of scope, so the answer is E.

8. D. The code compiles fine, so E is incorrect. Line 3 creates an array of six `ints`. The enhanced `for` loop adds the six `ints` together, so sum is 2+4+5+5+6+8=30. `scores.length` is 6 and 30/6 equals 5, which is printed on line 8. Therefore, the answer is D.

9. B. The expression on line 8 is `true` when `row * col` is an even number. Let's step through each iteration:

    - `row = 1` and `col = 1`: Line 8 is `false`, the `continue` is skipped, and `count` is incremented to 1.

    - `row = 1` and `col = 2`: Line 8 is `true`, the `continue` executes, and control jumps to the next iteration of the outer `for` loop.

    - `row = 2` and `col = 1`: Line 8 is `true` again, so we jump to the next iteration of the outer loop.

- row = 3 and col = 1: Line 8 is false so count gets incremented to 2.
- row = 3 and col = 2: Line 8 is true, the continue executes, and the outer loop is done.

Therefore, the output is 2 and the answer is B.

10. D. You need to tackle these types of questions by analyzing one iteration through the loop at a time. Let's analyze each step:

- m = 9 and n = 1: m>n is true, m is decremented to 8, n is incremented to 3, and x is 8 +3 = 11.
- m = 8 and n = 3: m>n is true, m is decremented to 7, n is incremented to 5, and x is 11 + 7 + 5 = 23.
- m = 7 and n = 5: m>n is true, m is decremented to 6, n is incremented to 7, and x is 23 + 6 + 7 = 36.
- m = 6 and n = 7: m>n is false, so the loop terminates.

The final value of x is 36, so the answer is D.

11. E. This is a tough question. The code does not compile, so A, B, and C are incorrect. Line 3 is fine — you can declare an infinite while loop. The compiler is aware that line 3 is an infinite loop and that line 6 is an unreachable statement, so the compiler generates an error at line 6. Therefore, the answer is E.

12. E. The loop control variable y equals 1 and does not change in this do-while loop. Because 1 <= 10 is always true, this is an infinite loop and 1 followed by a space displays indefinitely, so the answer is E.

13. A. The variable y is declared within the do statement on line 8, so it is out of scope of line 10. Therefore, line 10 generates a compiler error and the answer is A.

14. C. Line 14 compiles fine. A control structure that requires a boolean expression can also use java.lang.Boolean values. The loop control variable i goes from 10 down to 5, then the loop stops executing. Shifting result to the left 1 on line 13 is the equivalent of multiplying by 2, so result takes on the successive values 2, 4, 8, 16, and 32 through the five iterations. Therefore, the answer is C.

15. C and E. The code compiles, so A is incorrect. The command line does not enable assertions, so E is true and B is false even though the assertion is false. Because no AssertionError is thrown, line 5 executes and outputs 7, so C is true and D is false. Therefore, the answer is C and E.

16. B and E. The code compiles fine, so A is false. The command line enables assertions, so C is false. Line 11 changes x to 5, so the assert on line 5 fails and an AssertionError is thrown, so B is true. The AssertionError causes line 6 to not execute, so D is false and E is true. Therefore, the answer is B and E.

17. B, C, and E. A java.io.IOException is thrown by many methods in the java.io package, but it is always thrown programmatically. The same is true for NumberFormatException; it is thrown programmatically by the wrapper classes of java.lang. The other three exceptions are all thrown by the JVM when the corresponding problem arises; therefore, the answer is B, C, and E.

18. E. The code does not compile, so A is incorrect. The readFromFile method compiles fine because it properly declares the IOException that might be thrown on lines 5 and 7, so B, C, and D are incorrect. The main method invokes readFromFile and needs to handle or declare the IOException. Because it does neither, line 14 generates a compiler error and the answer is E.

19. C. The main method invokes go and A is printed on line 3. The stop method is invoked and E is printed on line 15. Line 17 throws a NullPointerException, so stop is immediately popped off the method call stack and line 18 does not execute. The exception is not caught in go, so the go method is popped off the call stack, but not before its finally block executes and C is printed on line 9. Because main does not catch the exception, the stack trace displays and no further output occurs, so "AEC" was the output printed before the stack trace. Therefore, the answer is C.

20. E. The order of catch blocks is important because they are checked in the order they appear after the try block. Because ArithmeticException is a child class of RuntimeException, the catch block on line 7 is unreachable. (If an ArithmeticException is thrown in the try block, it will be caught on line 5.) Line 7 generates a compiler error because it is unreachable code, so the answer is E.

21. B. The code compiles fine, so E is incorrect. The while loop iterates through the String one character at a time and increments count if the character is a vowel. Because the given word has 16 vowels, the output is 16 and the answer is B.

22. B. The code compiles fine, so E is incorrect. The main method invokes start on a new Laptop object. Line 4 prints Starting up, then line 5 throws an Exception. Line 6 catches the exception, line 7 prints Problem, and then line 8 calls System.exit, which terminates the JVM. The finally block does not execute because the JVM is no longer running, so the answer is B.

23. C. The parseName method is invoked within main on a new Dog object. Line 5 prints 1. The try block executes and 2 is printed. Line 8 throws a NumberFormatException, so line 9 does not execute. The exception is caught on line 10 and line 11 prints 4. Because the exception is handled, execution resumes normally. parseName runs to completion and line 19 executes, printing 5. That is the end of the program, so the output is 1245 and the answer is C.

24. D. The parseName method is invoked on a new Cat object. Line 5 prints 1. The try block is entered and line 7 prints 2. Line 8 throws a NumberFormatException. It is not caught, so parseName is popped off the method call stack. main does not catch the exception either, so the program terminates and the stack trace for the NumberFormatException is printed. Therefore, the answer is D.

25. E. Believe it or not, the code compiles fine, so F is incorrect. The best way to explain the answer is by reformatting the code so the lines are indented properly, as follows:

```
3.   int x = 10;
4.   if(x < 0)
5.       System.out.print("anywhere");
```

```
6.  else if(x < 5)
7.      if(x == 10)
8.          System.out.print("here");
9.      else if(x >= 5)
10.         System.out.print("there");
11.     else
12.         System.out.print("somewhere");
13. else
14.     System.out.print("nowhere");
```

The x < 0 comparison on line 4 is false, as is x < 5 on line 6. The else on line 13 matches up with the if on line 5, so line 14 executes and nowhere is printed. Therefore, the answer is E.

26. E. A finally block can only appear at the end of a try statement. Therefore, this code does not compile and the answer is E.

27. A, B, D, and G. The main method invokes run on a new Mouse object. Line 5 prints 1 and line 7 prints 2, so A and B are correct. Line 8 throws a NullPointerException which causes line 9 to be skipped, so C is incorrect. The exception is caught on line 10 and line 11 prints 4, so D is correct. Line 12 throws the exception again, which causes run to immediately get popped off the method call stack, so line 14 does not execute and E is incorrect. The main method does not catch the exception either, so line 20 does not execute and F is incorrect. The uncaught NullPointerException causes the stack trace to be printed, so G is correct. Therefore, the answers are A, B, D, and G.

Chapter

4

API Contents

SCJP EXAM OBJECTIVES COVERED IN THIS CHAPTER:

✓ Develop code that uses the primitive wrapper classes (such as Boolean, Character, Double, Integer, etc.), and/or autoboxing and unboxing. Discuss the differences between the String, StringBuilder, and StringBuffer classes.

✓ Given a scenario involving navigating file systems, reading from files, writing to files, or interacting with the user, develop the correct solution using the following classes (sometimes in combination), from java.io: BufferedReader, BufferedWriter, File, FileReader, FileWriter, PrintWriter, and Console.

✓ Develop code that serializes and/or de-serializes objects using the following APIs from java.io: DataInputStream, DataOutputStream, FileInputStream, FileOutputStream, ObjectInputStream, ObjectOutputStream and Serializable.

✓ Use standard J2SE APIs in the java.text package to correctly format or parse dates, numbers, and currency values for a specific locale; and, given a scenario, determine the appropriate methods to use if you want to use the default locale or a specific locale. Describe the purpose and use of the java.util.Locale class.

✓ Write code that uses standard J2SE APIs in the java.util and java.util.regex packages to format or parse strings or streams. For strings, write code that uses the Pattern and Matcher classes and the String.split method. Recognize and use regular expression patterns for matching (limited to: . (dot), * (star),+(plus), ?, \d, \s, \w, [], ()). The use of *, +, and ? will be limited to greedy quantifiers, and the parenthesis operator will only be used as a grouping mechanism, not for capturing content during matching. For streams, write code using the Formatter and Scanner classes and the PrintWriter.format/printf methods. Recognize and use formatting parameters (limited to: %b, %c, %d, %f, %s) in format strings.

These objectives are Section 3 of the SCJP exam objectives. The exam tests your knowledge of the primitive wrapper classes, input and output streams, the java.text package, formatting and parsing data using locales, and regular expressions. This chapter covers these topics in detail, starting with a discussion of the wrapper classes.

The Primitive Wrapper Classes

Data in a Java application is either an object or a primitive data type. There are situations in Java where only an object can be used and primitive types do not work. For example, the classes in the Collections API can only hold Object references. The wrapper classes provide the ability to treat primitive types as objects by wrapping the primitive in an Object. This section discusses how to wrap a primitive type into its corresponding wrapper class.

The exam objectives state that you should be able to "develop code that uses the primitive wrapper classes." The *wrapper classes* are defined in the java.lang package and are used in situations where an object is required but the data is a primitive type. The primitive type is "wrapped" into an object and can be "unwrapped" whenever the primitive value is needed. There is a wrapper class in the java.lang package for each of the eight primitive types:

Byte This type wraps a byte.

Short This type wraps a short.

Integer This type wraps an int.

Long This type wraps a long.

Float This type wraps a float.

Double This type wraps a double.

Character This type wraps a char.

Boolean This type wraps a boolean.

Wrapper classes have the following properties:

- Each of the wrapper classes contains a single field that holds the value it is wrapping.
- The value of the wrapped primitive type cannot be changed.
- Each class has a constructor that takes in the data type it wraps.
- Except for Character, each class has a constructor that takes in a String that is automatically parsed into the corresponding primitive type.

- Each wrapper class has a "value" method that unwraps the primitive type. For example, the `Float` class has a `floatValue` method that returns the `float`.

Let's look at an example. The following code wraps an `int` into an `Integer` object:

```
int x = 357;
Integer w = new Integer(x);
```

The `Integer` class has a method named `intValue` that unwraps the `int`:

```
int y = w.intValue();
```

Autoboxing

As of Java 5.0, primitive types can be automatically boxed and unboxed into their corresponding wrapper classes, eliminating the need for instantiating a new wrapper type to box a primitive, or using a value method to retrieve the wrapped primitive.

Let's look at an example where a wrapper class is necessary. The following class contains a method named `addScore` with an `Object` parameter. Because a primitive type is not an `Object`, a primitive type needs to be wrapped before it can be passed into `addScore`. Study the following code and try to determine its output:

```
1.  public class ScoreKeeper {
2.      public java.util.ArrayList<Object> scores =
3.              new java.util.ArrayList<Object>();
4.
5.      public void addScore(Object score) {
6.          scores.add(score);
7.      }
8.
9.      public void printScores() {
10.         for(Object score : scores) {
11.             System.out.println(score);
12.         }
13.     }
14.
15.     public static void main(String [] args) {
16.         ScoreKeeper keeper = new ScoreKeeper();
17.         Integer one = new Integer(50);
18.         Double two = new Double(23.4);
19.         Float three = new Float(18.5);
20.         keeper.addScore(one);
```

```
21.          keeper.addScore(two);
22.          keeper.addScore(three);
23.          keeper.printScores();
24.     }
25. }
```

Within main, an int, double, and float are wrapped into their corresponding wrapper class and passed into the addScore method of a new ScoreKeeper object. The code compiles because Integer, Double, and Float are subclasses of Object. Each object is saved in the ArrayList, and invoking printScores generates the following output:

```
50
23.4
18.5
```

Parsing Strings Using the Wrapper Classes

Each wrapper class (except for Character) contains a useful method for parsing String objects into primitive types. The name of the method is parse Xxx, where Xxx is the data type being parsed to. For example, parseInt in the Integer class parses a String to an int, parseShort in the Short class parses a String to a short, and so on. The following statements parse a String into a double:

```
String s = "123.4";
double d = Double.parseDouble(s);
double twice = d * 2;
System.out.println(twice);
```

The String "123.4" is parsed into a double, multiplied by 2, and the output is

```
246.8
```

Each parse method throws a NumberFormatException if the given String does not contain a value that is parseable to the appropriate type.

The wrapper classes are used whenever a primitive type needs to be treated as an Object. Java 5.0 introduced an autoboxing feature that hides the wrapper classes behind the scenes. The next section discusses autoboxing and unboxing in detail.

Autoboxing and Unboxing

As of Java 5.0, you no longer need to write the code to wrap primitive types into their corresponding wrapper class; the compiler now does this for you behind the scenes. The term *autoboxing* refers to the compiler automatically converting a primitive type into its corresponding wrapper class. The term *unboxing* refers to the compiler automatically unwrapping a primitive type from its wrapper object. Autoboxing and unboxing do not require any special syntax. The compiler realizes situations where primitives need to be boxed or unboxed. For example, if an `int` needs to be treated as an object, it automatically becomes an `Integer`. Similarly, an `Integer` automatically becomes an `int` whenever necessary.

Before autoboxing, you would wrap a primitive by instantiating a new wrapper object:

```
Integer w = new Integer(10);
```

With autoboxing, you simply assign a wrapper class reference to a primitive type:

```
Integer w = 10;
```

Behind the scenes, the compiler instantiates a new `Integer` object for the `int` 10.

Similarly, the compiler unboxes a wrapped primitive whenever necessary. The following statements are valid:

```
5. Double pi = 3.14159;
6. double radius = 10.0;
7. double area = pi * radius * radius;
```

The `Double` object on line 5 is automatically instantiated and wraps the value 3.14159. On line 7, `pi` is automatically unwrapped into a `double` before the multiplication occurs. Before unboxing, we would have used the `doubleValue` method:

```
double area = pi.doubleValue() * radius * radius;
```

The autoboxing occurs whenever the compiler realizes that a primitive needs to be wrapped in its corresponding wrapper class. For example, the `ScoreKeeper` class from the previous section contains the following method:

```
public void addScore(Object score) {
    scores.add(score);
}
```

The following statements are valid method invocations of `addScore`:

```
keeper.addScore(50);
keeper.addScore(23.4);
keeper.addScore(18.5F);
```

Behind the scenes, the 50 is converted to an `Integer`, 23.4 is converted to a `Double`, and 18.5F is converted to a `Float`.

Testing for Equality Using Autoboxing

With the introduction of autoboxing, your code can essentially ignore the distinction between a primitive type and its wrapper. One situation where you might need to make the distinction is when you test for equality. When using ==, wrapped types are not unboxed. For example, see if you can determine the output of the following code:

```
13. Integer one = new Integer(128);
14. Integer two = new Integer(128);
15. if(one == two)
16.     System.out.println("true");
17. else
18.     System.out.println("false");
19.
20. int three = 128;
21. if(one == three)
22.     System.out.println("true");
23. else
24.     System.out.println("false");
```

Line 15 is comparing two references that do not point to the same object, so the result is false. On line 21, the Integer is unboxed to an int, so the comparison is made between two equal ints, resulting in true. The output of the previous code is

```
false
true
```

Autoboxing and unboxing eliminates the tedious code of instantiating wrapper objects using the new keyword and unwrapping the primitive types using the corresponding value methods. Autoboxing is a new feature of Java, so there will certainly be a question or two on the exam about it.

Strings

A *string* is a sequence of characters. Strings are not primitive types in Java; they are objects. The Java API has three classes to represent string objects, each one declared in the java.lang package: String, StringBuilder, and StringBuffer. The exam objectives state that you need to be able to "discuss differences between the String, StringBuilder, and StringBuffer classes." The main differences between these classes are as follows:

String String represents an immutable sequence of characters. The string literals in your code are of type String.

StringBuilder StringBuilder represents a mutable sequence of characters. String-Builder is like String except the individual characters can be modified and the length can change. The methods in this class are not synchronized, so do not use an instance of this class in a situation where multiple threads can access the instance.

StringBuffer StringBuffer represents a thread-safe, mutable sequence of characters. The methods in this class are exactly identical to the methods of StringBuilder. The only difference between the two classes is that the methods in StringBuffer are synchronized.

The simplest class to use is String, but it tends to be inefficient when working with character sequences that need to be changed often because a String object is immutable. Use StringBuilder and StringBuffer in situations where you need to manipulate strings, because they contain methods like append, insert, and concat that change the string without creating a new object each time.

This section discusses each of these classes in detail, starting with the String class.

The *String* Class

The String class represents an immutable array of characters. String literals are automatically instantiated into String objects. For example, "Hello" in the following statement is a String object:

```
String s = "Hello";
```

You can also instantiate a String dynamically using one of the String constructors:

```
char [] abc = {'a', 'b', 'c'};
String s2 = new String(abc);
```

The JVM stores string literals in a special memory called the string pool. Because String objects are immutable, instances in the string pool can be shared. For example, the following two String references point to the same instance, and the output is "true":

```
String one = "today";
String two = "today";
if(one == two)
    System.out.println("true");
else
    System.out.println("false");
```

Use equals to Compare Strings

You should use the equals method when comparing if two String objects are identical because not all String objects appear in the string pool. For example, see if you can determine the output of the following code:

```
String one = "today";
String three = new String("today");
if(one == three)
    System.out.println("true");
else
    System.out.println("false");
```

The one reference points to a String object in the string pool while the three reference points to a dynamically created String object on the heap, so one and three do not point to the same instance and the output of the previous code is "false".

One nice feature of using String objects is the simple way they are concatenated using the + operator. For example, the following statements create a "Tooth Fairy" string:

```
String first = "Tooth";
first += " " + "Fai" + "ry";
```

It is valid to concatenate a String to any primitive type or Object. Primitive types are converted to a String object internally by the JVM. Object types have their toString method invoked automatically. For example, the following statements are valid. See if you can determine their output:

```
String prefix = "x = ";
int x = 123;
System.out.println(prefix + x);
java.util.Date d = new java.util.Date();
System.out.println("The date is " + d);
```

The int x is converted to a String before the concatenation occurs. Similarly, the toString method is invoked on d before concatenating to the String object "The date is". The output of the code is

```
x = 123
The date is Mon Oct 06 08:26:47 MDT 2008
```

You should be aware that String objects tend to be inefficient when they are concatenated. Remember, a String object is immutable, meaning it cannot be changed. Therefore, concatenating two String literals involves creating a new String object and having the old ones get garbage collected. For example, concatenating " ", "Fai", and "ry" results in four String objects being instantiated and three of them eligible for garbage collection immediately, as Figure 4.1 shows.

FIGURE 4.1 String concatenation can result in multiple String objects created and garbage collected.

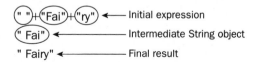

The circled String objects are eligible for garbage collection once the result is evaluated.

Optimizing String Concatenation

It is possible that a Java implementation optimizes String concatenation to minimize the number of intermediate String objects created. The Java Language Specification contains the following statement:

> An implementation may choose to perform conversion and concatenation in one step to avoid creating and then discarding an intermediate String object. To increase the performance of repeated string concatenation, a Java compiler may use the StringBuffer class or a similar technique to reduce the number of intermediate String objects that are created by evaluation of an expression.

In other words, a JVM may or may not optimize String concatenation. Even if the JVM does optimize this step, a temporary StringBuffer object is created behind the scenes. Either way, you should avoid the overuse of String concatenation because it can be inefficient, especially when building strings or modifying them regularly. In these situations, a StringBuffer or StringBuilder object is a better choice, which we discuss in the next section.

See if you can determine how many String objects appear in memory from the following statements:

```
10. String alpha = "";
11. for(char current = 'a'; current <= 'z'; current++) {
12.     alpha += current;
13. }
14. System.out.println(alpha);
```

The empty String on line 10 is instantiated, and then line 12 appends an "a". However, because the String object is immutable, a new String object is assigned to alpha and the "" object becomes eligible for garbage collection. The next time through the loop, alpha is assigned a new String object "ab" and the "a" object becomes eligible for garbage collection. The next iteration assigns alpha to "abc" and the "ab" object becomes eligible for garbage collection, and so on.

This sequence of events continues, and after 26 iterations through the loop, a total of 27 objects are instantiated, 26 of which are immediately eligible for garbage collection. A better technique in this situation would be to use the StringBuffer or StringBuilder classes, which I discuss in detail in the next section.

The *StringBuilder* and *StringBuffer* Classes

The java.lang package contains two classes for representing strings as a mutable sequence of characters: StringBuilder and StringBuffer. The StringBuffer class has been around since the first version of Java, while StringBuilder was added in J2SE 5.0. The two classes have the exact same method signatures and constructor parameters. The only difference between them is that StringBuffer is thread-safe and StringBuilder is not. If you are working with arrays of characters in a multithreaded application, use the StringBuffer class. Otherwise, if threads are not an issue for your particular situation, use the StringBuilder class.

Let's look at an example. The following for loop is similar to the example in the previous section, except it uses a single StringBuilder object instead of 27 String objects:

```
15. StringBuilder alpha = new StringBuilder(26);
16. for(char current = 'a'; current <= 'z'; current++) {
17.     alpha.append(current);
18. }
19. System.out.println(alpha);
```

The StringBuilder class contains a constructor that takes in an int to represent the initial capacity. On line 15, a new StringBuilder object is instantiated with an initial capacity of 26. This does not mean only 26 characters can appear in alpha. The capacity merely specifies an initial buffer. If the capacity of a StringBuilder object is reached, the length of the StringBuilder object is automatically increased. We can improve performance if we give a StringBuilder a capacity, but it does not affect the behavior of the object.

The call to append on line 17 increases the size of the StringBuilder object by one each time through the for loop and appends the value of current to the end of alpha. The StringBuilder object grows as needed, but there is only one instance in memory, as Figure 4.2 shows.

FIGURE 4.2   The sequence of characters increases by one each time through the loop.

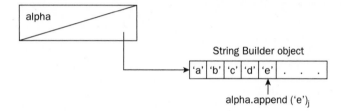

The output of the code is

abcdefghijklmnopqrstuvwxyz

The principal methods of the StringBuilder and StringBuffer classes are their append and insert methods. The append and insert methods are overloaded to accept any of the primitive types, Object, String, or StringBuffer. To demonstrate the method signatures, here are the append and insert methods in StringBuilder for appending and inserting a float:

- public StringBuilder append(float f) appends the given float to the end of the character sequence.

- public StringBuilder insert(int offset, float f) inserts the given float at the value of the offset. The first index of the sequence is 0, the second index is 1, and so on.

The overloaded methods for the other data types take on the same form as the methods above. The append and insert methods are identical in StringBuffer, except that the return values are of type StringBuffer:

- public StringBuffer append(float f)

- public StringBuffer insert(int offset, float f)

The append method appends the data to the end of the character sequence, while the insert method inserts the data at the given offset. Notice that the return value of append and insert is the original StringBuilder or StringBuffer object, which allows for the chaining of method calls. For example, see if you can figure out the character sequence that the following code generates:

```
24.   StringBuffer sb = new StringBuffer();
25.   sb.append("cet").insert(2,"ntra").insert(0,"con").append("ing");
26.   System.out.println(sb);
```

Let's break this code down step by step:

1. The initial StringBuffer object instantiated on line 24 is empty.

2. On line 25, the methods are executed left to right, so the first append call puts "cet" in the sequence.

3. The insert of "ntra" occurs after the second character (because the offset is 2), so the StringBuffer now contains "centrat".

4. The "con" is inserted at the beginning of the sequence, resulting in "concentrat".

5. The "ing" is appended to the sequence.

Therefore, the output of the code is

```
concentrating
```

As I mentioned earlier, the append and insert methods are overloaded for all the Java primitive types. For example, the following statements insert an int and append a double to a StringBuffer object:

```
StringBuffer numbers = new StringBuffer(" * 5.0 = ");
numbers.insert(0, 100).append(500.0);
System.out.println(numbers);
```

The output of the statements is

```
100 * 5.0 = 500.0
```

The StringBuilder and StringBuffer classes also contain other string manipulation methods, including the following ones:

- public StringBuffer delete(int start, int end) removes the characters at the specified start and end indexes, excluding the end character, and shortens the sequence accordingly.

- public StringBuffer deleteCharAt(int index) removes the character at the specified index and shortens the sequence by one.

- public StringBuffer reverse() replaces the character sequence with the reverse of itself.

- With public StringBuffer replace(int start, int end, String str), the characters from start to end-1 are replaced with the characters of the given String.

To demonstrate these methods, see if you can determine the result of the following code:

```
12. StringBuilder x = new StringBuilder("starter");
13. x.deleteCharAt(6).reverse().replace(0,2,"d");
14. System.out.println(x);
```

Here is what the code does:

1. The initial sequence of characters is "starter".

2. On line 13, deleteCharAt removes the "r" at the end, resulting in "starte".

3. The reverse method reverses the sequence, resulting in "etrats".

4. The call to `replace` deletes the first two characters (the character at the end position is not deleted), so `"et"` is replaced with a `"d"`, resulting in `"drats"`.

Therefore, the outcome of the code is

```
drats
```

As far as the SCJP exam goes, focus on understanding the `insert` or `append` methods of `StringBuilder` and `StringBuffer` because they are the most commonly used methods in the two classes. Now we change topics and discuss the various classes in Java for performing input and output.

Input and Output

The `java.io` package contains a variety of classes that can perform just about any type of input or output you might need to perform in your Java applications. The trick to mastering the `java.io` package is to understand the difference between stream classes and reader and writer classes, as well as the difference between low-level and high-level streams. This section discusses these differences together with the specific classes of the `java.io` package that you need to know for the SCJP exam.

Let's start with a discussion on streams vs. readers and writers. If you look at the classes in the `java.io` package, you will notice a set of classes whose names end in `"InputStream"` or `"OutputStream"`, together with a set of classes that end in `"Reader"` and `"Writer"`. There is a difference between the two:

- The stream classes are used for inputting and outputting all types of binary data.
- The reader and writer classes are used exclusively for inputting and outputting character and string data.

For example, the `DataInputStream` class is a useful input stream that can read all the primitive types, as well as strings and other binary types. The `FileReader` class is a reader that can only read a character or an array of characters from a file.

Most of the input classes have a corresponding output class for writing the data. For example, `DataOutputStream` writes data that can be read by a `DataInputStream`, and a `PipedWriter` outputs characters to a stream that a `PipedReader` can read from in a different thread.

Now let's discuss the differences between the stream classes and the readers and writers.

Streams vs. Readers and Writers

The stream classes work with raw bytes of data. The parent class of all input streams is the abstract class `InputStream` and the parent class of all the output streams is `OutputStream`. Figure 4.3 shows the input stream classes in the `java.io` package, and Figure 4.4 shows the output streams.

FIGURE 4.3 The input streams of the java.io package

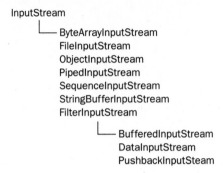

FIGURE 4.4 The output streams of the java.io package

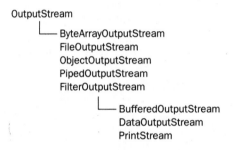

If you are dealing with data that includes other types than just strings or characters, use the input and output streams shown in Figures 4.3 and 4.4. However, if the data you are streaming is either characters or strings, use the reader and writer classes shown in Figures 4.5 and 4.6. Notice the readers subclass, the abstract Reader class, and the writers subclass, the Writer class.

FIGURE 4.5 The reader classes of the java.io package

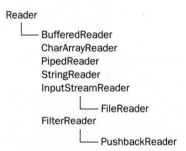

FIGURE 4.6   The writer classes of the java.io package

```
Writer
    └── BufferedWriter
        CharArrayWriter
        PipedWriter
        PrintWriter
        StringWriter
        OutputStreamWriter
            └── FileWriter
        FilterWriter
```

To demonstrate how the classes work, let's look at an example of a program that reads characters from a file. The following code reads in a single character at a time from a file named alphabet.txt, which contains the 26 characters of the alphabet in lowercase:

```
FileReader in = new FileReader("alphabet.txt");
int c = 0;
while((c =  in.read()) != -1) {
    System.out.print((char) c);
}
```

The output of the code is

abcdefghijklmnopqrstuvwxyz

In the real world, reading one character from a file is not done because it is inefficient and typically the data in the file represents data types beyond characters. Typically, you take a FileReader and attach a high-level stream to it to buffer and filter the data, which we discuss in the next section.

Low-Level vs. High-Level Streams

Another important concept to understand about the java.io package is the difference between a low-level stream and a high-level stream (where stream in this context also refers to reader and writer streams):

- Low-level input and output streams connect to the source of the data.
- High-level input and output streams are chained to an existing stream. Most high-level streams filter the data and convert it into Java data types.

For example, a FileReader is a low-level stream because it connects to a file on your file system. The purpose of FileReader is not to filter the data or format it any way. Its purpose is strictly to communicate with the file. If you want to read the characters from the file in a more useful manner than one character at a time, you can attach a high-level stream to the low-level stream. For example, BufferedReader is a high-level stream that can be chained to a FileReader and read in lines of characters at a time, converting the line of characters to a String. The next section, "File Input and Output," contains an example that demonstrates this technique.

Table 4.1 lists the low-level and high-level streams from the java.io package.

TABLE 4.1   The Low-Level and High-Level Streams in the java.io Package

Low-level Streams		High-level Streams	
FileReader	FileInputStream	BufferedReader	BufferedInputStream
FileWriter	FileOutputStream	BufferedWriter	BufferedOutputStream
ByteArrayInputStream	CharArrayWriter	DataInputStream	ObjectInputStream
StringReader	StringWriter	PipedInputStream	OutputStreamWriter
InputStream	OutputStream	PipedOutputStream	InputStreamReader
		PushbackInput Stream	LineNumberReader
		PushbackReader	
		PushbackReader	

Determining Low-level vs. High-level Streams

If you ever need to determine whether a java.io stream is a high-level or low-level stream, just look at the constructors of the class. If the constructors take in an existing stream object, then it is a high-level stream; otherwise, it is a low-level stream.

For example, the DataInputStream class has only one constructor:

```
public DataInputStream(InputStream is)
```

You cannot instantiate a DataInputStream unless you already have an existing stream to pass in to the constructor. Therefore, DataInputStream must be a high-level stream.

Compare DataInputStream to FileInputStream, which has three constructors:

```
public FileInputStream(File file)
public FileInputStream(FileDescriptor fdObj)
public FileInputStream(String name)
```

Each constructor takes in some variation of a file, which is the source of the data and not another stream class. Therefore, FileInputStream is a low-level stream.

Now that we have discussed the differences between input and output streams versus readers and writers and also the difference between low-level and high-level streams, let's see how to put this information to good use by demonstrating how to read and write from files.

File Input and Output

The exam objectives state that "given a scenario involving navigating file systems, reading from files, writing to files, or interacting with the user, develop the correct solution using the following classes (sometimes in combination), from java.io: BufferedReader, BufferedWriter, File, FileReader, FileWriter, PrintWriter, and Console." This section discusses the details of these classes and how to use them to read and write data from files. We start with the FileReader and FileWriter classes.

The *FileReader* and *FileWriter* Classes

The FileReader and FileWriter classes are used for reading and writing character data from files. Let's look at an example. Suppose you want to read the data from the following text file named states.txt:

```
New York
Alabama
South Dakota
Nevada
```

Because the data is in a file, we need to use either FileInputStream or FileReader to read the data. Because the file only contains characters, FileReader is the better choice here. The states are separated by the linefeed character, so we need to read the text in line by line, not a built-in capability of the FileReader class. However, if we chain a BufferedReader object to the FileReader, we can use the readLine method of BufferedReader to easily read in each state in the file, as the following program shows:

```
1.  import java.io.*;
2.
3.  public class States {
4.      public static void main(String [] args) {
5.          try {
6.              FileReader fileReader = new FileReader("states.txt");
7.              BufferedReader in = new BufferedReader(fileReader);
8.              String currentState = in.readLine();
```

```
9.                  while(currentState != null) {
10.                     System.out.println("State: " + currentState);
11.                     currentState = in.readLine();
12.                 }
13.             }catch(IOException e) {
14.                 e.printStackTrace();
15.             }
16.     }
17. }
```

Here is what the States program does:

1. A new `FileReader` is instantiated on line 6. If the file `states.txt` is not found or cannot be read from, a `FileNotFoundException` is thrown.

2. A `BufferedReader` is chained to the `FileReader` to buffer the data.

3. Line 8 reads in the first line of text from the file.

4. On line 9, if the previous line of text read from the file is not `null`, we print it to the console and read in the next line of the file on line 11.

5. The `while` loop continues line by line until the end of the file is reached, at which point the `readLine` method returns `null`.

The output of the States program is

```
State: New York
State: Alabama
State: South Dakota
State: Nevada
```

Figure 4.7 shows the `BufferedReader` chained to the `FileReader`. A `BufferedReader` cannot exist on its own. It is a high-level stream so it must be attached to an existing stream.

FIGURE 4.7   A `BufferedReader` is chained to a `FileReader`.

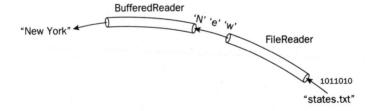

> **Buffering File Input and Output**
>
> The BufferedReader class does more than read the characters from a file line by line. It buffers the characters to minimize the overhead of actually reading from the file system each time a character is read. You can set the size of the buffer by using the following BufferedReader constructor:
>
> ```
> public BufferedReader(Reader in, int size)
> ```
>
> Similarly, the BufferedWriter class is used to buffer characters written to a file and contains the following constructor:
>
> ```
> public BufferedWriter(Writer out, int size)
> ```
>
> If you are working with other data types besides characters, use the FileOutputStream and FileInputStream classes to read and write to the file, and use the BufferedInputStream and BufferedOutputStream classes if you want to also buffer that data.

The *File* Class

The exam objectives mention using the java.io.File class in combination with the stream classes. The File class represents the pathname of a file or directory, and the class contains useful methods for determining information about the file or directory. Some uses of the File class include the following:

- Determining if a file exists using the exists method, which returns a boolean
- Determining if a file can be read from, written to, or executed using the respective canRead, canWrite, or canExecute methods
- Creating a new file using the createNewFile method
- Making a new directory using the mkdir method
- Deleting a file or directory using the delete method
- Listing the contents of a directory using the list and listFiles methods

To demonstrate using the File class, the following code creates a new file and writes strings to it using a FileWriter object. The FileWriter is chained to a BufferedWriter, which in turn is chained to a PrintWriter, a useful class for printing all data types. (System.out is a PrintWriter object.) Study the code and see if you can determine what it does:

```
1.  package com.sybex.io;
2.
3.  import java.io.*;
```

```
4.
5.  public class FileDemo {
6.      public static void main(String [] args) {
7.          File test = new File("./test.html");
8.          if(!test.exists()) {
9.              try {
10.                 test.createNewFile();
11.             }catch(IOException e) {
12.                 System.out.println(e.getMessage());
13.                 return;
14.             }
15.         }
16.         try {
17.             FileWriter fw = new FileWriter(test);
18.             BufferedWriter bw = new BufferedWriter(fw, 1024);
19.             PrintWriter out = new PrintWriter(fw);
20.             out.println("<html><body><h1>");
21.             out.println(args[0]);
22.             out.println("</h1></body></html>");
23.             out.close();
24.             bw.close();
25.             fw.close();
26.         }catch(IOException e) {
27.             e.printStackTrace();
28.         }
29.     }
30. }
```

The following sequence of events occurs when running the FileDemo program:

1. Line 7 creates a new File object for the pathname "./test.html". Keep in mind this does not create a new file on your file system. The File class represents pathnames to files and directories, not actual files and directories.

2. Line 10 creates a new file named test.html on the file system if no such file already exists in the current directory.

3. Line 17 instantiates a new FileWriter object that opens the file and prepares it for writing. If the file contained any existing data, that data is now lost. (If you need to append to a file, use the FileWriter constructor that takes in an additional boolean argument.)

4. Line 18 chains a BufferedWriter to the FileWriter with an initial buffer size of 1,024.

5. Line 19 chains a `PrintWriter` to the `BufferedWriter`.

6. Lines 20–22 write some HTML to the file.

7. Lines 23–25 close the streams.

Suppose we run the program with the following command line:

```
java com.sybex.io.FileDemo "This is a new file"
```

A file named `test.html` is created in the current working directory and the contents of the file look like

```
<html><body><h1>
This is a new file
</h1></body></html>
```

You probably won't use this example in the real world to write a dynamic web page, but the program does demonstrate how you can use the `File` class. It also demonstrates how to chain a low-level writer (`FileWriter`) to a high-level writer (`BufferedWriter`), and even how to chain a high-level writer (`BufferedWriter`) to another high-level writer (`Print-Writer`) to achieve the buffered, filtered stream that Figure 4.8 illustrates.

FIGURE 4.8   Data written to the PrintWriter is buffered and eventually written to the file.

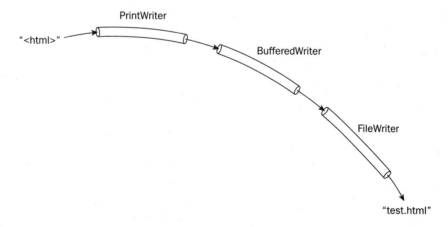

The following section demonstrates the concept of chaining streams together using byte streams instead of character streams.

The *FileInputStream* and *FileOutputStream* Classes

The `FileInputStream` and `FileOutputStream` classes represent low-level streams that read and write byte streams from files. As with `FileReader` and `FileWriter`, chain `FileInputStream` and `FileOutputStream` to high-level streams to buffer and filter the data into appropriate data types.

The following `CopyFile` program demonstrates these two classes by reading the bytes from one file and copying them into another, making a byte-by-byte copy of the file:

```
1.   package com.sybex.io;
2.
3.   import java.io.*;
4.
5.   public class CopyFile {
6.       public static void copy(File src, File dest)
7.                                   throws IOException {
8.           FileInputStream in = new FileInputStream(src);
9.           FileOutputStream out = new FileOutputStream(dest);
10.          int c;
11.          try {
12.              while((c = in.read()) != -1) {
13.                  out.write(c);
14.              }
15.          }finally{
16.              in.close();
17.              out.close();
18.          }
19.      }
20.
21.      public static void main(String [] args) {
22.          try {
23.              File source = new File("States.class");
24.              File destination = new File("copyofStates.class");
25.              copy(source, destination);
26.          }catch(IOException e) {
27.              e.printStackTrace();
28.          }
29.      }
30. }
```

The following breakdown illustrates what the `CopyFile` program does:

1. Within main on lines 23 and 24, two `File` objects are instantiated to represent the pathnames to the source and destination files.

2. The copy method is called on line 25, and the two `File` references are copied into the src and dest parameters.

3. Line 8 instantiates a `FileInputStream` for `src` and line 9 instantiates a `FileOutput-Stream` for `dest`.

4. The `while` loop on line 12 reads one byte at time from the source file. If the `read` method returns -1, the end of the file has been reached and the `while` loop terminates. Otherwise, the byte is written to the destination file.

5. Be sure to close all streams, as done on lines 16 and 17.

Notice that the source file I chose to copy was a bytecode file, which is not just character data. (The `Reader` and `Writer` classes would not have worked for this application because the data is raw bytes.) An exact copy of `States.class` is created in a new file named `copyofStates.class`.

The next section discusses two useful high-level streams, `DataInputStream` and `DataOutputStream`, which filter byte streams into primitive types and strings.

The *DataInputStream* and *DataOutputStream* Classes

The `CopyFile` program from the previous section used only low-level streams, but most input and output use the high-level streams as well. For example, the `DataInputStream` and `DataOutputStream` classes are high-level streams that contain methods for reading and writing the eight Java primitive types as well as `String` objects. The following `ContactManager` program demonstrates the `DataInputStream` and `DataOutputStream` classes. The program uses the following `Contact` class, a basic representation of a person's contact information:

```
1.    package com.sybex.io;
2.
3.    public class Contact {
4.        public String name;
5.        public int age;
6.        public long cellPhone;
7.
8.        public Contact(String name, int age, long cellPhone) {
9.            this.name = name;
10.           this.age = age;
11.           this.cellPhone = cellPhone;
12.       }
13.
14.       public String toString() {
15.           return name + " " + age + " " + cellPhone + "\n";
16.       }
17.   }
```

The ContactManager program writes the fields of a Contact object to a given File, and also reads the fields from a File and creates new Contact objects with the read data. Study the code and see if you can determine its output:

```
1.   package com.sybex.io;
2.
3.   import java.io.*;
4.   import java.util.ArrayList;
5.
6.   public class ContactManager {
7.
8.       public static void addContact(Contact contact, File dest)
9.                               throws IOException {
10.          FileOutputStream fos = new FileOutputStream(dest, true);
11.          BufferedOutputStream bos = new BufferedOutputStream(fos);
12.          DataOutputStream out = new DataOutputStream(bos);
13.          out.writeUTF(contact.name);
14.          out.writeInt(contact.age);
15.          out.writeLong(contact.cellPhone);
16.          out.close();
17.          bos.close();
18.          fos.close();
19.      }
20.
21.      public static ArrayList<Contact> getContacts(File source)
22.                              throws IOException {
23.          ArrayList<Contact> contacts = new ArrayList<Contact>();
24.
25.          FileInputStream fis = new FileInputStream(source);
26.          BufferedInputStream bis = new BufferedInputStream(fis);
27.          DataInputStream in = new DataInputStream(bis);
28.          while(in.available() > 0) {
29.              String name = in.readUTF();
30.              int age = in.readInt();
31.              long cellPhone = in.readLong();
32.              Contact current = new Contact(name, age, cellPhone);
33.              contacts.add(current);
34.          }
35.
36.          return contacts;
37.      }
```

```
38.
39.     public static void main(String [] args) {
40.         try {
41.             Contact one = new Contact("Bugs Bunny", 22,
42.                                         2025551212L);
43.             Contact two = new Contact("Daffy Duck", 33,
44.                                         3035551212L);
45.             File contactsFile = new File("mycontacts.dat");
46.
47.             addContact(one, contactsFile);
48.             addContact(two, contactsFile);
49.
50.             System.out.println(getContacts(contactsFile));
51.         }catch(IOException e) {
52.             e.printStackTrace();
53.         }
54.     }
55. }
```

Let's step through the ContactManager program and discuss what it does:

1. Within main, two Contact objects are instantiated on lines 41–44.

2. The File object on line 45 represents the pathname to the file that we will be writing to and reading from, which is mycontacts.dat.

3. The addContact method is invoked on line 47, passing in the Bugs Bunny object. Within addContact, a FileOutputStream is instantiated on line 10 using mycontacts.dat. The true argument says to append to the file. Without the true argument, any existing data in the file is lost.

4. Line 11 chains a BufferedOutputStream to the FileOutputStream and line 12 chains a DataOutputStream to the buffer.

5. The writeUTF method is for writing String objects, and on line 13 "Bugs Bunny" is written to the file. Similarly, the int 22 is written on line 14 and the long 2025551212 is written on line 15.

6. The streams are closed and the method returns. The process repeats for Daffy Duck on line 48.

7. Line 50 invokes the getContacts method for mycontacts.dat, so control jumps to line 21.

8. Lines 25–27 chain together the streams to read, buffer, and filter the data in mycontacts.dat through a DataInputStream.

9. Lines 29–31 read in the data in the same order that it was written, and the data is used to instantiate a new Contact object. Line 33 adds the Contact object to the ArrayList from line 23.

10. The `while` loop on line 28 repeats until all the data is read from the file. For each set of data in the file, a `Contact` object is instantiated and added to the `ArrayList`, which is returned on line 36 and printed to the console on line 50. The `toString` method is invoked on each `Contact` and printed to the console.

The output of the `ContactManager` program is

```
[Bugs Bunny 22 2025551212
, Daffy Duck 33 3035551212
]
```

> The square brackets and comma in the output of ContactManager are the output of the ArrayList object. The toString method of ArrayList returns the elements of the collection in a comma-separated list, which is useful for debugging but probably not something you will use in a production scenario.

I doubt anyone would use the `ContactManager` program to actually manage your contacts in real life, but it does demonstrate a typical use of the classes in the `java.io` package: chaining streams together to buffer and filter the data into whatever format your program needs.

You might be tempted to write code like `ContactManager` that writes the fields of an object to a file. It seems like a good way to save the state of your objects, and it would make sense to do this except for the fact that Java has a built-in mechanism called serialization for saving the state of objects. In the upcoming section "Object Serialization," I provide a different version of `ContactManager` that writes `Contact` objects to a file in an easier fashion.

The next section discusses a stream that is both a low-level and a high-level stream: the `PrintWriter` class.

The *PrintWriter* Class

The purpose of a `PrintWriter` object is to print data types and objects to a character stream. The `PrintWriter` class contains the same `print` and `println` methods as `PrintStream` (the data type of `System.out` and `System.err`), except that `PrintWriter` outputs data as characters instead of bytes.

Let's start with a simple example of using `PrintWriter` to print data types to a file as characters. See if you can determine the result of the following statements:

```
6.   int i = 101;
7.   double d = 1.0/3.0;
8.   StringBuilder s = new StringBuilder("hello");
9.   boolean b = true;
10.
```

```
11. FileWriter fw = new FileWriter("characters.txt");
12. PrintWriter out = new PrintWriter(fw);
13. out.print(i);
14. out.println(d);
15. out.println(s);
16. out.println(b);
17. out.close();
18. fw.close();
```

The new `FileWriter` on line 11 creates a file named `characters.txt`, which is chained to a `PrintWriter` on line 12. Line 13 prints i without an ending line feed, so d gets printed on the same line as i. The `StringBuilder` s and the `boolean` b are printed next on their own lines, and the resulting file looks like this:

```
1010.3333333333333333
hello
true
```

The `int`, `double`, and `boolean` are converted to characters and output to the file. The value of d prints a long list of 3s because it is the fraction one third. The `print` and `println` methods cannot be used to control the format of d. If you need control over formatting, use the `format` method of `PrintWriter`, which is discussed next.

The *format and printf* Methods

The `format` method of a `PrintWriter` object writes a formatted string to the stream using a specified format string and arguments. Along with general knowledge of the `PrintWriter` class, the exam objectives specifically state that you need to be able to "write code using `PrintWriter.format/printf` methods." In addition, you must be able to "recognize and use formatting parameters (limited to: %b, %c, %d, %f, %s) in format strings." The Print-Writer class has been a part of the Java language since JDK 1.1, but the `format` and `printf` methods were introduced in Java 5.0.

As a convenience to C programmers familiar with C's `printf` function, `PrintWriter` also contains a `printf` method. The signatures of the two methods are

- `public PrintWriter format(String fmt, Object... args)`
- `public PrintWriter printf(String fmt, Object... args)`

Aside from their names, there is no difference between the `format` and `printf` methods. Their output and behavior is identical. The return value of both is the `PrintWriter` object, which allows for chaining of method calls. The `fmt` parameter consists of fixed text and one or more embedded *format specifiers*. The args parameter is a variable-length argument that contains a comma-separated list of data types that are written to the stream in the format specified by their corresponding format specifier. Here is an example of a call to format:

```
6.  PrintWriter out = new PrintWriter(System.out);
7.  double d = 0.1/0.3;
8.  String intro = "d = ";
9.  out.format("%s%7.3f", intro, d);
10. out.flush();
```

The PrintWriter on line 6 is chained to System.out, so it outputs characters to the console. The format specifier on line 9 is "%s%7.3f". The "s" denotes string conversion and is associated with the intro argument. The "f" denotes floating-point conversion and is associated with the d argument. The 7.3 before the f denotes the width (7) and precision (3) to output d in. Figure 4.9 shows how the format specifier lines up with the arguments to format.

FIGURE 4.9   Understanding format specifiers for the format method

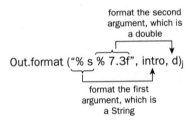

The output of the previous code is

```
d =    0.333
```

The double d has a width of 7, which includes the decimal point and two spaces preceding it. Because the intro string already has a space after its equals sign, there are exactly three spaces between the equals sign and the "0.333".

The syntax for a format specifier is as follows:

```
%[argument_index$][flags][width][.precision]conversion
```

The argument_index is optional and denotes the position of the argument in the argument list. The flags value is optional and varies depending on the specifier. The width value is the minimum number of characters to output. For floating-point numbers, the precision value is the number of digits to write after the decimal point.

Java has over 15 format conversions, but the exam objectives only require you to know the five specifiers shown in Table 4.2.

TABLE 4.2   The Format Specifiers

Conversion Specifier	Description
%b	Specifies a boolean
%c	Specifies a character
%d	Specifies an integer number
%f	Specifies a decimal number
%s	Specifies a string

The best way to understand the format specifiers is by looking at examples. Study the following code and see if you can determine its result:

```
11.  FileWriter fw = new FileWriter("format.txt");
12.  PrintWriter pw = new PrintWriter(fw);
13.  double r = Math.random();
14.  int x = 1, y = 2;
15.  pw.format("The number %4.2f is between %d and %d%n", r, x, y);
16.  pw.printf("%2$d %3$s %1$d%n", x, y, "is bigger than");
17.  pw.flush();
```

The output is formatted to a file named `format.txt`. Line 15 formats a `double` and two `ints`. The `%n` conversion outputs a line separator. Line 16 demonstrates the `argument_index` parameter, which appears before the dollar sign in a format specifier. For example, `"%2$d"` formats the second argument as an integer, and `"%3$s"` formats the third argument as a string. The resulting `format.txt` file looks like this:

```
The number 0.67 is between 1 and 2
2 is bigger than 1
```

The call to `printf` on line 16 could have been a call to `format` because the two methods are identical. In terms of the exam, make sure you know the conversions in Table 4.1 and the syntax for format specifiers. The `Formatter` and `Console` classes, discussed in the sidebar "The Formatter Class" and the next section, "The Console Class," use the same syntax.

The Formatter Class

The Formatter class is an interpreter for the format strings used in format/printf methods. The class is similar to the PrintWriter class except that Formatter defines only the format methods and not the printf methods. You invoke format in the way you do PrintWriter: passing in a format specifier followed by a comma-separated list of arguments.

For example, the following statements create a Formatter object and format a string of primitive types. Study the code and see if you can determine its output:

```
StringBuilder sb = new StringBuilder();
Formatter fmt = new Formatter(sb);
double d = 0.1/0.3;
int x = 123;
fmt.format("d=%5.3f and x=%6d", d, x);
System.out.println(sb.toString());
```

In this example, the Formatter writes its output to a StringBuilder object. The double d is formatted with a width of 5 and precision of 3. The int x is formatted with a width of 6, and the resulting StringBuffer looks like this:

```
d=0.333 and x=   123
```

As you can see, working with Formatter is similar to working with PrintWriter.

The *Console* Class

The java.io.Console class represents the JVM's console, typically the command prompt where the Java application is executed from. The System.in and System.out objects also represent the console, but they are byte streams. The Console class, new to the language as of Java 6.0, represents a single Console object in your JVM that provides access to the console input and output as character streams.

The Console class is unique in that it does not have any constructors. There is only one instance of this class, obtained by invoking the static method System.console(). This method returns null if no console device is available in your environment.

The Console class contains similar format and printf methods as the PrintWriter class:

-    public Console format(String fmt, Object... args)
-    public Console printf(String fmt, Object... args)

As with PrintWriter, these two methods in Console are synonyms and behave in the same manner. Let's look at an example. See if you can determine the format of the output of the following code:

```
4.  Console console = System.console();
5.  if(console == null) {
6.      throw new IOException("Console not available");
7.  }
8.  String formula = "Formula = ";
9.  double radius = 2.0;
10. console.format("%10s%12.10f * %3$4.2f * %3$4.2f%n",
11.              formula, Math.PI, radius);
12. double area = Math.PI * radius * radius;
13. console.format("%10s%16.13f%n", "Result = ", area);
```

Line 4 obtains a reference to the Console object, and line 5 makes sure that it worked by checking for a null return value. Line 10 formats four conversions, but notice there are only three arguments. The third argument, radius, is formatted twice (demonstrating that arguments can be reused in the format specifier). Also the two strings formula and "Result = " have the same width so that they line up nicely. The output of the code is sent to the console and looks like this:

```
Formula = 3.1415926536 * 2.00 * 2.00
 Result = 12.5663706143592
```

You can also use the Console object to read keyboard input from the user. The Console class defines four methods for reading in a single line of text from the console:

- public String readLine() reads in a single line as a String.
- public String readLine(String fmt, Object... args) displays a formatted prompt, then reads a single line as a String.
- public char [] readPassword() reads a line of text as a char array with echoing disabled.
- public char [] readPassword(String fmt, Object... args) displays a formatted prompt and then reads a line of text as a char array with echoing disabled.

The readPassword methods provide support for secure password entry by disabling the input and also by storing the input in an array of chars, allowing you to overwrite the password in memory after it has been used without waiting for the garbage collector.

The following code demonstrates reading input using the Console object by prompting the user for a username and password. Study the code and see if you can determine its output:

```
10. Console console = System.console();
11. if(console == null) {
12.     throw new IOException("Console not available");
13. }
14. String userprompt = "Enter username:";
15. String passprompt = "Password:";
```

```
16. String verifyprompt = "Verify password:";
17.
18. String username = console.readLine("%18s ", userprompt);
19. char [] password = console.readPassword("%18s ", passprompt);
20. char [] verify = console.readPassword("%18s ", verifyprompt);
21. if(password == null || !Arrays.equals(password, verify)) {
22.     System.out.println("Passwords do not match");
23.     return;
24. }
25. if(!Arrays.equals(password, "qwerty123".toCharArray())) {
26.     System.out.println("Invalid login");
27.     return;
28. }
29. System.out.println("Login successful!");
30. //Remove password from memory
31. for(int i = 0; i < password.length; i++) {
32.     password[i] = 'x';
33.     verify[i] = 'x';
34. }
```

The following breakdown illustrates what the code does:

1. Line 10 obtains a reference to the Console object and lines 11–13 verify that the Console is available.

2. Line 18 displays "Enter username:" formatted as 18 characters and the program waits for the user to input a line of text at the console.

3. Lines 19 and 20 prompt the user to input a password twice. The program waits for input each time and users cannot see their input.

4. Line 21 uses the Arrays.equals method for comparing two arrays of type char. If password is null or the two input passwords are different, the method returns.

5. Line 25 compares the password input by the user to "qwerty123".

6. The for loop on line 31 overwrites the two passwords input by the user with xs (this is done for security purposes).

The output varies depending on what the user inputs. The following output occurs if the user inputs any username and "qwerty123" for both passwords:

```
Enter username: raposa
        Password:
  Verify password:
Login successful!
```

The output does not show the passwords because the readPassword method disables the echoing of user input.

NOTE The Console class is preferred over using System.out and System.in when working with formatted output to the console or console input from the user. Because the class is new in Java 6.0, expect a question or two about Console on the exam.

Next we discuss a different exam objective: object serialization. I explain how it works in the next section and discuss the various classes and interface involved.

Object Serialization

The exam objectives state that you need to be able to "develop code that serializes and/or de-serializes objects using the following APIs from java.io: DataInputStream, DataOutput-Stream, FileInputStream, FileOutputStream, ObjectInputStream, ObjectOutputStream and Serializable." In other words, you need to understand the details of Java object serialization. The earlier section titled "The DataInputStream and DataOutputStream Classes" discussed saving the state of an object using DataInputStream and DataOutputStream. This section focuses on the ObjectInputStream and ObjectOutputStream classes and the Serializable interface.

Object serialization refers to taking the state of an object and writing it to a stream. You can use serialization to persistently store your objects in files. You can also serialize an object and send it across the network to another Java program or save it in a database. *Deserialization* refers to the process of reading the data from an object stream and reconstituting the object in memory. Not all objects can be serialized; only objects whose classes implement the java.io.Serializable interface. Let's take a look at this interface and what it means to implement it.

The *Serializable* Interface

The Serializable interface is a tagging interface, which means it does not have any methods in it. A class implements Serializable to let the JVM know that instances of the class can be serialized. There is no extra work on your part to make a class serializable because there are no methods in the interface. Your main concern with implementing Serializable is ensuring that all the fields in your class are also Serializable. If an attempt is made to serialize an object and a field is reached during the serialization process that is not serializable, the JVM throws a NotSerializableException and the serialization fails. The compiler does not verify whether or not your fields are Serializable. Denote a field as *transient* (using the transient keyword) to tell the JVM to ignore the field during the serialization and deserialization process.

Why Not Make Everything Serializable?

You might be wondering why Java doesn't just make all objects serializable automatically. The reason is that for some objects it does not make sense to save their state. For example, the Thread class is not serializable, nor are any of the stream classes in the `java.io` package. It would be too difficult to try to save the state of a thread or stream object, and their state is often not the kind of information that you want or need to save anyway. However, most classes in the Java API are serializable and many of the classes you write will likely be serializable as well. For example, the String class implements `Serializable`, as do most of the data structure classes in the Collections API of the `java.util` package. If you are not sure whether or not an object is serializable, check the Java API documentation and see if its corresponding class implements the `Serializable` interface.

Let's take a look at an example by revisiting the Contact class from earlier in this chapter. I renamed the class Contact2 to distinguish it from the earlier version, and I added a GregorianCalendar field to represent the person's birthday. The Contact2 class implements Serializable, and I also made the fields private to demonstrate that the access specifier on a field does not have an effect on serialization. The city field is declared transient to demonstrate the effect of the transient keyword.

```
package com.sybex.io;

import java.util.GregorianCalendar;

public class Contact2 implements java.io.Serializable {
    private String name;
    private int age;
    private long cellPhone;
    private GregorianCalendar birthday;
    private transient String city;

    public Contact2(String name, int age, long cellPhone,
                    GregorianCalendar birthday, String city) {
        this.name = name;
        this.age = age;
        this.cellPhone = cellPhone;
        this.birthday = birthday;
        this.city = city;
    }

    public String toString() {
```

```
        return name + " " + age + " " + cellPhone;
    }

    public String getCity() {
        return city;
    }
}
```

The Contact2 class implements Serializable, so each of its nontransient fields better be Serializable as well. The primitive types are no problem because all the primitive types are serializable. You won't be surprised to find that the String class implements Serializable, as does the GregorianCalendar class. Therefore, we should be able to serialize objects of type Contact2 using the ObjectOutputStream class.

The *ObjectOutputStream* Class

An ObjectOutputStream writes Serializable objects to an output stream. It is a high-level stream that needs to be chained to a low-level stream that represents the destination of the serialized objects. The upcoming SerializeDemo program demonstrates using FileOutput-Stream with ObjectOutputStream.

The ObjectOutputStream class contains methods for writing primitive types and String objects, but the principal method of ObjectOutputStream is public void writeObject(Object obj) throws IOException.

The writeObject method serializes the Object argument passed in. If the Object passed in is not serializable, a NotSerializableException is thrown. If the Object is serializable, all the information necessary to deserialize the object is written to the stream, including the class name, class signature, and the values of the nonstatic and nontransient fields.

Let's look at an example that serializes Contact2 objects to a file. Study the following SerializeDemo program and see if you can determine its result:

```
1.  package com.sybex.io;
2.
3.  import java.io.*;
4.  import java.util.GregorianCalendar;
5.
6.  public class SerializeDemo {
7.      public static void main(String [] args) {
8.          try {
9.              GregorianCalendar bday1 =
10.                     new GregorianCalendar(1950, 3, 21);
11.             GregorianCalendar bday2 =
12.                     new GregorianCalendar(1956, 5, 30);
13.             Contact2 one = new Contact2("Bugs Bunny", 22,
```

```
14.                         2025551212L, bday1, "Toontown");
15.             Contact2 two = new Contact2("Daffy Duck", 33,
16.                         3035551212L, bday2, "Toontown");
17.
18.             File contactsFile = new File("mycontacts.ser");
19.             FileOutputStream fos =
20.                     new FileOutputStream(contactsFile);
21.             ObjectOutputStream out = new ObjectOutputStream(fos);
22.
23.             out.writeObject(one);
24.             out.writeObject(two);
25.
26.             out.close();
27.             fos.close();
28.         }catch(IOException e) {
29.             e.printStackTrace();
30.         }
31.     }
32. }
```

There is no output, but the SerializeDemo program does create a new file named my contacts.ser that contains two serialized objects of type Contact2. The lines of code to focus on in this program are lines 23 and 24. Calling writeObject and passing in a Contact2 reference serializes the object and writes it to the mycontacts.ser file.

Now that we have seen how to serialize objects, let's look at the code to deserialize them using the ObjectInputStream class.

The *ObjectInputStream* Class

An ObjectInputStream deserializes objects from an input stream. It is a high-level stream that needs to be chained to a low-level stream that represents the source of the serialized objects. You should know how to use FileInputStream with ObjectInputStream, and I discuss an example of using these two classes as we deserialize the two Contact2 objects from the SerializeDemo program in the previous section.

The ObjectInputStream class contains read methods that correspond to the write methods of ObjectOutputStream, including public Object readObject() throws IOException, ClassNotFoundException.

The readObject method deserializes the next object in the stream. Note the reference type of the return value is Object. Typically we need to cast the reference to its appropriate class type.

The following DeserializeDemo program deserializes two objects from the mycontacts. ser file created in SerializeDemo. Assuming the SerializeDemo program is executed once, see if you can determine the output of this program:

```
1.   package com.sybex.io;
2.
3.   import java.io.*;
4.   import java.util.GregorianCalendar;
5.
6.   public class DeserializeDemo {
7.       public static void main(String [] args) {
8.           try {
9.               File contactsFile = new File("mycontacts.ser");
10.              FileInputStream fis =
11.                      new FileInputStream(contactsFile);
12.              ObjectInputStream in = new ObjectInputStream(fis);
13.
14.              while(fis.available() > 0) {
15.                  Object obj = in.readObject();
16.                  if(obj instanceof Contact2) {
17.                      Contact2 contact = (Contact2) obj;
18.                      System.out.println(contact);
19.                      System.out.println("city = "
20.                                  + contact.getCity());
21.                  }
22.              }
23.
24.              in.close();
25.              fis.close();
26.          }catch(IOException e) {
27.              e.printStackTrace();
28.          }catch(ClassNotFoundException c) {
29.              c.printStackTrace();
30.          }
31.      }
32. }
```

The while loop on line 14 reads in objects from the mycontacts.ser file until the stream is empty. Two objects are in the file, so the while loop executes twice. The instanceof comparison on line 16 is true for both objects and line 18 prints the Contact2 object, outputting the result of its toString method. I added line 19 to explicitly illustrate that the city field did not get serialized because it was declared transient. Transient fields are ignored during serialization and initialized to their "zero" value during deserialization, which for references is null. The output of the DeserializeDemo program is

```
Bugs Bunny 22 2025551212
city = null
Daffy Duck 33 3035551212
city = null
```

By the way, the GregorianCalendar objects were also serialized, but the toString method for GregorianCalendar prints out a lot of information, so I purposely left it out of the toString method of Contact2. (We discuss formatting dates in detail later in this chapter.) If you open mycontacts.ser in a text editor, you will clearly see the two GregorianCalendar objects serialized in the file.

Now that we have seen how to serialize and deserialize objects, let's turn our attention to formatting and parsing data that uses the java.text package.

Formatting and Parsing Data

The java.text package contains classes and interfaces for handling text, dates, numbers, and messages independent of the language that is being used in the application. According to the exam objectives, you need to be able to "use standard J2SE APIs in the java.text package to correctly format or parse dates, numbers, and currency values for a specific locale." This section discusses these topics in detail, including how to

- Format and parse numbers and currency using the DecimalFormat and NumberFormat classes in java.text.
- Format and parse dates using the java.text.DateFormat class.

Format and Parse Numbers and Currency

The java.text.NumberFormat class is the abstract parent class of the number formatting classes. The class contains static methods for getting appropriate formatter instances based on the type of number you are formatting. For example, if you want to format currency, use the static getCurrencyInstance method. Because formatting currency varies depending on the language and culture of the users of your program, you can also specify the locale of your specific users. Use a java.util.Locale object to represent your desired locale.

The following list gives the static methods in NumberFormat for obtaining instances of NumberFormat:

- public static final NumberFormat getInstance() is a general-purpose number format that uses the default locale.
- public static NumberFormat getInstance(Locale loc) is the same as the previous method except that the format uses the specified locale.
- public static final NumberFormat getNumberInstance() is intended for formatting and parsing numbers in the default locale.

- `public static NumberFormat getNumberInstance(Locale loc)` is used for formatting and parsing numbers in the given locale.

- `public static final NumberFormat getCurrencyInstance()` returns a currency format for the default locale.

- `public static NumberFormat getCurrencyInstance(Locale loc)` returns a currency format for the given locale.

- `public static final NumberFormat getIntegerInstance()` is used for formatting and parsing integers. Floating-point numbers are rounded using the half-even rounding mode. (See the Java API documentation for `NumberFormat` if you are interested in learning about the half-even rounding mode. It is not a topic you need to know for the SCJP exam.)

- `public static NumberFormat getIntegerInstance(Locale loc)` returns an integer format for the given locale.

- `public static final NumberFormat getPercentInstance()` is intended for formatting and parsing percentages using the default locale.

- `public static NumberFormat getPercentInstance(Locale loc)` returns a percentage format for the given locale.

Each method is overloaded with a `Locale` object so that you can use a formatter for a specific locale. The no-argument versions of these methods use the default locale, which vary depending on the platform that the program executes on. After you obtain a `Number-Format` instance, use its `format` and `parse` methods to format and parse numbers and currency. Let's start with a discussion on the `format` methods.

The *NumberFormat.format* Methods

Use one of the `format` methods of the `NumberFormat` class to format a number. The class defines several overloaded versions of `format`, including

- `public final String format(long number)`
- `public final String format(double number)`

The `format` method formats the given number based on the locale associated with the `NumberFormat` object. The following code demonstrates using a `NumberFormat` object with the German language locale. Study the code and see if you can determine its output:

```
NumberFormat nf = NumberFormat.getInstance(Locale.GERMAN);
double d = 123.57;
System.out.println(nf.format(d));
```

If you are not familiar with how numbers are formatted in German, decimal numbers use a comma instead of a decimal point, so the output is

```
123,57
```

See if you can determine the output of the following statements:

```
NumberFormat pf = NumberFormat.getPercentInstance();
double p = 0.47;
System.out.println(pf.format(p));
```

Because no Locale is specified, the NumberFormat object uses the default locale. Running the program on a Windows machine in the United States outputs

```
47%
```

Notice that the decimal 0.47 is converted to the number 47 followed by the percent symbol, which is the syntax expected in the United States.

Working with Locales

A locale represents a specific geographical, political, or cultural region. The java.util .Locale class represents a locale. To obtain a Locale object, you can either instantiate a new one by passing a language into one of its constructors, or you can use one of the many static Locale fields in the Locale class. For example, the following statement creates a new Locale object for the Portuguese language:

```
Locale por = new Locale("pt");
```

The string "pt" represents the two-letter code for Portuguese as specified by ISO 639.2. View a complete list of language codes online at http://www.loc.gov/standards/ iso639-2/.

The static fields of Locale represent locales for commonly used languages and countries. For example, if you need a formatter for the Japanese language, use the Locale .JAPANESE object.

To format currency, use a NumberFormat object obtained from the getCurrencyInstance methods. The following statements format a double as currency in the country locale of France:

```
NumberFormat cf = NumberFormat.getCurrencyInstance(Locale.FRANCE);
double c = 59.99321;
FileWriter fw = new FileWriter("numberformat.txt");
PrintWriter pw = new PrintWriter(fw);
pw.println(cf.format(c));
pw.flush();
pw.close();
fw.close();
```

France uses the euro for its currency, and the output in the numberformat.txt file looks like this:

59,99

Notice the double c was rounded to two decimal places, a comma appears instead of a decimal point, and the euro symbol appears after the digits. (I had to write the output to a file because my Windows console was not properly displaying the euro symbol.)

The *DecimalFormat* Class

The NumberFormat class has a child class named DecimalFormat that adds a variety of features for formatting floating-point numbers, including the ability to specify precision, leading and trailing zeros, and prefixes and suffixes. You can obtain a DecimalFormat object in two ways:

- Instantiate a new DecimalFormat using one of its constructors, which is useful when working with the default locale.

- When using a specific locale, invoke the static getInstance method in NumberFormat and cast the return value to a DecimalFormat.

A DecimalFormat object has a pattern to represent the format of the decimal number. The pattern consists of symbols, which include pound signs (#) and zeros to denote placeholders. The pound signs are placeholders that are ignored if the number has fewer digits than the pattern. The zeros are placeholders that represent leading and trailing zeros if the number has fewer digits than the pattern.

The pattern is best understood by an example. The following code creates several DecimalFormat objects that format a large floating-point number. Study the code and see if you can determine its output:

```
8.  double d = 1234567.437;
9.  DecimalFormat one = new DecimalFormat("###,###,###.###");
10. System.out.println(one.format(d));
11.
12. DecimalFormat two = new DecimalFormat("000,000,000.00000");
13. System.out.println(two.format(d));
14.
15. DecimalFormat three = new DecimalFormat("$#,###,###.##");
16. System.out.println(three.format(d));
```

The DecimalFormat object on line 15 demonstrates adding a symbol to the pattern, in this case a dollar sign. The output of the code is

```
1,234,567.437
001,234,567.43700
$1,234,567.44
```

The DecimalFormat object on line 12 puts leading and trailing zeros on the number, and the one from line 15 prefixes a dollar sign and the decimal value is rounded up.

When using a locale, a `DecimalFormat` object is obtained by calling `getInstance` in `NumberFormat` and casting the return value, as demonstrated in the following code. Study the code and see if you can determine its output:

```
18. NumberFormat nf = NumberFormat.getInstance(Locale.GERMAN);
19. if(nf instanceof DecimalFormat) {
20.     DecimalFormat df = (DecimalFormat) nf;
21.     df.applyPattern("##,#00.00#");
22.     double d1 = 23184.348;
23.     double d2 = 3.1;
24.     System.out.println(df.format(d1));
25.     System.out.println(df.format(d2));
26. }
```

On line 18 the locale is set to the German language, and `getInstance` typically returns a `DecimalFormat` object, so line 19 is `true` for most environments. The pattern on line 21 contains both pound signs and zeros and uses English-style commas and a decimal point. In German, the commas are replaced by a decimal point and vice versa. The output of the code is

```
23.184,348
03,10
```

The double 3.1 is formatted with a leading and trailing zero because the pattern calls for at least two digits before and after the decimal.

The *NumberFormat.parse* Method

The `NumberFormat` class defines a `parse` method for parsing a `String` into a number using a specific locale. The signature of the `parse` method is `public Number parse(String source) throws ParseException`.

The result of parsing depends on the locale. For example, if the locale is the United States and the number contains commas, the commas are treated as formatting symbols. If the locale is a country or language that uses commas as a decimal separator, the comma is treated as a decimal point. In other words, the value of the resulting number depends on the locale.

Let's look at an example. The following code parses the same string with different locales. Study the code and see if you can determine its output:

```
6.  NumberFormat en = NumberFormat.getInstance(Locale.US);
7.  NumberFormat fr = NumberFormat.getInstance(Locale.FRANCE);
8.
9.  try {
10.     String s = "123,45";
11.     System.out.println(en.parse(s));
```

```
12.        System.out.println(fr.parse(s));
13. }catch(ParseException e) {
14.        e.printStackTrace();
15. }
```

The string being parsed is "123,45". In the U.S. locale, the comma is treated as a visual format and is ignored, so the resulting number is the integer 12345. In the France locale, the comma is a decimal separator, so the resulting number is the double 123.45. The output of the code is

```
12345
123.45
```

The parse method only parses the beginning of a string. After it reaches a character that cannot be parsed, the parsing stops and the value is returned. See if you can determine the output of the following statements:

```
NumberFormat nf = NumberFormat.getInstance();

try {
    String one = "456abc";
    String two = "-2.5165e10";
    String three = "x85.3";
    System.out.println(nf.parse(one));
    System.out.println(nf.parse(two));
    System.out.println(nf.parse(three));
}catch(ParseException e) {
    e.printStackTrace();
}
```

The NumberFormat object uses the default locale to parse "456abc". When the 'a' character is reached, the parsing stops and 456 is returned. Similarly, the String two is parsed into -2.5165. Parsing "x85.3" throws a ParseException because the beginning of the string cannot be parsed. The output of the code is

```
456
-2.5165
java.text.ParseException: Unparseable number: "x85.3"
```

 I do not think the exam will test your knowledge of such details about the parse method and the point at which parsing fails, but it is a good trait to understand. Instead, expect a question that successfully parses a string to a number.

The parse method is also used for parsing currency. Study the following code and see if you can determine its output:

```
29. NumberFormat cf = NumberFormat.getCurrencyInstance();

30. try {
31.     String amt = "$12,345.99";
32.     double value = (Double) cf.parse(amt);
33.     System.out.println(value);
34. }catch(ParseException e) {
35.     e.printStackTrace();
36. }
```

The currency string "$12,345.99" on line 31 contains a dollar sign and a comma. The parse method strips out the characters and converts the value to a number. Assuming a U.S. locale, the output of the code is

```
12345.99
```

The return value of parse is a Number object. Number is the parent class of all the java.lang wrapper classes, so the return value can be cast to its appropriate data type. On line 32, the Number is cast to a Double and then automatically unboxed into a double.

The NumberFormat and DecimalFormat classes have other features and capabilities, but the topics covered in this section address the content you need to know for the SCJP exam. The next section discusses how to format and parse dates.

Format and Parse Dates

The java.text.DateFormat class is an abstract class that formats and parses dates and times for a specific locale. Similar to NumberFormat, DateFormat objects are obtained by invoking one of the static factory methods in the DateFormat class. You can create a date format for working with just dates, or a date/time format for working with dates and times, as follows:

- public static final DateFormat getDateInstance() is intended for formatting dates in the default locale.

- public static final DateFormat getDateInstance(int style, Locale loc) gets the date formatter with the specified style and locale. The possible formatting styles are FULL, LONG, MEDIUM, and SHORT, static constants defined in the DateFormat class.

- public static final DateFormat getTimeInstance() is used for formatting times in the default locale.

- public static final DateFormat getTimeInstance(int style, Locale loc) gets the time formatter with the specified style and locale. The possible time formatting styles are FULL, LONG, MEDIUM, and SHORT.

- public static final DateFormat getDateTimeInstance() is used for formatting dates and times in the default locale.

- `public static final DateFormat getDateTimeInstance(int dateStyle, int timeStyle, Locale loc)` gets a date/time formatter with the specified date style, time style, and locale.

The DateFormat class also defines a third overloaded version for each of these methods that takes in the style `int`s but not the `Locale` reference, so the default locale is used for those methods. After you obtain a DateFormat object, you use its `format` and `parse` methods to format and parse dates and times in the specified locale, which we discuss next.

The *DateFormat.format* Methods

The DateFormat class defines three `format` methods, but you only need to know one of these for the exam: `public final String format(Date date)`.

The date parameter is of type `java.util.Date`, a useful class that represents a specific instance in time as milliseconds. A Date object is instantiated by passing in a `long` that represents the time in milliseconds from January 1, 1970 at 00:00:00 GMT. (The no-argument constructor of Date returns the current time on the underlying platform.) The `format` method returns the String representation of the given Date based on the specified locale of the DateFormat object.

Let's look at an example. The following code creates a Date object that lies on January 31, 1984, and formats the date in both the SHORT and FULL styles:

```
DateFormat df = DateFormat.getDateInstance(DateFormat.SHORT);
DateFormat full =DateFormat.getDateInstance(DateFormat.FULL);

Date d = new Date(444444444000L);
System.out.println(df.format(d));
System.out.println(full.format(d));
```

The output of the statements is

```
1/31/84
Tuesday, January 31, 1984
```

To include the time in the format of a date, use a DateFormat object from the get DateTimeInstance method. The following statement formats the same Date object from the previous code using a MEDIUM date style and a FULL time style:

```
DateFormat dtf = DateFormat.getDateTimeInstance(
                        DateFormat.MEDIUM,
                        DateFormat.FULL);
System.out.println(dtf.format(d));
```

The output of the previous statements depends on the time zone and locale, but it will look something like this:

```
Jan 31, 1984 5:47:24 PM MST
```

Let's try a similar format with the same date but a different locale. The following statements use a DateFormat object for the country Germany:

```
DateFormat de = DateFormat.getDateTimeInstance(
                            DateFormat.MEDIUM,
                            DateFormat.FULL,
                            Locale.GERMANY);
System.out.println(de.format(d));
```

The output of the statements looks something like this:

```
31.01.1984 17.47 Uhr MST
```

Between the various date styles, time styles, and locales, you have a lot of options for formatting dates and times using the DateFormat class. The class is also used for parsing dates, as the next section shows.

The *DateFormat.parse* Method

The DateFormat class contains the following parse method for parsing strings into dates:
public Date parse(String source) throws ParseException.

The return value is of type java.util.Date, and the ParseException is thrown when the beginning of the string cannot be parsed into a date successfully.

The format of the String object depends on both the style and the locale of the DateFormat object. The following statements parse a date string in the SHORT style of the U.S. locale, and then format the resulting Date object in the FULL style of the France locale:

```
7.  DateFormat shortFormat = DateFormat.getDateInstance(
8.                              DateFormat.SHORT,
9.                              Locale.US);
10. String s = "01/31/1984";
11. try {
12.    Date date = shortFormat.parse(s);
13.    DateFormat fullFormat = DateFormat.getDateInstance(
14.                            DateFormat.FULL,
15.                            Locale.FRANCE);
16.    System.out.println(fullFormat.format(date));
17. }catch(ParseException e) {
18.    e.printStackTrace();
19. }
```

The shortFormat object has the SHORT date style and U.S. locale, and on line 12 it parses the string "01/31/1984". The resulting Date object is printed on line 16 using a FULL style with the France locale. The output is

```
mardi 31 janvier 1984
```

The parse method throws a ParseException if the beginning of the string cannot be parsed. As with the parse method in NumberFormat, the parse method in DateFormat successfully parses a string if the beginning of the string is in the proper format.

The DateFormat class is useful when you develop Java applications that need to work with formatted dates and times. The next section discusses some useful classes for working with regular expressions.

Regular Expressions

A *regular expression* is a sequence of characters that describes a pattern of characters. The pattern describes a set of strings based on common characteristics. The syntax for a regular expression is not unique to Java, and they are used in many different programming languages. Java uses the Pattern and Matcher classes in the java.util.regex package for using regular expressions in your Java applications.

For the exam you should be able to write code that uses the Pattern and Matcher classes and the String.split method. You also need to be able to "recognize and use regular expression patterns for matching (limited to: . (dot), * (star), + (plus), ?, \d, \s, \w, [], ())." The objectives specifically state that what you need to know about "the use of *, +, and ? will be limited to greedy quantifiers, and the parentheses operator will only be used as a grouping mechanism, not for capturing content during matching." This section discusses these topics in detail, starting with a discussion on the Pattern and Matcher classes.

The *Pattern* and *Matcher* Classes

The Pattern class represents a compiled regular expression. You do not instantiate a Pattern object; instances are obtained from the static compile method defined in the Pattern class public static Pattern compile(String regex).

Regular expressions need to be compiled into a pattern. The resulting Pattern object is used to obtain a Matcher instance. A Matcher object represents the engine that performs the actual parsing on the character sequence to see if it matches the pattern.

The following statements represent a typical usage of the Pattern and Matcher classes:

```
5.   String regex = "hello";
6.   Pattern pattern = Pattern.compile(regex);
7.   Matcher m1 = pattern.matcher("hello");
8.   Matcher m2 = pattern.matcher("goodbye");
9.   if(m1.matches()) {
10.      System.out.println("hello is a match");
```

```
11. }
12. if(m2.matches()) {
13.     System.out.println("goodbye is a match");
14. }
```

The regular expression "hello" on line 5 is an example of a string literal pattern, the simplest pattern in regular expressions. A character sequence matches the regular expression "hello" only if the character sequence is "hello". The Pattern object on line 6 represents the compiled pattern. Two Matcher objects are instantiated for the pattern: "hello" and "goodbye". Line 9 is true because "hello" matches the pattern, and line 12 is false because "goodbye" does not match the pattern. The output of the code is

```
hello is a match
```

Regular Expression Metacharacters

A typical regular expression is more complex than a string literal like "hello". A special set of characters called *metacharacters* is used to specify wildcards, repetition, ranges, and more. Table 4.3 shows the metacharacters specifically mentioned in the SCJP exam objectives.

TABLE 4.3 Metacharacters of Regular Expressions

Metacharacter	Description
. (dot)	Any character
*	Match the preceding character any number of times
+	Match the previous character one or more times
?	Match the previous character 0 or 1 times only
\d	A digit 0–9
\s	A whitespace character
\w	A word character (any lowercase or uppercase letter, the underscore character, or any digit)
[ ]	Match anything inside the square brackets for one character position once
( )	Use parentheses for grouping together search expressions

Let's look at an example of the various metacharacters. Suppose we have the following Pattern:

```
14. String regex = ".ing";
15. Pattern pattern = Pattern.compile(regex);
```

The dot in a regular expression represents any character, so ".ing" says "match any word that begins with any character and ends in ing." Using this pattern, see if you can determine the output of the following statements:

```
16. String [] tests = {"ing", "ring", "trying", "running", "beings"};
17. for(String test: tests) {
18.     Matcher m = pattern.matcher(test);
19.     if(m.matches()) {
20.         System.out.println(test + " matches " + regex);
21.     }
22. }
```

The for loop on line 17 iterates through the tests array and creates a Matcher object for each String in the array. Line 19 invokes the matches method in Matcher, which returns true if the pattern matches the String. The only String in tests that consists of one character and ends in "ing" is "ring", so the output of the code is

```
ring matches .ing
```

If you want to match all words that end in "ing", then use the * metacharacter, which matches the preceding character any number of times. Assuming we use the same tests array from earlier, see if you can determine the matches of the following pattern:

```
String regex = ".*ing";
Pattern pattern = Pattern.compile(regex);
```

The regular expression ".*ing" matches any word ending in "ing", so the matches from the tests array are

```
ing matches .*ing
ring matches .*ing
trying matches .*ing
running matches .*ing
```

Use square brackets ([]) to denote a list or range of specific characters in a regular expression. For example, the pattern [aeiou] matches any vowel. Use a hyphen (-) to specify a range of characters. For example, the expression [q-v] is equivalent to [qrstuv]. The pattern [a-zA-Z] matches any uppercase or lowercase letter of the alphabet. See if you can determine the types of strings that match the following pattern:

```
String regex = "[qrstuv]*.ing";
Pattern pattern = Pattern.compile(regex);
```

The pattern matches any word that starts with any character between 'q' and 'v' (the [qrstuv]) repeated any number of times (the "*"), followed by any single character (the .), and ending with the literal string "ing". Using the tests array from the previous examples, the matches are

```
ring matches [qrstuv]*.ing
trying matches [qrstuv]*.ing
```

Together with *, the + and ? metacharacters also allow for repetition in a regular expression. The + matches the previous character or expression one or more times, while ? matches the previous character or expression zero or one times. For example, the pattern x+ matches 1 or more xs. The pattern [aeiou]? matches any vowel zero or one times.

See if you can determine the output of the following statements:

```
23. Pattern p = Pattern.compile("[0-4]+[a-z]*[5-9]?");
24. String [] values = {"4a", "112abc6", "2345", "01a",
25.                      "a5" , "4a56" };
26. for(String value: values) {
27.     Matcher m = p.matcher(value);
28.     if(m.matches()) {
29.         System.out.println(value + " matches [0-4]+[a-z]*[5-9]?");
30.     }
31. }
```

Figure 4.10 explains the pattern "[0-4]+[a-z]*[5-9]?" and the strings that match it.

FIGURE 4.10   Using the +, ?, and * metacharacters   [f0410.eps]

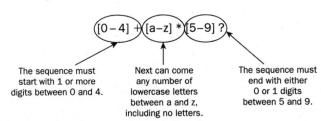

The string "a5" does not match because it does not start with a digit between 0 and 4. The string "4a56" does not match because it ends with two digits between 5 and 9. The other four strings in the values array match, so the output of the code is

```
4a matches [0-4]+[a-z]*[5-9]?
112abc6 matches [0-4]+[a-z]*[5-9]?
2345 matches [0-4]+[a-z]*[5-9]?
01a matches [0-4]+[a-z]*[5-9]?
```

Parentheses in a Regular Expression

Use parentheses to group together expressions in a regular expression. For example, the pattern a*b+ matches any number of a's followed by one or more b's. Matches include ab, aaaab, and b. Adding parentheses can change the pattern. For example, the pattern (a*b)+ matches any number of a's followed by one b, with that pattern repeated one or more times. Matches include ab, abaabab, and babb.

The *Pattern* Character Classes

The Pattern class uses several predefined *character classes* that represent commonly used character patterns in regular expressions. The exam objectives explicitly state knowledge of the following three character classes:

- \d, which denotes a digit; equivalent to [0-9]
- \s, which denotes a whitespace character; equivalent to [\t\n\x0B\f\r]
- \w, which denotes a word character; equivalent to [a-zA-Z_0-9]

Because the syntax of the character classes starts with a backslash, in Java you must escape them with an additional backslash. For example, the following regular expression matches one or more digits:

```
String digits = "\\d+";
```

See if you can determine the output of the following statements:

```
34. String s = "[A-Z]\\w*\\s+[A-Z]\\w+";
35. Pattern x = Pattern.compile(s);
36. String [] names = {"John Doe", "JohnDoe", "John\tDoe", "John doe",
37.                     "J D", "J   D5"};
38. for(String name: names) {
39.     Matcher m = x.matcher(name);
40.     if(m.matches()) {
41.         System.out.println(name + " matches " + s);
42.     }
43. }
```

Figure 4.11 breaks down the regular expression on line 34.

FIGURE 4.11   A regular expression that contains character classes

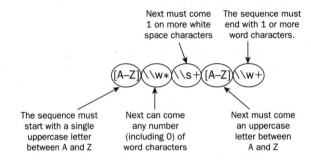

The string `"JohnDoe"` is not a match because it does not contain any whitespace characters. `"John doe"` is not a match because the second word does not start with a letter from A to Z. `"J D"` is not a match because the D is not followed by one or more word characters. The other strings in the `names` array match, so the output of the code is

```
John Doe matches [A-Z]\w*\s+[A-Z]\w+
John     Doe matches [A-Z]\w*\s+[A-Z]\w+
J    D5 matches [A-Z]\w*\s+[A-Z]\w+
```

As you can see, regular expressions can become quite complex, but their complexity makes them a powerful tool for matching character sequences. They also show up in other Java API classes and methods, including the `String.split` method, which we discuss next.

The *String.split* Method

The `String` class contains a method named `split` that takes in a regular expression and splits the `String` object into an array of `String` objects. The signature of the `split` method is `public String [] split(String regex)`.

The `String` argument is a regular expression, and the return value is one or more `String` objects in an array. The size of the array depends on how many matches of the regular expression are found. For example, the following statements split a `String` object into three `String` objects:

```
String greetings = "hi;hello;welcome";
String [] greetingsArray = greetings.split(";");
for(String greeting : greetingsArray) {
    System.out.println(greeting);
}
```

The regular expression in the call to `split` is the string literal `";"` that appears twice in the `greetings` `String`. The `greetingsArray` contains three elements. The output of the code is

```
hi
hello
welcome
```

The `split` method is useful for parsing character sequences where the delimiter is defined as a regular expression, as demonstrated by the following statements. See if you can determine the output of this code:

```
String data = "3035551212,123 Main St.\tDenver,CO:50431";
String [] results = data.split("[;,:\\t]");
for(String result : results) {
    System.out.println(result);
}
```

The regular expression [;,:\\t] splits the `String` at every semicolon, comma, colon, or tab. The output of the code is

```
3035551212
123 Main St.
Denver
CO
50431
```

Limiting the Results of the `split` Method

The `split` method also has an overloaded version that takes in an `int` that limits the number of times the regular expression is applied to the `String`. If you specify a limit, after the limit is reached the remaining characters are placed in the last element of the `String` array. For example, the following code invokes `split` with a limit of 3, so the resulting array will not be larger than three elements. See if you can determine the output:

```
String s = "abc,def,g,hi,jklm,o";
String [] array = s.split(",", 3);
for(String x : array) {
    System.out.println(x);
}
```

The "abc" and "def" are split into the array and the remaining characters are put in a `String` in the third element of the array. The output of the code is

```
abc
def
g,hi,jklm,o
```

As I mentioned earlier, regular expressions appear in other areas of the Java API, but the exam objectives only require knowledge of the `Pattern` and `Matcher` classes and the `String.split` method. Now that we have discussed regular expressions, we can explore the `Scanner` class.

The Scanner Class

The Scanner class is a text scanner that can parse primitive data type and strings into tokens. The delimiter for the tokens is either whitespace or a regular expression. The source of the text can be from a `String`, `File`, or `InputStream` object. You can also assign a `Locale` to a Scanner object.

A Scanner is constructed by passing in the source of the data. Here are some of the constructors in Scanner:

- `public Scanner(File source) throws FileNotFoundException`
- `public Scanner(InputStream source)`
- `public Scanner(String source)`

By default, the delimiter for parsing the text is whitespace. To assign a regular expression as the delimiter, invoke one of the `useDelimiter` methods of Scanner:

- `public Scanner useDelimiter(Pattern pattern)`
- `public Scanner useDelimiter(String pattern)`

The Scanner class defines a collection of "next" and "hasNext" methods for parsing tokens, including a version for strings and each of the primitive types. For example, `nextInt()` returns the next int in the input, and `hasNextInt()` returns `true` if the next token is an int. Similarly, `nextDouble()` and `hasNextDouble()` are used to read in doubles. The `next()` method of the Scanner class reads in the next token as a `String`, no matter its data type.

Let's look at an example. The following code parses a `String` into tokens using whitespace as the delimiter. Study the code and see if you can determine its output:

```
String source = "abc de fgh 123 ijk";
Scanner scan = new Scanner(source);
while(scan.hasNext()) {
    if(scan.hasNextInt()) {
        int x = scan.nextInt();
        System.out.println("int = " + x);
    } else {
        String token = scan.next();
        System.out.println(token);
    }
}
```

The `source` `String` has four spaces that split the string into five tokens. Notice the fourth token is parsed as an `int`. The output is

abc
de

```
fgh
int = 123
ijk
```

The following example demonstrates using a delimiter that is a regular expression by invoking the useDelimiter method. Study the code and see if you can determine its output:

```
String status = "probable,questionable;doubtful:out";

Scanner in = new Scanner(status);
in.useDelimiter("[,;:]");
while(in.hasNext()) {
    String token = in.next();
    System.out.println(token);
}
```

The delimiter pattern [,;:] is any character that is a comma, semicolon, or colon. Therefore, the output of the code is

```
probable
questionable
doubtful
out
```

Using Scanner for Keyboard Input

A common use of the Scanner class is for keyboard input. Use System.in as the source of the text and the "next" methods wait for the user to input data. The following example reads in three tokens from the console separated by whitespace:

```
25. Scanner console = new Scanner(System.in);
26. System.out.print("Enter a String, int and double: ");
27. String first = console.next();
28. int middle = console.nextInt();
29. double last = console.nextDouble();
30. System.out.println("first = " + first);
31. System.out.println("middle = " + middle);
32. System.out.println("last = " + last);
```

Whitespace includes spaces and line feeds so that the user can input the tokens on a single line separated by spaces. A sample execution of the code is

```
Enter a String, int and double: first 123 4.567
first = first
middle = 123
last = 4.567
```

The Scanner class has other features, such as the ability to find the next occurrence of a token, skip tokens, and work with locales. However, the information provided in this section is sufficient for the types of questions that you can expect on the SCJP exam regarding Scanner.

Summary

This chapter covered the "API Contents" section of the SCJP exam objectives. We discussed many useful classes in the Java language, starting with the primitive wrapper classes in java .lang. Each primitive type has a corresponding class that is used to "wrap" the primitives into objects. As of Java 5.0, a primitive type is automatically boxed into its corresponding wrapper class and automatically unboxed whenever necessary.

Strings were discussed in detail, including the differences between the String, String-Builder, and StringBuffer classes. The String class represents an immutable string of characters. StringBuilder and StringBuffer represent mutable strings of characters, and the two classes have the same method signatures and constructor parameters. The only difference between them is that StringBuffer is thread-safe and StringBuilder is not.

A key topic discussed in this chapter was the input and output of data, including the difference between byte streams and character streams (readers and writers). Low-level streams connect to the source of the data, and high-level streams are chained to existing streams. We saw how to buffer data streams using the BufferedInputStream, Buffered-OutputStream, BufferedReader, and BufferedWriter classes. We also discussed how to read and write primitive types and strings using the DataInputStream and DataOutput-Stream classes.

The java.io.File class represents the pathname of a file or directory, and the class contains methods for determining information about the file or directory is represents. The FileInputStream and FileOutputStream classes read and write raw bytes to files, and the FileReader and FileWriter classes read and write characters streams to files. We saw how to use the format/printf methods of the PrintWriter class to format strings. We also discussed the Console class, which represents the JVM environment's console.

Serialization refers to taking the state of an object and writing it to a stream. An object's class must implement java.io.Serializable to be serialized. Use the ObjectInputStream and ObjectOutputStream classes to read and write objects to a stream.

We spent a large portion of this chapter discussing how to format numbers, currency, dates, and strings, including how to use the java.util.Locale class to perform these operations within a given locale. Use the format methods of the java.text.Number Format class to format numbers and currency for a specific locale. The DecimalFormat class is a child class of NumberFormat and formats floating-point numbers for a specific locale. We discussed how to use the parse method of NumberFormat to parse numbers and currency. We also discussed how to format and parse dates using the DateFormat class of java.text.

A regular expression is a sequence of characters that describe a pattern of characters. We discussed how to represent a regular expression in Java using the `compile` method of the `Pattern` class, and how to search for a match to a `Pattern` using the `matcher` method of the `Matcher` class. The `String.split` method splits a `String` object into an array of `String` objects based on a regular expression. The `Scanner` class is a text scanner that parses primitive data types and strings into tokens using a delimiter, and is also useful for reading keyboard input from the console.

Be sure to test your knowledge of these API contents by answering the Review Questions at the end of the chapter. Make sure you have a good understanding of the following Exam Essentials before you attempt the Review Questions.

Exam Essentials

Understand autoboxing and unboxing.   Since the addition of autoboxing and unboxing to Java, the need for using the wrapper classes explicitly has been minimized greatly. Be sure to understand when a primitive type is autoboxed or unboxed.

Be familiar with the various string methods.   The concat method in `String` creates a new `String` object. Understand how the append and `insert` methods of `StringBuilder` and `StringBuffer` behave.

Be familiar with the basic methods of the `File` class.   The `java.io.File` class only represents a pathname to a file or directory and does not contain any methods for accessing or modifying the contents of a file. However, you *can* use the `File` class to create and delete files and directories.

Understand Java object serialization.   Understand what it means for an object to be serializable and how to serialize and deserialize an object using the `ObjectOutputStream` and `ObjectInputStream` classes.

Know how to format and parse numbers, currency, and dates for a given locale.   You won't be expected know all the foreign locales, but you should be able to format or parse a number, currency, or date in the U.S. locale using the `NumberFormat`, `DecimalFormat`, and `DateFormat` classes in `java.text`.

Be able to interpret simple regular expressions.   Know the patterns and metacharacters you need to for the exam. You won't see a complex and confusing regular expression on the exam, but you should be able to answer questions that contain simple regular expressions used in places like `Pattern`, `Scanner`, and `String.split`.

Understand the format specifiers for `format/printf`.   Expect to see a question or two on the exam that uses the format specifiers found in the `format/printf` methods of the `PrintWriter` and `Formatter` classes. The exam objectives specifically list %b, %c, %d, %f, and %s.

Review Questions

1. What is the result of the following code?

```
3.   byte twelve = -12;
4.   Byte b1 = new Byte(twelve);
5.   Byte b2 = new Byte(twelve);
6.   if(b1.byteValue() == b2) {
7.       System.out.println("equal");
8.   } else {
9.       System.out.println("not equal");
10.  }
```

A. Line 6 generates a compiler error.

B. An exception is thrown on line 6.

C. equal

D. not equal

2. What is the result of the following program?

```
1.   public class Unboxer {
2.       private Integer x;
3.
4.       public boolean compare(int y) {
5.           return x == y;
6.       }
7.
8.       public static void main(String [] args) {
9.           Unboxer u = new Unboxer();
10.          if(u.compare(21)) {
11.              System.out.println("true");
12.          } else {
13.              System.out.println("false");
14.          }
15.      }
16.  }
```

A. true

B. false

C. Line 5 does not compile.

D. Line 5 throws an exception.

E. Line 10 does not compile.

3. What is the result of the following program?

```
1.  public class Question03 {
2.      public static void doSomething(int i){
3.          System.out.println("method one");
4.      }
5.
6.      public static void doSomething(Byte b){
7.          System.out.println("method two");
8.      }
9.
10.     public static void main(String[] args) {
11.         byte b = -12;
12.         doSomething(b);
13.     }
14. }
```

A. method one

B. method two

C. Compiler error on line 11

D. Compiler error on line 12

4. What is the result of the following program?

```
1.  import java.util.Locale;
2.  import java.text.NumberFormat;
3.
4.  public class MyParser {
5.      public static void main(String [] args) {
6.          NumberFormat nf =
7.              NumberFormat.getInstance(Locale.FRANCE);
8.          String value = "444,33";
9.          System.out.println(nf.parse(value));
10.     }
11. }
```

A. 444.33

B. 444,33

C. Line 9 causes an exception to be thrown.

D. Line 7 generates a compiler error.

E. Line 9 generates a compiler error.

5. Given the following code:

```
6.  try {
7.      File f = new File("./test/");
8.      if(!f.exists()) {
9.          f.mkdir();
10.     }
11.
12.     File g = new File("./test/something.txt");
13.     g.createNewFile();
14. }catch(IOException e) {
15.     e.printStackTrace();
16. }
```

and assuming that the current directory from which this program is executed does not contain any subdirectories and that no exceptions are thrown, which of the following statents are true? (Select two answers.)

A. A new subdirectory named `test` is created in the current directory.

B. A new file named `something.txt` is created in the current directory.

C. A new file named `something.txt` is created in the test subdirectory.

D. The `mkdir` and `createNewFile` methods are not defined for objects of type `java.io.File`.

E. A new file named `test` is created in the current directory.

6. Which of the following statements are true? (Select three.)

A. All string literals are automatically instantiated into a `String` object.

B. The `StringBuilder` and `StringBuffer` classes define the exact same public methods.

C. In a multithreaded environment, use `StringBuilder` instead of `StringBuffer`.

D. A `StringBuilder` object is immutable.

E. A `StringBuffer` object can increase its length when appending characters.

7. What is the result of the following code?

```
4.  String s = "Hello";
5.  String t = new String(s);
6.
7.  if("Hello".equals(s)) {
8.      System.out.print("one");
9.  }
10.
11. if(t == s) {
12.     System.out.print("two");
```

```
13. }
14.
15. if(t.equals(s)) {
16.     System.out.print("three");
17. }
```

A. one

B. onethree

C. twothree

D. onetwothree

E. The code does not compile.

8. What is the result of the following code?

```
NumberFormat fmt =
        NumberFormat.getCurrencyInstance(Locale.US);
float f = 99.999F;
System.out.println(fmt.format(f));
```

A. $99.99

B. $99.999

C. $100.00

D. 99.999

E. The output is indeterminate and depends on the locale of the JVM environment.

9. What is the result of the following code?

```
7.  StringBuilder sb = new StringBuilder();
8.  sb.append("aaa").insert(1, "bb").insert(4, "ccc");
9.  System.out.println(sb);
```

A. bbaaaccc

B. abbaaccc

C. abbaccca

D. bbaaccca

E. The code does not compile.

10. Given the following class definition:

```
1.  import java.io.*;
2.
3.  public class MyReader {
4.      BufferedReader in;
5.
```

```
6.        public MyReader(File file) throws IOException {
7.            FileReader fr = new FileReader(file);
8.            in = new BufferedReader(fr);
9.        }
10.
11.       public void go() throws IOException {
12.           String s = null;
13.           while((s = in.readLine()) != null) {
14.               System.out.print(s);
15.           }
16.       }
17.
18.       public static void main(String [] args) {
19.           try {
20.               File file = new File("data.txt");
21.               new MyReader(file).go();
22.           }catch(IOException e) {
23.               e.printStackTrace();
24.           }
25.       }
26. }
```

what is the output of the MyReader program if the file "data.txt" is in the same directory as MyReader.class and contains the following contents:

H
E
L
L
O

A. The characters HELLO with each character on a separate line.

B. The characters HELLO on the same line.

C. The character 'H'.

D. An IOException is thrown on line 13.

E. The code does not compile.

11. Suppose you need to write data that consists of ints, doubles, booleans, and strings
to a file that maintains the format of the original data. The data needs to be buffered to
improve performance. Which three java.io classes can be chained together to best achieve
this result?

A. FileWriter

B. FileOutputStream

C. BufferedOutputStream

D. DataOutputStream

E. PrintWriter

F. PipedOutputStream

12. What is output of the following code?

```
5.   PrintWriter pw = new PrintWriter(System.out);
6.   double d = 2.73258;
7.   int x = 3;
8.   pw.format("%4.2f%s %d%n", d, " is almost", x);
9.   pw.close();
```

A. 2.73 is almost 3

B. 2.73 is almost3

C. 02.73 is almost 3

D. 2.733 is almost 3

E. There is no output.

13. What is the result of the following code?

```
7.   PrintWriter pw = new PrintWriter(System.out);
8.   pw.format("%2$d is bigger than %2$d", 10, 5);
9.   pw.close();
```

A. 10 is bigger than 5

B. 5 is bigger than 10

C. 10 is bigger than 10

D. 5 is bigger than 5

E. Line 8 generates a compiler error.

14. Given the following program:

```
1.   import java.io.*;
2.
3.   public class Employee {
4.       private String name;
5.       private float salary;
6.       private int id;
7.
8.       public Employee(String name, float salary, int id)
9.       {
10.          this.name = name;
```

```
11.          this.salary = salary;
12.          this.id = id;
13.     }
14.
15.     public static void main(String [] args)
16.                    throws IOException {
17.         Employee e = new Employee("Jim", 100.0F, 44);
18.         FileOutputStream fs =
19.                new FileOutputStream("e.ser");
20.         new ObjectOutputStream(fs).writeObject(e);
21.     }
22. }
```

which one of the following statements is true?

A. A new file named e.ser is created and contains a serialized Employee object.

B. The private fields of the Employee object are not serialized.

C. Line 3 generates a compiler error.

D. Line 20 generates a compiler error.

E. Line 20 throws a NotSerializableException.

15. Given the following code:

```
5. java.io.Console out = System.console();
6. String s = out.readPassword("%s", "Enter a password: ");
7. System.out.println("You entered " + s);
```

which of the following statements are true? (Select two.)

A. Line 5 generates a compiler error.

B. Line 6 generates a compiler error.

C. Line 7 generates a compiler error.

D. The out reference on line 5 may be null.

E. The readPassword method does not use a format specifier.

16. What is the result of the following program?

```
1.   import java.io.*;
2.
3.   public class SerializeA {
4.       public static void main(String [] args) throws
5.                IOException, ClassNotFoundException {
6.           A ref = new A(12);
```

```
7.          FileOutputStream fos =
8.              new FileOutputStream("a.ser");
9.          new ObjectOutputStream(fos).writeObject(ref);
10.         FileInputStream fis =
11.             new FileInputStream("a.ser");
12.         A ref2 = (A)
13.             new ObjectInputStream(fis).readObject();
14.         System.out.print(ref2.a);
15.     }
16. }
17.
18. class A implements Serializable {
19.     public int a;
20.
21.     public A(int a) {
22.         this.a = a;
23.         System.out.print("A");
24.     }
25. }
```

A. A0

B. AA12

C. A12

D. An exception is thrown at runtime because the A class does not have a no-argument constructor.

E. The code does not compile because the A class does not properly implement the Serializable interface.

17. What is the result of the following code?

```
4.  NumberFormat n =
5.      NumberFormat.getPercentInstance(Locale.US);
6.  double d = 3.1415;
7.  System.out.println(n.format(d));
```

A. 314%

B. 3.1415%

C. 314.15%

D. 3.14%

E. The code does not compile.

18. What is the result of the following code?

```
10. DecimalFormat df = new DecimalFormat("#,#00.00##");
11. double d = 3.141592653;
12. System.out.println(df.format(d));
```

   A. 03.1415

   B. 3.0016

   C. 3.1416

   D. 03.1416

   E. 00.0015

19. What is the result of the following code?

```
10. try {
11.     NumberFormat nf =
12.         NumberFormat.getPercentInstance(Locale.US);
13.     String s = "75%";
14.     double d = (Double) nf.parse(s);
15.     System.out.println(d);
16. }catch(ParseException e) {
17.     System.out.println("Something failed");
18. }
```

   A. 75%

   B. 0.75

   C. 0.00

   D. Something failed.

   E. Line 14 generates a compiler error.

20. Given the following code:

```
3.  try {
4.      DateFormat df =
5.          DateFormat.getDateInstance(DateFormat.SHORT,
6.                                      Locale.US);
7.      String s = "10/19/1987";
8.      Date d = df.parse(s);
9.      System.out.println(d.getTime());
10. }catch(ParseException e) {
11.     System.out.println("Something failed");
12. }
```

which of the following statements are true? (Select two.)

    A. Line 8 throws a `ParseException` because `"19"` is not a valid month.

    B. Line 8 generates a compiler error.

    C. Line 8 successfully parses the `String s` into a `java.util.Date` object that represents October 19, 1987.

    D. The U.S. locale does not support the SHORT date style.

    E. The output is a `long` that represents the number of milliseconds from January 1, 1970 to October 19, 1987.

21. Given the following code:

```
Pattern p = Pattern.compile("x.y");
String [] values = {"xy", "xay", "xaby", "xa"};
for(String value : values) {
    if(p.matcher(value).matches()) {
        System.out.println(value);
    }
}
```

which of the following strings is output? (Select one.)

    A. xy

    B. xay

    C. xaby

    D. xa

    E. None of the above

22. What is the output of the following code?

```
3.  String stuff = "of coursewyeswnowmaybe";
4.  String [] values = stuff.split("w");
5.  System.out.println(values.length);
```

    A. 0

    B. 3

    C. 4

    D. 5

    E. A `NullPointerException` is thrown.

23. What is the result of the following code?

```
3.  Pattern pattern =
4.          Pattern.compile("(\\d[a-z])+\\s\\w?");
5.  String [] values = {"9a4b x", "3a z", "a", "1a2b3c "};
6.  int counter = 0;
```

```
7.  for(String value : values) {
8.      if(pattern.matcher(value).matches()) {
9.          counter++;
10.     }
11. }
12. System.out.println(counter);
```

A. 0

B. 1

C. 2

D. 3

E. 4

24. What is the result of the following code?

```
2.  String s = "Good morning sunshine the earth says hello";
3.  Scanner in = new Scanner(s);
4.  in.useDelimiter("\\s[s]");
5.  int counter = 0;
6.  while(in.hasNext()) {
7.      in.next();
8.      counter++;
9.  }
10. System.out.println(counter);
```

A. 3

B. 4

C. 8

D. 9

E. 0

Answers to Review Questions

1. C. The code compiles and executes successfully, so A and B are incorrect. The comparison on line 6 is byte comparison, because b1.byteValue() is a byte and b2 is automatically unboxed to a byte. Because both bytes are -12, the comparison is true and line 7 outputs equal. Therefore, the answer is C.

2. D. The code compiles fine, so C is incorrect. On line 5, the Integer x is automatically unboxed into an int. However, x is null in this program because it is an uninitialized field of Unboxer. Attempting to unbox a null reference results in a NullPointerException, so the answer is D.

3. A. The code compiles fine, so C and D are incorrect. Line 12 invokes the overloaded doSomething method and passes in a byte argument, which is a valid argument for both doSomething methods. The compiler has to pick one, and it chooses the method with the nearest compatible parameter, which is the int parameter of the doSomething method on line 2. Therefore, the output is method one and the answer is A.

4. E. The parse method in the NumberFormat class throws the checked exception ParseException, which must be handled or declared. The code does neither, so a compiler error occurs on line 9 and therefore the answer is E.

5. A and C. D is incorrect: the File class contains a mkdir and createNewFile method used for creating new directories and files on the file system. Because we are assuming that the current directory does not contain any subdirectories, the ./test/ subdirectory cannot already exist. Therefore, line 8 is true and line 9 creates a new subdirectory named test. The only reason line 13 would fail is if the file something.txt already existed in /test, but because /test is a new, empty directory, the createNewFile method is successful and a new file named something.txt is created in the /test subdirectory. Therefore, the answers are A and C.

6. A, B, and E. String literals are automatically instantiated into String objects, so A is true. B is also true; the two classes contain the same methods. The only difference between StringBuilder and StringBuffer is that StringBuffer is thread-safe, which is why C is false. You should use StringBuffer if using mutable strings in a multithreaded application. D is false; the StringBuilder and StringBuffer classes represent mutable character sequences. E is true; a StringBuffer and StringBuilder can grow and shrink to match the number of characters in the sequence.

7. B. The code compiles fine, so E is incorrect. Line 7 is a valid statement and evaluates to true, so one is output. The reference s points to a String object in the string pool and t points to a String object on the heap. Because s and t do not point to the same object in memory, line 11 is false. Line 15 is true because s and t both point to a Hello string. Therefore, the output is onethree and the answer is B.

8   C. E is incorrect because the `Locale.US` is specified for `fmt`, so the output does not depend on the JVM's environment or platform. The currency format rounds decimals up to two decimal places, so `99.999` is rounded up to `100.00` and printed in the U.S. locale. The output is `$100.00`, and therefore the answer is C.

9   C. The code compiles fine, so E is incorrect. The `StringBuilder` contains `aaa` after the `append("aaa")` method call. The `insert(1, "bb")` inserts `bb` at position 1, resulting in `abbaa`. The `insert(4, "ccc")` inserts `ccc` at position 4, resulting in `abbaccca`. Therefore, the answer is C.

10.   B. The code compiles and runs fine, so D and E are incorrect. The `File` object represents the filename `data.txt`. The constructor of `MyReader` chains a `FileReader` and `BufferedReader` to `data.txt`. The go method reads in the contents of `data.txt` one line at a time and prints each character without a linefeed, so the output is `HELLO` and the answer is B.

11.   B, C, and D. The data to be output consists of more than strings or characters, so writer classes are not appropriate. `FileOutputStream` is needed to write to the file. `BufferedOutputStream` is needed to buffer the data, and the best choice for writing various primitive types and strings is `DataOutputStream`, so the answer is B, C, and D.

12.   A. The format specifier formats d with a width of 4 and precision 2, which results in `2.73`. The string is almost is printed, followed by a space. (There is a space between `%s` and `%d` in the format specifier.) The value of x is printed as 3, and then a linefeed (`%n`). The result is `2.73 is almost 3`, so the answer is A.

13.   D. The `"2$"` portion of `"%2$d"` denotes the second argument to be formatted, which is the 5. Therefore, 5 is output twice and the 10 does not appear in the result. The output is `5 is bigger than 5` and the answer is D.

14.   E. The code compiles fine, so C and D are incorrect. Line B is a false statement because the access specifier of a field does not have an effect on serialization. An attempt is made on line 20 to serialize an `Employee` object, but the `Employee` class does not implement the `Serializable` interface. Therefore, a `NotSerialiableException` is thrown, so A is false and E is true. Therefore, the answer is E.

15.   B and D. Line 5 compiles fine and is how you obtain a reference to the `Console` object. The `System.console()` method might return `null` if the environment does not have a console, so D is true. Line 6 does not compile because the return value of `readPassword` is a char array, not a `String`, so B is true. E is false; the first argument of `readPassword` is a format specifier. Therefore, the answer is B and D.

16.   C. The code compiles fine and the A class properly implements `Serialiable`, so E is incorrect. D is incorrect because no constructors are invoked on a class being deserialized. (A nonserializable parent class constructor may be invoked.) Instantiating A on line 6 invokes the constructor on line 21 and A is printed. After the object is deserialized, line 14 prints the value of `ref2.a`, which is 12, so the final output is `A12` and therefore the answer is C.

17 A. The code compiles fine, so E is incorrect. The percent format for the U.S. locale formats a double as a percentage. The decimal point is not displayed, so B, C, and D are incorrect. The number is multiplied by 100 and the percent sign is appended to the end. After any necessary rounding, the output is displayed, which in this example is 314%. Therefore, the answer is A.

18. D. The DecimalFormat object calls for at least two digits before the decimal point, so a leading 0 appears before the 3, making B and C incorrect. The format also calls for at least two digits past the decimal but no more than four. The decimal portion of d has more than four digits, so the format rounds the result up in this case because a 9 follows the 5. Therefore, the output is 03.1416 and the answer is D.

19. B. The code compiles fine, so E is incorrect. The NumberFormat object is a percent format and the string being parsed is "75%". The return value of parse on line 14 is a Number object. Casting it to a Double (its actual type) and assigning it to a double causes the value to be automatically unboxed. Printing it on line 15 results in 0.75, so the answer is B.

20. C and E. The code compiles successfully, so B is incorrect. D is just an odd statement that I made up to try to confuse you, so it is incorrect also. A is incorrect; the SHORT format lists the month first in the U.S. locale, so 10 is the month and 19 is the day of the month. C is correct; the parse method successfully creates a Date object for October 19, 1987. As odd as E sounds, it is true. Date objects measure time as the number of milliseconds from January 1, 1970, a date referred to as the epoch.

21. B. The regular expression "x.y" matches character streams of length three that begin with x, end with y, and with any character in the middle. The string "xay" matches, but none of the others do, so the answer is B.

22. C. The split method splits the stuff string into an array of substrings using the character 'w' as the delimiter. The resulting substrings are "of course", "yes", "no", and "maybe", so values.length is 4 and the answer is C.

23. D. A match for the pattern has to start with (\\d[a-z])+, which specifies a digit followed by a lowercase character, with that pattern repeating one or more times. The \\s denotes exactly one whitespace character. The \\w? denotes 0 or 1 word characters. The string "a" does not match because it lacks a beginning digit and a whitespace character. The other three strings in the array match this pattern, so the value of counter is 3 and the answer is D.

24. A. The delimiter of the Scanner is "\\s[s]", which describes a whitespace character followed by an s. The string being scanned has two delimiter matches: at _sunshine and _says. Within the while loop, the Scanner reads in Good morning, then unshine the earth, and then ays hello. Therefore, the while loop executes 3 times and the answer is A.

Chapter
5

Concurrency

SCJP EXAM OBJECTIVES COVERED IN THIS CHAPTER:

- ✓ Write code to define, instantiate, and start new threads using both java.lang.Thread and java.lang.Runnable.

- ✓ Recognize the states in which a thread can exist, and identify ways in which a thread can transition from one state to another.

- ✓ Given a scenario, write code that makes appropriate use of object locking to protect static or instance variables from concurrent access problems.

- ✓ Given a scenario, write code that makes appropriate use of wait, notify, or notifyAll.

These objectives are found in Section 4 of the SCJP exam objectives. The exam tests your knowledge of writing and using threads in Java, including thread states, synchronization, and the wait and notify methods of Object. This chapter covers these topics in detail.

Overview of Threads

Before we discuss the details and semantics of concurrency and threads, I want to discuss some terminology. Concurrency refers to doing multiple tasks at the same time. Your computer's operating system runs programs concurrently, and a program that runs on a computer is referred to as a process. A process consists of allocated memory and resources, including the executable code of your program.

Concurrency in processes is handled at the operating system level, and a typical Java program is not interested in multiple processes. Instead, Java programs often need to perform simultaneous tasks within a single process by using multiple threads to implement concurrency. A *thread* is a path of execution, a block of code that executes within a process and has access to the process memory. Each thread within a process executes concurrently, and the JVM schedules the threads with the CPU. The number of threads running at any given time depends on the number of CPUs on the machine. For example, if your machine has one CPU, only one thread can be executing at a time. What are the other threads doing when the CPUs are busy? Depending on their state, they are either waiting for the JVM to schedule them with the next available CPU or waiting for a particular event to occur.

Every stand-alone Java program has *system threads* that run in the background of the application. For example, garbage collection is a task that always needs to be running and is implemented in a system thread. From a programmer's point of view, you are typically more concerned with *user-defined threads*, the threads that you write to perform a specific task. A stand-alone Java application starts with a single thread associated with the main method. This *main thread* can start new user-defined threads, allowing you to break down your program into simultaneous, logical units of work.

This chapter discusses in detail the steps involved in writing and starting new user-defined threads. We will also discuss the various states that a thread can be in, along with thread synchronization and the wait and notify methods of Object. Let's start with a discussion on how to write and start a thread.

Writing a Thread

For the exam you need to understand how to instantiate and start a thread using the Thread class and Runnable interface. A thread has two components:

- A *thread object* that gets started and has a priority and state, and is scheduled to run by the JVM
- A *runnable target* that contains the code that executes when the thread object finally gets to the CPU

The Thread class represents a thread object in Java, and the Runnable interface is used to define a runnable target. You can write a thread two ways in Java:

- Write a class that implements Runnable and then pass an instance of your Runnable class into the constructor of a new Thread object. When the Thread object is started and reaches the CPU, the run method of the Runnable object is invoked.
- Write a class that subclasses the Thread class and overrides the run method. (The Thread class implements Runnable.) When your Thread object is started and reaches the CPU, the overridden run method is invoked.

In either option, you implement the run method defined in the Runnable interface and instantiate a new Thread object. The run method has the following signature:

```
public void run()
```

The run method represents the code that executes when the Thread object gets scheduled to run. Before a thread can run, it needs to be started. Once started, a thread is alive until the run method finishes executing, either by running to completion or throwing an exception. We will discuss this topic in detail in the section "Thread States," but first let's discuss the details of writing a thread using both of the options mentioned previously.

 Real World Scenario

Writing Threads

From an object-oriented point of view, the preferred option for writing a thread is to implement Runnable. The Runnable target creates a nice separation between the Thread object, which is busy getting scheduled, synchronizing, and other thread-related activities, and the runnable target, which is the code that executes when the thread gets scheduled.

If you write a class that extends Thread, you are implying that the class you are writing "is a" thread object and are therefore extending the capabilities of the Thread class. However, if you extend thread only to override the run method, then from an object-oriented point of view you are not extending Thread for inheritance reasons.

Therefore, in the real world you typically create a thread by writing a class that implements Runnable and associating it as a target of a new Thread object. That being said, we will discuss in detail both ways to write a thread in Java because the exam objectives specifically state knowledge of both techniques.

Implementing the *Runnable* Interface

You can write a thread in Java by writing a new class that implements the Runnable interface and assigning an instance of the class to a new Thread object. A Runnable target is associated with a new Thread object using one of the following constructors in the Thread class:

- `public Thread(Runnable target)`
- `public Thread(Runnable target, String name)`
- `public Thread(ThreadGroup group, Runnable target)`
- `public Thread(ThreadGroup group, Runnable target, String name)`
- `public Thread(ThreadGroup group, Runnable target, String name, long stackSize)`

You can assign a Thread object a name so that your application can monitor its threads. You can also specify a stack size that, according to the Java API documentation, is highly platform dependent. The stack size is the approximate number of bytes of address space that the virtual machine is to allocate for this thread's stack.

NOTE Using the Thread constructors that declare a ThreadGroup parameter, you can assign your Thread object to a ThreadGroup. A ThreadGroup allows you to organize and manage the threads of your application into groups. The SCJP exam does not require knowledge of the ThreadGroup class.

Let's look at an example of creating a new thread by writing a class that implements the Runnable interface. The following SayHello class implements the Runnable interface and has one field, one constructor, and the necessary run method:

```
1.  public class SayHello implements Runnable {
2.      private String greeting;
3.
4.      public SayHello(String greeting) {
```

```
5.              this.greeting = greeting;
6.          }
7.
8.      public void run() {
9.          for(int i = 1; i <= 10; i++) {
10.             System.out.print(greeting);
11.         }
12.         System.out.println("End of run");
13.      }
14. }
```

The run method on line 8 prints a String ten times. Line 12 prints "End of run" just before the run method completes. Keep in mind that implementing Runnable does not make the SayHello object a thread. An instance of SayHello needs to be associated with a new Thread object, and then that Thread object is started by invoking its start method. Only when the start method is invoked does an additional thread get added to the current process.

The following CountToTen program starts a new Thread using a SayHello instance. Study the code and see if you can determine its result:

```
public class CountToTen {
    public static void main(String [] args) {
        SayHello hello = new SayHello("Hi");
        Thread t = new Thread(hello);
        t.start();

        for(int k = 1; k <= 10; k++) {
            System.out.print(k);
        }
        System.out.println("End of main");
    }
}
```

The output of the CountToTen programs looks like

```
12345678910End of main
HiHiHiHiHiHiHiHiHiHiEnd of run
```

The Output of a Multithreaded Program

Now is a good time to point out that you cannot exactly determine the output of a multithreaded program because you do not control when the threads get to execute. The actual output of the CountToTen program is indeterminate because it can change every time the program is executed.

Given that, I ran CountToTen many times and each result was the same as the previous one. The most likely reason that the output was similar each time is that the program's threads do not perform a lot of computations. The code is executed so quickly that the main thread ends before the new thread has a chance to run. To test this hypothesis, I modified the for loops in both SayHello and CountToTen so that they executed 50 times instead of 10 times, and here is a sample output of that result:

```
123456789101112HiHiHiHiHiHiHiHiHiHiHiHiHiHiHiHiHiHiHiHiHiHiHiHiHi
HiHiHiHiHiHiHi131415161718192021222324252627282930313233343536373839
4041424344454647HiHiHiHiHiHiHiHiHiHiHiHiHiHiHiHiEnd of run
484950End of main
```

Notice how this time the two threads took turns on the CPU. The main thread printed the numbers 1 to 12, and then gave up the CPU while the SayHello thread printed "Hi". The output varies on different executions of the program, and you might see entirely different results running this code on different platforms and environments.

Let's look at another example of writing a thread, except this time I demonstrate extending the Thread class instead of implementing Runnable.

Extending the *Thread* Class

You can create a thread by writing a class that extends the Thread class and overriding the run method. (A class that extends Thread is still a Runnable object because the Thread class implements Runnable.) The following class demonstrates this technique:

```
1.  public class MyThread extends Thread {
2.      private String message;
3.      private boolean keepGoing;
4.
5.      public MyThread(String m) {
6.          message = m;
7.          keepGoing = true;
8.      }
```

```
9.
10.     public void setKeepGoing(boolean b) {
11.         keepGoing = b;
12.     }
13.
14.     public void run() {
15.         while(keepGoing) {
16.             System.out.print(message + " ");
17.             try {
18.                 Thread.sleep(1000);
19.             }catch(InterruptedException e) {}
20.         }
21.         System.out.println("gone!");
22.     }
23. }
```

In the run method of MyThread, the message field is printed in a while loop. The call to Thread.sleep on line 18 causes the currently running thread (which is the MyThread instance) to sleep for at least 1,000 milliseconds (one second). Therefore, this run method prints a String over and over again with at least a one-second delay between printings.

The following Main program instantiates and starts a MyThread object. Because this example extended Thread, there is no need to instantiate two objects. (When implementing Runnable, you instantiate both the Runnable target and a Thread object.) The MyThread object represents both the thread object and the runnable target. Study the Main program and see if you can determine its result:

```
1.  public class Main {
2.      public static void main(String [] args) {
3.          MyThread myThread = new MyThread("going");
4.          myThread.start();
5.          try {
6.              Thread.sleep(6000);
7.          }catch(InterruptedException e) {}
8.
9.          myThread.setKeepGoing(false);
10.         System.out.println("End of main");
11.     }
12. }
```

Line 3 instantiates a new MyThread object with the message "going". Because MyThread extends the Thread class, it inherits the start method of Thread, so line 4 starts the new MyThread object. The main thread then sleeps on line 6 for six seconds. While the main thread is sleeping, MyThread is printing "going" about every second. Upon awaking and getting scheduled by the JVM, line 9 sets the keepGoing field of MyThread to false. The output of Main looks like

```
going going going going going going End of main
gone!
```

As I mentioned in the previous section, the output of a multithreaded application is indeterminate. The above output of Main is a common output because of the timing of the calls to sleep. MyThread prints "going" every second and Main sleeps for six seconds, then tells MyThread to stop printing, so I am not surprised that "going" is printed six times. However, depending on the JVM and other factors of the environment, it is possible for "going" to be printed a different number of times.

 Real World Scenario

Stopping a Thread

The Thread class contains a method named stop, but this method is deprecated and you are highly discouraged from invoking it. The problem with the stop method is that the thread being stopped might contain object locks that other threads are waiting for, and the stopped threads might not let go of those locks when stop is called.

If you need one thread to be able to stop another thread, follow the design of the MyThread class in this section. Notice that the while loop on line 15 of MyThread checks the boolean field keepGoing after each printing of the message. The idea behind this design is that another thread can communicate with a MyThread object by setting keepGoing to false (via the setKeepGoing method of MyThread). Setting the boolean to false won't stop the thread immediately, but the thread only does a small amount of work before checking the boolean again. Providing a mechanism in your threads so that they can be stopped cleanly by another thread is commonly done in multithreaded Java applications.

Now that you have seen the details of writing a thread by implementing Runnable or extending Thread, let's discuss the important topic of thread state and what happens to your threads when they are not running on the CPU.

Thread States

A thread takes on various states from the time that it starts to the point when its run method completes execution. You should be able to recognize the various thread states and how a thread transitions from one state to another. This section discusses the details of these various states.

The Thread class defines the following method for obtaining the current state of a thread:

```
public Thread.State getState()
```

Thread.State is an enumeration defined in the Thread class that represents all the possible states of threads. The Thread.State enumeration has the following values:

NEW   The thread has been instantiated but not started yet.

RUNNABLE   The thread is either currently running on the CPU or waiting to be scheduled by the JVM for execution.

BLOCKED   The thread is waiting for a monitor lock to become available. A thread becomes blocked when attempting to enter a block of synchronized code.

WAITING   The thread is waiting for another thread to perform a particular action. For example, the thread might be waiting for another thread to call Object.notify on a specific object or waiting for another thread to terminate due to a call to Thread.join.

TIMED_WAITING   This state is similar to WAITING except the thread only waits until a specified time elapses. A thread enters this state with a call to Thread.join or Object.notify with a timeout, or Thread.sleep.

TERMINATED   The thread has run to completion. A terminated thread cannot be started again.

Now we discuss each of these states and how a thread transitions from one state to another.

New Threads

A Thread object is required to create a thread in Java. After a Thread object is instantiated but before its start method is invoked, the thread is referred to as being in the *new thread* state. Let's look at an example. Suppose we have the following Runnable class named ReadAFile whose run method scans the contents of a file and prints them to the console output:

```java
import java.io.*;
import java.util.Scanner;

public class ReadAFile extends Thread {
    private Scanner in;
    private boolean keepGoing = true;

    public ReadAFile(File f) throws FileNotFoundException {
        in = new Scanner(f);
    }

    public void stopReading() {
        keepGoing = false;
    }

    public void run() {
        while(keepGoing  && in.hasNext()) {
            System.out.print(in.next());
        }
    }
}
```

The following statements instantiate a ReadAFile object and then wrap that object into a new thread:

```java
File source = new File("somedata.txt");
ReadAFile target = new ReadAFile(source);
Thread t = new Thread(target);
```

At this point in the program, t points to a new Thread object but the JVM has not created a new thread in the process yet. Only when the start method is invoked on the Thread does the JVM add a new thread to the process, at which point a new thread transitions into a *runnable thread*, as Figure 5.1 shows.

FIGURE 5.1   A new thread transitions to a runnable thread when its start method is invoked.

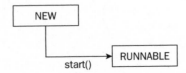

Starting a Thread Twice Is Not Valid

A new thread cannot be started twice. For example, the following code compiles fine:

```
23. File source = new File("somedata.txt");
24. ReadAFile target = new ReadAFile(source);
25. Thread t = new Thread(target);
26. t.start();
27. t.start();
```

However, the call to start on line 27 throws an IllegalThreadStateException at runtime:

```
Exception in thread "main" java.lang.IllegalThreadStateException
        at java.lang.Thread.start(Thread.java:595)
        at ReadAFile.main(ReadAFile.java:27)
```

Keep an eye out for this scenario on the exam.

Runnable Threads

A *runnable thread* is a thread that is either executing or waiting to be scheduled. The JVM schedules which thread to execute based on the *thread priority*. The priority is an integer value, and a thread inherits its priority from the thread that started it. Priority can be changed at any time using the setPriority method of the Thread class:

```
public final void setPriority(int p)
```

Typically you set a thread's priority to be MIN_PRIORITY, NORM_PRIORITY, or MAX_PRIORITY, static fields in the Thread class. The setPriority method throws an IllegalArgumentException if the argument is not between MIN_PRIORITY and MAX_PRIORITY.

Java programmers should assume the scheduler uses *preemptive scheduling*, meaning that if a thread is executing and another thread of a higher priority becomes runnable, it preempts the lower-priority thread, as Figure 5.2 shows. (Preemptive scheduling is not an absolute guarantee, so your algorithm logic should not rely on it.)

FIGURE 5.2   The JVM scheduler determines which thread to schedule on a CPU.

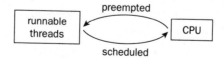

Threads that have the same priority execute in a round-robin fashion, meaning that the currently executing thread runs until it either terminates or transitions into a waiting state.

Use the static `yield` or `sleep` method of the `Thread` class if you are concerned a thread is hogging the CPU. The `sleep` method causes a thread to transition into the `TIMED_WAITING` state until the specified amount of time elapses. The `yield` method causes the currently running thread to give up the CPU, allowing another thread to be scheduled. Figure 5.3 shows the transitions for `sleep` and `yield`.

FIGURE 5.3 The thread state transition of the sleep and yield methods

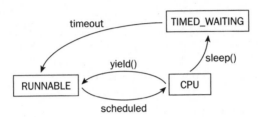

Notice that invoking `yield` does not change the state of a thread; it just pushes the thread to the back of the line of other runnable threads. The `sleep` method actually transitions a thread from `RUNNABLE` to `TIMED_WAITING`. When the specified time elapses, the thread becomes `RUNNABLE` and goes to the back of the line of runnable threads.

To demonstrate the `yield` method, I added a call to `yield` in the `run` method of the `SayHello` class from the previous section:

```
public void run() {

    for(int i = 1; i <= 10; i++) {
        System.out.print(greeting);
        Thread.yield();
    }
    System.out.println("End of run");
}
```

Similarly, I added a call to `yield` in the `CountToTen` program, which now yields after printing each `int`:

```
for(int k = 1; k <= 10; k++) {
    System.out.print(k);
    Thread.yield();
}
```

Running the program again results in an entirely different output than before the yields were added:

```
1Hi2Hi3Hi4Hi5Hi6Hi7Hi8Hi9Hi10HiEnd of main
End of run
```

The two threads have the same priority and politely yield to each other. As you can see by the output, each thread is getting equal time on the CPU. In a real-world scenario, you might not call yield quite this often, but in general it is a good method to call whenever you want your threads to get along with other threads and not hog the CPU unnecessarily.

Blocked Threads

Threads access shared memory in a process and therefore need to be synchronized. The upcoming section "Thread Synchronization" discusses the synchronized keyword and the details you need to know about thread synchronization. Synchronization in Java is done at the object level, where threads ask for an object's lock before entering synchronized code. If a thread asks for a lock and the lock is already in use by another thread, it becomes a *blocked thread*. A blocked thread stays blocked until the requested lock becomes available, at which point it returns to the runnable state, as Figure 5.4 shows.

FIGURE 5.4   A thread goes from RUNNABLE to BLOCKED when a synchronized lock is unavailable.

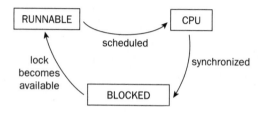

The getState method of a blocked thread returns the BLOCKED value of the Thread .State enumeration.

Waiting and Timed-Waiting Threads

The Java language has built-in threading capabilities, as demonstrated by the wait and notify methods of the Object class. The wait method invoked on an Object causes the thread to wait until another thread calls notify on the same Object. We discuss the details in the section "The wait, notify, and notifyAll Methods," but for now let's see the effect these methods have on the state of a thread.

The wait method in Object has three overloaded versions:

```
public final void wait() throws InterruptedException
public final void wait(long timeout) throws InterruptedException
public final void wait(long timeout, int nanos) throws InterruptedException
```

The wait method causes the thread to wait for either notify or notifyAll to be invoked on the same object or wait for the specified time to elapse. The wait and notify methods cannot be invoked unless the thread has the object's lock. When wait is invoked, the lock is released and the state of the thread changes to WAITING or TIMED_WAITING, depending on which version of the wait method is invoked. When notify is invoked on the object, the waiting threads move to the BLOCKED state because the lock of the object is not available (the thread that called notify has it). Figure 5.5 shows the thread state transition of wait and notify.

FIGURE 5.5   The thread state transition caused by the wait and notify methods

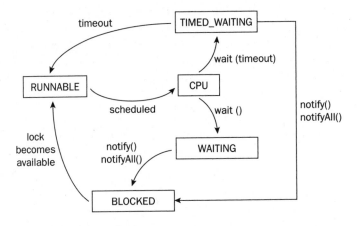

Two events need to occur for a waiting thread to become runnable again: notify or notifyAll needs to be invoked and then the lock of the object needs to become available.

WAITING vs. TIMED_WAITING

Invoking wait() moves a thread into the WAITING state and invoking wait(long timeout) or wait(long timeout, int nanos) moves a thread into the TIMED_WAITING state.

A TIMED_WAITING thread and a WAITING thread both move into the BLOCKED state after notify or notifyAll. However, a WAITING thread waits indefinitely, while a TIMED_WAITING thread only waits for as long as the specified timeout value. A thread can also move into the TIMED_WAITING state by invoking the sleep and join methods of Thread that have long parameters for specifying a time-out.

Terminated Threads

A *terminated thread* is a thread that has run to completion, and its corresponding enumerated state is TERMINATED. A thread terminates when its run method completes, either by returning or throwing an exception. A thread cannot be started again, and a terminated thread is often referred to as a dead thread. Figure 5.6 shows the state transition of a terminated thread.

FIGURE 5.6   When a thread runs to completion, its state changes to TERMINATED.

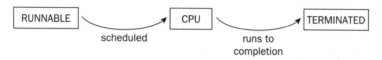

The only way to transition into the TERMINATED state is from RUNNABLE. A thread in the TERMINATED state cannot be started again or an IllegalThreadStateException is thrown.

Now that we have discussed the various states that a thread can be in, the next section looks at the BLOCKED state of a thread and synchronization.

Thread Synchronization

Thread synchronization involves using an object's lock to protect its fields, a topic you need to understand for the exam. We synchronize threads because they share the same memory, and it is possible for two threads to cause inconsistent or unreliable data in your application by modifying fields of an object at the same time. We use object locking to force threads to play nice with other threads and ensure that the data in our program remains consistent.

To demonstrate the need for synchronization, let's look at a multithreaded program whose threads interfere with each other. The following MyStack class simulates a simple stack of ten ints. The index field points to the next available spot in the stack. The push method contains a call to Thread.yield on line 8 at an important step in the program's business logic. You would probably not put a yield call here in a real-world scenario, but because you never know when a thread is going to be preempted, we will attempt to simulate preempting at this point in the code. Study the class and see if you can determine how the push and pop methods work:

```
1.  public class MyStack {
2.      private int [] values = new int[10];
3.      private int index = 0;
4.
5.      public void push(int x) {
6.          if(index <= 9) {
```

```
7.              values[index] = x;
8.              Thread.yield();
9.              index++;
10.        }
11.     }
12.
13.     public int pop() {
14.        if(index > 0) {
15.            index--;
16.            return values[index];
17.        } else {
18.            return -1;
19.        }
20.     }
21.
22.     public String toString() {
23.        String reply = "";
24.        for(int i = 0; i < values.length; i++) {
25.            reply += values[i] + " ";
26.        }
27.        return reply;
28.     }
29. }
```

If two threads each push an int onto the stack at the same time, it is possible that data in the stack will be corrupted, as demonstrated by the following Pusher class. The Pusher class extends Thread and pushes five ints onto an instance of MyStack in its run method:

```
public class Pusher extends Thread {
    private MyStack stack;

    public Pusher(MyStack stack) {
        this.stack = stack;
    }

    public void run() {
        for(int i = 1; i <= 5; i++) {
            stack.push(i);
        }
    }
}
```

The following code instantiates one MyStack object, which is shared between two Pusher threads. The two threads run and each pushes five ints onto the MyStack object:

```
MyStack stack = new MyStack();
Pusher one = new Pusher(stack);
Pusher two = new Pusher(stack);
one.start();
two.start();

try {
    one.join();
    two.join();
}catch(InterruptedException e) {}

System.out.println(stack.toString());
```

The main thread calls join on the two Pusher threads, which causes the main thread to wait until both Pusher threads run to completion. Then the toString method displays the contents of the values array. Because the code uses threads, the output varies depending on the environment that the code executes in, but here is a sample output:

```
1 2 2 3 3 4 4 5 5 0
```

Notice that the contents of this array are not consistent with the logic of the program. Each Pusher thread pushed the numbers 1 through 5 onto the stack, so there should appear two 1s, two 2s, and so on. Instead, there is only one 1 on the stack and a 0 appears at the end, so only nine elements were actually pushed on the stack.

The problem is that when an int is pushed onto the stack, both the values array and the index need to be updated in an *atomic* manner (without being interrupted). By yielding in the middle of a push, the stack is left in an invalid state. When the 1 is pushed on the stack by the first thread, the following statement (from line 7 of MyStack) executes:

```
values[0] = 1;
```

Before the thread can increment index by 1, it yields to the second thread, which immediately pushes a 1 onto the stack also. But index is still 0, so the second thread executes the same statement:

```
values[0] = 1;
```

At this point in the program, the array data has been corrupted because both threads pushed a 1 onto the first element in the stack. The problem is that the second thread should not have been allowed to invoke the push method of the MyStack object while the first thread was in the middle of a push. These two threads need to be synchronized, which we will fix in the next section, but first I need to discuss the details of an object's monitor lock.

The Monitor Lock

Every `Object` in Java has an entity called its *monitor lock* (often referred to as the *monitor* or *lock*) that threads use to synchronize access to the data of the object. The monitor lock of an `Object` has the following features:

- A thread uses the `synchronized` keyword to "acquire" an object's lock.

- If the lock is available, the thread is said to "own" the lock.

- Once the thread leaves the synchronized block of code, the thread "releases" the lock.

- If a thread attempts to acquire a lock and the lock is not available, the thread transitions into the blocked state. The thread remains blocked until the lock becomes available again.

A thread attempts to acquire a monitor lock on a specific object in the following two ways:

- The thread enters a synchronized block of code, in which case the thread attempts to acquire the monitor lock of the object specified with the `synchronized` keyword.

- The thread invokes a `synchronized` method, in which case the thread attempts to acquire the monitor lock of the object the method is invoked on.

Both of these scenarios involve using the `synchronized` keyword, either at the method level or on a block of code. Let's look at an example that demonstrates both of these scenarios, starting with a synchronized block of code.

Synchronized Blocks

Use the `synchronized` keyword to create a synchronized block of code. The syntax is

```
synchronized(reference) {
    //synchronized block
}
```

The *reference* is any `Object` reference, and if the monitor lock of that `Object` is available, then the thread acquires it; otherwise, the thread blocks until the lock becomes available.

Let's look at an example. Suppose we have the following class named `BankAccount`:

```
public class BankAccount {
    private double balance;

    public void deposit(double amount) {
        System.out.println("Making a deposit: " + amount);
        balance += amount;
```

```
      }

      public void withdraw(double amount) {
            System.out.println("Making a withdrawal: " + amount);
            balance -= amount;
      }

      public double getBalance() {
          return balance;
      }
}
```

Making a withdrawal or deposit on a bank account is a good candidate for synchronization. (I doubt you or your bank would be happy with a program that occasionally loses a deposit or withdrawal because of interfering threads.) A thread that needs to access a BankAccount object should obtain its monitor lock first, as demonstrated in the following method:

```
4.  public static void doSomeBanking(BankAccount account) {
5.       synchronized(account) {
6.            account.deposit(50.00);
7.            account.withdraw(20.00);
8.       }
9.       System.out.println(account.getBalance());
10. }
```

On line 5, the current thread attempts to acquire the lock on a BankAccount object using its reference. Line 5 has two possible outcomes:

- The lock is available and the current thread becomes the owner of the lock. Lines 6 and 7 execute and then the lock is released on line 8.

- The lock is not available and the current thread becomes blocked. The thread does not become runnable again until the lock becomes available.

Assuming lines 6 and 7 execute (unless we are in a deadlock situation), the output is

```
Making a deposit: 50.0
Making a withdrawal: 20.0
30.0
```

The getBalance method is invoked outside of synchronized code, which might be acceptable because the method does not alter any data in the fields. However, it is not uncommon for a "get" method to be invoked within synchronized code.

Real World Scenario

Beware of Deadlock

Like many tasks in Java, starting a thread is easy. However, making sure your threads play nice with the other threads in your application is often a difficult task in the real world. After your threads start asking for monitor locks, you have to worry about the possibility of deadlock. If a thread attempts to acquire a lock and, for whatever reason, the lock never becomes available, then your thread has become deadlocked and will never become runnable again.

For example, using the BankAccount class defined in this section, suppose we have the following Teller thread that transfers $50.00 from one BankAccount object to another, obtaining the lock of both objects before making the transfer:

```java
public class Teller extends Thread {
    private BankAccount src, dest;

    public Teller(BankAccount src, BankAccount dest) {
        this.src = src;
        this.dest = dest;
    }

    public void run() {
        synchronized(src) {
            Thread.yield();
            synchronized(dest) {
                src.withdraw(50.00);
                dest.deposit(50.00);
            }
        }
    }
}
```

Notice the conveniently placed call to Thread.yield after the first lock is acquired but before the attempt at acquiring the second lock. You would not normally call yield here, but I want to emphasize the importance of never knowing when a thread is preempted. Try to determine the output of the following code:

```java
public class DeadlockDemo {
    public static void main(String [] args) {
        BankAccount a = new BankAccount();
```

```
        a.deposit(100.00);
        BankAccount b = new BankAccount();

        Teller t1 = new Teller(a, b);
        Teller t2 = new Teller(b, a);
        t1.start();
        t2.start();

        try {
            t1.join();
            t2.join();
        }catch(InterruptedException e) {}

        System.out.println("a balance = " + a.getBalance());
        System.out.println("b balance = " + b.getBalance());
    }
}
```

The output varies depending on the environment, but deadlock can occur immediately, in which case the output is

```
Making a deposit: 100.0
```

Here is what happens: the deposit of $100.00 is successfully made on BankAccount a, but the two Teller threads deadlock before any other output occurs. The t1 thread grabs the lock on a, then yields. The t2 thread grabs the lock on b, then yields. The t1 thread now attempts to acquire the b lock, but t2 owns it, so t1 becomes blocked. The t2 thread attempts to acquire the a lock, but t1 owns it so t2 becomes blocked. Neither thread will ever become runnable again because the locks they are waiting for will never be freed. In addition, the main thread of the DeadlockDemo program is also blocked forever because it called join on both t1 and t2, and neither of those two threads can run to completion.

Starting threads is easy but working with them can be difficult. The BankAccount example shown here is the typical example used to demonstrate deadlock. By the way, there are several fixes to this problem. One common design pattern is to order your locks. If a thread needs multiple locks, then those objects should have some type of ordering so that all threads ask for multiple locks in the same order. For example, when t1 and t2 needed the a and b locks, both threads should have attempted to acquire the a lock first. When the t2 thread attempts to grab the a lock and t1 already owns it, t2 is blocked but does not own any monitor locks, leaving the b lock available for the t1 thread to complete its task successfully and avoid this deadlock scenario.

Synchronized Methods

A *synchronized method* is similar to a synchronized block of code except the lock being acquired is on the object the synchronized method is invoked on. Think of a synchronized method as a synchronized block of code that attempts to acquire the this reference. Use the synchronized keyword in the method declaration to denote a method as synchronized.

Let's revisit the MyStack class from earlier in this section. The push and pop methods are good candidates for synchronized methods because they perform atomic tasks. The following version of the class, MyStack2, demonstrates the syntax for declaring synchronized methods:

```java
public class MyStack2 {
    private int [] values = new int[10];
    private int index = 0;

    public synchronized void push(int x) {
        if(index <= 9) {
            values[index] = x;
            Thread.yield();
            index++;
        }
    }

    public synchronized int pop() {
        if(index > 0) {
            index--;
            return values[index];
        } else {
            return -1;
        }
    }

    public synchronized String toString() {
        String reply = "";
        for(int i = 0; i < values.length; i++) {
            reply += values[i] + " ";
        }
        return reply;
    }
}
```

All three methods of MyStack2 are declared as synchronized. This simple change to the class now makes it thread-safe, and the issue of data corruption that existed in MyStack is resolved. The following code creates two threads that each push the `ints` 1 to 5 onto the same `MyStack2` object, except this time the threads do not interfere with each other. The `Pusher2` class is the same as `Pusher` from earlier except it has a field of type `MyStack2` instead of `MyStack`.

```
MyStack2 stack = new MyStack2();
Pusher2 one = new Pusher2(stack);
Pusher2 two = new Pusher2(stack);
one.start();
two.start();

try {
    one.join();
    two.join();
}catch(InterruptedException e) {}

System.out.println(stack.toString());
```

Here is a sample output:

```
1 1 2 2 3 3 4 4 5 5
```

Because the `MyStack2` object has synchronized methods, the `push` and `pop` methods successfully modify the `values` and `index` fields of `MyStack2` without leaving the object in an inconsistent state.

Now that we have seen the `synchronized` keyword, we can discuss the `wait` and `notify` methods of the `Object` class. These two methods can only be invoked within a synchronized block of code, and they provide a communication mechanism between threads that need to work concurrently.

The *wait, notify,* and *notifyAll* Methods

The `wait`, `notify`, and `notifyAll` methods are defined in the `Object` class, so they can be invoked on any Java object. As we discussed in the "Thread States" section, the `wait` method causes the current thread to stop running until another thread calls `notify` or `notifyAll` on the same object that the waiting thread called `wait` on. You should know the following two important details about `wait`, `notify`, and `notifyAll`:

- A thread can only invoke `wait`, `notify`, or `notifyAll` on an object if the thread owns the object's monitor lock. In other words, these methods must be invoked in synchronized code.

- The wait method releases the object's lock before transitioning into the WAITING or TIMED_WAITING state.

If the wait method does not release the lock, no other thread can invoke notify because the notify method requires the lock.

The wait and notify methods are used in a producer/consumer model where one thread is "producing" something and another thread is "consuming" something. If the producer is too fast, it might need to wait for the consumer. Once the consumer catches up, it can notify the producer to start producing again.

To demonstrate a producer and consumer model, let's use the thread-safe MyStack2 class from the previous section. The class contains two fields:

```
public class MyStack2 {
    private int [] values = new int[10];
    private int index = 0;


    //remainder of class definition
}
```

Suppose a thread (our producer) pushes values onto the stack, and another thread (our consumer) pops values off the stack. If the stack is empty, the popping thread can wait for the pushing thread to push something onto the stack. Once a push occurs, the pushing thread can notify the popping thread to resume execution.

Let's start with the consumer thread. The following class named Consumer tries to pop values off of a MyStack2 object. Study the code and see if you can determine what it does:

```
1.  public class Consumer extends Thread {
2.      private MyStack2 stack;
3.
4.      public Consumer(MyStack2 stack) {
5.          this.stack = stack;
6.      }
7.
8.      public void run() {
9.          while(true) {
10.             synchronized(stack) {
11.                 int x = stack.pop();
12.                 if(x == -1) {
13.                     try {
14.                         System.out.println("Waiting...");
15.                         stack.wait();
16.                     }catch(InterruptedException e) {}
17.                 } else {
18.                     System.out.println("Just popped " + x);
19.                 }
```

```
20.                    }
21.                }
22.            }
23. }
```

On line 15 the Consumer thread invokes `wait` on a `MyStack2` object if the stack is empty (returns -1). The thread needs to own the lock of `stack`, which it acquires on line 10.

The following Producer thread calls `notify` after each push onto the stack:

```
1.   public class Producer extends Thread {
2.       private MyStack2 stack;
3.
4.       public Producer(MyStack2 stack) {
5.           this.stack = stack;
6.       }
7.
8.       public void run() {
9.           while(true) {
10.
11.              int random = (int) (Math.random() * 5);
12.              stack.push(random);
13.              System.out.println("Just pushed " + random);
14.              synchronized(stack) {
15.                  System.out.println("Notifying...");
16.                  stack.notify();
17.              }
18.              try {
19.                  Thread.sleep(2000);
20.              }catch(InterruptedException e) {}
21.          }
22.      }
23. }
```

I added a call to `Thread.sleep` on line 19 of the Producer thread to slow the program down. The call to `notify` on line 16 is made on a `MyStack2` object. The following code instantiates a Consumer and Producer, each with a reference to the same `MyStack2` object:

```
4.   MyStack2 stack = new MyStack2();
5.   Consumer c = new Consumer(stack);
6.   c.start();
7.
8.   Producer p = new Producer(stack);
9.   p.start();
```

The following sequence of events occurs when the code executes:

1.   Assuming the Consumer thread runs first (which is only an assumption and not a guarantee), its run method is invoked.

2.   On line 10, the thread attempts to acquire the monitor lock of the stack. Again, let's assume the lock is available.

3.   The Consumer pops an int off the stack. With our assumptions so far, the value returned is -1 because the Producer has not had a chance to push anything onto the stack yet.

4.   The Consumer calls wait on line 15 and gives up the monitor lock of the stack.

5.   The Producer thread is started and its run method is invoked. A random int between 0 and 4 is pushed onto the stack on line 12.

6.   On line 14, the Producer thread attempts to acquire the lock of the stack. This step is necessary because the call to notify can only occur if the thread owns the lock on the stack.

7.   On line 16, the notify method awakens the Consumer thread and its state changes from WAITING to BLOCKED. Notice the Consumer thread is not RUNNABLE at this point in time. Why? Because the Producer thread still has the lock on the stack and the Consumer thread was within synchronized code when it invoked wait.

8.   The Producer thread gives up the lock of the MyStack2 object on line 17, causing the Consumer thread to transition to the RUNNABLE state.

9.   The Producer thread sleeps, allowing the Consumer thread to obtain the lock of the stack and pop the recently pushed value. The stack is now empty because the Producer is sleeping, so the Consumer waits again.

This process repeats indefinitely because the threads run in infinite while loops. The output changes each time because we are dealing with threads and also because the numbers pushed onto the stack are random. Here is a typical output of the code:

```
Waiting...
Just pushed 1
Notifying...
Just popped 1
Waiting...
Just pushed 3
Notifying...
Just popped 3
Waiting...
Just pushed 4
Notifying...
Just popped 4
Waiting...
```

The output is the most common I got from running the program many times (aside from the random numbers changing), but as with any multithreaded application, the output might vary depending on the environment.

The notifyAll Method

If your program has multiple threads waiting for a call to notify, then you can use the notifyAll method of Object. The notifyAll method wakes up all threads waiting for an object's lock.

Keep in mind that all of these threads that are awakened are all competing for the same object's lock before they can proceed. However, they are no longer in the WAITING or TIMED_WAITING state because they have transitioned to the BLOCKED state, making each thread one step closer to RUNNABLE, as Figure 5.5 shows.

The producer and consumer in the stack example could easily be switched. If a thread attempts to push an int on a full stack, it could wait for another thread to pop an int off the stack, assuming the popping thread calls notify on the stack after each pop. For example, assuming the pushing thread is waiting for a pop, the following statements add a call to notify to the Consumer class on line 19 on the stack object after a pop occurs:

```
10.   synchronized(stack) {
11.       int x = stack.pop();
12.       if(x == -1) {
13.           try {
14.               System.out.println("Waiting...");
15.               stack.wait();
16.           }catch(InterruptedException e) {}
17.       } else {
18.           System.out.println("Just popped " + x);
19.           stack.notify();
20.       }
21.   }
```

Having a thread invoke both wait and notify is a fairly common occurrence in producer/consumer situations where threads rely on each other to complete certain tasks.

The notify method wakes a single thread that is waiting on the object's monitor. If multiple threads are waiting, you do not have any control over which ones are chosen to be awakened. The thread chosen is arbitrary and is based on the JVM implementation that the code is running in.

The `wait` and `notify` methods are an example of how threads are a built-in aspect of the Java programming language. The methods have been a part of the language since the first version of Java, and their main usage is in implementing a producer/consumer model. If you also understand that a thread needs to own the object's lock to invoke its `wait` or `notify` methods, you will have the information you need for answering the `wait` and `notify` questions on the SJCP exam.

Summary

This chapter covered the "Concurrency" objectives of the SCJP exam. The goal of this chapter was to demonstrate how to create a thread in Java and also to understand the various states of a thread once it is started.

You can write a thread in Java in two ways: write a class that implements the `Runnable` interface and wrap a new `Thread` object around an instance of your `Runnable` class, or write a class that extends `Thread` and override the `run` method. From an object-oriented point of view, writing a class that implements `Runnable` is the preferred technique.

We discussed the various states of a thread object and how a thread transitions from one state to another. A thread in Java is NEW, RUNNABLE, BLOCKED, WAITING, TIMED_WAITING, or TERMINATED. A NEW thread has been instantiated but not yet started. A RUNNABLE thread is either currently executing on the CPU or waiting to be scheduled. A BLOCKED thread has requested an unavailable lock and is waiting for that lock to be released by whichever thread currently owns the lock. A WAITING thread has invoked the `wait` method on an object and is waiting indefinitely for a `notify` or `notifyAll` to be invoked on the object. A thread enters the TIMED_WAITING state by invoking `wait` or `join` with a specified timeout or by invoking the `Thread.sleep` method. A TERMINATED thread has run to completion; it cannot be started again.

Threads have a priority, and we discussed thread scheduling and the preemptive behavior of threads. We also discussed the static `sleep` and `yield` methods of `Thread` and their effects on the currently running thread. The `sleep` method causes the currently running thread to temporarily cease executing for a specified amount of time. The `yield` method causes the currently running thread to temporarily pause and allow other threads of the same priority to execute.

Threads need to be synchronized when accessing the same data in a process. Every `Object` in Java has an entity called its monitor lock that threads use to synchronize access to the data of the object. Use the `synchronized` keyword to have a thread attempt to acquire the monitor lock of an object. The `synchronized` keyword can obtain the lock of a specific object's reference. You can also declare a method `synchronized`, in which case the monitor lock of the object the method was invoked on is acquired.

We also discussed the `wait`, `notify`, and `notifyAll` methods of `Object`. These methods are used in a producer/consumer model where one thread is "producing" something and another thread is "consuming" something. The object's lock must be owned by the current thread before invoking these methods or an exception occurs at runtime.

Be sure to test your knowledge of concurrency by answering the Review Questions at the end of the chapter. Make sure you have a good understanding of the following Exam Essentials before you attempt the Review Questions, and good luck!

Exam Essentials

Know the two different ways to write a thread in Java.   A thread in Java is created by either extending the `Thread` class or writing a class that implements `Runnable` and associating an instance with a new `Thread`.

Understand the various states of a thread and the ways that a thread can transition from one state to another.   For example, a `NEW` thread transitions to `RUNNABLE` by invoking its `start` method. A `RUNNABLE` thread transitions to `BLOCKED` when attempting to acquire an unavailable lock. A `RUNNABLE` thread transitions to `TERMINATED` upon running to completion.

A thread cannot be started more than once.   A thread can only be started once. An attempt to start a thread that has already been started results in an `IllegalThreadStateException`.

Understand the synchronized keyword.   The `synchronized` keyword is used by a thread to attempt to acquire an object's monitor lock. The `synchronized` keyword is used to write a synchronized block of code or to denote a method as synchronized.

Understand the join method.   A thread that calls `join` on another thread blocks until the other thread runs to completion.

The output of a multithreaded application is indeterminate.   In many situations, the output is indeterminate because there are multiple possible results of the code.

Understand the producer/consumer model.   Be able to answer conceptual questions about the producer/consumer model, along with a programmatic understanding of how to use the `wait` and `notify` methods.

Review Questions

1. Given the following DoSomething class definition:

```
1.   public class DoSomething implements Runnable {
2.       public void run() {
3.           System.out.println("Do something");
4.       }
5.   }
```

what is output of the following statements?

```
10. DoSomething r = new DoSomething();
11. Thread t = new Thread(r);
12. System.out.println(t.getState());
```

   A. Do something

   B. The output is indeterminate.

   C. NEW

   D. RUNNABLE

   E. TERMINATED

2. Given the following DoSomething class definition:

```
1.   public class DoSomething implements Runnable {
2.       public void run() {
3.           System.out.print("Do something");
4.       }
5.   }
```

what is output of the following program?

```
1.   public class Main {
2.       public static void main(String [] args)
3.                   throws InterruptedException {
4.           DoSomething r = new DoSomething();
5.           Thread t = new Thread(r);
6.           t.start();
7.           t.join();
8.           System.out.print(" else ");
9.       }
10. }
```

   A. Do something else

   B. else Do something

C. else

D. Do something

E. The output is indeterminate.

3. Given the following `PrintA` class definition:

```
1.  public class PrintA extends Thread {
2.      public void run() {
3.          System.out.print("A");
4.      }
5.  }
```

which of the statements is true about the following `PrintB` program? (Select one.)

```
1.  public class PrintB {
2.      public static void main(String [] args) {
3.          Thread a = new PrintA();
4.          a.run();
5.
6.          System.out.print("B");
7.      }
8.  }
```

A. The program generates an exception at runtime.

B. The program does not compile.

C. The output varies and is either AB or BA.

D. The output is always AB.

4. Which of these statements is true about the following `PrintSomething` program? (Select one.)

```
1.  public class PrintSomething implements Runnable {
2.      private String value;
3.
4.      public PrintSomething(String value) {
5.          this.value = value;
6.      }
7.
8.      public void run() {
9.          try {
10.             Thread.sleep((int) (Math.random() * 4000));
11.         }catch(InterruptedException e) {}
12.         System.out.print(value);
13.     }
14.
```

```
15.     public static void main(String [] args) {
16.         Runnable x = new PrintSomething("x");
17.         Runnable y = new PrintSomething("y");
18.         Thread one = new Thread(x);
19.         Thread two = new Thread(y);
20.         two.start();
21.         one.start();
22.     }
23. }
```

A. The output is always xy.

B. The output is always yx.

C. The output can be either xy or yx.

D. Lines 16 and 17 generate compiler errors.

E. Lines 18 and 19 generate compiler errors.

5. Given the following MyTarget class definition:

```
1.  public class MyTarget {
2.      public void run() {
3.          for(int i = 1; i <= 10; i++) {
4.              System.out.print("x");
5.          }
6.      }
7.  }
```

what is result of the following program?

```
1.  public class PrintX {
2.      public static void main(String [] args) {
3.          MyTarget target = new MyTarget();
4.          Thread t = new Thread(target);
5.          t.start();
6.          System.out.print("y");
7.      }
8.  }
```

A. xxxxxxxxxxy

B. yxxxxxxxxxx

C. Ten xs and one y printed in an indeterminate order.

D. xxxxxxxxxxy or yxxxxxxxxxx

E. The code does not compile.

6. What state can a WAITING thread transition into? (Select one.)

   A. NEW

   B. RUNNABLE

   C. BLOCKED

   D. TIMED_WAITING

   E. TERMINATED

7. If the state of a thread is BLOCKED, what must its previous state have been? (Select all that apply.)

   A. NEW

   B. RUNNABLE

   C. WAITING

   D. TIMED_WAITING

   E. TERMINATED

8. Fill in the blanks: A thread that invokes wait is a _____ and a thread that invokes notify or notifyAll is a _____.

9. Given the following BankAccount class definition, which of the following statements are true? (Select two.)

```
1.  public class BankAccount {
2.      private double balance;
3.
4.      public synchronized void deposit(double amount) {
5.          balance += amount;
6.      }
7.
8.      public void withdraw(double amount) {
9.          synchronized(this) {
10.             balance -= amount;
11.         }
12.     }
13.
14.     public double getBalance() {
15.         return balance;
16.     }
17. }
```

   A. The lock being acquired on line 4 is for the this reference.

   B. A thread must have the appropriate monitor lock before invoking the deposit method.

   C. Line 4 generates a compiler error.

    D. The `getBalance` method can be invoked even if the object's monitor is owned by another thread.

    E. Line 9 generates a compiler error.

10. Given the following `Paint` class definition, which of the following statements is true? (Select one.)

```
1.   public class Paint {
2.       private static int color = 1;
3.
4.       public synchronized static void setColor(
5.                                       int newColor) {
6.           color = newColor;
7.       }
8.
9.       public synchronized static int getColor() {
10.          return color;
11.      }
12. }
```

    A. The `color` field is protected from concurrent access problems.

    B. Line 2 generates a compiler error.

    C. Lines 4 and 9 generate compiler errors.

    D. Lines 6 and 10 generate compiler errors.

11. Given the following `MyConsumer` class definition:

```
1.   public class MyConsumer extends Thread {
2.       private StringBuffer sb;
3.
4.       public MyConsumer(StringBuffer sb) {
5.           this.sb = sb;
6.       }
7.       public void run() {
8.           if(sb != null && sb.length() == 0) {
9.               try {
10.                  System.out.println("Waiting");
11.                  sb.wait();
12.              }catch(InterruptedException e) {}
13.          }
14.          sb.reverse();
15.      }
16. }
```

which of the statements is true about the following MyProducer program? (Select one.)

```
1.   public class MyProducer {
2.       public static void main(String [] args) {
3.           StringBuffer sb = new StringBuffer("");
4.           MyConsumer consumer = new MyConsumer(sb);
5.           consumer.start();
6.           Thread.yield();
7.           sb.append("abc");
8.           synchronized(sb) {
9.               sb.notifyAll();
10.          }
11.          System.out.println(sb);
12.      }
13. }
```

A. The output is Waiting following by cba.

B. The output is abc.

C. Either A or B always occurs.

D. The code may generate an exception at runtime.

E. The code does not compile.

12. What is the result of the following Reverser program?

```
1.   public class Reverser extends Thread {
2.       private StringBuffer sb;
3.
4.       public Reverser(StringBuffer sb) {
5.           this.sb = sb;
6.       }
7.
8.       public void run() {
9.           sb.reverse();
10.      }
11.
12.      public static void main(String [] args) {
13.          StringBuffer s = new StringBuffer("xyz");
14.          Reverser r = new Reverser(s);
15.          r.start();
16.          System.out.print(s);
17.          r.start();
18.          System.out.print(s);
19.      }
20. }
```

A. xyzzyx

B. zyxxyz

C. Either xyzzyx or zyxxyz

D. The code generates an exception at runtime.

E. The code does not compile.

13. Given the following statements:

```
5.  Thread t = new Thread(new Runnable() {
6.      public void run() {
7.          System.out.println("do something");
8.      }
9.  });
10. t.start();
```

what is the state of the thread t immediately after line 10 executes?

A. NEW

B. RUNNABLE

C. BLOCKED

D. TERMINATED

E. The state of the thread is indeterminate.

14. Given the following statements:

```
7.  Thread t = new Thread(new Runnable() {
8.      public void run() {
9.          System.out.println("do something");
10.     }
11. });
12. try {
13.     t.sleep(1000);
14. }catch(InterruptedException e) {
15.     System.out.println(e);
16. }
```

what is the state of the thread t immediately after line 13 executes?

A. NEW

B. RUNNABLE

C. TIMED_WAITING

D. WAITING

E. The state of the thread is indeterminate.

15. Given the following `Calendar` class:

```
public class Calendar {
    private static int FIRST_DAY = 1;

    public static synchronized void setFirstDay(int value) {
        FIRST_DAY = value;
    }

    public static int getFirstDay() {
        return FIRST_DAY;
    }
}
```

which of the following statements is true? (Select one)

A. The code does not compile.

B. Invoking `setFirstDay` generates an exception at runtime.

C. A thread that enters the `setFirstDay` method must own the lock of the `Calendar`'s `Class` object.

D. A thread that enters the `setFirstDay` method must own the lock of any instance of `Calendar`.

E. The `getFirstDay` method must also be synchronized.

Answers to Review Questions

1. C. The thread t is instantiated but has not been started yet. That is the definition of a new thread, so its state is NEW and the answer is C.

2. A. The call to join on line 7 of Main causes the main thread to wait until t is done executing. The t thread prints Do something and then ends, and line 8 prints else. Therefore, the answer is A.

3. D. The code compiles fine and runs fine, so A and B are incorrect. On line 4 of the PrintB class, the run method of the new thread is invoked. However, the run method does not start a new thread in the process. (Only a call to start starts a new thread.) In other words, this program is not multithreaded and the call to run occurs within the main thread. The output of this program is always AB and therefore the answer is D.

4. The code compiles fine, so D and E are incorrect. The order of the output of these two threads is indeterminate because they are scheduled by the JVM and there is no guarantee of the order in which they will execute (even if the call to sleep did not occur in the run method). Therefore, the output can either be xy or yx and the answer is C.

5. E. The MyTarget class does not implement Runnable, so line 4 of PrintX does not compile. Therefore, the answer is E.

6. C. When a WAITING thread receives a notify or notifyAll, it transitions into the BLOCKED state because the monitor lock it needs is not available. (The thread that called notify or notifyAll owns it.) Therefore, the answer is C.

7. B, C, and D. A NEW thread can only transition into the RUNNABLE state, so A is incorrect. A RUNNABLE thread transitions into BLOCKED when attempting to acquire an unavailable monitor lock, so B is correct. A WAITING or TIMED_WAITING thread transitions into BLOCKED on a notify or notifyAll, so C and D are correct. The state of a TERMINATED thread never changes, so E is incorrect. Therefore, the answers are B, C, and D.

8. consumer, producer. The wait and notify methods are used in producer/consumer models. If a consumer thread has nothing to consume, it waits. When a producer thread produces, it notifies. Therefore, a thread that invokes wait is a consumer and a thread that invokes notify or notifyAll is a producer.

9. A and D. The code compiles fine, so C and E are incorrect. Synchronized methods attempt to acquire the lock on the this reference, so A is true. B is false; a thread can invoke deposit without the lock. If the thread does not have the lock, it will have to acquire it. D is true; the getBalance method is not synchronized, so it is possible to invoke getBalance while another thread is in the middle of a deposit or withdraw. Therefore, the answers are A and D.

10. A. A static method can be declared as synchronized. The this reference it is attempting to acquire is to the Class object of the Paint class and not an actual instance of Paint. The code compiles fine. Because the color field is private and the only way to access it is through synchronized methods, it is protected from concurrent access problems and the answer is A.

11. D. The code compiles fine, so E is incorrect. A thread cannot invoke `wait` on an object unless that thread owns the object's monitor lock. In other words, a call to `wait` must appear within a synchronized method or block of code. Line 11 of the `MyConsumer` class generates an `IllegalMonitorStateException` at runtime because the thread does not own the lock of `sb`. Therefore, the answer is D.

12. D. You cannot start a thread twice. Line 17 compiles, but the `r` thread has already been started, so line 17 generates an `IllegalThreadStateException`. Therefore, the answer is D.

13. B. The state of `t` is `NEW` after it is instantiated on line 9, and `t` becomes `RUNNABLE` once it is started. Therefore, the answer is B.

14. A. This question is tricky. The state of `t` is `NEW` after it is instantiated on line 7. Because `t` is never started, it does not change states. The `sleep` method is `static` and causes the current thread to sleep, not the thread `t`. Therefore, the answer is A.

15. C. The code compiles and runs fine, so A and B are incorrect. E is false; there is no such requirement of the `getFirstDay` method. D is also false; owning the lock of a particular `Calendar` object is not sufficient for entering `setFirstDay`. The thread that enters `setFirstDay` must own the lock of the `Class` object of `Calendar`. Therefore, the answer is C.

Chapter

6

Object-Oriented Concepts

SCJP EXAM OBJECTIVES COVERED IN THIS CHAPTER:

- ✓ Develop code that implements tight encapsulation, loose coupling, and high cohesion in classes, and describe the benefits.

- ✓ Given a scenario, develop code that demonstrates the use of polymorphism. Further, determine when casting will be necessary and recognize compiler vs. runtime errors related to object reference casting.

- ✓ Explain the effect of modifiers on inheritance with respect to constructors, instance or static variables, and instance or static methods.

- ✓ Given a scenario, develop code that declares and/or invokes overridden or overloaded methods and code that declares and/or invokes superclass, or overloaded constructors.

- ✓ Develop code that implements "is-a" and/or "has-a" relationships.

These objectives are Section 5 of the SCJP exam objectives. The exam tests your knowledge of object-oriented (OO) programming, including encapsulation, inheritance, polymorphism, and good OO design that includes loose coupling and high cohesion. This chapter covers all of these topics in detail.

Encapsulation, Coupling, and Cohesion

The concepts of encapsulation, coupling, and cohesion are not unique to Java and represent good design techniques in any object-oriented programming language. This section discusses each of these design concepts in detail, starting with tight encapsulation.

Tight Encapsulation

Encapsulation refers to the combining of fields and methods together in a class such that the methods operate on the data, as opposed to users of the class accessing the fields directly. The term *tight encapsulation* refers to using encapsulation every time on all the fields of a class, and only providing access to the fields via methods. With tight encapsulation, no fields of an object can be modified or accessed directly; you can only access the fields through a method call.

To implement tight encapsulation, make the fields of a class `private` and provide `public` accessor ("getter") and mutator ("setter") methods. Because a mutator or accessor method must be invoked to access the fields of the object, tight encapsulation has several key benefits:

- You can monitor and validate all changes to a field.

- Similarly, you can monitor and format all access to a field.

- The actual data type of a field can be hidden from the user, allowing you to change the data type without affecting the code that uses the object, as long as you do not alter the signatures of the corresponding accessor and mutator method.

To demonstrate, let's first look at a class that does not implement tight encapsulation. The following class, named `Student1`, represents a student with fields for the year (Freshman, Sophomore, Junior, Senior) and percentage grade of a student. The fields of `Student1` are `public` and can be accessed directly:

```
public class Student1 {
    public String year;
    public double grade;
}
```

Because the class does not implement tight encapsulation, the fields of a Student1 object can take on any values. The following code is valid, although from an application point of view the values do not make sense:

```
Student1 s = new Student1();
s.year = "Memphis, TN";
s.grade = -24.5;
```

The string "Memphis, TN" is not a valid year, and we can assume that a student's grade should never be negative. With tight encapsulation, these issues can easily be avoided because users of the class cannot access its fields directly. By forcing a method call to change a value, you can validate any changes to the fields of the object.

The following Student2 class is similar to Student1 but implements tight encapsulation. It is not possible for year to be an invalid value or grade to be negative or greater than 105.0:

```
1.  public class Student2 {
2.      private String year;
3.      private double grade;
4.
5.      public void setYear(String year) {
6.          if(!year.equals("Freshman") &&
7.              !year.equals("Sophomore") &&
8.              !year.equals("Junior")   &&
9.              !year.equals("Senior")) {
10.             throw new IllegalArgumentException(
11.                                 year + " not a valid year");
12.         } else {
13.             this.year = year;
14.         }
15.     }
16.
17.     public String getYear() {
18.         return year;
19.     }
20.
21.     public void setGrade(double grade) {
22.         if(grade < 0.0 || grade > 105.0) {
23.             throw new IllegalArgumentException(
```

```
24.                                    grade + " is out of range");
25.          } else {
26.              this.grade = grade;
27.          }
28.      }
29.
30.      public double getGrade() {
31.          return grade;
32.      }
33. }
```

See if you can determine the result of the following statements:

```
Student2 s2 = new Student2();
s2.setYear("Junior");
s2.setGrade(-24.5);
```

Invoking setYear with the argument "Junior" changes the year field to "Junior". Invoking setGrade with the argument -24.5 causes an IllegalArgumentException to be thrown on line 23. Due to tight encapsulation, it is not possible for the values of Student2 to contain invalid values.

Information Hiding

One of the key benefits of tight encapsulation is *information hiding*, where the user of an object is unaware of how the object stores its data. With information hiding and tight encapsulation, if you ever need to alter or modify a field, the users of the class are unaffected by the change as long as you do not modify the method signatures in the class.

For example, suppose we decide to store the grade of Student2 as a float instead of a double. If we leave the signatures of setGrade and getGrade alone, the change will not affect code elsewhere:

```
public class Student2 {
        private float grade;

    public void setGrade(double grade) {
        if(grade < 0.0 || grade > 105.0) {
```

```
                    throw new IllegalArgumentException(grade + " is out of range");
            } else {
                this.grade = (float) grade;
            }
        }


    public double getGrade() {
        return grade;
    }


    //remainder of class definition remains unchanged...
}
```

The field grade is now a float and a cast is needed within setGrade to assign the double parameter to grade. Any object invoking setGrade still passes in a double, and a double is still returned from getGrade, but behind the scenes the data is stored as a float, and the change to the Student2 class has no effect on the code that already interacts with Student2 objects.

The benefits of encapsulation outweigh any overhead of the additional method calls, and any good OO design uses tight encapsulation in all classes. The next section discusses another important object-oriented design concept: loose coupling.

Loose Coupling

Coupling is the extent to which one object depends on another object to achieve its goal. For example, an Employee class might depend on an Address class to represent the home address of an employee, so the Employee class is coupled to the Address class. At some point in your application, your classes need to interact with each other, so you cannot avoid coupling entirely. However, the goal of good OO design is to implement *loose coupling*, where you minimize the dependencies an object has on other objects.

If objects are tightly coupled, changing the code in one class has a major effect on the dependent class, requiring code changes to both classes. For example, suppose we have the following Address class:

```
public class Address {
    public String street;
    public String city;
    public int zip;
}
```

The following `Employee` class is tightly coupled to `Address` because `Employee` makes multiple accesses to the `Address` class, directly accessing the `street`, `city`, and `zip` fields of `Address`:

```
public class Employee {
    private Address home;

    public Employee(String street, String city, int zip) {
        home = new Address();
        home.street = street;
        home.city = city;
        home.zip = zip;
    }
}
```

Making changes to `Address` has a direct effect on `Employee`. For example, if we need to change the `city` field in `Address` from a `String` to a `StringBuffer`, the `Employee` class no longer compiles. The ripple effect of tight coupling can quickly get out of hand, and it can become tedious and difficult to maintain the code.

You can avoid this situation by using loose coupling. With loose coupling, changing code in one class can have a minimal effect on its dependent classes. In addition, loose coupling increases the reusability of your classes because a class is more readily used and extended when it is not dependent on other classes.

Loose Coupling and Tight Encapsulation

Implementing loose coupling actually works in close association with tight encapsulation. One of the design techniques of loose coupling is to make the fields of a class `private` and only access them through `public` methods, which is exactly how we implement tight encapsulation. By making the fields `private` and using tight encapsulation, we loosen the coupling between classes because the fields of a class are not accessed directly, as we demonstrate in the `Employee2` class in a moment.

To demonstrate loose coupling, let's modify the `Address` class so that it uses tight encapsulation, shown here in a new class named `Address2`:

```
public class Address2 {
    private String street;
    private String city;
```

```
        private int zip;

        public void setStreet(String s) {
            street = s;
        }

        public void setCity(String c) {
            city = c;
        }

        public void setZip(int z) {
            zip = z;
        }
    }
```

The following `Employee2` class is similar to `Employee` from earlier except that it changes the fields of `Address2` via `public` mutator methods:

```
public class Employee2 {
    private Address2 home;

    public Employee2(String street, String city, int zip) {
        home = new Address2();
        home.setStreet(street);
        home.setCity(city);
        home.setZip(zip);
    }
}
```

If the `city` field of `Address` is changed from a `String` to a `StringBuffer`, no changes need to be made to the `Employee2` class as long as the signature of `setCity` is unchanged. In this situation, the benefit of loose coupling is achieved by using tight encapsulation.

One other design technique for achieving loose coupling involves minimizing the interaction between two objects. For example, in the constructor of `Employee2`, several methods are invoked on `Address2` to initialize its fields. A better, loosely coupled design is to perform the initialization steps in one method call, such as a constructor. For example, suppose we add the following constructor to `Address2`:

```
    public Address2(String s, String c, int z) {
        street = s;
        city = c;
        zip = z;
    }
```

The following `Employee3` class is even more decoupled from `Address2` because it performs the initialization of the `home` field in one step instead of invoking multiple methods of `Address2`:

```java
public class Employee3 {
    private Address2 home;

    public Employee3(String street, String city, int zip) {
        home = new Address2(street, city, zip);
    }
}
```

Unnecessary coupling decreases the reusability of the coupled objects and increases the difficulty of modifying your code, so loose coupling is an important design to implement in your Java applications. The next section discusses yet another important OO design concept: high cohesion.

High Cohesion

Cohesion refers to how closely related the specific tasks are of an object. *High cohesion* is when an object performs a collection of closely related tasks. *Low cohesion* is when an object performs multiple tasks that are not related to each other. Using low cohesion creates code that is difficult to maintain and reuse; therefore, high cohesion is an important design goal of any OO application. Classes that implement high cohesion are more reusable and easier to test and understand.

To demonstrate cohesion, consider the following `Payroll` class that performs various tasks related to paying employees of a company. Based on the names of the methods of `Payroll`, see if you can determine if it follows the design principle of high or low cohesion:

```java
public class Payroll {
    public void computeEmployeePay() {
        System.out.println("Compute pay for employees");
    }

    public void computeEmployeeTaxes() {
        System.out.println("Compute taxes for employees");
    }

    public void addNewEmployee(Employee e) {
        System.out.println("New employee hired...");
    }
}
```

The Payroll class has three specific tasks: computing the employees' pay, computing their taxes, and adding new employees. Computing pay and taxes are related, but adding a new employee to the company seems unrelated to the specific tasks of computing paychecks. Therefore, the Payroll class uses low cohesion and is therefore not a well-designed class.

To make Payroll highly cohesive, remove the **addNewEmployee** method from Payroll and add it to a new class that is related to the tasks of hiring employees. For example, the following HumanResources class seems like a good class to contain such a method:

```
public class HumanResources {
    public void addNewEmployee(Employee e) {
        System.out.println("New employee hired...");
    }

    public void removeEmployee(Employee e) {
        System.out.println("Employee leaving...");
    }
}
```

Now the hiring and removing of employees is separate from paying employees, which results in a highly cohesive design. If we need to alter how employees are added or removed from the company, the Payroll class will be unaffected by such a change. Similarly, if we need to change how employees are paid, changes can be made to the Payroll class without affecting the HumanResources class.

High Cohesion and Loose Coupling

Implementing high cohesion works in close association with loose coupling. If a class is highly cohesive, it is easier to minimize the number of interactions the object has with other objects, which results in looser coupling. On the other hand, if a class performs various unrelated tasks and therefore has low cohesion, more objects will need to communicate with the class, which results in tighter coupling.

In general, your OO applications should strive to decrease dependencies between unrelated objects (loose coupling), while striving to create objects that perform specific, related tasks (high cohesion). The result is code that is easier to maintain and reuse.

There is a direct relationship and benefit to using tight encapsulation, loose coupling, and high cohesion. Using tight encapsulation and high cohesion tends to result in loose coupling, all of which result in code that is more maintainable and reusable.

The next section discusses two more important OO design relationships that you should adhere to in your Java applications: the is-a and the has-a relationships.

OO Design Relationships

You need to be able to develop code that implements is-a and/or has-a relationships for the exam. When you design applications, you make decisions as to how your objects are related to each other. Some objects are extensions of existing objects, making inheritance a good design choice. Some objects are made up of other objects, in which case composition is the better design choice.

The is-a relationship is a simple check to verify that you are using inheritance properly. Specifically, you should be able to state that a child object "is a" parent object. The has-a relationship is a simple check to verify that you are using composition properly. Specifically, if an object "has a" specific attribute or property, the attribute or property is a good candidate for a field within the object's class.

This section discusses the details you need to know regarding the is-a and has-a relationships, starting with the is-a relationship.

The "is-a" Relationship

In Java, a child class is allowed only one parent and can subclass any other non-final class. From a design point of view, your inheritance should satisfy the *is-a relationship*, a simple test to determine if you are using a proper approach and good code design in your application regarding inheritance. The test is simple, but the result is very important: you should be able to state that your child object "is a" parent object.

For example, suppose a class named Cat extends a Pet class. Because a cat "is a" pet, this inheritance is probably a good design. Figure 6.1 shows what these classes might look like.

FIGURE 6.1   A cat is a pet, so Cat extending Pet is a good design.

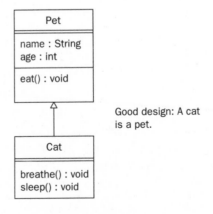

Good design: A cat is a pet.

Suppose I need to write a class to represent employees of a company. Because the Pet class contains fields like name and age, I might be tempted to write an Employee class that extends Pet to reuse the code in Pet, as Figure 6.2 shows.

FIGURE 6.2 Good inheritance design needs to satisfy the "is a" relationship.

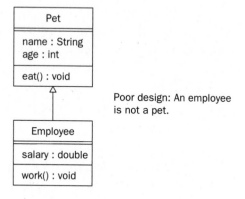

Poor design: An employee is not a pet.

Although this design might work functionally and allow me to store an employee's name and age in the fields of Pet, the design is not a good one because an employee is not a pet.

A better design is for the Employee class to extend a class like Person, because most likely an employee "is a" person. Figure 6.3 shows what these classes might look like.

FIGURE 6.3 An employee is a person, so Employee extending Person is a good design.

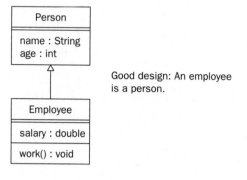

Good design: An employee is a person.

The is-a Relationship and Polymorphism

The is-a relationship is more than a test to verify good inheritance design. It is also useful in understating object-oriented programming and polymorphism. For example, using the Cat and Pet classes from Figure 6.1, the following statement is valid in Java:

```
Pet c = new Cat();
```

Why can a Pet reference point to a Cat object? Because a Cat object "is a" Pet object. We discuss this topic in detail in the upcoming section "Polymorphism."

The is-a relationship is not unique to Java. Inheritance in any OO programming language should satisfy the is-a relationship. Now let's look at another design test: the has-a relationship.

The "has-a" Relationship

Composition refers to a class that contains a reference to another class. The *has-a relationship* is a test to decide when a class should use composition. For example, suppose we have a class called Address that we want to use with an Employee class to represent an employee's home and mailing addresses. Because an employee "has a" address, composition is a good design choice. Figure 6.4 illustrates this relationship.

FIGURE 6.4   An employee "has a" address, so making Address a field of Employee is a good design.

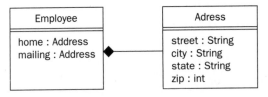

Good design: An employee has a home
and mailing address.

We saw in the previous section that Employee extending Person is a good design because an employee is a person. However, inheritance is not a good design with Address and Employee because an address is not an employee, nor is an employee an address.

As with the is-a relationship, the has-a relationship is an object-oriented concept not exclusive to Java. Sometimes the relationships between objects is not as obvious as the `Employee`, `Person`, and `Address` classes, but you should strive to adhere to the is-a and has-a relationships as much as possible. The benefits of adhering to these relationships include the following:

- The resulting code is more logical.
- The code is easier to understand.
- The classes are easier to reuse in other relationships and applications.
- The code is easier to maintain, especially if the needs and requirements of the program change.

Combining the is-a and has-a relationships with the other OO design goals of tight encapsulation, loose coupling, and high cohesion results in flexible, logical, and maintainable code.

We now change subjects and discuss the details of modifiers on the fields and methods of inherited classes.

Modifiers and Inheritance

You will be tested on your knowledge about the various Java modifiers and their effect on inheritance. In particular, the exam will test your knowledge of the access modifiers: `public`, `private`, `protected`, and the default access, as well as the `abstract` and `final` modifiers. This section discusses the details of these modifiers on inheritance, starting with the access modifiers.

The Access Modifiers

The Java language has four access modifiers, and it is important to understand their effect on fields and methods. (Expect several questions on the exam that test your understanding of the access modifiers.) The access modifiers are as follows:

public   A `public` field, method, or constructor in a class is accessible to any other class.

private   A `private` field, method, or constructor is only accessible from within the class it is declared.

protected   A `protected` field, method, or constructor is accessible from other classes in the same package or subclasses.

No modifier (the default access)   A field, method, or constructor with default access is accessible only from other classes in the same package.

Let's look at an example. The following Phone class is declared in the com.sybex.demos package and demonstrates members with each level of access:

```
1.  package com.sybex.demos;
2.
3.  public class Phone {
4.      public int number;
5.      int extension;
6.      private String ringTone;
7.
8.      public Phone(int n, int e) {
9.          number = n;
10.         extension = e;
11.     }
12.
13.     protected Phone(int n, int e, String r) {
14.         this(n, e);
15.         ringTone = r;
16.     }
17.
18.     void placeCall(int numberToDial) {
19.         System.out.println("Calling " + numberToDial);
20.     }
21.
22.     protected String getRingTone() {
23.         return ringTone;
24.     }
25. }
```

The Phone class has the following properties:

- The class is public, so it is accessible from anywhere. More precisely, the Phone class can be used in any other class.
- Its number field and the constructor on line 8 are also public, so they are accessible from any other class.
- The ringTone field is private and only accessible from within the class, as done on lines 15 and 23.
- The extension field has the default access and is only accessible from other classes in the com.sybex.demos package.
- The constructor on line 13 and the getRingTone method are protected, so they are accessible from any child classes of Phone and also any other classes in the com.sybex .demos package.

The following CellPhone class subclasses Phone and is in the same package, so CellPhone has access to all the public, protected, and default members of Phone:

```
1.  package com.sybex.demos;
2.
3.  public class CellPhone extends Phone {
4.      private int minutesUsed;
5.      private int minutesRemaining;
6.
7.      public CellPhone(int n, int minutes) {
8.          super(n, 0);
9.          minutesRemaining = minutes;
10.     }
11.
12.     public CellPhone(int n, int minutes, String ringTone) {
13.         super(n, 0, ringTone);
14.         minutesRemaining = minutes;
15.     }
16.
17.     public void placeCall(int numberToDial) {
18.         super.placeCall(numberToDial);
19.         minutesUsed += 10;
20.         minutesRemaining -= 10;
21.     }
22. }
```

The following comments are about the CellPhone class:

- Line 8 invokes the public constructor of Phone, which is allowed because the constructor is public.

- Line 13 invokes the protected constructor of Phone, which is allowed because CellPhone is a child of Phone.

- Line 18 invokes the placeCall method of Phone, which is allowed because CellPhone and Phone are in the same package.

Therefore, the CellPhone class compiles fine and is a valid extension of Phone. Now let's look at an example that does not compile. Study the following RotaryPhone class and see if you can determine what is wrong with the code:

```
1.  package com.sybex.demos.oldphones;
2.
3.  import com.sybex.demos.Phone;
4.
```

```
5.   public class RotaryPhone extends Phone {
6.       private int number;
7.
8.       public RotaryPhone(int n, int e, String r) {
9.           super(n, e, r);
10.          this.number = super.number;
11.      }
12.
13.      public void placeCall(int numberToDial) {
14.          super.placeCall(numberToDial);
15.          System.out.println("Using ring tone " + ringTone);
16.      }
17. }
```

The RotaryPhone class makes some valid and invalid attempts at accessing the members of Phone:

- Line 9 invokes the protected constructor of Phone, which is valid because RotaryPhone is a child of Phone.

- Line 10 is valid because the number field in Phone is public and therefore accessible to any other class.

- Line 14 does not compile because the placeCall method has default access and RotaryPhone is not in the same package as Phone.

- Line 15 does not compile because ringTone is private in Phone and therefore not accessible outside of the Phone class.

Attempting to compile RotaryPhone generates the following compiler errors:

```
RotaryPhone.java:14: placeCall(int) is not public in
 com.sybex.demos.Phone; cannot be accessed from outside package
        super.placeCall(numberToDial);
              ^

RotaryPhone.java:15: ringTone has private access in
 com.sybex.demos.Phone
        System.out.println("Using ring tone " + ringTone);
                                                 ^

2 errors
```

In the real world you would implement tight encapsulation, so the number field of Phone would not be public. However, the Phone class is meant to demonstrate the effect of the access modifiers, and you can expect exam questions that contain classes like Phone that do not follow good OO design but instead are testing your knowledge of a specific Java concept.

Make sure that you have a good understanding of the four access modifiers. We now discuss the effect of the `abstract` modifier on inheritance in Java.

The *abstract* Modifier

As you probably recall, we discussed the details of abstract methods and method overriding in Chapter 2, "Declarations, Initialization, and Scoping." The emphasis in this section is to discuss the specific details of the `abstract` modifier and its effect on inheritance. The *abstract modifier* declares a class or method as abstract and has the following effect on the class or method:

- An abstract class cannot be instantiated.
- An abstract method must be overridden.
- A class that contains an abstract method must also be declared `abstract`.
- A child class must override the abstract methods in its parent class or the child class must also be declared `abstract`.
- The access modifier in the child class must be at least as accessible as the access modifier of the abstract parent method.

For example, the following Shape class contains an abstract method named `computeArea`:

```java
public abstract class Shape {
    private String color;

    public Shape(String color) {
        this.color = color;
    }

    protected abstract double computeArea();
}
```

Any non-abstract child class of Shape must declare a `protected` or `public` `computeArea` method. For example, the following class does not compile:

```java
public class InvalidShape extends Shape {

    public InvalidShape(String color) {
        super(color);
    }

    double computeArea() {
        System.out.println("Computing area...");
        return 0.0;
    }
}
```

The computeArea method in InvalidShape has the default access, a weaker access than protected. The following compiler error is generated:

```
InvalidShape.java:7: computeArea() in InvalidShape cannot override
 computeArea() in Shape; attempting to assign weaker access privileges;
 was protected
    double computeArea() {
        ^
```

```
1 error
```

The computeArea method in InvalidShape can only have public or protected access.

Private and Abstract Methods

An abstract method cannot be declared private because a private method is not visible in a child class and therefore cannot be overridden. For example, the following code does not compile:

```
public abstract class Shape {
    private abstract double computeArea();
}
```

The following compiler error is generated:

```
Shape.java:2: illegal combination of modifiers: abstract and private
    private abstract double computeArea();
        ^
```

```
1 error
```

As you can see, the compiler states that abstract and private are not a valid combination of modifiers.

The abstract modifier is only applied to classes and methods. Constructors cannot be overridden, so it does not make sense for a constructor to be abstract. For example, the following Square class does not compile:

```
public abstract class Square {
    private int side;

    public abstract Square(int s) {
        side = s;
    }
}
```

The compiler error generated is

```
Square.java:4: modifier abstract not allowed here
    public abstract Square(int s) {
                  ^
```

```
1 error
```

A constructor cannot be abstract because it cannot be overridden. You can specify that a method cannot be overridden as well using the `final` modifier, discussed in the next section.

The *final* Modifier

The *final modifier* is applied to local variables, fields, methods, or classes. The properties of the `final` modifier are

- A `final` variable or field cannot be changed. These are referred to as *constants*.
- A `final` method cannot be overridden. (We discussed `final` methods in Chapter 2.)
- A `final` class cannot be subclassed.

A `final` variable or field cannot be changed once it is assigned. The following `MyLogger` class contains a `final` field, a `final` parameter, and a `final` local variable:

```
1.  import java.io.File;
2.
3.  public final class MyLogger {
4.      private final File DEST;
5.
6.      public MyLogger(File d) {
7.          DEST = d;
8.      }
9.
10.     public void logMessage(final String MESSAGE) {
11.         final long TIME = new java.util.Date().getTime();
12.         //write time and message to file...
13.     }
14. }
```

The field `DEST` on line 4 and the parameter `MESSAGE` on line 10 are referred to as *blank finals*. They are constants that do not have an initial value, and once they are assigned a value, they cannot be changed. The `TIME` variable on line 11 is assigned the current time and cannot be changed.

The `MyLogger` class is also declared `final`, meaning that it cannot be subclassed. For example, the following `InvalidLogger` class does not compile because it attempts to extend `MyLogger`:

```
public class InvalidLogger extends MyLogger {
    public InvalidLogger(java.io.File dest) {
        super(dest);
    }
}
```

The compiler generates the following error:

```
InvalidLogger.java:1: cannot inherit from final MyLogger
public class InvalidLogger extends MyLogger {
                  ^

1 error
```

Naming Convention for Final Variables

The naming conventions of Java specify that variable names of constants be in all uppercase letters. For example:

```
final long TIME = new java.util.Date().getTime();
```

If the variable name is a compound word, use the underscore character to separate the words. For example:

```
final String COMPANY_NAME = "Sybex";
```

For more information on Java naming conventions, visit `http://java.sun.com/docs/codeconv`.

The `final` modifier on a field does not affect how the field is inherited. A subclass still inherits the field in the same manner as a non-final field; `final` methods are also inherited in the same manner as non-final methods. The only difference is that a `final` method cannot be overridden in the child class.

Static methods can also be declared `final`, meaning they cannot be overridden. For example, the following `MyStaticLogger` class declares a `final static` method named `logMessage`:

```
import java.io.File;


public class MyStaticLogger {
```

```
    private static final File DEST;

    static {
        DEST = new File("mylogfile.txt");
    }

    public final static void logMessage(final String MESSAGE) {
        final long TIME = new java.util.Date().getTime();
        //write time and message to file...
    }
}
```

The following MyNewLogger class extends MyStaticLogger and attempts to override logMessage:

```
public class MyNewLogger extends MyStaticLogger {
    public static void logMessage(final String MESSAGE) {
        System.out.println("Using MyNewLogger...");
        //write message to DEST file
    }
}
```

The compiler generates the following error:

```
MyNewLogger.java:2: logMessage(java.lang.String) in MyNewLogger cannot
 override logMessage(java.lang.String) in MyStaticLogger; overridden
 method is static final
    public static void logMessage(final String MESSAGE) {
                       ^
1 error
```

Recall from Chapter 2 that a non-final static method can be overridden in Java, which is referred to as method hiding. For example, if logMessage in MyStaticLogger is not declared final, then overriding logMessage in MyNewLogger would be valid.

Now that we have discussed the details of the various modifiers, let's change subjects and discuss the object-oriented concept of polymorphism and how to use polymorphism in your Java applications.

Polymorphism

Polymorphism refers to how an object in Java can take on "many forms." Be prepared to develop code that demonstrates the use of polymorphism.

The concept of polymorphism is a result of inheritance and implementing interfaces:

- A child class takes on the form of its parent class.
- A class takes on the form of its implemented interfaces.

This section discusses how to use polymorphism in your code. We also discuss the casting of references, the `instanceof` operator, polymorphic parameters, and heterogeneous collections.

Understanding Polymorphism

To understand how polymorphism works in Java, let's look at an example of a class that extends another class and implements an interface. Suppose we have the following `Pet` class to represent the parent class of various types of pets:

```java
public class Pet {
    private String name;
    private int age;

    public Pet(String name, int age) {
        this.name = name;
        this.age = age;
    }

    public void eat() {
        System.out.println(name + " is eating");
    }
}
```

In addition, suppose we have the following interface named `Mammal` to represent the behaviors of mammals:

```java
public interface Mammal {
    public void breathe();
}
```

The following `Cat` class both extends `Pet` and implements the `Mammal` interface:

```java
public class Cat extends Pet implements Mammal {
    public Cat(String name, int age) {
        super(name, age);
    }

    public void breathe() {
```

```
        System.out.println("Cat is breathing");
    }

    public void sleep() {
        System.out.println("Cat is sleeping");
    }
}
```

The is-a relationship is helpful when trying to understand polymorphism. Because Cat extends Pet, a Cat object is a Pet object. Because Cat implements Mammal, a Cat object is also a Mammal object. Therefore, the following statements are valid:

```
Cat c = new Cat("Garfield", 3);
Pet p = c;
Mammal m = c;
```

The reference p can only refer to Pet objects, but because a Cat object is a Pet object, assigning p to c is valid. Similarly, the reference m can only refer to Mammal objects, but because a Cat object is a Mammal, assigning m to c is also valid. As Figure 6.5 shows, there is only one Cat object in memory, but the object is taking on three different forms. The c reference is treating the object as a Cat, the p reference is treating the object as a Pet, and the m reference is treating the object as a Mammal.

FIGURE 6.5 The single Cat object takes on different forms.

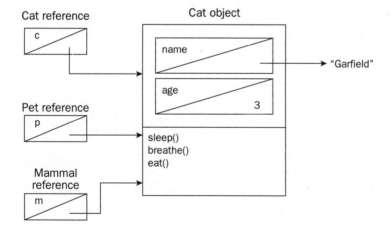

Using the references from Figure 6.5, the following statements are valid without requiring any casting:

```
c.sleep();
c.breathe();
c.eat();
p.eat();
m.breathe();
```

Using the reference c, you can invoke all the methods of Cat, Pet, and Mammal. Using the reference p, you can only invoke the eat method of Pet. Even though the corresponding Cat object contains sleep and breathe methods, the p reference does not see those methods because the p reference thinks it is pointing to a Pet object (not a Cat). Similarly, using the m reference, you can only invoke the breathe method, even though the object has an eat and a sleep method. Casting is required if you want to invoke the "hidden" methods of the Cat object using the m and p references.

Virtual Method Invocation

Now that we have discussed polymorphism, we can discuss the concept of a *virtual method*. All methods in Java are virtual methods, meaning that if a method is overridden, the overridden method is always invoked at runtime, even if the compiler sees the parent class method at compile time. For example, suppose we have the following parent class named ButtonListener with a single method named buttonClicked:

```java
public class ButtonListener {
        public void buttonClicked() {
                System.out.println("Inside ButtonListener");
        }
}
```

The following ChildListener class extends ButtonListener and overrides the buttonClicked method:

```java
public class ChildListener extends ButtonListener {
    public void buttonClicked() {
        System.out.println("Inside ChildListener");
    }
}
```

Using polymorphism, the following statements are valid. Study them carefully and see if you can determine the output:

```
7.  ButtonListener listener = new ChildListener();
8.  listener.buttonClicked();
```

The `listener` reference is of type `ButtonListener`, but it points to a `ChildListener` object. On line 8, the compiler looks for a `buttonClicked` method in `ButtonListener` and finds one, so the code compiles file. However, at runtime, the `buttonClicked` method in `ChildListener` is invoked. This type of behavior is referred to as *virtual method invocation*, where the runtime type of an object is used to determine the overridden method invoked at runtime, as opposed to invoking the method the compiler found at compile time. The output of the previous statements is

```
Inside ChildListener
```

Virtual method invocation is an essential concept in Java that you must understand if you are going to become a serious Java developer.

Casting Polymorphic References

Polymorphic references often need to be cast to their appropriate child class type. The exam tests your knowledge of issues that arise at compile time and runtime involving the casting of these references. In general, the only time casting is necessary is when you need to invoke a method defined in a child class using a parent class or interface reference *and* the method is not overridden. (If the method is overridden, invoking the parent class method causes the child class method to execute at runtime because methods in Java are virtual.)

For example, the `Cat` class contains a `sleep` method that does not override any methods in `Pet` or `Mammal`. To invoke `sleep` using a `Pet` reference, you need to cast the reference first, as demonstrated in the following statements:

```
16. Pet pet = new Cat("Alley", 7);
17. pet.eat();     //no cast needed
18. ((Cat) pet).sleep();     //cast is needed
19. ((Mammal) pet).breathe();     //cast is needed
20. ((Cat) pet).breathe();   //Same as previous line of code
```

The `pet` reference is of type `Pet`, so invoking `eat` on line 17 does not require a cast. However, invoking `sleep` on line 18 requires `pet` to be cast to `Cat`. Invoking `breathe` requires `pet` to be cast to either `Mammal` or `Cat`, as demonstrated on lines 19 and 20. The output of the previous statements is

```
Alley is eating
Cat is sleeping
Cat is breathing
Cat is breathing
```

You need to be careful when casting because it is possible to fool the compiler with a cast that fails at runtime. For example, suppose we have a class called Dog that also extends Pet:

```
public class Dog extends Pet {
    public Dog(String name, int age) {
        super(name, age);
    }

    public void eat() {
        System.out.println("Dog is eating");
    }
}
```

Notice that the Dog class overrides eat from Pet. Study the following code carefully and see if you can determine if it compiles and its result:

```
22. Pet one = new Dog("Fido", 2);
23. one.eat();
24. ((Dog) one).eat();
25. ((Cat) one).eat();
```

On line 23, the compiler sees the eat method of Pet, but at runtime the eat method in Dog is invoked. Line 24 casts one to a Dog, which is valid and the eat method in Dog is invoked again. Line 25 compiles because the Cat class inherits an eat method from Pet, so invoking eat on a Cat is normally a valid statement and the code compiles fine. However, the one reference does not point to a Cat object, and the JVM throws an exception at runtime, as seen in the following output:

```
Dog is eating
Dog is eating
Exception in thread "main" java.lang.ClassCastException:
Dog cannot be cast to Cat
        at PolymorphismDemo.main(PolymorphismDemo.java:25)
```

As you can see, we need to be careful when casting a reference "down the inheritance tree" so that we are casting the reference to its appropriate type. To avoid a ClassCastException, use the instanceof operator, discussed in the next section.

The *instanceof* Operator

The instanceof operator is a Boolean operator used to compare a reference to a class type. If the reference is of the given class type, then the result is true; otherwise, it's false. The syntax for instanceof is

reference instanceof *ClassName*

For example, the following statement avoids the `ClassCastException` from the previous example by using the `instanceof` operator to determine the runtime type of the reference `mypet`:

```java
Pet mypet = new Dog("Fido", 2);
if(mypet instanceof Cat) {
    ((Cat) mypet).eat();
} else if(mypet instanceof Dog) {
    ((Dog) mypet).eat();
}
```

If `mypet` points to a `Cat`, we cast it to a `Cat` before invoking `eat`. If `mypet` points to a `Dog`, we cast it to a `Dog` before invoking `eat`. The previous statements compile and run successfully without a `ClassCastException` ever occurring.

The casting might seem odd, and you might be wondering why we don't just make the `mypet` reference be of type `Dog` instead of `Pet`. The answer is that there are many real-world situations in Java where a parent class reference is used to point to a child object, including polymorphic parameters and heterogeneous collections, which I discuss next.

Polymorphic Parameters

A common use of polymorphism is with *polymorphic parameters* of a method. If a method parameter is a class type, the argument passed in can be any child type of the class as well. For example, the following `Vet` class contains a `vaccinate` method that takes in a `Pet` reference:

```java
public class Vet {
    public void vaccinate(Pet pet) {
        if(pet instanceof Dog) {
            System.out.println("Vaccinating a dog");
            Dog dog = (Dog) pet;
            //use the dog reference
        } else if(pet instanceof Cat) {
            System.out.println("Vaccinating a cat");
            Cat cat = (Cat) pet;
            //use the cat reference
        }
    }
}
```

The argument passed into `vaccinate` can certainly be a `Pet` object, but you can also pass in a `Cat` object, a `Dog` object, or any other object that is a child class of `Pet`. The result is often a parent class reference pointing to a child class object, and we can use the `instanceof` operator if we need to cast the reference to its appropriate child class type, as demonstrated in the `vaccinate` method.

Using `Object` as a Parameter

If you need to write a method that takes in any type of argument, use `Object` as the data type of the parameter. This situation is quite common in the Java API. For example, the `writeObject` method of `ObjectOutputStream` takes in an `Object`:

```
public final void writeObject(Object obj)
```

Because of polymorphism, every object in Java is of type `Object`. Therefore, any reference can be passed into the `writeObject` method. Of course, as we saw in Chapter 4, "API Contents," the `Object` passed in to `writeObject` needs to be of type `Serializable` or an exception is thrown. The `writeObject` method uses the `instanceof` operator to determine if the argument passed in implements `Serializable`. The code looks similar to the following:

```
if(!(obj instanceof Serializable)) {
    throw new NotSerializableException(obj.getClass());
}
```

 ## Real World Scenario

Using Polymorphic Parameters

I developed an application that required an event to be logged every time a customer preference is changed. For example, a customer can choose whether or not to receive emails with promotions, special offers, and news items, and these preferences are stored in a database. The corresponding Java objects to represent the various preferences all extend a class named Preference. The event logging method is defined as

```
public void preferenceChanged(Preference pref) {
    logger.writeUTF(pref.toString());
}
```

The `logger` variable is a `DataOutputStream` that writes to a file. Instead of defining multiple overloaded preferenceChanged methods, this single method can log any Preference that is changed. If a new type of preference comes along, the preferenceChanged method can remain unchanged as long as the new preference extends the Preference class.

Heterogeneous Collections

A *heterogeneous collection* is a collection of objects that are not the same data type but have a common parent class. Continuing with the `Pet` class example, suppose we define an `ArrayList` of `Pet` references:

```
ArrayList<Pet> pets = new ArrayList<Pet>();
```

Any object of type `Pet` can be added to the `pets` collection. For example, the following statements add three different types of objects to `pets`:

```
pets.add(new Pet("", 4));
pets.add(new Cat("Alley", 7));
pets.add(new Dog("Fido", 2));
```

Each statement is valid, and the `ArrayList` now contains one `Pet` object, one `Cat` object, and one `Dog` object. This type of collection is made possible because of polymorphism. As far as the `ArrayList` is concerned, the only objects in `pets` are of type `Pet` because the collection consists of `Pet` references. However, because of polymorphism, the collection actually contains different types of objects like `Cat` and `Dog` objects.

Summary

This chapter covered the "OO Concepts" objectives of the SCJP exam. The goal of this chapter was to discuss the details of object-oriented programming and the standard design rules to follow when you develop OO applications.

We discussed the details of tight encapsulation, loose coupling, and high cohesion. Tight encapsulation is when you make the fields of your class private and only allow access to the field via public methods. The benefit of tight encapsulation is that you control the changes made to your fields and also hide from the users the implementation details of the class.

Loose coupling is when you design your objects to minimize the number of dependencies on other objects. Loose coupling goes hand in hand with tight encapsulation and allows for changes in a class to have a minimal effect on the other classes it is coupled with.

High cohesion is when you design your objects to perform specific, closely related tasks. A highly cohesive object does a specific job and does that job well, without relying on a lot of input from other objects. High cohesion works hand in hand with loose coupling and allows for more logical code that is easier to understand.

The two OO design relationships that we discussed were the is-a and has-a relationships. The is-a relationship is a simple but important test to determine if you are implementing a good inheritance design. Whenever you use inheritance, you should be able to state that a child object "is a" parent object. Similarly, the has-a relationship is used to verify that you are using composition properly. If a class has an object field, you should be able to state that the class "has a" object as one of its attributes.

We discussed the effect of access modifiers and inheritance. There are four access modifiers in Java that can be applied to the field, methods, and constructors of a class. The `public` modifier provides access to everyone; the `private` modifier provides access from only within the class; the `protected` modifier provides package-level access as well as child classes; and the default access is package-level only. We also discussed the effects of the `abstract` and `final` modifiers on methods and inheritance. An `abstract` method must be overridden by any non-`abstract` child class, and a `final` method cannot be overridden in any child class.

The topic of polymorphism was discussed in detail. Polymorphism is when an object takes on many forms. The typical use of polymorphism in Java is when a parent class reference points to a child class object. In this situation, the child object is said to "take on the form" of the parent class. We discussed how to use the `instanceof` operator to ensure valid casting, and we also discussed polymorphism in action with the examples of polymorphic parameters and heterogeneous collections.

Be sure to test your knowledge of these OO concepts by answering the Review Questions that follow the section on Exam Essentials. Attempt to answer the questions without looking back at the pages of this chapter. Make sure you have a good understanding of the following Exam Essentials before you attempt to answer the Review Questions, and good luck!

Exam Essentials

Understand encapsulation, coupling, and cohesion.   Be sure to know what it means for the fields of a class to be tightly encapsulated, where the fields of a class are private and accessed via `public` methods. Also, you need to know the benefits of loose coupling and high cohesion, which results in code that is more reusable and easier to maintain.

Understand polymorphism and the "is-a" relationship.   An object takes on many forms. For example, a parent class reference can refer to a child class object because the child object "is-a" parent. Use the is-a relationship as a simple test to ensure you are using inheritance properly. Use the has-a relationship to determine if you are using composition properly.

Recognize valid reference casting.   Given multiple class definitions, you need to be able to determine if a reference cast is successful at compile or runtime. The compiler cannot always determine if a cast is appropriate, so be able to recognize when a `ClassCastException` is thrown.

Know the four levels of access in Java.   The members of a class can be `public`, `private`, `protected`, or have the default access. You need to recognize whether an attempt to access a field, method, or constructor of a class is allowed.

Understand polymorphism.   Polymorphism, where an object can take on many forms, is one of the most important concepts in OO programming. Be sure to recognize when a parent class reference is pointing to a child class object, as well as when that reference needs to be cast to a child class type.

Understand the `instanceof` operator.   Use the `instanceof` operator to avoid a `ClassCast-Exception` when you are unsure of the actual data type of a reference that needs casting.

Understand virtual method invocation.   By default, Java methods behave like virtual methods, meaning that overridden methods are invoked at runtime, no matter which method the compiler sees at compile time.

Review Questions

1. Fill in the blank: If all of the non-`final` fields of a class are `private` and the class contains `public` methods to view or modify the fields, this is an example of _____.

    A. Tight encapsulation

    B. Loose coupling

    C. High cohesion

    D. The is-a relationship

    E. The has-a relationship

2. Given the following `Television` class definition:

```
public class Television {
    public int channel;
    private boolean on;
    private int volume;

    public void changeChannel(int newChannel) {
        channel = newChannel;
    }

    public int getChannel() {
        return channel;
    }

    public void turnOn() {
        on = true;
    }

    public void turnOff() {
        on = false;
    }

    public void turnUp() {
        volume += 1;
    }
}
```

```
    public void turnDown() {
        volume -= 1;
    }
}
```

which of the following OO design patterns does the `Television` class more closely adhere to?

A. Tight encapsulation

B. Tight coupling

C. High cohesion

D. Low cohesion

3. Fill in the blank: Minimizing the dependencies an object has on other objects is referred to as _____.

A. Tight encapsulation

B. Loose coupling

C. High cohesion

D. The is-a relationship

E. The has-a relationship

4. Which of the following is not a benefit of tight encapsulation and loose coupling?

A. Information hiding

B. Code changes have a smaller ripple effect on other classes.

C. Easier reuse of code

D. Decreases the need to test the code

5. Which one of the following uses of inheritances is probably not a good design?

A. Car extends `Vehicle`

B. Elephant extends `Mammal`

C. Laptop extends `Computer`

D. Square extends `Triangle`

E. Apple extends `Fruit`

6. Given the following class definitions:

```
1.  public class Parent {
2.      protected void sayHi() {
3.          System.out.print("Hi");
4.      }
5.  }
```

```
6.
7.   class Child extends Parent {
8.       public void sayHi() {
9.           System.out.print("Hello");
10.      }
11. }
```

what is output of the result of the following statements?

```
15. Parent p = new Child();
16. p.sayHi();
```

A. Hi

B. Hello

C. Compiler error on line 8

D. Compiler error on line 15

E. Line 16 causes an exception to be thrown.

7. What is the result of the following code?

```
1.  public class Beverage {
2.      private int ounces = 12;
3.      boolean carbonated = false;
4.
5.      public static void main(String [] args) {
6.          System.out.println(new SodaPop());
7.      }
8.  }
9.
10. class SodaPop extends Beverage {
11.     public String toString() {
12.         return ounces + " " + carbonated;
13.     }
14. }
```

A. 12 false

B. Compiler error on line 6

C. Compiler error on line 10

D. Compiler error on line 11

E. Compiler error on line 12

8. What is the result of the following code?

```
1.  public class Fruit {
2.      private String color = "Green";
```

```
3.
4.        public static void main(String [] args) {
5.            Fruit apple = new Fruit();
6.            apple.color = "Red";
7.            System.out.println(apple.color);
8.        }
9.    }
```

A. Red

B. Green

C. Compiler error on line 5

D. Compiler error on lines 6 and 7

E. Line 6 throws an exception at runtime.

9. Given the following `MyWindowCloser` class definition:

```
1.  public abstract class MyWindowCloser {
2.      protected abstract void closeWindow(String id);
3.  }
```

which of the following methods could appear in a child class of `MyWindowCloser`? (Select three answers.)

A. `protected void closeWindow(String id)`

B. `private void closeWindow()`

C. `protected int closeWindow(String id)`

D. `void closeWindow(String id)`

E. `public void closeWindow(String x)`

10. What is the result of the following code?

```
1.  public abstract class Catchable {
2.      protected abstract void catchAnObject(Object x);
3.
4.      public static void main(String [] args) {
5.          java.util.Date now = new java.util.Date();
6.          Catchable target = new MyStringCatcher();
7.          target.catchAnObject(now);
8.      }
9.  }
10.
11. class MyStringCatcher extends Catchable {
12.     public void catchAnObject(Object x) {
13.         System.out.println("Caught object");
14.     }
```

```
15.
16.     public void catchAnObject(String s) {
17.         System.out.println("Caught string");
18.     }
19. }
```

A. Caught object

B. Caught string

C. Compiler error on line 2

D. Compiler error on line 12

E. Compiler error on line 16

11. What is the result of the following code?

```
1.  public abstract class A {
2.      private void doSomething() {
3.          System.out.println("A");
4.      }
5.
6.      public static void main(String [] args) {
7.          A a = new B();
8.          a.doSomething();
9.      }
10. }
11.
12. class B extends A {
13.     protected void doSomething() {
14.         System.out.println("B");
15.     }
16. }
```

A. A

B. B

C. Compiler error on line 7

D. Compiler error on line 8

E. Compiler error on line 13

12. What is the result of the following code?

```
1.  public class X {
2.      protected final void doSomething() {
3.          System.out.println("X");
4.      }
```

```
5.
6.        public static void main(String [] args) {
7.            X x = new Y();
8.            x.doSomething();
9.        }
10. }
11.
12. class Y extends X {
13.        protected void doSomething() {
14.            System.out.println("Y");
15.        }
16. }
```

A. X

B. Y

C. Compiler error on line 2

D. Compiler error on line 8

E. Compiler error on line 13

13. Given the following class definitions:

```
1.  public class Pet implements Runnable {
2.       public void run() {}
3.
4.       public static void main(String [] args) {
5.            _____ x = new Cat();
6.       }
7.  }
8.
9.  class Cat extends Pet {
10. }
11.
12. class Dog extends Pet {
13. }
```

which of the following answers can fill in the blank on line 5 and have the code compile successfully? (Select three.)

A. Pet

B. Runnable

C. Cat

D. Dog

E. Thread

14. Given the following `Vehicle` and `Car` class definitions:

```
1.  package my.vehicles;
2.
3.  public class Vehicle {
4.      public String make;
5.      protected String model;
6.      private int year;
7.      int mileage;
8.  }
```

```
1.  package my.vehicles.cars;
2.
3.  import my.vehicles.*;
4.
5.  public class Car extends Vehicle {
6.      public Car() {
7.
8.      }
9.  }
```

which of the following statements can appear on line 7 so that the `Car` class compiles successfully? (Select all that apply.)

A. `make = "Honda";`

B. `model = "Pilot";`

C. `year = 2009;`

D. `mileage = 15285;`

E. None of the above

15. What is the result of the following code?

```
1.  public class Browser {
2.      public static void main(String [] args) {
3.          Browser b = new Firefox();
4.          IE e = (IE) b;
5.          e.go();
6.      }
7.
8.      public void go() {
9.          System.out.println("Inside Browser");
10.     }
11. }
```

12.
13. class Firefox extends Browser {
14.   public void go() {
15.   System.out.println("Inside Firefox");
16.   }
17. }
18.
19. class IE extends Browser {
20.   public void go() {
21.   System.out.println("Inside IE");
22.   }
23. }

A. Inside Browser

B. Inside Firefox

C. Inside IE

D. Compiler error on line 4

E. Line 4 generates an exception at runtime.

16. Using the class definitions from Question 15, what is the result of the following statements?

4. Browser ref = new IE();
5. if(ref instanceof Firefox) {
6.   System.out.println("Firefox");
7. } else if(ref instanceof Browser) {
8.   System.out.println("Browser");
9. } else if(ref instanceof IE) {
10.   System.out.println("IE");
11. } else {
12.   System.out.println("None of the above");
13. }

A. Firefox

B. Browser

C. IE

D. None of the above

E. The code does not compile.

17. Using the class definitions from Question 15 along with the following OperatingSystem class:

1. public class OperatingSystem {
2.   private Browser browser;

```
3.
4.        public void setBrowser(Browser b) {
5.            browser = b;
6.        }
7.
8.        public static void main(String [] args) {
9.            OperatingSystem os = new OperatingSystem();
10.           os.setBrowser(_____);
11.       }
12. }
```

which of the following statements can appear in the blank on line 10 so that the OperatingSystem class compiles successfully?

A. new Browser()

B. new Firefox()

C. new IE()

D. new Object()

E. new String("Hello")

18. Given the following class definitions:

```
1.   import java.util.Stack;
2.
3.   public class FairyTale {
4.       public static void main(String [] args) {
5.           Stack<FairyTale> tales =
6.                       new Stack<FairyTale>();
7.           tales.add(_____);
8.       }
9.   }
10.
11.  class SnowWhite extends FairyTale {}
12.
13.  class Cinderella {}
```

which of the following statements can appear in the blank on line 7 so that the code compiles successfully? (Select all that apply.)

A. new Cinderella()

B. new SnowWhite()

C. new FairyTale()

D. None of the above

19. What is the result of the following code?

```
1.  public abstract class Book {
2.       public abstract void read();
3.
4.       public static void main(String [] args) {
5.            Book book = new NonFictionBook();
6.            book.read();
7.       }
8.  }
9.
10. class NonFictionBook extends Book {
11.      public void read(int time) {
12.           System.out.println("Reading a NonFictionBook");
13.      }
14. }
```

A. Reading a NonFictionBook

B. Compiler error on line 5

C. Compiler error on line 6

D. Compiler error on line 10

E. An exception occurs at runtime on line 6.

20. What is the result of the following program?

```
1.  public abstract class Book {
2.       public final void read() {
3.            System.out.println("Reading a Book");
4.       }
5.
6.       public static void main(String [] args) {
7.            Book book = new NonFictionBook();
8.            book.read();
9.       }
10. }
11.
12. class NonFictionBook extends Book {
13.      public void read() {
14.           System.out.println("Reading a NonFictionBook");
15.      }
16. }
```

A. Reading a Book

B. Reading a NonFictionBook

C. Compiler error on line 7

D. Compiler error on line 8

E. Compiler error on line 13

Answers to Review Questions

1. A. Making all of the fields of a class `private` and providing `public` setter and getter methods is the definition of tight encapsulation, so the answer is A.

2. C. The `Television` class has a `public` field `channel`, so it does not follow tight encapsulation and A is incorrect. It does not refer to any other classes, so it is loosely coupled and B is incorrect. The methods of `Television` perform tasks reminiscent of a TV and are closely related, which is the goal of high cohesion, making D incorrect and C the correct answer.

3. B. The definition of loose coupling is to minimize an object's dependencies on other objects, so the answer is B.

4. D. Information hiding is a benefit of tight encapsulation, so A is incorrect. Easier code changes and reuse of code are benefits of both tight encapsulation and loose coupling. No matter how well you design your application, there is always a need to test your code, so D is the correct answer.

5. D. The only inheritance that does not satisfy the is-a relationship is D, because a square is not a triangle. Therefore, the answer is D.

6. B. The code compiles and runs fine, so C, D, and E are incorrect. The compiler sees the `sayHi` method of `Parent` on line 16, but at runtime the `sayHi` method of `Child` is invoked because the `Child` class overrides the `sayHi` method. Therefore, the output is `Hello` and the answer is B.

7. E. The code does not compile, so A is incorrect. On line 12, the child class `SodaPop` attempts to access the ounces field of its parent class `Beverage`. Because the `ounces` field is `private`, `SodaPop` does not have access to it and a compiler error is generated. Therefore, the answer is E.

8. A. The code compiles and runs fine, so C, D, and E are incorrect. The `main` method is defined within `Fruit`, so `main` has access to the `private` field `color`. (If `main` were defined in a different class, then lines 6 and 7 would not compile.) Line 6 changes the color to `Red` and line 7 prints it out, so the answer is A.

9. A, B, and E. C is incorrect because it attempts to change the return value of `closeWindow` in the parent, which is not allowed. D is incorrect because it has the default access, which is a weaker access than `protected` in the parent. A and E successfully override the `closeWindow` method in `MyWindowCloser`, so they are valid methods that could appear in a child class. B is also valid because it is overloading the `closeWindow` method (not overriding the method) in the parent and can have any access modifier. Therefore, the correct answers are A, B, and E.

10. A. An `abstract` method can be `protected`, and a child class can override the method with `public` access. The `catchAnObject` method on line 16 is a valid overloading of the method. The code compiles fine, so C, D, and E are incorrect. Line 7 invokes `catchAnObject` with a `Date` object, which through polymorphism causes the method on line 12 to be invoked. Therefore, the output is `Caught object` and the answer is A.

11. A. Tough question! The code actually compiles fine, so C, D, and E are incorrect. A private method cannot be overridden, so doSomething in B is not overriding doSomething in A. The method call to doSomething on line 8 is referring to the private method on line 2, and that is also the method that gets invoked at runtime because it is not overridden. Therefore, the output is A and the correct answer is A.

12. E. The code does not compile, so A and B are incorrect. The parent class X declares a final method named doSomething, and the child class Y attempts to override it on line 13. Because a final method cannot be overridden, a compiler error occurs on line 13 and the answer is E.

13. A, B, and C. The object on the right-hand side of the equation on line 5 is a Cat object, so the reference on the left-hand side needs to be compatible with Cat. Because Cat extends Pet, Pet is valid, so A is correct. Because Pet implements Runnable and Cat extends Pet, Runnable is valid so B is correct. C is correct because a Cat reference can certainly point to a Cat object. D is incorrect; Dog is not compatible with Cat. E is incorrect; Thread is not related to the Cat class in any way.

14. A and B. The make field in Vehicle is public, so it is accessible anywhere. Therefore, A is a correct answer. The model field is protected, so it is accessible in child classes. Because Car extends Vehicle, B is a correct answer. The year field is private in Vehicle, so C does not compile. The mileage field has the default access, but Car is in a different package than Vehicle, so D is incorrect.

15. E. The code compiles file, so D is incorrect. However, a ClassCastException is thrown at runtime on line 4 when the reference b, which points to a Firefox object, is cast to an IE reference. Therefore, the answer is E.

16. B. The ref reference points to an IE object, so the comparison line 5 is false. However, the comparison line 7 is true because an IE object is a Browser object, so line 8 displays Browser. Therefore, the answer is B.

17. A, B, and C. The parameter of setBrowser is Browser, so any Browser object of child of Browser can be passed into setBrowser. Therefore, A, B, and C are correct. D is incorrect because Object is not a child of Browser. (Browser is a child of Object, but that relationship is in the wrong direction for setBrowser to be invoked successfully.) Similarly, since String is not a child of Browser, E is also incorrect.

18. B and C. The tales reference is a Stack of FairyTale objects, which can include any child classes of FairyTale. Putting a SnowWhite object on the stack and a FairyTale object are both valid, so B and C are correct. Because Cinderella does not extend FairyTale, A is incorrect.

19. D. The code does not compile, so A is incorrect. The problem with the code is that NonFictionBook extends Book but does not override read. The read method in NonFictionBook is an overloaded version of read, so NonFictionBook must be declared abstract. Because it is not declared abstract, the compiler points to line 10 as the cause of the error, so the answer is D.

20. E. The code does not compile, so A and B are incorrect. Lines 7 and 8 are valid, so C and D are incorrect. The problem with this code is the Book declares the read method as final, and the child class NonFictionBook attempts to override it. The compiler error is on line 13, so the answer is E.

Chapter 7

Collections and Generics

SCJP EXAM OBJECTIVES COVERED IN THIS CHAPTER:

✓ Given a design scenario, determine which collection classes and/or interfaces should be used to properly implement that design, including the use of the Comparable interface.

✓ Distinguish between correct and incorrect overrides of corresponding hashCode and equals methods, and explain the difference between == and the equals method.

✓ Write code that uses the generic versions of the Collections API, in particular, the Set, List, and Map interfaces and implementation classes. Recognize the limitations of the non-generic Collections API and how to refactor code to use the generic versions. Write code that uses the NavigableSet and NavigableMap interfaces.

✓ Develop code that makes proper use of type parameters in class/interface declarations, instance variables, method arguments, and return types; and write generic methods or methods that make use of wildcard types and understand the similarities and differences between these two approaches.

✓ Use capabilities in the java.util package to write code to manipulate a list by sorting, performing a binary search, or converting the list to an array. Use capabilities in the java.util package to write code to manipulate an array by sorting, performing a binary search, or converting the array to a list. Use the java.util.Comparator and java.lang .Comparable interfaces to affect the sorting of lists and arrays. Furthermore, recognize the effect of the "natural ordering" of primitive wrapper classes and java.lang .String on sorting.

These objectives are Section 6 of the SCJP exam objectives. The exam tests your knowledge of the Collections API, including the use of generics. This chapter covers all of these topics in detail.

Overview of Collections

A *collection* is a group of objects contained in a single element. Examples of collections include an array of integers, a vector of strings, or a hash map of vehicles. The *Java Collections Framework* is a unified set of classes and interfaces defined in the java.util package for storing collections. For the exam, you need to understand the different types of collections in the Collections Framework, including lists, maps, and sets. You need to recognize which collection to use given a specific scenario. The exam also tests your knowledge of the Comparable interface and the difference between == and the equals method. This section discusses all of these topics, starting with a discussion on the collections interfaces, which provide the foundation of the Collections Framework.

The Collections Interfaces

The java.util package contains a group of interfaces referred to as the *collections interfaces* to represent the various types of collections. The root interface of the collections interfaces is Collection. There are different types of collections, and the subinterfaces of Collection reflect these various types of collections, as follows:

Lists   A *list* is an ordered collection of elements that allows duplicate entries. Lists implement the List interface, and elements in a list can be accessed by an integer index.

Sets   A *set* is a collection that does not allow duplicate entries. Sets implement the Set interface.

Queues   A *queue* is a collection that orders its elements in a specific order for processing. A typical queue processes its elements in a first-in, first-out (FIFO) fashion, but other ordering is possible. Queues implement the Queue interface.

Maps   A *map* is a collection that maps keys to values, with no duplicate keys allowed. The elements in a map are key-value pairs. Maps implement the Map interface, which is unique because the Map interface is not a subinterface of Collection like the other types of collections.

Figure 7.1 shows the `Collection` interface and its core subinterfaces.

FIGURE 7.1   The `Collection` interface is the root of all collections except maps.

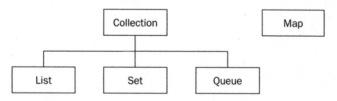

Maps are the only collections that do not implement the `Collection` interface because elements in a map are key-value pairs of data while elements in a collection are single items. The `Map` interface contains methods for working with keys and values that do not apply to `Collection` objects.

The `Collection` interface contains useful methods for working with lists, sets, and queues, including:

`public boolean add(E e)`   Adds an element to the collection.

`public boolean remove(Object e)`   Removes a single instance of the given object from the collection.

`public boolean contains(Object e)`   Returns `true` if the given `Object` appears in the collection.

`public Iterator<E> iterator()`   Returns an iterator over the elements in the collection.

All of the interfaces and classes in the Collections Framework are generics, as evidenced by the E parameter of the add method and the <E> generic return type of the iterator method. Generics are an important aspect of the Collections Framework and are discussed in detail in the section, "Using Generics," later in this chapter.

Let's look at each of the collection types and their corresponding interfaces and classes, starting with lists.

Lists

A list is an ordered collection that can contain duplicate entries. Items in a list can be retrieved and inserted at a specific position in the list based on an integer index, much like an array. You can search a list, iterate through its elements, and perform operations on a range of values in the list. Lists are commonly used because there are many situations in programming where you need to keep track of a list of objects. For example, suppose you have a website that sells electronic equipment and you execute a database query that returns all cameras for sale. You could use a list to hold the data and iterate through the list to display the cameras in an HTML table.

Figure 7.2 shows the List interface and the classes in the Collections Framework that implement List.

FIGURE 7.2   The List interface and its implementing classes

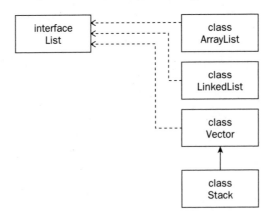

The different list classes each provide their own unique functionality:

ArrayList   A resizable list implemented as an array. When elements are added and removed, the ArrayList grows and shrinks accordingly. You can control the internal size of the array to improve performance.

LinkedList   A list that implements a linked list data structure. Items can be added and removed from the beginning or end of the linked list. LinkedList is unique in that it also implements the Queue and Deque interfaces.

Vector   A Vector is essentially the same as an ArrayList except that the methods in Vector are synchronized.

Stack   A list that implements a stack data. Items are pushed onto the top and popped off the top of the stack, a last-in, first-out (LIFO) behavior.

The basic operations of List include the ability to add a single element at a specified index, add a collection of elements, replace or remove a specific element, and retrieve an element at a specified index.

Sets

A set is a collection of elements that does not allow duplicates and models the mathematical concept of abstract sets. For example, the Set interface contains an andAll method for performing set unions and a retainAll method for performing set intersections. Use a set when you need a collection where duplicates are not allowed. Attempts to add a duplicate element to a set are ignored. For example, suppose that you need to write an application that searches a book for keywords and keeps track of the page numbers where the keywords appear. After a page number is found, add it to the set. If a keyword appears twice on a page, adding the page number again to the set has no effect, which is the desired behavior in this situation.

Figure 7.3 shows the Set interfaces and their implementing classes.

FIGURE 7.3   The Set interfaces and their implementing classes

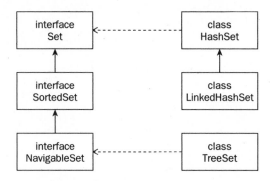

The different set classes each provide their own unique functionality:

HashSet   A set that stores its elements in a hash table. There is no ordering to the items, and HashSet uses the hashCode method of its elements to determine their placing in the set.

LinkedHashSet   A set that stores its elements in a linked list hash table. The items are hashed based on their hashCode and also ordered in a doubly linked list.

TreeSet   A set that stores its elements in a tree data structure that is also sorted and navigable. The add, remove, and contains methods are guaranteed to work in log(n) time, where n is the number of elements in the tree.

The basic operations of Set include the ability to add or remove a single element or collection of elements, and to perform unions and intersections.

Queues

A queue is a collection whose elements are added and removed in a specific order. Queues are typically used for storing elements prior to processing them. For example, suppose you have an order processing application that places new orders into a queue. The warehouse could retrieve the order from the queue to fulfill the order, and the billing department could retrieve the order from the queue to collect payment. Queues typically process elements in a FIFO behavior, but the actual behavior depends on the type of queue you are using.

A *deque* (pronounced "deck") is a double-ended queue that allows for elements to be inserted and removed at both ends of the queue. Deques implement the Deque interface, a subinterface of Queue. Figure 7.4 shows the hierarchy of queue interfaces and classes.

FIGURE 7.4   The Queue and Deque interfaces and implementing classes

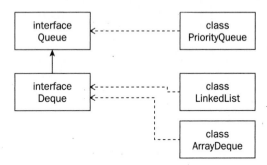

The different queue and deque classes each have their own specific behaviors:

PriorityQueue   A queue where the elements are ordered based on an ordering you specify (as opposed to ordering based on FIFO).

LinkedList   The same LinkedList class we saw earlier in the discussion on lists. LinkedList also implements the Queue and Deque interfaces, providing a queue or deque that is implemented as a linked list data structure.

ArrayDeque   A queue and deque implemented as a resizable array with no capacity restrictions.

The basic operations of Queue include adding a single element, polling the queue to retrieve the next element, or peeking at the queue to see if there is an element available in the queue. The Deque operations are similar except elements can be added, polled, or peeked at both the beginning and end of the deque.

Maps

A map is a collection that maps keys to values. Each key maps to one value, and duplicate keys are not allowed in a map. A map is similar to a function in mathematics. Use a map when the data you are storing has a key value that is more meaningful than a simple integer index (like arrays and lists use). For example, suppose you need to write a phonebook application. A person's name and phone number are paired together, and we usually search a phonebook by a person's name. Therefore, a phonebook map could use a person's name as the key and their phone number as the value of that key.

Figure 7.5 shows the Map interface, its subinterfaces, and the various map classes in the Collections Framework.

FIGURE 7.5   The Map interfaces and implementing classes

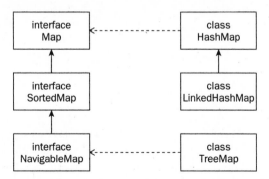

The following overview shows the implementing classes of Map:

HashMap   A map that stores its elements in a hash table. There is no ordering to the elements, and they are placed in the hash table based on their hashCode.

LinkedHashMap   A map that stores its element in a hash table and doubly linked lists. The linked list provides an ordering to the elements.

TreeMap   A map that stores its elements in a tree data structure with a natural or user-defined ordering. TreeMap provides $\log(n)$ time for the methods that view or change elements in the tree.

The Map interface provides methods for accessing the elements of the collection as a set of keys, a list of values, or a set of key-value mappings. We discuss maps in detail in the section "Using Generics" later in this chapter as well as the details for using lists, sets, and queues. But before we move on to generics, I need to discuss one more topic on the subject of collections: the Comparable interface.

Using a Map to Count Keywords

A common use for search engines is to determine the relevance of the content on a web page, and an important factor that search engines use is the number of times a particular word or phrase appears on the page. This scenario is a good example of when to use a Map object, where the key of the map is the keyword on the web page and the value of the map is the number of occurrences. The code might look something like the following:

```java
import java.util.HashMap;

public class KeywordCounter {
    public HashMap<String, Integer> keywords = new HashMap<String, Integer>();

    public void keywordFound(String keyword) {
        Integer count = keywords.get(keyword);
```

```
            if(count == null) {
                keywords.put(keyword, 1);
            } else {
                keywords.put(keyword, count + 1);
            }
        }
    }
```

The keywordFound method takes in a String object to represent a keyword. If the String is not in the map, then count is null and the keyword is added with a value of 1. If the keyword is in the map already, it is replaced with the same keyword but an incremented value. The following statements create a new KeywordCounter and add various strings to the map:

```
KeywordCounter webpage = new KeywordCounter();
webpage.keywordFound("java");
webpage.keywordFound("ejb");
webpage.keywordFound("java");
webpage.keywordFound("jsp");
for(String keyword : webpage.keywords.keySet()) {
    System.out.println(keyword + " = " +
                        webpage.keywords.get(keyword));
}
```

The output of this code is

```
ejb = 1
jsp = 1
java = 2
```

The *Comparable* Interface

The Comparable interface in the java.util package creates an ordering for a collection of objects by providing a method to compare two objects. The Comparable interface contains only one method:

```
public int compareTo(T o)
```

The T parameter denotes a generic type. The return value of compareTo is an int, which represents one of three outcomes:

Zero   The two objects are equal.

Negative   This object is less than the specified object o.

Positive   This object is greater than the specified object o.

The ordering of objects that the compareTo method provides is referred to as the *natural ordering* of the class. For example, the String class implements Comparable, and the natural ordering of String objects is lexicographical, which is close to alphabetical except uppercase letters always appear before lowercase letters. See if you can determine if the following compareTo method calls return a positive number, a negative number, or 0:

```
4.   String a = "hello";
5.   String b = "goodbye";
6.   String c= "Hello";
7.
8.   System.out.println(a.compareTo(b));
9.   System.out.println(c.compareTo(b));
10.  System.out.println(a.compareTo(c));
11.  System.out.println(a.compareTo(a));
```

The output of the statements is

```
1
-31
32
0
```

The first int displayed from line 8 is positive because the string "hello" is greater than "goodbye". The actual value of the positive number is normally irrelevant, and for String objects it represents the difference between the first unequal characters between the two strings. Line 9 compares "Hello" to "goodbye" and outputs -31 because H is uppercase and appears before all lowercase letters. Therefore, "Hello" is less than "goodbye". Similarly, "hello" is greater than "Hello" on line 10, which outputs 32. Line 11 outputs 0 because the two strings are equal.

The Difference Between == and *equals*

We discussed the differences between the == operator and the equals method of Object in Chapter 1, "Fundamentals." The == operator compares if two references point to the same object, and the equals method uses your own business logic to determine if two objects are equal. To refresh your memory, see if you can determine the output of the following:

```
4.    String x = "hi";
5.    String y = new String("hi");
6.    if(x == y) {
7.        System.out.println("x == y");
8.    }
9.    if(x.equals(y)) {
10.       System.out.println("x.equals(y)");
11.   }
```

Because x and y point to different objects, line 6 is false. Because the two objects are equal in the sense of String equality, line 9 is true. Therefore, the output of the previous code is

```
x.equals(y)
```

The equals method plays an important role in the Java Collections Framework. Sets do not allow duplicate elements and maps do not allow duplicate keys. The set and map classes use the equals method of the objects in the collection to determine if two objects are equal. If you are using collections, you should include an equals method in your classes. When overriding equals, be sure to override hashCode so that two equal objects generate the same hashCode, as demonstrated by the following Product class:

```java
public class Product {
    String description;
    double price;
    int id;

    public boolean equals(Object obj) {
        if(!(obj instanceof Product)) {
            return false;
        }
        Product other = (Product) obj;
        return this.id == other.id;
    }

    public int hashCode() {
        return id;
    }
}
```

Notice that the two `Product` objects are equal if they have the same `id`, and two equal Product objects generate the same `hashCode`.

---

compareTo **Consistent with** equals

If you write a class that implements `Comparable`, you introduce new business logic for determining equality. The `compareTo` method returns 0 if two objects are equal, while your `equals` method returns `true` if two objects are equal. A natural ordering that uses `compareTo` is said to be *consistent with equals* if and only if `x.equals(y)` is true whenever `x.compareTo(y)` equals 0. You are strongly encouraged to make your `Comparable` classes consistent with `equals` because not all collection classes behave predictably if the `compareTo` and `equals` methods are not consistent. For example, the following `Product` class defines a `compareTo` method that is consistent with `equals`:

```
public class Product implements Comparable<Product> {
    int id;

    public boolean equals(Object obj) {
        if(!(obj instanceof Product)) {
            return false;
        }
        Product other = (Product) obj;
        return this.id == other.id;
    }

    public int compareTo(Product obj) {
        return this.id - obj.id;
    }
}
```

If two Product objects are equal, they have the same `id`. Therefore, the return value of `compareTo` is 0 when comparing two equal Product objects, so this `compareTo` method is consistent with `equals`.

Now that we have discussed the various types of collections in the Collections Framework, let's put this knowledge to use by instantiating and using the collection classes in the next section. Because all of the collections classes use generics and the exam requires knowledge of generics, the next section discusses both topics simultaneously.

Using Generics

You will be tested on your knowledge of the generic versions of the Set, List, and Map interfaces and implementation classes. You also need to understand the limitations of nongeneric collection objects. *Generics* refers to a new feature added to J2SE 5.0 that provides support for parameterized data types. Before J2SE 5.0, Collection objects stored Object references, meaning that the compiler did not know the actual contents of a collection. Generics provide compile-time type safety for collections by allowing your Collection objects to specify what types they contain.

This section discusses generics and how to use them in collections, starting with a discussion on the limitations of nongeneric collections.

Limitations of Nongeneric Collections

Let's look at an example that does not use generics to demonstrate the various limitations of nongenerics. Suppose we create an ArrayList to contain String objects that represents the keywords of the subject of this book. The following code does not use generics and has a problem. Do you see what the problem is?

```
7.  ArrayList keywords = new ArrayList();
8.  keywords.add("java");
9.  keywords.add("certification");
10. keywords.add("exam");
11. keywords.add(new java.util.Date());
12.
13. for(Object x : keywords) {
14.     String temp = (String) x;
15.     System.out.println(temp.toUpperCase());
16. }
```

The ArrayList can contain any Object, even though we only want it to store Strings. Line 11 adds a Date object, which is a problem with nongenerics because the compiler cannot stop us from putting a Date object in the ArrayList. Another problem is on line 14, where each reference in the ArrayList is cast to a String so we can invoke toUpperCase. The cast throws an exception when it gets to the Date object, as the following output shows:

```
JAVA
CERTIFICATION
EXAM
Exception in thread "main" java.lang.ClassCastException: java.util.Date
 cannot be cast to java.lang.String
```

```
    at GenericsDemo.main(GenericsDemo.java:14)
```

We could use `instanceof` to avoid this situation, but that adds yet another step of complexity to what should be a fairly simple task. Now let's look at this example again, except we will use generics to specify the data type of the elements in the `ArrayList`.

As of J2SE 5.0, the class declaration of `ArrayList` is

```
public class ArrayList<E>
```

The `<E>` represents a generic element. The `E` is not required and can be any variable name, but the naming convention for generics uses single uppercase letters to denote generic types, and `E` is commonly used for elements. The `<E>` denotes that an `ArrayList` can specify a data type when it is constructed. For example, the following code instantiates an ArrayList for `String` objects:

```
18. ArrayList<String> keywords2 = new ArrayList<String>();
19. keywords2.add("java");
20. keywords2.add("certification");
21. keywords2.add("exam");
22. keywords2.add(new java.util.Date());
```

The `ArrayList` of keywords2 can only contain `String` objects, and the compiler enforces this rule. Lines 19–21 compile fine, but line 22 generates the following compiler error:

```
GenericsDemo.java:22: cannot find symbol
symbol   : method add(java.util.Date)
location: class java.util.ArrayList<java.lang.String>
keywords2.add(new java.util.Date());
```

The add method of `ArrayList` only accepts `String` references. Notice how generics allow issues like this one to be discovered at compile time. The other benefit of generics is that you do not need to cast the data when accessing elements in the collection. For example, any time an element in keywords2 is accessed, it is returned as a `String`:

```
for(String keyword : keywords2) {
    System.out.println(keyword.toUpperCase());
}
```

No casting appears in the code, which improves both the readability and reliability of the code. A `ClassCastException` is not possible in the `for-each` loop, demonstrating how generics and `for-each` loops work together to simplify working with collections.

Generics have greatly improved the Java Collections Framework. Generics allow the compiler to enforce the data types that can be added to a collection, as well as retrieve elements from the collection in their appropriate data type. Your Java code is simpler and easier to read. Now that we have seen an example of generics, let's discuss what you need to know about using generics with lists, sets, and maps.

Lists

The Collections Framework has several implementations of the List interface, including ArrayList, LinkedList, Vector, and Stack. Instantiating a list using generics requires specifying the data type that the list contains. The use of generics is seen in the class declaration of the list classes. For example, the Vector class is declared as

```
public class Vector<E> extends AbstractList<E>
       implements List<E>, RandomAccess, Cloneable, Serializable
```

The E is a generic and represents a placeholder for the data type of the elements to be stored in the Vector. You specify the data type for E when constructing a Vector. For example, a Vector of Date objects is instantiated as

```
Vector<Date> december = new Vector<Date>();
```

Only Date objects can be stored in the december vector, and all get methods of december return Date references.

Let's look at an example of using lists. The following ArrayList can only contain String types:

```
List<String> list = new ArrayList<String>();
```

The following statements demonstrate some of the basic methods in the List interface for adding and removing items from list. Study the code and see if you can determine the result:

```
7.  list.add("SD");
8.  list.add(0, "NY");
9.  list.set(1, "FL");
10. list.remove("NY");
11. list.remove(0);
```

The sequence of events for the previous statements is as follows:

1. The ArrayList is initially empty. Line 7 adds "SD" to the end of list, which is at index 0.

2. Line 8 inserts "NY" at index 0. The list now contains "NY" and "SD".

3. Line 9 sets "FL" at index 1, replacing "SD". The list now contains two String objects: "NY" and "FL".

4. Line 10 removes "NY" "from the list, leaving just "FL".

5. Line 11 removes the element at index 0, which is "FL". The ArrayList is now empty again.

The List interface contains other useful methods. Using the same ArrayList named list from the previous code, see if you can determine the output of the following statements:

```
12. list.add("OH");
13. list.add("CO");
14. list.add("NE");
15. list.add("NJ");
16. String state = list.get(2);
17. System.out.println(state);
18. if(list.contains("CO")) {
19.     System.out.println(list.indexOf("CO"));
20. }
21. Iterator<String> iter = list.iterator();
22. while(iter.hasNext()) {
23.     System.out.println(iter.next());
24. }
25. list.clear();
26. System.out.println(list.size());
```

The sequence of events for the previous statements is as follows:

1. Lines 12–15 add four strings to list.

2. Line 16 sets state to the element at index 2, which is the third element, "NE". Because of generics, there is no need to cast the return value of get to a String.

3. Line 18 is true and line 19 displays the index of "CO", which is 1.

4. Line 21 returns an Iterator for list, a common technique for iterating through a list. Using generics, the Iterator declares its elements as String types, which is consistent with the data types in list.

5. The while loop on lines 22–24 demonstrates the hasNext and next methods of Iterator, displaying each String in list on a separate line.

6. Line 25 removes all elements from the list, so printing the size on line 26 outputs 0.

The output of the code is

```
NE
1
OH
CO
NE
NJ
0
```

The methods demonstrated here are in the List interface and therefore are available to all List objects. Each implementation class of List also adds additional behaviors relevant to the type of list. For example:

- The LinkedList class implements a doubly linked list and contains the methods addFirst, addLast, removeFirst, and removeLast for adding and removing elements at the beginning or end of the linked list.

- The Stack class contains the methods push and pop for pushing and popping elements onto the stack, as demonstrated in the sidebar "The Stack Class."

- The Vector class contains methods for array-like behaviors, like elementAt, insertElementAt, and removeElementAt.

- The ArrayList class is a simple (but useful) implementation of the List interface and basically contains the same methods as the List interface.

The Stack Class

The Stack class in java.util implements a Stack data structure as a list. The Stack class defines a push method that pushes an item on the stack and a pop method that removes the top object from the stack. For example, the following statements create a Stack for storing Integer objects and push two elements onto the stack:

```
Stack<Integer> mystack = new Stack<Integer>();
mystack.push(new Integer(100));
mystack.push(200);
```

Due to generics, only Integer types can be pushed on the Stack mystack. (Pushing 200 is allowed because of Java's autoboxing feature.) The following line of code does not compile:

```
mystack.push("Not an Integer");
```

The compiler error looks like

```
ListDemo.java:9: push(java.lang.Integer) in
java.util.Stack<java.lang.Integer> cannot be applied to
(java.lang.String)
mystack.push("Not an Integer");
        ^
```

The pop method of stack removes the top element and returns a reference to it. For example:

```
Integer top = mystack.pop();
for(Integer i : mystack) {
    System.out.println(i);
}
```

The for-each loop executes only once because the 200 was popped off the top of the stack, leaving only 100. The output of the previous statements is

100

Use the Stack class for situations that require LIFO behavior.

Use lists when you work with ordered collections where duplicates are allowed and you need control over where the items appear in the collection. If duplicates are not allowed, a set might be more appropriate for your needs, as discussed in the next section.

Sets

The Collections Framework has several implementations of the Set interface, including HashSet, LinkedHashSet, and TreeSet. Use a Set object when duplicates are not allowed in your collection. The equals method is used to determine if elements are duplicated. All the Set classes use generics. For example, the HashSet class is declared as

```
public class HashSet<E> extends AbstractSet<E>
        implements Set<E>, Cloneable, Serializable
```

The E is a generic type that represents the data type of the elements that can be stored in the HashSet.

To demonstrate using sets, suppose we have the following class called Product to represent a product for sale. According to the equals method, two Product objects are equal if they have the same id.

```
public class Product {
    String description;
    double price;
    int id;

    public Product(String d, double p, int i) {
        description = d;
        price = p;
        id = i;
    }

    public boolean equals(Object obj) {
        if(!(obj instanceof Product)) {
            return false;
        }
```

```
        Product other = (Product) obj;
        return this.id == other.id;
    }

    public int hashCode() {
        return id;
    }

    public String toString() {
        return id + " " + description;
    }
}
```

Let's add some Product objects to a set. Using generics, the following statements create a HashSet for Product objects. Study the code carefully and see if you can determine its result:

```
7.  Product one = new Product("Laptop", 1299.99, 101);
8.  Product two = new Product("Television", 1099.00, 202);
9.  Product three = new Product("Cellphone", 200.00, 303);
10. Product four = new Product("PC", 699.99, 101);
11. Set<Product> set = new HashSet<Product>();
12. set.add(one);
13. set.add(two);
14. set.add(three);
15. set.add(four);
16. set.add(null);
17. set.add(null);
18. for(Product p : set) {
19.     System.out.println(p);
20. }
```

The four Product objects are added to set using the add method of Set. Notice that the objects one and four have the same id and are therefore equal, so adding four on line 15 does not modify the set. A HashSet allows a null entry, but only once. Adding null on line 16 modifies the set, while line 17 does not. Sets are not ordered, so the elements of the set are displayed in the for-each loop in no particular order. The output of the code is

```
null
101 Laptop
202 Television
303 Cellphone
```

The add method was invoked six times on set, but the HashSet only contains four elements because duplicate elements are not added. Because we are using generics, only Product objects can be added to set based on its construction on line 11.

Another Set implementation is LinkedHashSet, which is basically identical to HashSet except the insertion order is maintained behind the scenes by a doubly linked list. The iterator method returns the set in the order the elements were inserted. For example, see if you can determine the output of the following LinkedHashSet iterator that uses the same four Product objects from the previous code example:

```
Set<Product> linkedset = new LinkedHashSet<Product>();
linkedset.add(two);
linkedset.add(three);
linkedset.add(null);
linkedset.add(two);
linkedset.add(four);
linkedset.add(one);
Iterator<Product> products = linkedset.iterator();
while(products.hasNext()) {
    System.out.println(products.next());
}
```

The linkedset object maintains the insertion order, so the iterator outputs the four unique Product objects in the order that they were added:

```
202 Television
303 Cellphone
null
101 PC
```

Inserting two a second time did not change linkedset. Adding one did not change the linkedset because four was already added and the four and one Product objects are equal.

Another Set implementation in the Collections Framework is TreeSet, useful for working with large sets of data that require multiple searches or insertions. The TreeSet uses a tree data structure, so access is guaranteed in $\log(n)$ time, where n is the number of elements in the tree. The TreeSet class also orders the elements in the set and contains methods like first, last, ceiling, and floor for accessing specific elements and subsets. Use TreeSet when your collection does not allow duplicates and you want control over how the elements in the set are ordered.

The NavigableSet Interface

A TreeSet object has a specific ordering, and the TreeSet class implements the NavigableSet interface, which declares methods for navigating and searching a set. The interface contains the following generic methods, where E represents the data type of the elements in the set:

- Iterator<E> iterator() returns an iterator in ascending order.

- Iterator<E> descendingIterator() returns an iterator in descending order.

- E lower(E e) returns the greatest element in this set strictly less than the given element.

- E floor(E e)returns the greatest element in this set less than or equal to the given element.

- E ceiling(E e) returns the least element in this set greater than or equal to the given element.

- E higher(E e) returns the least element in this set strictly greater than the given element.

- NavigableSet<E> subSet(E fromElement, boolean fromInclusive, E toElement, boolean toInclusive) returns a view of the portion of this set whose elements range from fromElement to toElement.

The interface also defines headSet and tailSet methods for retrieving subsets from the beginning or end of the set.

Let's look at an example. The following code adds a collection of Integer objects to a TreeSet named tree:

```
TreeSet<Integer> tree = new TreeSet<Integer>();
for(int i = 1; i <= 20; i++ ) {
    tree.add(i);
}
```

The tree contains 20 Integer objects whose values are 1 to 20. The following statements demonstrate some of the methods in NavigableSet. Study the code and see if you can determine its output:

```
12. Integer ceiling = tree.ceiling(10);
13. System.out.println("ceiling of 10 = " + ceiling);
14. Integer higher = tree.higher(10);
15. System.out.println("floor of 10 = " + higher);
```

```
16. NavigableSet<Integer> subset = tree.subSet(new Integer(7), false,
                                    new Integer(14), true);
17. for(Integer x : subset) {
18.     System.out.print(x + " ");
19. }
```

The previous statements break down as follows:

1. Line 12 retrieves the ceiling of 10, which is the smallest element greater than or equal to 10, which is 10.

2. Line 14 retrieves the higher of 10, which is the smallest element greater than 10, which is 11.

3. Line 16 retrieves a subset of tree from 7 (noninclusive) and 14 (inclusive), which is 8 to 14. The for-each loop on line 17 outputs this subset.

The output of the code is

```
ceiling of 10 = 10
floor of 10 = 11
8 9 10 11 12 13 14
```

The TreeSet class is the only class in the Collections Framework that implements the NavigableSet interface, and the exam requires basic knowledge of the methods listed previously.

Now let's discuss the details of using the various types of maps in the Collections Framework.

Maps

The Map interface is the parent interface of the various maps in the Collections Framework. Maps are unique in that they do not implement the Collection interface like all the other collections classes. The elements in a map are pairs of data: a value and a key that maps to that value. Think of a map as an array, except instead of integer indexes to access elements, you use a key that can be any data type. Maps do not allow duplicate keys, but there is no restriction on duplicate values.

The Map implementations are HashMap, LinkedHashMap, and TreeMap. Like all the other Collections Framework classes and interfaces, maps use generics. Maps are different, though, because you specify two data types when you construct a Map object: the data type of the key and the data type of the value. For example, the declaration of the TreeMap class looks like this:

```
public class TreeMap<K,V> extends AbstractMap<K,V>
        implements NavigableMap<K,V>, Cloneable, Serializable
```

The K and V are generic types for the key and value, respectively. The following statement declares a new TreeMap whose keys are String objects and whose values are Long objects:

```
TreeMap<String, Long> phoneBook = new TreeMap<String, Long>();
```

Unlike Collection objects where you "add" an element, with maps you "put" an element in the map. For example, the following statements put several paired values into the phoneBook map:

```
phoneBook.put("Nguyen, Scott", 2015551111L);
phoneBook.put("Negreanu, Dan", 2015552222L);
phoneBook.put("Ivey, Phil", 2015553333L);
phoneBook.put("Rosario, Shirley", 2015554444L);
phoneBook.put("Boyd, Russ", 2015555555L);
```

The keys in this map are the names and the values are the phone numbers. The L after the phone numbers ensures that the values are autoboxed into Long objects. A TreeMap orders the elements in the tree based on the natural ordering of the keys, so the elements in phoneBook are in alphabetical order.

The Map interface contains several methods for obtaining elements. You can obtain a specific value given a key, the entire list of values, and specific keys. The following statements demonstrate some of the Map methods. Because of generics, no casting is needed when you retrieve elements from the map. Study the code and see if you can determine its result:

```
14. Long number = phoneBook.get("Ivey, Phil"); //a value from a key
15. Set<String> keys = phoneBook.keySet();
16. for(String key : keys) {
17.    System.out.println(key + ": " + phoneBook.get(key));
18. }
19.
20. Map.Entry<String, Long> last = phoneBook.lastEntry();
```

```
21. System.out.println("Last entry = " + last.getKey()
                        + " " +  last.getValue());
22.
23. String firstKey = phoneBook.firstKey();
24. System.out.println("First key = " + firstKey);
```

A description of the previous statements follows:

1. Line 14 shows how to use the get method to obtain a value given a key. The value of number is 2015553333.

2. Line 15 shows how to use the keySet method to obtain a Set of just the keys. The keys are String objects in phoneBook, as seen by the data type of the keys reference.

3. The for-each loop on line 16 uses the get method to obtain the value, displaying each key-value pair in phoneBook.

4. Map.Entry is an object for storing map elements. The last reference on line 20 points to the last map entry in phoneBook, which based on the natural ordering of String objects is "Rosario, Shirley".

5. Line 21 demonstrates the getKey and getValue methods of Map.Entry, which return "Rosario, Shirley" and 2015554444, respectively.

6. Line 23 demonstrates the firstKey method, which returns the first key in the set. In phoneBook, that is "Boyd, Russ".

The output of the previous statements is

```
Boyd, Russ: 2015555555
Ivey, Phil: 2015553333
Negreanu, Dan: 2015552222
Nguyen, Scott: 2015551111
Rosario, Shirley: 2015554444
Last entry = Rosario, Shirley 2015554444
First key = Boyd, Russ
```

TreeMap is a good choice for a phone book because elements are retrieved and inserted in log(*n*) time, where *n* is the number of elements. A TreeMap with hundreds of thousands of entries has a relatively efficient access time.

The HashMap and LinkedHashMap classes have similar put and get methods for adding and retrieving elements. Elements in a HashMap are iterated in arbitrary order, while a LinkedHashMap maintains the elements in their order of insertion. Use a HashMap if ordering does not matter, a LinkedHashMap if insertion order is sufficient, and a TreeMap if you need to control the specific ordering of elements.

The NavigableMap Interface

The TreeMap class implements the NavigableMap interface, which contains methods similar to the NavigableSet interface for navigating and searching a map. Here are some of the methods in NavigableMap:

- Map.Entry<K,V> ceilingEntry(K key) returns a key-value mapping associated with the least key greater than or equal to the given key.

- K ceilingKey(K key) returns the least key greater than or equal to the given key.

- Map.Entry<K,V> floorEntry(K key) returns a key-value mapping associated with the greatest key less than or equal to the given key.

- K floorKey(K key) returns the greatest key less than or equal to the given key.

- NavigableSet<K> descendingKeySet() returns a reverse order NavigableSet view of the keys contained in this map.

- NavigableMap<K,V> descendingMap() returns a reverse order view of the mappings contained in this map.

- NavigableMap<K,V> subMap(K fromKey, boolean fromInclusive, K toKey, boolean toInclusive) returns a view of the portion of this map whose keys range from fromKey to toKey.

The interface also defines headMap and tailMap methods for obtaining subsets at the beginning and end of the map. Let's look at an example. The following TreeMap contains 26 character and integer pairs:

```
TreeMap<Character, Integer> ascii = new TreeMap<Character, Integer>();
int value = 97;
for(char c = 'a'; c <= 'z'; c++) {
    ascii.put(c, value++);
}
```

Study the following code and see if you can determine its result:

```
12. Map.Entry<Character, Integer> ceiling = ascii.ceilingEntry('h');
13. System.out.println("ceiling: " + ceiling);
14. SortedMap<Character, Integer> tailMap = ascii.tailMap('t');
15. Set<Character> tailKeys = tailMap.keySet();
16. for(Character key : tailKeys) {
17.     System.out.print(key + " ");
18. }
19. System.out.println();
20. NavigableSet<Character> keys = ascii.descendingKeySet();
```

```
21. for(Character key : keys) {
22.     System.out.print(key + " ");
23. }
```

A breakdown of the previous statements follows:

- Line 12 returns the least element greater than or equal to `'h'`, which is the pair (`'h'`, 104).

- Line 14 retrieves the tail of the map after the element `'t'`. Line 15 retrieves just the keys from `tailMap`, and the for-each loop on line 16 displays these keys.

- Line 20 is the keys from `ascii` in descending order, which are printed in the for-each loop on line 21.

  The output of the previous statements is

```
ceiling: h=104
t u v w x y z
z y x w v u t s r q p o n m l k j i h g f e d c b a
```

As you can see, a `NavigableMap` object provides many useful methods for navigating and searching a map. The `TreeMap` class is the only class in the Collections Framework that implements the `NavigableMap` interface.

Now that we have discussed generics and you've used them with the Collections Framework, let's see how to introduce generics into your own code. The following section discusses the details of writing and using generic types and methods.

Generic Types and Methods

Generic types are not exclusive to the Collections Framework. You can define your own classes, interfaces, and methods that use generic types. The exam requires a general understanding of this technique, and this section examines the details of using generics in your own classes, including a discussion on the following:

- Generic classes
- Generic interfaces
- Generic methods
- Bounded generic types
- Generic wildcards

  Let's start with generic classes.

Generic Classes

You can introduce generics into your own classes and interfaces. The syntax for introducing a generic is to declare a *formal type parameter* in angle brackets, <>. For example, the following class named `Cupboard` has a generic type variable declared after the name of the class:

```
public class Cupboard<T> {
    private T item;

    public Cupboard(T item) {
        System.out.println("Cupboard for " + item.getClass());
        this.item = item;
    }

    public T getItem() {
        return item;
    }
}
```

The generic type T is available anywhere within the `Cupboard` class, and its compile-time type is determined when a user declares and instantiates a `Cupboard` object. The following statements are valid and create three `Cupboard` objects, each denoting a different data type for the `item` field:

```
4.  Cupboard<String> c1 = new Cupboard<String>("dishes");
5.  Cupboard<Integer> c2 = new Cupboard<Integer>(123);
6.  Cupboard<Double> c3 = new Cupboard<Double>(3.14159);
7.  String s = c1.getItem();
8.  Integer x = c2.getItem();
9.  Double d = c3.getItem();
```

Notice that c1 assigns the generic of `Cupboard` to be a `String` type, and then passes in a `String` to the constructor. The variable c2 sets its generic type to be `Integer` and passes in an `Integer` (autoboxed) into the constructor. Similarly, c3 uses a `Double` for its generic. The constructor of `Cupboard` prints out the class type of the generic, so the output of the previous statements is

```
Cupboard for class java.lang.String
Cupboard for class java.lang.Integer
Cupboard for class java.lang.Double
```

The calls to `getItem` on lines 7–9 do not need a cast. The compiler knows the data type of the return value for each `Cupboard` instance, a key benefit to using generics.

Type Erasure

Specifying a generic type allows the compiler to enforce proper use of the generic type. For example, specifying the generic type of a Cupboard as String is like replacing the T in the Cupboard class with String:

```
Cupboard<String> c1 = new Cupboard<String>("dishes");
```

However, behind the scenes, the compiler replaces all references to T in Cupboard with Object. In other words, after the code compiles, your generics are actually just Object types. The Cupboard class looks like the following output:

```
public class Cupboard {
    private Object item;

    public Cupboard(Object item) {
        System.out.println("Cupboard for " + item.getClass());
        this.item = item;
    }

    public Object getItem() {
        return item;
    }
}
```

Displaying item.getClass() doesn't simply output Object each time due to polymorphism. The class name displayed is the actual data type that the field item refers to. Also, if getItem returns an Object, a cast is needed at runtime. The compiler adds the appropriate cast for you whenever you invoke getItem.

This process of removing the generics syntax from your code is referred to as *type erasure*. Type erasure allows your code to be compatible with older versions of Java that did not contain generics.

As with classes, you can use generics in interface declarations, which I discuss in the next section.

Generic Interfaces

An interface can declare a formal type parameter in the same fashion as a class. For example, the following Breakable interface uses a generic type as the argument to its doBreak method:

```
public interface Breakable<T> {
    public void doBreak(T t);
}
```

A class can implement `Breakable` by specifying a data type for `T` in the `implements` statement, as the following `Glass` class demonstrates:

```
public class Glass implements Breakable<String> {

    public void doBreak(String message) {
        System.out.println("Breaking a Glass: " + message);
    }
}
```

The `Glass` declaration denotes `String` as the data type for `T` in `Breakable`, so the `doBreak` method must have a `String` parameter.

The other technique for a class to implement `Breakable` is to specify another generic as the data type:

```
public class Dish<U> implements Breakable<U> {
    public void doBreak(U u) {
        System.out.println("Breaking " + u.toString());
    }
}
```

The data type for the `Breakable` generic `T` will be the same as the data type for the generic `U` in `Dish`, which is specified when a `Dish` is constructed. For example:

```
Dish<Float> dish = new Dish<Float>();
dish.doBreak(2.7F);
```

The `Dish` object uses a `Float` for its generic, so the parameter for invoking `doBreak` is a `Float`. The output of the previous statement is

```
Breaking 2.7
```

As a side note, the `U` in `Dish` is arbitrary and in the real world I would probably use a `T`. I just wanted to emphasize that the `Dish` is assigning the generic `T` in `Breakable` to another generic.

Naming Conventions for Generics

You can name your generic types using any valid identifier. However, the standard naming convention is to use a single, uppercase letter. Again, use any letter you want, but in general the following letters are used:

- E for an element
- K for a map key

- V for a map value

- N for a number

- T for a generic data type

Use S, U, V, and so on for multiple types in the same class.

Declaring a generic type at the class level allows the generic to be used anywhere within the class. You can also declare generics at the method level, which I discuss in the next section.

Generic Methods

A method or constructor can contain generic type parameters, which makes the method or constructor generic. You define a generic method by declaring a generic type in angle brackets before the return value of the method. The scope of the generic type is only within the method.

To demonstrate, the following Box class contains a generic method named ship. The data type of the argument is the generic denoted by <T> preceding the method signature, which means that the parameter's type is not determined until compile time, allowing the ship method to be invoked with any object type. See if you can determine the result of the Box program:

```
1.   import java.awt.Frame;
2.
3.   public class Box {
4.       public static <T> void ship(T item) {
5.           System.out.println("Shipping " + item.toString());
6.           if(item instanceof Frame) {
7.               Frame frame = (Frame) item;
8.               frame.setSize(200,200);
9.               frame.setVisible(true);
10.          }
11.      }
12.
13.      public static void main(String [] args) {
14.          Box.ship("a String object");
15.          Box.ship(args);
16.          Box.ship(new Frame());
17.      }
18. }
```

On line 6, if the data type of the argument passed in is Frame, the Frame is given a size and displays. Within main, line 14 passes in a String object, so the T is a String during that invocation. On line 15, an array of String objects is passed in, so T is of type String [] for that invocation. Line 16 passes in a new Frame object, so line 6 is true and a 100×100-pixel window displays after line 9 executes. The ship method also prints the toString method of each argument, so the output to the command prompt is

```
Shipping a String object
Shipping [Ljava.lang.String;@3e25a5
Shipping java.awt.Frame[frame0,0,0,0x0,invalid,hidden,
layout=java.awt.BorderLayout,title=,resizable,normal]
```

The Syntax for Invoking a Generic Method

Generics have an optional syntax for specifying the type for a generic method. You can place the data type of the generic in angle brackets, <>, after the dot operator and before the method call. For example, the following statements are valid method invocations of the ship method in the Box class:

```
Box.<String>ship("a String object");
Box.<String []>ship(args);
Box.<Frame>ship(new Frame());
```

The syntax makes the code more readable and also gives you control over the generic type in situations where the type might not be obvious.

Let's look at another example of a generic method. Suppose we add the following method to the Box class, which uses the generic Dish class discussed earlier in this section:

```
public static <U> void wrap(List<Dish<U>> list) {
    for(Dish<U> dish : list) {
        System.out.println("Wrapping " + dish);
    }
}
```

The wrap method takes in a List of Dish objects with any data type for the Dish's generic. The for-each loop prints out each Dish<U> in the list. The following statements demonstrate invoking the wrap method:

```
Dish<String> d1 = new Dish<String>();
Dish<String> d2 = new Dish<String>();
Dish<String> d3 = new Dish<String>();
List<Dish<String>> dishes = new ArrayList<Dish<String>>();
```

```
dishes.add(d1);
dishes.add(d2);
dishes.add(d3);
Box.wrap(dishes);
```

The call to wrap passes in a List<Dish<String>> object, and the output looks like this:

```
Wrapping Dish@1389e4
Wrapping Dish@c20e24
Wrapping Dish@2e7263
```

If the syntax of List<Dish<String>> looks confusing, welcome to Java generics! Often the syntax for generics requires the nesting of data types, which tends to result in code that is not always intuitive. As we will see in the next section, the bounded generic types only add another layer of complexity to this syntax.

Bounded Generic Types

A generic type parameter opens the door for any data type to be used as the generic type. There might be situations where you want to use generics but also restrict the type used. A *bounded parameter type* is a generic type that specifies a bound for the generic. You can specify a parent class for a generic type using the extends keyword, creating an upper-bound generic, as the following example shows:

```
public class Hello<T extends List> { }
```

The previous declaration states that T is a generic type that must extend (or, in this case, implement) the List interface. Using extends in a generic creates an upper bound on the actual type used for the generic. For example, the following statements are valid for the Hello class because ArrayList and Stack both implement List:

```
Hello<ArrayList> h1 = new Hello<ArrayList>();
Hello<Stack> h2 = new Hello<Stack>();
```

However, the following statement is not valid because a HashMap is not a List:

```
Hello<HashMap> h3 = new Hello<HashMap>(); //not valid
```

The compiler error looks like

```
Hello.java:7: type parameter java.util.HashMap is not within its bound
Hello<HashMap> h3 = new Hello<HashMap>();
```

Understanding Polymorphism and Generics

Be careful when you work with polymorphism and generic types that do not use the extends keyword. There is no implied upper bound when a specific generic type is declared without the extends keyword. To demonstrate, let's use the Cupboard class from earlier in this section that used a formal type parameter:

```
public class Cupboard<T> {
    //definition of class
}
```

The following statement is valid because we are assigning a Cupboard<Number> object to a Cupboard<Number> reference:

```
Cupboard<Number> a = new Cupboard<Number>(123);
```

Now consider the following statement that assigns a Cupboard<Double> object to a Cupboard<Number> reference. Is it valid?

```
Cupboard<Number> b = new Cupboard<Double>(456.0);
```

Surprisingly, the answer is no: the previous statement does not compile and generates the following compiler error:

```
SubtypeDemo.java:5: incompatible types
found   : Cupboard<java.lang.Double>
required: Cupboard<java.lang.Number>
Cupboard<Number> b = new Cupboard<Double>(456.0);
               ^
```

Even though a Double is a Number, a Cupboard<Double> is *not* a Cupboard<Number>. If you want to use a polymorphic reference, you need to use an upper bound. For example, the following statement is valid:

```
Cupboard<? extends Number> c = new Cupboard<Double>(789.0);
```

The ? is referred to as a wildcard and creates a reference that can point to any Cupboard<?> object where ? extends the Number class. The previous statement is valid because we are assigning a Cupboard<Double> object to a Cupboard<? extends Number> reference and Double extends Number.

We use the extends keyword to create an upper-bound generic type. In the next section I discuss how to use the super keyword together with a wildcard to create a lower-bound generic type, together with the other details that you need to know about using generic wildcards.

Let's look at a complete example. The following MyMath class contains a generic method named average with type <T extends Number>. (Number is the parent class of the numeric wrapper classes.) Study the following code and see if you can determine its result:

```
1.  public class MyMath {
2.      public static <T extends Number> double average(T one, T two) {
3.          double d1 = one.doubleValue();
4.          double d2 = two.doubleValue();
5.          double average = (d1 + d2)/2.0;
6.          return average;
7.      }
8.
9.      public static void main(String [] args) {
10.         Double x = 25.0;
11.         Integer y = 35;
12.         double ave = MyMath.average(x, y);
13.         System.out.println("average = " + ave);
14.     }
15. }
```

Within main on line 12, a Double and Integer are passed into the average method, which is valid because both Double and Integer are subclasses of Number. A nice advantage of using an upper-bound generic type is that within the average method, we can invoke the doubleValue method of Number on lines 3 and 4 without casting the one or two references. The compiler does not know the exact data type of one or two, but it does know that these two references are at least of type Number. Without the extends Number in the generic, lines 3 and 4 would not compile.

Using the average method, the following statement compiles because of the autoboxing feature of Java:

```
MyMath.average(12.0, -12);
```

However, the following statement does not compile because 'a' is a char and "Hello" is a String, neither of which extend Number:

```
MyMath.average('a', "Hello");
```

The compiler error looks like this:

```
MyMath.java:15: internal error; cannot instantiate <T>average(T,T)
at MyMath to (char,java.lang.String)
        MyMath.average('a', "Hello");
```

Generic Wildcards

A *wildcard generic type* is an unknown generic represented with a question mark, ?. The wildcard provides a polymorphic-like behavior for declaring generics. You can use generic wildcards in three ways:

- ?, an unbounded wildcard
- ? extends *type*, a wildcard with an upper bound
- ? super *type*, a wildcard with a lower bound

This section examines each of these wildcard uses, starting with the unbounded wildcard.

Unbounded Wildcards

The *unbounded wildcard* represents any data type, similar to the <T> syntax. Use the ? in situations where you do not need a formal parameter type like <T>. For example, the following for-each loop takes in a List of any type. Because the loop does not need to know the actual data type, it uses a wildcard:

```
public static void printList(List<?> list) {
    for(Object x : list) {
        System.out.println(x.toString());
    }
}
```

Any List of any generic type can be passed into the printList method. For example, the following statements invoke printList with an ArrayList<String> object:

```
ArrayList<String> keywords = new ArrayList<String>();
keywords.add("java");
keywords.add("generics");
keywords.add("collections");
printList(keywords);
```

The output of the statements is

```
java
generics
collections
```

Upper-Bound Wildcards

As discussed in the sidebar "Understanding Polymorphism and Generics," polymorphism is not quite as apparent with generics. For example, the following statement is valid:

```
ArrayList<Double> list = new ArrayList<Double>();
```

The reference `list` and the object it refers to are both of type `ArrayList<Double>`. However, the following statement is not valid:

```
ArrayList<Number> notvalid = new ArrayList<Double>();//doesn't compile
```

Even though `Double` is a child of `Number`, the compiler complains that `ArrayList<Double>` is incompatible with `ArrayList<Number>`. An `ArrayList<Number>` reference can only point to an `ArrayList` object whose generic is a `Number`. If you want a reference that can refer to an `ArrayList` whose generic is any `Number` (including subclasses of `Number`), you need to use the wildcard:

```
ArrayList<? extends Number> list2 = new ArrayList<Double>();
```

The generic `<? extends Number>` declares `list2` as a reference to an `ArrayList` object whose generic is `Number` or any subclass of `Number`.

The following statements are also valid:

```
ArrayList<? extends Number> list3 = new ArrayList<Integer>();
List<? extends Number> list4 = new Stack<Float>();
```

The `list3` reference is valid because `Integer` is a child of `Number`. The `list4` reference is valid because both `Float` is a child of `Number` and `Stack` implements `List`.

Lower-Bound Wildcards

Similar to using the `extends` keyword for creating an upper-bound wildcard, you can use the `super` keyword to create a lower-bound wildcard with a wildcard generic. For example, the following statement declares a generic type that must be an `IOException` or parent of `IOException`:

```
<? super IOException>
```

Using this generic type, see if you can determine whether or not the following statements are valid declarations:

```
6.  ArrayList<? super IOException> alist1 = new ArrayList<Exception>();
7.  ArrayList<? super IOException> alist2 =
                                  new ArrayList<IOException>();
8.  ArrayList<? super IOException> alist3 =
                      new ArrayList<FileNotFoundException>();
```

Line 6 is valid because `<Exception>` is a supertype of the generic `<? super IOException>` and `Exception` is a parent class of `IOException`. Line 7 is valid because the lower-bound generic `<? super IOException>` includes the `IOException` class. Line 8 *does not compile* because FileNotFoundException is not a parent class of IOException. The compiler error looks like the following output:

```
WildcardDemo.java:8: incompatible types
found    : java.util.ArrayList<java.io.FileNotFoundException>
required: java.util.ArrayList<? super java.io.IOException>
ArrayList<? super IOException> alist3 =
              new ArrayList<FileNotFoundException>();
```

Let's look at an example of a method that declares a lower-bound generic. The following showExceptions method prints a List of objects whose type is List<? super IOException>:

```
public static void showExceptions(List<? super IOException> list) {
    for(Object e : list) {
        System.out.println(e.toString());
    }
}
```

The following statements create an ArrayList<Exception>, a valid argument for showExceptions. Study the code and determine if it compiles and what the output is:

```
30. ArrayList<? super IOException> exceptions =
                              new ArrayList<Exception>();
31. IOException e1 = new IOException("Problem 1");
32. IOException e2 = new IOException("Problem 2");
33. FileNotFoundException e3 = new FileNotFoundException("Problem 3");
34. exceptions.add(e1);
35. exceptions.add(e2);
36. exceptions.add(e3);
37. showExceptions(exceptions);
```

The reference exceptions on line 30 is of type ArrayList<? super IOException> and the object it refers to is an ArrayList<Exception>. Therefore, line 30 is valid because Exception is the parent of IOException. Lines 31–36 add three Exception objects to the ArrayList. Line 37 passes exceptions to showExceptions. The argument of showExceptions is List<? super IOException>, so passing in an ArrayList<? super IOException> is also valid. The code compiles and runs fine, and the output is

```
java.io.IOException: Problem 1
java.io.IOException: Problem 2
java.io.FileNotFoundException: Problem 3
```

Understanding Generic Supertypes

You might find it confusing that a FileNotFoundException object can appear in the exceptions list, especially because FileNotFoundException is not a parent of IOException. The upper bound of the generic method showExceptions applies to the data type of the generic, which for <? super IOException> must be a parent class of Exception. The argument passed in was an ArrayList<Exception>, which is compatible with <? super IOException>. Because the data type of the generic is ArrayList<IOException>, any child of Exception can appear in the actual ArrayList, which is why FileNotFoundException can be in the list. In fact, any child object of Exception can appear in the exceptions object created on line 30 of the previous code snippet.

This ends our discussion on writing your own generic classes, interfaces, and methods. Now we change subjects and discuss how to sort and search lists using classes in the java.util package.

Working with Lists

For the exam you should be able to sort lists either in their natural order or using a Comparator object. The exam also requires knowledge of performing a binary search on lists. These objectives are indirectly referring to methods in the java.util.Collections class. In particular, the objectives refer to the static methods sort and binarySearch in Collections, which take in a List and an optional Comparator object.

In the next section I discuss the details that you need to know for the exam regarding the sorting and searching of lists using the Collections class, starting with the sort methods.

Sorting Lists

The Collections class (not to be confused with the Collection interface) contains dozens of useful static methods for working with and manipulating collections. The exam objectives specifically state knowledge of sorting lists, which is achieved using the two sort methods of Collections:

- public static <T extends Comparable<? super T>> void sort(List<T> list) sorts the given List according to its natural ordering, which is the ordering based on the implementation of the compareTo method in the Comparable interface. The elements in list must implement Comparable and must be *mutually comparable*, meaning each element can be compared to each other element without a ClassCastException being thrown.

- `public static <T> void sort(List<T> list, Comparator<? super T> c)` sorts the given `List` according to the ordering of the given `Comparator`. All elements in `list` must be mutually comparable.

Notice that in the first `sort` method the generic T is declared as `<T extends Comparable<? super T>>`, meaning the list object passed in must contain elements that implement the `Comparable` interface (because of extends `Comparable`) or whose parent class implements `Comparable` (based on `<? super T>`).

The second `sort` method does not have this restriction because the sorting is based on a `Comparator`, which is a separate object.

We discuss the difference between `Comparable` sorting and `Comparator` sorting next, starting with a discussion on the `Comparable sort` method.

Comparable Sorting

Let's look at an example of the first `sort` method shown previously that uses the natural ordering of objects. Recall that the natural ordering refers to the behavior of the `compareTo` method in the `Comparable` interface, so the elements being sorted must implement the `Comparable` interface. The following program sorts a list of `Character` objects in their natural order. Study the following program and see if you can determine its result:

```
1.  import java.util.*;
2.
3.  public class CharacterSorter {
4.      public static void main(String [] args) {
5.          char [] chars = args[0].toCharArray();
6.          List<Character> list = new ArrayList<Character>();
7.          for(char c : chars) {
8.              list.add(c);
9.          }
10.         Collections.sort(list);
11.         for(Character c : list) {
12.             System.out.print(c + " ");
13.         }
14.     }
15. }
```

The `CharacterSorter` program sorts an `ArrayList` of `Character` objects. Here is the sequence of events of the program:

1. Line 5 converts the first command-line argument into a char array.

2. Line 6 creates a new `ArrayList<Character>`, and the for-each loop on line 7 adds each char in chars to the list. Because of autoboxing, each char is wrapped in a `Character` object.

3. Line 10 invokes the `sort` method of `Collections`. The `sort` method modifies `list`, rearranging the `Character` objects into their natural order, which is strictly based on the order of their numeric Unicode values.

4. The `for-each` loop on line 11 displays the sorted list.

Suppose the program is executed with the following command:

```
java CharacterSorter soRTedChAractERs
```

The output is

```
A C E R R T a c d e h o r s s t
```

Notice that uppercase letters precede all lowercase letters because the numeric Unicode values of uppercase letters appear before the lowercase letters.

Natural Ordering of Wrapper Classes and Strings

The exam objectives mention knowledge of the natural ordering of the primitive wrapper classes and `String`. The natural ordering of the numeric classes `Byte`, `Short`, `Integer`, `Long`, `Float`, and `Double` matches their natural ordering in the number system, just as expected.

As we saw in the `CharacterSorter` program, `Character` objects are naturally ordered by their numeric Unicode values (which is not alphabetical because all uppercase letters appear before all lowercase letters).

For `Boolean` objects, `true` is considered greater than `false`. For example, the following statements output 1:

```
Boolean b = true;
System.out.println(b.compareTo(false));
```

As we saw in the earlier section "The Comparable Interface," the natural order of `String` objects is lexicographical, meaning that the first different character in two `String` objects determines the ordering. See if you can determine the output of the following statements:

```
String s1 = "hello";
String s2 = "hEllo";
String s3 = "hellothere";

List<String> list = new ArrayList<String>();
list.add(s1);
list.add(s2);
```

```
list.add(s3);
Collections.sort(list);
for(String s : list) {
    System.out.println(s);
}
```

All three `String` objects share the same first character, so their second character determines the ordering. Because E comes before e, `"hEllo"` comes before both `"hello"` and `"hellothere"`. Because `"hello"` and `"hellothere"` do not contain a different character to determine their order, `"hello"` comes first because it is the shorter `String`. The output of the previous statements is

```
hEllo
hello
hellothere
```

Sorting a list using the natural ordering requires each element in the `List` object to implement the `Comparable` interface and also that each element in the list be mutually comparable. For example, the following code does not compile. Can you see why?

```
6.  List<Object> items = new ArrayList<Object>();
7.  items.add("Java");
8.  items.add(new Integer(123));
9.  Collections.sort(items);
```

Lines 6–8 are valid and compile fine. The compiler error occurs at line 9. Because the `Collections.sort` method uses a generic type of `<T extends Comparable<? super T>`, only `List` objects whose generic type implements `Comparable` can be an argument for the `sort` method. The `Object` class does not implement `Comparable`, so line 9 generates the following compiler error:

```
MutuallyComparableDemo.java:9: cannot find symbol
symbol  : method sort(java.util.List<java.lang.Object>)
location: class java.util.Collections
Collections.sort(items);
```

The compiler is complaining that it cannot find a version of `sort` in `Collections` that takes in a `List<Object>`. Java generics are working their magic in this example, enforcing data type rules at compile time to avoid issues at runtime. If line 9 compiled successfully, then invoking `sort` would cause the `String` object `"Java"` to be compared to the `Integer` object wrapping 123, which would result in a `ClassCastException` at runtime because `"Java"` and 123 are not mutually comparable.

Comparator Sorting

The other version of the sort method in Collections does not require its elements to implement Comparable. Instead, it uses a separate object of type Comparator to determine the ordering:

```
public static <T> void sort(List<T> list, Comparator<? super T> c)
```

To use this version of Collections.sort, you need to write a class that implements the generic Comparator interface, making sure the generic type of the Comparator is T or a parent of T (based on the <? super T> in the method signature). The Comparator interface declares the following method:

```
int compare(T o1, T o2)
```

Define this method so that it returns 0 if o1 equals o2, a positive number if o1 is greater than o2, and a negative number if o1 is less than o2. The ordering is totally up to you, so the logic can be anything you define. For example, suppose we have the following class named Reverse that implements the Comparator interface with an Integer generic type:

```java
public class Reverse implements java.util.Comparator<Integer> {
    public int compare(Integer o1, Integer o2) {
        return o2 - o1;
    }
}
```

The logic in Reverse is the opposite of the natural order of Integer. For example, 10 is less than 5 using the logic of Reverse. To use this Comparator, create an instance and pass it into the sort method along with the List object to be sorted. Study the following code and see if you can determine its output:

```java
List<Integer> list = new ArrayList<Integer>();
list.add(-5);
list.add(12);
list.add(7);
list.add(7);
list.add(30);
Collections.sort(list, new Reverse());
for(Integer i : list) {
    System.out.println(i);
}
```

The ArrayList object contains five Integer objects. The call to Collections.sort includes a new Reverse object, which orders the numbers in reverse order. The output of the previous statements is

```
30
12
7
7
-5
```

The natural ordering is ignored when a Comparator is supplied to the sort method. Using a Comparator, you control the ordering of a list based on the needs of your business logic.

Converting a List to an Array

The sort methods in Collections perform the list search in $n \log(n)$ time, where n is the number of elements in the list. To achieve this type of performance, the sort methods actually convert the given List object to an array, sort the array, and then iterate over the list, resetting each element from the corresponding position in the array.

For the exam, you do not need to understand how the sort method works behind the scenes. However, the exam objectives specifically mention the ability to convert a list to an array, which is achieved using the generic toArray method of the List interface:

```
<T> T[] toArray(T[] a)
```

The toArray method returns an array that contains all the elements of the list. This generic version of toArray requires an array argument. The array passed in, if big enough, is used to contain the list elements (and also returned). If the array passed in is not big enough to hold the list, as in the following code, a new array is created and returned:

```
List<String> list = new ArrayList<String>();
list.add("one");
list.add("two");
list.add("three");
String [] array = list.<String>toArray(new String [0]);
for(String s : array) {
    System.out.print(s + " ");
}
```

> The output of the previous statements is
>
> ```
> one two three
> ```
>
> Notice that the invocation of toArray requires the generic type to be specified so that the toArray method knows what type of array to create and return. The syntax list.<String>toArray lets the toArray method know to return an array of String objects.

Sorting lists is a common task in programming, and the Collections.sort methods implement an efficient sorting algorithm that offers $n \log(n)$ performance, where n is the number of elements in the list. The next section discusses another common programming task: searching a list.

Searching Lists

The Collections class contains two methods for searching the elements in a List:

- public static <T> int binarySearch(List<? extends Comparable<? super T>> list, T key) searches the given List for the specified object. The list must be sorted first and the elements in the list must implement Comparable.

- public static <T> int binarySearch(List<? extends T> list, T key, Comparator<? super T> c) searches the given List for the specified object. The List must be sorted first, and the c parameter represents the Comparator object used to sort the list.

Both binarySearch methods require the given list to be sorted prior to searching. If the list is not sorted, the result of the search is undefined. The return value of both methods is the index in the list where the object was found or negative if the given object does not appear in the list.

Let's look at an example. The following list contains 20 Integer objects with random values:

```
6.  List<Integer> list = new ArrayList<Integer>();
7.  for(int i = 1; i <= 20; i++) {
8.      int x = (int) (Math.random() * 10);
9.      list.add(x);
10. }
```

Before it can be searched, the list must be sorted. The following statements sort the list and then search for the number 5:

```
11. Collections.sort(list);
12. for(Integer i : list) {
```

```
13.       System.out.print(i + " ");
14. }
15. System.out.println();
16. int index = Collections.binarySearch(list, new Integer(5));
17. if(index >= 0) {
18.       System.out.println("5 found at index " + index);
19. } else {
20.       System.out.println("5 not found");
21. }
```

The Integer class implements Comparable, and the method call on line 16 invokes the Comparable version of the binarySearch method. The value of index is the location in list where one of the 5s appears, or a negative value if list does not contain a 5. Here is a sample output of the previous statements:

```
0 0 0 1 1 2 3 3 3 5 5 5 5 5 6 8 8 9 9 9
5 found at index 9
```

If more than one element is found, the index returned is for one of the elements, but there is no guarantee as to which one.

The following example demonstrates the other version of binarySearch that uses a Comparator object. Use the Comparator version of binarySearch when the elements in the list do not implement the Comparable interface. For example, suppose we have a list of Product objects based on the Product class from earlier in this chapter:

```
public class Product {
    String description;
    double price;
    int id;

    public Product(String d, double p, int i) {
        description = d;
        price = p;
        id = i;
    }
    //remainder of class definition...
}
```

A Comparator object is required to sort and search a list of Product objects, as demonstrated by the following program. Study the code and see if you can determine its result:

```
1.   import java.util.*;
2.
3.   public class ProductSearch {
```

```
4.        static class ProductComparator implements Comparator<Product> {
5.            public int compare(Product a, Product b) {
6.                return (int) (a.price - b.price);
7.            }
8.        }
9.
10.       public static void main(String [] args) {
11.           List<Product> list = new ArrayList<Product>();
12.           Product toFind = new Product("shirt", 29.99, 101);
13.           list.add(toFind);
14.           list.add(new Product("shoes", 150.00, 202));
15.           list.add(new Product("tie", 12.50, 303));
16.           ProductComparator pc = new ProductComparator();
17.           Collections.sort(list, pc);
18.           for(Product p : list) {
19.               System.out.println(p.description + " " + p.price);
20.           }
21.           int index = Collections.binarySearch(list, toFind, pc);
22.           System.out.println("Index of shirt is " + index);
23.       }
24. }
```

The ProductComparator class sorts Product objects in ascending order by price. Three Product objects are added to the ArrayList from line 11, and then the list is sorted by price on line 17. Line 21 searches for the "shirt" product, and the resulting index is printed on line 22. The output of the previous program is

```
tie 12.5
shirt 29.99
shoes 150.0
Index of shirt is 1
```

Because the Product objects are sorted by price, the shirt is second in the list, so its index is 1.

Use the binarySearch methods to find a specific element in a list. Remember that a list must be sorted first before invoking binarySearch or the result is undefined. Use the Collections class to sort and search lists. The next section discusses the sorting and searching of arrays in Java using the Arrays class.

Working with Arrays

The exam objectives state that you should be able to sort arrays either in their natural order or using a Comparator object. The exam also requires knowledge of performing a binary search on arrays. These objectives are indirectly referring to the static sort and binarySearch methods of the java.util.Arrays class. We start with a discussion on sorting arrays.

Sorting Arrays

The Arrays class contains a collection of sort methods for sorting arrays of primitive types and objects. There is a pair of sort methods for each Java array type (except arrays of booleans). For example, the following sort methods are for sorting arrays of ints:

- `public static void sort(int[] a)`

- `public static void sort(int[] a, int fromIndex, int toIndex)`

Similarly, there are two sort methods for byte, short, long, float, double, and char arrays. The overloaded versions of sort allow for sorting a subset of the given array.

There is also a pair of sort methods for Object arrays:

- `public static void sort(Object[] a)`

- `public static void sort(Object[] a, int fromIndex, int toIndex)`

The Object array is sorted in its natural order and the elements in the array must implement Comparable and be mutually comparable.

The Arrays class also contains a generics version of sort that uses a Comparator to determine the ordering:

- `public static <T> void sort(T[] a, Comparator<? super T> c)`

- `public static <T> void sort(T[] a, int fromIndex, int toIndex, Comparator<? super T> c)`

Similar to sorting lists, a Comparator is useful when the objects being sorted do not implement Comparable or you need the objects sorted in a different order than their natural ordering.

Passing an array to a sort method alters the array. The values are rearranged in the appropriate order. Let's start with an example that sorts an array of primitive types. Study the following code and see if you can determine what it does:

```
6.  int [] values = new int[15];
7.  System.out.print("Initial values: ");
8.  for(int i = 0; i < values.length; i++) {
9.      values[i] = (int) (Math.random() * 10);
10.     System.out.print(values[i] + " ");
11. }
```

```
12.
13. Arrays.sort(values);
14.
15. System.out.print("\nSorted values: ");
16. for(int i : values) {
17.     System.out.print(i + " ");
18. }
```

The previous code breakdowns as follows:

1. Line 6 creates an array of 15 ints named values.

2. The for loop on line 8 fills the array with random numbers between 0 and 9 and displays those values.

3. Line 13 sorts the values array. Because the array is of type int, the array is ordered in its natural ordering.

4. The for loop on line 16 displays the array again.

Here is a sample output of the previous code:

```
Initial values: 8 0 7 9 9 9 0 5 7 1 5 0 9 3 8
Sorted values:  0 0 0 1 3 5 5 7 7 8 8 9 9 9 9
```

The array is sorted in its natural order, which for ints is numerical order. Now let's look at an example where a Comparator is used to determine the sort order. See if you can determine the ordering logic of the following comparator:

```java
public class EvenSorter implements java.util.Comparator<Integer> {
    public int compare(Integer a, Integer b) {
        return (b%2) - (a%2);
    }
}
```

If a and b are equal, the compare method returns 0. If both numbers are even or odd, the return value is also 0, so two even numbers are equal and two odd numbers are equal. If a is even and b is odd, the result is 1, so even numbers are greater than odd numbers. The following code sorts an array of random Integer objects using an EvenSorter comparator:

```java
Integer [] values = new Integer[15];
System.out.print("Initial values: ");
for(int i = 0; i < values.length; i++) {
    values[i] = (int) (Math.random() * 10);
    System.out.print(values[i] + " ");
}

Arrays.sort(values, new EvenSorter());
```

```
System.out.print("\nSorted values: ");
for(int i : values) {
    System.out.print(i + " ");
}
```

The odd numbers appear before all the even numbers. Here is a sample output of the previous code:

```
Initial values: 6 8 8 9 2 1 7 2 3 0 7 2 6 5 2
Sorted values:  9 1 7 3 7 5 6 8 8 2 2 0 2 6 2
```

Converting an Array to a List

You should be able to convert an array to a list, which is accomplished by using the static asList method in the Arrays class, as follows:

```
public static <T> List<T> asList(T... a)
```

The returned List is fixed in size and backed by the specified array, meaning that changes to the List object actually change the array, as long as you do not perform any operations that modify the length of the List. For example, see if you can determine the output of the following statements:

```
String [] array = {"one", "two", "three"};
List<String> list = Arrays.asList(array);
list.set(1, "four");
for(String s : array) {
    System.out.println(s);
}
```

The array contains three String objects, and passing it to asList creates a List with the same three String objects. Setting index 1 to "four" changes list and array, as shown by the output of the for-each loop:

```
one
four
three
```

Another use of the asList method is to create a fixed-size List using the variable-length arguments passed in. For example, the following statement creates a new List containing seven Integer objects:

```
List<Integer> numbers = Arrays.<Integer>asList(8, 6, 7, 5, 3, 0, 9);
```

Just remember that asList returns a fixed-size List. Attempting to add or remove an element from numbers results in an UnsupportedOperationException at runtime.

We just discussed how to use a `Comparator` object for sorting arrays either to alter the natural ordering or for sorting an array of objects that do not implement the `Comparable` interface. Now let's explore how to use the `binarySearch` method of `Arrays` to search arrays sorted either in the natural order or with a `Comparator`.

Searching Arrays

The `Arrays` class contains a collection of `binarySearch` methods for searching arrays of primitive types and objects. There is a pair of `binarySearch` methods for each Java array type (except arrays of `boolean`s). For example, the following `binarySearch` methods are for searching arrays of `long`s:

- `public static int binarySearch(long[] a, long key)` searches the entire array for the specified `long`. The array must be sorted first.
- `public static int binarySearch(long[] a, int fromIndex, int toIndex, long key)` searches a subset of the array for the specified `long`. The array must be sorted first.

Similarly, there are two `binarySearch` methods for `byte`, `short`, `int`, `float`, `double`, and `char` arrays. There is also a pair of `binarySearch` methods for `Object` arrays:

- `public static int binarySearch(Object[] a, Object key)`
- `public static int binarySearch(Object[] a, int fromIndex, int toIndex, Object key)`

The elements in the `Object` array must implement `Comparable` and be mutually comparable. The `Arrays` class also contains a generics version of `binarySearch` for arrays sorted using a `Comparator`, as follows:

- `public static <T> int binarySearch(T[] a, T key, Comparator<? super T> c)`
- `public static <T> int binarySearch(T[] a, int fromIndex, int toIndex, T key, Comparator<? super T> c)`

All of the `binarySearch` methods require the array to be sorted prior to searching. If the array is not sorted, then the result of the search is undefined. The return value of `binarySearch` is the index in the array where the key was found or negative if the given key does not appear in the array.

Let's look at an example. The following statements search an array of `long` elements. Study the code and see if you can determine its output:

```
6.  long [] values = {432432L, 2342323L, 1244L, 89349L, 7898239L};
7.  Arrays.sort(values);
8.  long key = 432432L;
9.  int index = Arrays.binarySearch(values, key);
10. System.out.println(key + " found at index " + index);
11. long key2 = 55555L;
12. int index2 = Arrays.binarySearch(values, key2);
13. System.out.println(key2 + " found at index " + index2);
```

Line 6 creates an array of five longs that is sorted on line 7. The array is searched on line 9 for the value 432432L and the index is returned. Line 12 searches the array for 55555L, which is not in the array. Therefore, index2 is a negative value. The output of the statements is

```
432432 found at index 2
55555 found at index -2
```

The number 432432 is third in the values array after it is sorted, so the index is 2. The number 55555 is not in the array, so the return value is computed as (-(insertion_point) - 1), where insertion_point is the index in the array where 55555 would appear in the array if it was inserted in order.

The following example demonstrates searching an array that is sorted using a Comparator. The code uses the Product class from earlier in this chapter and sorts the Product objects based on their description. Study the code and see if you can determine its output:

```
1.   import java.util.*;
2.
3.   public class ProductArraySearch {
4.       static class DescriptionSorter implements Comparator<Product> {
5.           public int compare(Product a, Product b) {
6.               return a.description.compareTo(b.description);
7.           }
8.       }
9.
10.      public static void main(String [] args) {
11.          Product toFind = new Product("milk", 2.95, 111);
12.          Product [] products = {
13.              toFind,
14.              new Product("eggs", 4.00, 222),
15.              new Product("butter", 2.75, 333),
16.              new Product("bread", 1.95, 444)
17.          };
18.
19.          DescriptionSorter dc = new DescriptionSorter();
20.          Arrays.<Product>sort(products, dc);
21.          for(Product p : products) {
22.              System.out.println(p.description + " " + p.price);
23.          }
24.          int index = Arrays.<Product>binarySearch(products,
                                                    toFind, dc);
```

```
25.          System.out.println("Index of milk is " + index);
26.     }
27. }
```

A breakdown of the `ProductArraySearch` program follows:

1. Line 4 declares a `Comparator` named `DescriptionSorter` that sorts `Product` objects in lexicographical order of the `description` string.

2. Line 12 fills the `products` array with four `Product` objects.

3. Line 20 sorts the `products` array using the `DescriptionSorter` comparator. The `for` loop on line 21 prints out the sorted array.

4. Line 24 searches the `products` array for the `"milk"` product, which appears at the end of the array.

5. Line 25 prints out the value of `index`.

The output of the program is

```
bread 1.95
butter 2.75
eggs 4.0
milk 2.95
Index of milk is 3
```

Because `"milk"` is at the end of the array, its index is 3. Notice that the products are sorted in alphabetical order by description. Use the generic version of `binarySearch` when you search an array sorted with a `Comparator` object.

Summary

This chapter covered the "Collections and Generics" objectives of the SCJP exam. The goal of this chapter was to discuss the details of using the Java Collections Framework, a collection of classes and interfaces in the `java.util` package that implement common data structures like lists, maps, and sets. The collection's classes and interfaces use generics, which provide a compile-time type safety for simplifying the use of collections.

The `Collection` interface is the parent interface of `List`, `Set`, and `Queue`. The map data structures implement the `Map` interface. A list is an ordered collection of elements that allows duplicate entries. The `List` implementations include `ArrayList`, `LinkedList`, `Vector`, and `Stack`. A set is a collection that does not allow duplicate entries. The `Set` implementations are `HashSet`, `LinkedHashSet`, and `TreeSet`. A queue is a collection that orders its elements in a specific order for processing. The `Queue` implementations include `LinkedList`, `PriorityQueue`, and `ArrayDeque`. A map is a collection that maps keys to values, with no duplicate keys allowed. The `Map` implementations are `HashMap`, `LinkedHashMap`, and `TreeMap`.

The collections classes use the `equals` method to determine the equality of two objects. The `Comparable` interface declares the `compareTo` method. Objects that implement `Comparable` are said to have a natural ordering, and the `compareTo` method is consistent with `equals` if it returns 0 for two objects that are equal in terms of the `equals` method. The `Comparator` interface declares the `compare` method and provides a mechanism for ordering objects in whatever order you define.

The generics feature, new to J2SE 5.0, provides support for parameterized data types. We discussed the details of using generics with the Collections Framework, along with defining your own classes, interfaces, and methods that take advantage of generics. Generics can use the wildcard ? to represent any generic type. Use the `extends` keyword to define an upper bound for a generic type and `super` to define a lower bound.

The `Collections` class contains `sort` methods for sorting lists and `binarySearch` methods for searching lists. The `Arrays` class contains `sort` methods for sorting arrays and `binarySearch` methods for searching arrays.

Be sure to test your knowledge of collections and generics by answering the Review Questions that follow the Exam Essentials. Attempt to answer the questions without looking back at the pages of this chapter. Make sure you have a good understanding of the following Exam Essentials before you attempt the Review Questions, and good luck!

Exam Essentials

Understand the different types of collection data structures.   Know the difference between lists, sets, queues, and maps. Be able to recognize which type of collection to use given a specific scenario. A list is an ordered collection of elements that allows duplicate entries, a set is a collection that does not allow duplicate entries, a queue is a collection that orders its elements in a specific order for processing, and a map is a collection that maps keys to values, with no duplicate keys allowed.

Understand the generics syntax.   Be sure you understand how to instantiate an object that uses generics, as well as invoke a generic method. Generics provide compile-time type safety for collections by allowing your `Collection` objects to specify what types they contain.

Understand generics and polymorphism.   You need to be able to recognize proper and improper use of polymorphic references and generics, especially with wildcards and upper and lower bounds. A question mark (?) represents an unknown generic, the `extends` keyword creates an upper-bound generic, and the `super` keyword creates a lower-bound generic.

Be familiar with the various collections class.   You are not expected to know all the details of all the collections classes, but you should be able to understand code that uses `ArrayList`, `Vector`, `Stack`, `LinkedList`, `HashSet`, `TreeSet`, `HashMap`, and `TreeMap`.

Understand natural ordering vs. comparators.   Classes that implement Comparable are said to have a natural ordering. If a class does not have a natural ordering, use a separate Comparator object to sort and search instances of the class. The Comparator interface declares the compare method that returns an int. The return value is a negative integer, zero, or a positive integer if the first argument is less than, equal to, or greater than the second, respectively.

Understand the difference between == and equals.   The comparison operator == returns true if the two references being compared point to the same object. The equals method compares two objects and uses business logic. If you override equals, make sure you also override the hashCode method in such a way that two equal objects produce the same hash code.

Understand the behavior and usage of the sort and binarySearch methods.   You should be able to understand code that uses the sort and binarySearch methods of the Collections (for lists) and Arrays (for arrays) classes. The Collections class defines two static sort methods: one for natural-order sorting and one for comparator sorting of lists. The Collections class also defines two static binarySearch methods, and the list must be sorted before it is searched. The Arrays class contains two overloaded sort methods for each type of array, which provides for both natural-order and comparator sorting. Similarly, the Arrays class contains binarySearch methods for searching the various types of arrays, and an array must be sorted before it is searched.

Review Questions

1. Suppose you have a collection of products for sale in a database and you need to display those products on a web page. The Java code on the server needs to be able to sort the products by price and category. Which of the following collections classes in the `java.util` package best suit your needs for this scenario?

   A. HashSet

   B. HashMap

   C. PriorityQueue

   D. Arrays

   E. ArrayList

2. Suppose you need to work with a collection of elements that need to be sorted in their natural ordering, iterated in descending order, and each element has a unique string associated with its value. Which of the following collections classes in the `java.util` package best suit your needs for this scenario?

   A. HashMap

   B. TreeMap

   C. HashSet

   D. Vector

   E. ArrayList

3. What is the result of the following statements?

   ```
   6.  List list = new ArrayList();
   7.  list.add("one");
   8.  list.add("two");
   9.  list.add(7);
   10. for(String s : list) {
   11.     System.out.print(s);
   12. }
   ```

   A. onetwo

   B. onetwo7

   C. onetwo followed by an exception

   D. Compiler error on line 9

   E. Compiler error on line 10

4. What is the result of the following statements?

   ```
   6.  List<String> list = new ArrayList<String>();
   7.  list.add("one");
   ```

```
8.  list.add("two");
9.  list.add(7);
10. for(String s : list) {
11.     System.out.print(s);
12. }
```

A. onetwo

B. onetwo7

C. onetwo followed by an exception

D. Compiler error on line 9

E. Compiler error on line 10

5. What is the result of the following statements?

```
3.  ArrayList<Integer> values = new ArrayList<Integer>();
4.  values.add(4);
5.  values.add(5);
6.  values.set(1, 6);
7.  values.remove(0);
8.  for(Integer v : values) {
9.      System.out.print(v);
10. }
```

A. 4

B. 5

C. 6

D. 46

E. 45

6. What is the result of the following statements?

```
10. Stack<String> greetings = new Stack<String>();
11. greetings.push("hello");
12. greetings.push("hi");
13. greetings.push("ola");
14. greetings.pop();
15. greetings.peek();
16. Iterator iter = greetings.iterator();
17. while(iter.hasNext()) {
18.     System.out.print(iter.next());
19. }
```

A. hello

B. hellohi

    C. hellohiola

    D. hihello

    E. The code does not compile.

7. Which of the following statements are valid? (Choose three.)

    A. `List<String> list = new Vector<String>();`

    B. `HashSet<Number> hs = new HashSet<Integer>();`

    C. `Map<String, ? extends Number> hm = new HashMap<String, Integer>();`

    D. `HashSet<? super ClassCastException> set = new HashSet<Exception>();`

    E. `List<Object> values = new LinkedHashSet<Object> ();`

8. What is the result of the following program?

```
1.  public class Hello<T> {
2.      T t;
3.
4.      public Hello(T t) {
5.          this.t = t;
6.      }
7.
8.      public String toString() {
9.          return t.toString();
10.     }
11.
12.     public static void main(String [] args) {
13.         System.out.print(new Hello<String>("hi"));
14.         System.out.print(new Hello("there"));
15.     }
16. }
```

    A. hi

    B. hi followed by a runtime exception

    C. hithere

    D. Compiler error on line 9

    E. Compiler error on line 14

9. Given the following statements:

```
6.  Set<Number> numbers = new HashSet<Number>();
7.  numbers.add(new Integer(86));
8.  numbers.add(75);
9.  numbers.add(new Integer(86));
10. numbers.add(null);
```

```
11. numbers.add(309L);
12. Iterator iter = numbers.iterator();
13. while(iter.hasNext()) {
14.     System.out.print(iter.next());
15. }
```

Which of the following statements are true? (Select two.)

A. The code compiles successfully.

B. The output is 8675null309.

C. The output is indeterminate.

D. Line 6 generates a compiler error.

E. Line 12 generates a compiler error.

10. What is the result of the following statements?

```
7.  TreeSet<String> tree = new TreeSet<String>();
8.  tree.add("one");
9.  tree.add("One");
10. tree.add("ONE");
11. System.out.println(tree.ceiling("On"));
```

A. one

B. One

C. ONE

D. On

11. Given the following declaration:

```
Map<String, Double> map = new HashMap<String, Double>();
```

which of the following statements are valid?

A. map.add("pi", 3.14159);

B. map.add("e", 2.71828D);

C. map.add("log(1)", new Double(0.0));

D. map.add('x', new Double(123.4));

E. None of the above.

12. What is the result of the following program?

```
import java.util.*;

public class MyComparator implements Comparator<String> {
    public int compare(String a, String b) {
```

```
            return a.toLowerCase().compareTo(b.toLowerCase());
        }

        public static void main(String [] args) {
            String [] values = {"abc", "Abb", "aab"};
            Arrays.sort(values, new MyComparator());
            for(String s : values) {
                System.out.print(s + " ");
            }
        }
    }
```

A. aab Abb abc

B. Abb aab abc

C. abc Abb aab

D. aab abc Abb

E. The code does not compile.

13. What is the result of the following statements?

```
3. Map<Integer, Integer> map = new HashMap<Integer, Integer>(10);
4. for(int i = 1; i <= 10; i++) {
5.     map.put(i, i * i);
6. }
7. System.out.println(map.get(4));
```

A. Compiler error on line 3

B. Compiler error on line 5

C. Compiler error on line 7

D. 16

E. 25

14. What is the result of the following statements?

```
10. int [] random = {6, -4, 12, 0, -10};
11. int x = 12;
12. int y = Arrays.binarySearch(random, x);
13. System.out.println(y);
```

A. 2

B. 4

C. The result is undefined.

D. Line 12 throws an exception at runtime.

E. Compiler error on line 12

15. Given the following class definition:

```
1.  import java.io.*;
2.
3.  public class Helper {
4.      public static <U extends Exception> void
                            printException(U u) {
5.          System.out.println(u.getMessage());
6.      }
7.
8.      public static void main(String [] args) {
9.          _____
10.     }
11. }
```

which of the following statements can appear on line 9 so that the Helper class compiles successfully?

A. Helper.printException(new FileNotFoundException("A"));

B. Helper.printException(new Exception("B"));

C. Helper.<Throwable>printException(new Exception("C"));

D. Helper.<NullPointerException>printException(new NullPointerException ("D"));

E. Helper.printException(new Throwable("E"));

16. Given the following class definition:

```
1.  import java.util.*;
2.
3.  public class Wildcard {
4.      public void showSize(List<?> list) {
5.          System.out.println(list.size());
6.      }
7.
8.      public static void main(String [] args) {
9.          Wildcard card = new Wildcard();
10.         _____
11.         card.showSize(list);
12.     }
13. }
```

which of the following statements can appear on line 10 so that the `Wildcard` class compiles successfully? (Select three answers.)

A. `Stack<?> list = new Stack<?>();`

B. `List<?> list = new ArrayList<String>();`

C. `ArrayList<? super Date> list = new ArrayList<Date>();`

D. `Vector<? extends Number> list = new Vector<Integer>();`

E. `List<Exception> list = new LinkedList<java.io.IOException>();`

17. What is the result of the following statements?

```
3. List<Integer> list =
                Arrays.<Integer>asList(10, 4, -1, 5);
4. Collections.sort(list);
5. Integer [] array =
                list.<Integer>toArray(new Integer[4]);
6. System.out.println(array[0]);
```

A. Compiler error on line 3

B. Line 4 throws an exception at runtime.

C. Compiler error on line 5

D. -1

E. 10

18. What is the result of the following program?

```
1.  import java.util.*;
2.
3.  public class StringSearch {
4.      static class ReverseLexi implements
                                Comparator<String> {
5.          public int compare(String a, String b) {
6.              return b.compareToIgnoreCase(a);
7.          }
8.      }
9.
10.     public static void main(String [] args) {
11.         List<String> list = new ArrayList<String>();
12.         list.add("ab");
13.         list.add("ba");
14.         list.add("bd");
15.         list.add("aa");
```

```
16.          ReverseLexi comparator = new ReverseLexi();
17.          Collections.sort(list, comparator);
18.          int index = Collections.binarySearch(list,
 "ab", comparator);
19.          System.out.println(index);
20.      }
21. }
```

A. 1

B. 2

C. 3

D. 4

E. The code does not compile.

19. What is the result of the following statements?

```
6.  String [] names = {"Tom", "Dick", "Harry"};
7.  List<String> list = names.asList();
8.  list.set(0, "Sue");
9.  System.out.println(names[0]);
```

A. Sue

B. Tom

C. Compiler error on line 7

D. Compiler error on line 8

E. Line 9 causes an exception at runtime.

20. What is the result of the following code?

```
4.  List<String> names = Arrays.asList("Tom", "Dick",
 "Harry", "Sue");
5.  Collections.sort(names);
6.  int x = Collections.binarySearch(names, "Tom");
7.  System.out.println(x);
```

A. 0

B. 1

C. 2

D. 3

E. -1

21. What is the result of the following statements?

```
10. List<String> one = new ArrayList<String>();
11. one.add("abc");
12. List<String> two = new ArrayList<String>();
13. two.add("abc");
14. if(one == two) {
15.     System.out.println("A");
16. } else if(one.equals(two)) {
17.     System.out.println("B");
18. } else {
19.     System.out.println("C");
20. }
```

A. A

B. B

C. C

D. Compiler error on line 14

E. Compiler error on line 16

22. What is the result of the following code?

```
10. List<String> one = new ArrayList<String>();
11. one.add("abc");
12. List<String> two = new Vector<String>();
13. two.add("abc");
14. if(one == two) {
15.     System.out.println("A");
16. } else if(one.equals(two)) {
17.     System.out.println("B");
18. } else {
19.     System.out.println("C");
20. }
```

A. A

B. B

C. C

D. Compiler error on line 14

E. Compiler error on line 16

Answers to Review Questions

1. **E.** The HashSet and HashMap classes do not provide ordering or sorting of items, so they are not good choices in this scenario. A PriorityQueue is used for processing items based on a priority, which is not relevant to our needs. The Arrays class is not a collections class; it is a utility class with only static methods. An ArrayList can be ordered and sorted easily using the Collections class, which makes it a good choice for this scenario. Therefore, the answer is E.

2. **B.** Because each element has a unique string associated with its value, a map is the best choice, so C, D, and E are incorrect. A HashMap does not provide specific ordering, so A is incorrect. A TreeMap is always sorted in natural order, and because it implements NavigableMap, it contains a descending iterator. Therefore, the best choice for this scenario is TreeMap and the answer is B.

3. **E.** The code does not compile, so A, B, and C are incorrect. D is also incorrect; line 9 compiles fine because the code is not using generics and any Object can be added to list. Line 10 does not compile because list contains Object references and the for-each loop is attempting to assign them to String. Therefore, the answer is E.

4. **D.** The code does not compile, so A, B, and C are incorrect. E is also incorrect; line 10 compiles fine because list contains String objects. Line 9 does not compile because list is instantiated using generics; only String objects can be added to list and 7 is an int. Therefore, the answer is D.

5. **C.** Here is the sequence of events:

    1. Line 4 adds 4 to values at index 0.

    2. Line 5 adds 5 to values at index 1.

    3. Line 6 replaces 5 with 6 at index 1.

    4. Line 7 removes 4 from index 0, leaving only the 6 in values.

    The for-each loop only iterates one time and 6 is displayed, so the answer is C.

6. **B.** The code compiles fine, so E is incorrect. The strings "hello", "hi", and "ola" are pushed onto the stack. The call to pop on line 14 removes "ola" from the stack. The call to peek on line 15 returns "hi" but does not remove it from the stack. That leaves "hello" and "hi" on the stack, and they are iterated in that order. Therefore, the output is hellohi and the answer is B.

7. **A, C, and D.** A is valid because Vector implements List and the <String> generics are identical. B does not compile because <Integer> is not compatible with <Number>. (There is no implied polymorphism with generic types.) C is valid because HashMap implements Map and Integer is a child of Number. D is valid because Exception is a parent class of ClassCastException. E is not valid because LinkedHashSet does not implement List.

8. C. The code compiles and runs fine, so B, D, and E are incorrect. Line 14 does cause a "Note" from the compiler about using "unchecked or unsafe operations," but it is not a compiler error. The compiler has to deduce that "T" is of type String for the Hello object on line 14, which it successfully does. Line 9 compiles fine because all objects have a toString method. Lines 13 and 14 print "hi" and "there" respectively, so the output of the code is "hithere" and the answer is C.

9. A and C. The code compiles fine, so A is correct and D and E are incorrect. B is not correct because a Set does not guarantee any specific iteration order, and the iteration order can change over time. Therefore, C is correct and the answers are A and C.

10. B. To find the ceiling of "On", you need to know the natural ordering of the four String objects, which is "ONE", "On", "One", and then "one". The ceiling method returns the least String in tree greater than "On", which is "One". Therefore, the answer is B.

11. E. This is a trick question! Each of the answers attempts to "add" a key-value pair to the map, but the Map interface does not declare an add method. Instead, you "put" elements in a map using the put method, so none of the statements are valid and the answer is E. (By the way, if you change add to put, then A, B, and C would be correct and D would generate a compiler error because 'x' is not a String.)

12. A. The code compiles fine, so E is incorrect. The values array is sorted using the MyComparator class, which sorts strings in alphabetical order because it ignores uppercase characters. The order of values alphabetically is aab, Abb, and abc, so the answer is A.

13. D. The code compiles fine, so A, B, and C are incorrect. The for loop puts 10 pairs in the map. The keys range from 1 to 10 and they map to their squared value. For example, 1 maps to 1, 2 maps to 4, 3 maps to 9, 4 maps to 16, and so on. Line 7 prints out the value whose key is 4, which is 16. Therefore, the answer is D.

14. C. The code compiles and runs fine, but an array must be sorted before invoking the Arrays.binarySearch method. Therefore, the result is undefined and the answer is C.

15. A, B, and D. The generic for the printException method must be an Exception or a child of Exception. A is valid because FileNotFoundException is a child of Exception. B is valid because the generic is Exception. C and E are not valid because Throwable is not a child class of Exception. D is valid and demonstrates the syntax for specifying the type explicitly when invoking a generic method. Therefore, A, B, and D are the correct answers.

16. B, C, and D. The showSize method can accept a List object with any generic type. A is not a valid statement (regardless of the showSize method) because when you instantiate a generic type, you cannot use a wildcard in the new statement. You must declare a specific data type. E is not a valid statement either (regardless of the showSize method); <IOException> and <Exception> are not compatible. The other three statements are valid List declarations, and because any generic List can be passed into showSize because of the wildcard <?>, the answers are B, C, and D.

17. D. The code compiles and runs fine, so A, B, and C are incorrect. The asList method creates a fixed-size list with four Integer objects. Line 4 sorts the numbers into their natural order. Line 5 converts the list to an array using the generic toArray method of List. Line 6 prints out the first element in the array, which is the smallest value: -1. Therefore, the answer is D.

18. B. The code compiles fine, so E is incorrect. The array is sorted in reverse alphabetical order, so the order of the sorted list is `"bd"`, `"ba"`, `"ab"`, then `"aa"`. The index of `"ab"` is 2, which is displayed on line 19. Therefore, the answer is B.

19. C. The code does not compile. An array is converted to a list using the static `Arrays.asList` method. Line 7 attempts to invoke `asList` as if it is a method of the array object, which it is not. Line 7 generates a compiler error and therefore the answer is C.

20. D. The `names` list is sorted on line 6, so its order is `"Dick"`, `"Harry"`, `"Sue"`, and then `"Tom"`. The `binarySearch` call on line 6 assigns x to the index of `"Tom"`, which is 3. Therefore, the answer is D.

21. B. The code compiles fine, so D and E are incorrect. Line 14 is `false` because one and two do not point to the same object. Line 16 is `true`; the `equals` method of `List` returns `true` if and only if both lists have the same size, and all corresponding pairs of elements in the two lists are equal. Because one and two are both of size 1 and contain the same `String` object `"abc"`, they are equal and line 17 prints out B. Therefore, the answer is B.

22. B. The code compiles fine, so D and E are incorrect. The only difference between Question 21 and Question 22 is line 12: this time the two reference points to a `Vector` instead of an `ArrayList`. Line 14 is `false` because one and two do not point to the same object. Line 16 is actually `true`; the `equals` method of `List` does not make a distinction about the actual `List` implementation, so an `ArrayList` can equal a `Vector` as long they have the same size and all corresponding pairs of elements in the two lists are equal. Because one and two are both of size 1 and contain the same `String` object `"abc"`, they are equal and line 17 prints out B. Therefore, the answer is B.

Appendix

About the Companion CD

IN THIS APPENDIX:

✓ What you'll find on the CD

✓ System requirements

✓ Using the CD

✓ Troubleshooting

What You'll Find on the CD

The following sections are arranged by category and summarize the software and other goodies you'll find on the CD. If you need help with installing the items provided on the CD, refer to the installation instructions in the "Using the CD" section of this appendix. Some programs on the CD might fall into one of these categories:

Shareware programs are fully functional, free, trial versions of copyrighted programs. If you like particular programs, register with their authors for a nominal fee and receive licenses, enhanced versions, and technical support.

Freeware programs are free, copyrighted games, applications, and utilities. You can copy them to as many computers as you like—for free—but they offer no technical support.

GNU software is governed by its own license, which is included inside the folder of the GNU software. There are no restrictions on distribution of GNU software. See the GNU license at the root of the CD for more details.

Trial, *demo*, or *evaluation* versions of software are usually limited either by time or by functionality (such as not letting you save a project after you create it).

Sybex Test Engine

For Windows

The CD contains the Sybex test engine, which includes all of the Assessment Test and chapter review questions in electronic format, as well as two bonus exams located only on the CD.

PDF of the Book

For Windows

We have included an electronic version of the text in .pdf format. You can view the electronic version of the book with Adobe Reader.

Adobe Reader

For Windows

We've also included a copy of Adobe Reader so you can view PDF files that accompany the book's content. For more information on Adobe Reader or to check for a newer version, visit Adobe's website at www.adobe.com/products/reader/.

Electronic Flashcards

For PC, Pocket PC, and Palm

These handy electronic flashcards are just what they sound like. One side contains a question or fill-in-the-blank question, and the other side shows the answer.

System Requirements

Make sure your computer meets the minimum system requirements shown in the following list. If your computer doesn't match up to most of these requirements, you may have problems using the software and files on the companion CD. For the latest and greatest information, please refer to the ReadMe file located at the root of the CD.

- A PC running Microsoft Windows 98, Windows 2000, Windows NT4 (with SP4 or later), Windows Me, Windows XP, or Windows Vista

- An Internet connection

- A CD-ROM drive

Using the CD

To install the items from the CD to your hard drive, follow these steps:

1. Insert the CD into your computer's CD-ROM drive. The license agreement appears.

Windows users: The interface won't launch if you have Autorun disabled. In that case, click Start ➢ Run (for Windows Vista, Start ➢ All Programs ➢ Accessories ➢ Run). In the dialog box that appears, type D:\Start.exe. (Replace D with the proper letter if your CD drive uses a different letter. If you don't know the letter, see how your CD drive is listed under My Computer.) Click OK.

2. Read the license agreement, and then click the Accept button if you want to use the CD.

The CD interface appears. The interface allows you to access the content with just one or two clicks.

Troubleshooting

Wiley has attempted to provide programs that work on most computers with the minimum system requirements. Alas, your computer may differ, and some programs may not work properly for some reason.

The two likeliest problems are that you don't have enough memory (RAM) for the programs you want to use or you have other programs running that are affecting installation or running of a program. If you get an error message such as "Not enough memory" or "Setup cannot continue," try one or more of the following suggestions and then try using the software again:

Turn off any antivirus software running on your computer. Installation programs sometimes mimic virus activity and may make your computer incorrectly believe that it's being infected by a virus.

Close all running programs. The more programs you have running, the less memory is available to other programs. Installation programs typically update files and programs; so if you keep other programs running, installation may not work properly.

Have your local computer store add more RAM to your computer. This is, admittedly, a drastic and somewhat expensive step. However, adding more memory can really help the speed of your computer and allow more programs to run at the same time.

Customer Care

If you have trouble with the book's companion CD, please call the Wiley Product Technical Support phone number at (800) 762-2974. Outside the United States, call +1(317) 572-3994. You can also contact Wiley Product Technical Support at http://sybex.custhelp.com. John Wiley & Sons will provide technical support only for installation and other general quality-control items. For technical support on the applications themselves, consult the program's vendor or author.

To place additional orders or to request information about other Wiley products, please call (877) 762-2974.

Glossary

A

abstract class   A class declared with the `abstract` keyword. An abstract class cannot be instantiated.

abstract method   An instance method declared with the `abstract` keyword. An abstract method does not contain a method body and must be overridden by any nonabstract child classes.

abstract modifier   Declares a class or method as abstract. An abstract class cannot be instantiated; an abstract method must be overridden in any concrete subclass.

accessor methods   A JavaBeans "get" method that is used to access the value of a field.

additive operators   The operators + and -; they can be evaluated on any of the primitive types except `boolean`.

anonymous inner class   A local inner class that does not have a name. It is declared and instantiated all in one statement using the `new` keyword.

argument   A variable that is passed into a method.

arithmetic operators   Refers to the operators +, -, *, /, %, ++ and --.

array   A contiguous chunk of memory on the heap representing a fixed-size collection of values that all have the same data type.

array initializer   A shorthand notation for declaring an array and filling it with values, all in a single statement.

array reference   A reference that denotes the data type of the values to be stored in the array, using square brackets to denote the array reference.

assert statement   Used to insert an assertion at a particular point in your code. An assert statement uses the `assert` keyword followed by a `boolean` expression and an optional error message.

assertion   A `boolean` expression placed at particular points in your code where you think something should always be true.

assignment operators   The simple assignment = and 11 compound assignment operators: +=, -=, *=, /=, %=, &=, ^=, |=, <<=, >>=, and >>>=.

atomic   A task that needs to be completed without interruption. The term is often used to describe a task that needs to execute in a synchronized block of code.

autoboxing   Refers to the compiler automatically converting a primitive type into its corresponding wrapper class.

B

bitwise   Refers to the &, ^, and | operators.

bitwise and logical operators   The &, ^, |, &&, and || operators.

blank finals   A constant variable that is not assigned an initial value. A blank final becomes constant once it is assigned a value.

blocked thread   A thread in the BLOCKED state. A blocked thread becomes runnable when the monitor lock it is attempting to acquire becomes available.

bounded parameter type   A generic type that specifies a bound for the generic.

break statement   Transfers flow of control out of an enclosing statement. A break statement can appear within a `switch`, `for`, `while`, or do statement.

by value   Refers to how arguments are passed to methods in Java. Passing arguments by value means that a copy of the argument is passed to the corresponding parameter of the method.

bytecode   Compiled Java code. Bytecode appears in `.class` files.

C

call stack   Refers to the stack of methods executing within a single thread. The first method invoked in a thread sits at the bottom of the call stack, and subsequent method calls are pushed onto the top of the stack.

catch clauses   A block of code using the `catch` keyword that follows a try block. The catch block is often referred to as an exception handler since the `catch` block can handle an exception and stop it from traversing further down the method call stack.

character classes   Represents commonly used character patterns in regular expressions.

checked exception   Any exception that is a subclass of `java.lang.Exception` but not a subclass of `java.lang.RuntimeException`. Checked exceptions must be handled or declared.

class   A description of an object. A class in Java is defined in a `.java` source file and compiled into a `.class` file.

class method   A method within a class declared as static.

classpath   The path on your file system where your `.class` files are saved. The classpath is defined by the CLASSPATH environment variable.

class variable   A field within a class declared as static.

cohesion   Refers to how closely related the specific tasks are of an object.

collection   A group of objects contained in a single element.

collections interfaces   Refers to the interfaces in the Java Collections Framework that represent the various types of collections.

composition   Refers to a class containing a reference to another class. Good composition design satisfies the has-a relationship.

compound assignment operators   Refers to the assignment operators +=, -=, *=, /=, %=, &=, ^=, |=, <<=, >>=, and >>>=.

concrete subclass   A subclass of an abstract class that is not abstract.

concurrency   Performing multiple tasks at the same time. In Java, concurrency refers to a program that contains multiple threads.

conditional operator   The operator a ? b : c, where a is a boolean expression, b is the expression evaluated when a is true, and c is the expression evaluated when c is false.

consistent with equals   A natural ordering that uses compareTo is said to be *consistent with equals* if and only if x.equals(y) is true whenever x.compareTo(y) equals 0.

constants   Final fields or local variables; they cannot be changed.

constructor   A special method within a class that gets invoked when an object is instantiated. A constructor must match the name of the class and cannot declare a return value. The purpose of a constructor is to initialize the fields of the object.

continue statement   A statement within a repetition control structure that transfers flow of control to the loop-continuation point of the loop. A continue statement can appear within a for, while, or do statement.

coupling   The extent to which one object depends on another object to achieve its goal.

covariant return types   When the return type of the overriding method is a child class of the return type of the overridden method.

D

default constructor   A compiler-generated constructor that is automatically generated by the compiler if a class does not explicitly define a constructor. The default constructor takes in no arguments and only contains a call to the no-argument parent class constructor.

deserialization   Refers to the process of reading the data from an object stream and reconstituting a serialized object in memory.

deque   Pronounced "deck," it is short for "double-ended queue," a collection that allows for elements to be inserted and removed at both ends of the queue.

do-while loop   A repetition control structure that is useful for repeating a block of code an indeterminate number of times, but at least once. A do-while loop is declared using the do keyword.

E

encapsulation   Refers to the combining of fields and methods together in a class such that the methods operate on the data, as opposed to users of the class accessing the fields directly.

enhanced for loop   Referred to as a for-each loop, the enhanced for loop is a new type of loop introduced in Java 5.0 that provides a simpler syntax for iterating through collections.

enhanced for statement   An enhanced for statement, also referred to as a for-each loop, is a looping control structure designed for iterating through arrays and collections. The syntax is simpler than a basic for loop and makes your code more readable.

enum   A Java class that represents an enumeration.

enumeration   A fixed set of constants.

error   An exception that is a child class of java.lang.Error. An error is associated with problems that arise outside of your application, and you typically do not attempt to recover from errors.

exception   An event that occurs during the execution of a program that disrupts the normal flow of control. In Java, an exception is an object that a method "throws" down the method call stack by handing it to the JVM and letting the JVM search for a handler.

explicit initialization   Refers to when an instance variable is assigned a value at the same time that the instance variable is declared.

F

fields   Another name for the instance variables of a class.

final method   A method declared with the final keyword. A final method cannot be overridden.

final modifier   When applied to fields and variables, creates constants. When applied to a method, the method cannot be overridden. When applied to a class, the class cannot be subclassed.

finally block   A block of code that follows a try statement and executes after the try block, regardless of whether an exception occurs within the try block.

for loop   A repetition control structure that uses the for keyword and is useful for repeating a block of code a fixed number of times.

for-each loop   Another name for an enhanced `for` statement.

formal type parameter   Refers to the parameter used in a class, interface, method, or constructor that uses generics. The formal type parameter is declared in angle brackets. For example, `T` is the formal type parameter of the expression `<T>`.

format specifiers   The expression used in the format methods of the `java.io` `.PrintWriter` class. Examples include `%b` for Booleans, `%c` for characters, `%d` for integers, `%f` for decimal numbers, and `%s` for strings.

free store   Another term used to refer to the heap.

G

generics   Refers to the new Java feature added to J2SE 5.0 that provides support for parameterized data types.

Handle or Declare Rule   A rule enforced by the compiler that states if a statement throws a checked exception, it must either attempt to catch the exception or declare the exception in the enclosing method declaration using the `throws` keyword.

H

has-a relationship   A simple test to decide when a class should use composition.

heap   Represents a large pool of unused memory allocated to your Java application. All objects in Java reside in the heap memory.

heterogeneous collection   A collection of objects that are not the same data type but have a common parent class.

high cohesion   An OO design where an object performs a collection of closely related tasks.

I

identifier   The name of a variable, method, class, interface, or enum.

if-else statement   Also referred to as an `if-then` or `if-then-else` statement, it is the most basic of decision-making control structures in Java.

immutable   Refers to an object that cannot be changed.

import   The Java keyword used to import a package into a source file.

information hiding   A result of tight encapsulation, where a class does not expose to its users how the fields of the class are stored.

inner class   A nonstatic nested class.

instance initializer   A block of code declared in a class that executes for each new instance of the class. An instance initializer executes immediately after the parent class constructor finishes and before the body of the class constructor executes.

instance method   A nonstatic method of a class.

instance variables   The nonstatic fields of a class.

instantiation process   The events that occur during the creation of a new object.

interface   A reference type, similar to a class, that can only contain static constants, abstract methods, and nested types.

is-a relationship   A simple test to determine if you are using a proper approach and good code design in your application regarding inheritance. Simply put, you should be able to state that a child object "is a" parent object.

J

JavaBeans   A technology for developing software components in Java.

Java Collections Framework   A unified set of classes and interfaces defined in the `java.util` package for storing collections.

L

label   An identifier that appears before a statement and is followed by a colon. A break or `continue` statement can refer to a label to clarify which loop to break or continue on.

labeled break   A break statement that specifies a label, useful for breaking out of an outer loop or switch.

labeled continue   A `continue` statement that specifies a label, useful for continuing on an outer loop.

list   An ordered collection of elements that allows duplicate entries, and each element is accessed by an integer index.

local inner class   An inner class defined within a method.

local variable   A variable defined within a method, which includes method parameters.

lock   Short for "monitor lock."

loose coupling   The minimizing of the dependencies an object has on other objects.

low cohesion   When an object performs multiple tasks that are not related to each other.

M

main thread   Refers to the thread created by the JVM when invoking the `main` method of a stand-alone Java application.

map   A collection that maps keys to values, with no duplicate keys allowed. The elements in a map are key-value pairs.

member inner class   A nonstatic nested class defined at the member level of a class.

metacharacters   A special set of characters used to specify wildcards, repetition, and ranges in regular expressions.

method declaration   The definition of a Java method comprising of six components of a method: modifiers, return type, method name, parameter list, exception list, and method body.

method hiding   When a child class contains a static method that is also defined in its parent, following the rules of method overriding.

method overloading   When a class contains multiple methods with the same name but different parameter lists.

method overriding   When a child class contains the same instance method as its parent class.

method signature   A method's name and parameter types.

monitor   Short for "monitor lock."

monitor lock   An entity that every Java `Object` has, the monitor lock is used by threads to synchronize access to the `Object`.

multiplicative operators   The operators `*`, `/`, and `%`.

mutator methods   A JavaBean "set" method that is used to alter the value of a field.

mutually comparable   A collection of elements is said to be mutually comparable if any two elements in the list can be compared to each other using the `compareTo` method without a `ClassCastException` being thrown.

N

natural ordering   Refers to an ordered collection whose elements implement the `Comparable` interface.

nested class   A class defined within another class.

new thread   A thread in the NEW state, it refers to a new thread object that has been instantiated but not started yet.

O

object   An instance of a class.

object serialization   Refers to taking the state of an object and writing it to a stream.

order of precedence   The order in which operators are evaluated.

P

package   A grouping of classes, interfaces, enumerations, and annotated types.

parameter   The name of the variable in the method signature that gets assigned the value of the argument.

polymorphic parameters   Refers to a method parameter that is class type. Due to polymorphism, child objects of the parameter type can also be passed into the method.

preemptive scheduling   Refers to the JVM scheduling higher-priority threads over lower-priority threads. A lower-priority thread is preempted by a higher-priority thread.

primitive types   The built-in data types of the Java language. There are eight primitive types in Java: byte, short, int, long, float, double, char, and boolean.

process   A program that runs in an environment. A process consists of allocated memory and resources.

Q

queue   A collection that orders its elements in a specific order for processing. A typical queue processes its elements in a first-in, first-out fashion, but other ordering is possible.

R

reference types   Variables that are class types, interface types, and array types.

regular expression   A sequence of characters that describes a pattern of characters. The pattern describes a set of strings based on common characteristics.

relational operators   The comparison operators <, <=, >, and >=.

runnable target   The code that executes when its corresponding thread object is scheduled to run on the CPU.

runnable thread   A thread in the RUNNABLE state. A runnable thread is either running on the CPU or waiting to be scheduled.

runtime exception   Any exception that is a subclass of java.lang.RuntimeException. The Handle or Declare Rule does not apply to runtime exceptions.

S

scope   The portion of code where a variable can be accessed.

set   A collection that does not allow duplicate entries.

shift operators   Operators used to shift the bits of a numerical value. Java has three shift operators: << for a left shift, >> for a signed right shift, and >>> for an unsigned right shift.

simple assignment   Refers to the assignment operator =.

static field   Another name for a class variable.

static import   A type of import introduced in Java 5.0 that allows for class variable names to be imported into a source file.

static initializer   A block of code that executes once when a class is loaded by the class loader. The syntax for a static initializer is the static keyword followed by a set of curly braces.

static method   Another name for a class method, a static method is a method containing the static keyword in its declaration.

static nested class   A static class defined at the member level of an enclosing class.

static variable   Another name for a class variable.

string   A sequence of characters.

string pool   A feature of the JVM where String literals are stored. The JVM can optimize the use of string literals by allowing only one instance of a string in the pool.

switch statement   A decision-making control structure based on testing a byte, short, char, int, or enumerated type for equality to a list of case statements. A switch is similar to an if-then-else statement, except that a switch statement can only test for equality and it is possible for multiple blocks of code in a switch to execute.

synchronized block of code   A block of code created using the synchronized keyword along with a reference to the object whose monitor lock is being acquired.

synchronized method   A method in a class declared with the synchronized keyword. A thread invoking a synchronized method must acquire the object's this reference.

system threads   Threads created automatically by the JVM that run in the background.

T

terminated thread   A thread in the TERMINATED state. A terminated thread has run to completion.

ternary operator   Another name for the conditional operator.

thread   A path of execution; a block of code that executes within a process and has access to the process memory.

thread object   The part of a thread that gets started, has a priority and state, and is scheduled to run by the JVM.

thread priority   An integer value that is a property of every thread object. The JVM uses a thread's priority as one of its factors in deciding which thread to schedule.

tight encapsulation   Refers to using encapsulation every time on all the fields of a class, and only providing access to the fields via methods.

tokens   Separators, keywords, literals, operators, and identifiers in a source code file.

transient   A modifier for class fields that tells the JVM to ignore the field during the serialization and deserialization process.

try statement   A block of code containing one or more statements that may throw an exception. The statements within a `try` block are referred to as protected code.

type erasure   Refers to the changes that the compiler does to your code to remove the generics syntax and replace the generic types with `Object` references.

U

unbounded wildcard   The ? in generics, which represents any data type.

unboxing   Refers to the compiler automatically unwrapping a primitive type from its wrapper object.

unnamed package   The package that contains all Java elements that are not specifically declared in a package.

user-defined threads   A thread you write to perform a specific task.

V

variable   An allocated piece of memory for storing data. A variable has an identifier and a specific data type.

variable-length argument list   A parameter that contains the ellipsis (...) after its data type can take in any number of arguments. This comma-separated list of arguments must appear at the end of the argument list and is treated as an array.

virtual method   All methods in Java are virtual methods, meaning that if a method is overridden, the overridden method is always invoked at runtime, even if the compiler sees the parent class method at compile time.

virtual method invocation   Refers to the behavior of virtual methods, where the runtime type of an object is used to determine the overridden method invoked at runtime, as opposed to invoking the method the compiler found at compile time.

W

wildcard generic type   An unknown generic represented with a question mark (?).

while loop   A repetition control structure that uses the while keyword and is useful for repeating a block of code an indeterminate number of times.

wrapper classes   Refers to the eight classes defined in the java.lang package that are used to "wrap" primitive types into objects.

Index

Note to the reader: Throughout this index **boldfaced** page numbers indicate primary discussions of a topic. *Italicized* page numbers indicate illustrations.

F

O

Wiley Publishing, Inc.
End-User License Agreement

The Absolute Sun Certified Programmer for the Java Platform, Standard Edition 6 Book/CD Package on the Market!

Get ready for Sun's Certified Java Programmer for Java Standard Edition 6 certification with the most comprehensive and challenging sample tests anywhere!

The Sybex Test Engine features:

- All the review questions, as covered in each chapter of the book

- Challenging questions representative of those you'll find on the real exam

- Two full-length bonus exams available only on the CD

- An Assessment Test to narrow your focus to certain objective groups.

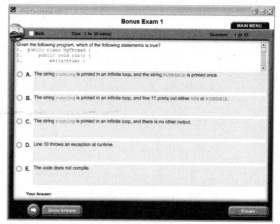

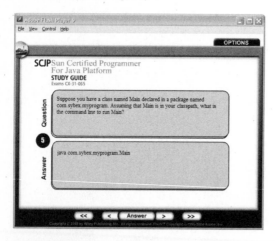

Search through the complete book in PDF!

- Access the entire *SCJP: Sun Certified Programmer for Java Platform, Standard Edition 6 Study Guide* complete with figures and tables, in electronic format.

- Search the *SCJP: Sun Certified Programmer for Java Platform, Standard Edition 6 Study Guide* chapters to find information on any topic in seconds.

Use the Electronic Flashcards for PCs or Palm devices to jog your memory and prep last-minute for the exam!

- Reinforce your understanding of key concepts with these hardcore flash-card-style questions.

- Download the Flashcards to your Palm device and go on the road. Now you can study for the SCJP (CX-310-065) exam any time, anywhere.

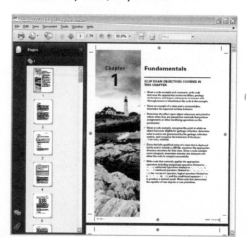